CHRYSLER

300/CHARGER, MAGNUM
2005-10 REPAIR MANUAL

Covers U.S. and Canadian models of
Chrysler 300, 2005 through 2010,
Dodge Charger, 2006 through 2010 &
Magnum, 2005 through 2008

Does not include information specific to SRT8, diesel engine or all-wheel drive models

by Joe L. Hamilton

PUBLISHED BY **HAYNES NORTH AMERICA**, Inc.

Printed in Malaysia
©2007, 2011, 2013 Haynes North America, Inc.
ISBN-13: 978-1-62092-056-5
ISBN-10: 1-62092-056-5
Library of Congress Control Number 2013938137

Haynes Publishing Group
Sparkford Nr Yeovil
Somerset BA22 7JJ England

Haynes North America, Inc
859 Lawrence Drive
Newbury Park
California 91320 USA

ABCDE
FGHIJ
KL

12V4

Contents

1

TUNE-UP AND ROUTINE MAINTENANCE – 1-1

2

2.7L V6 ENGINE – 2A-1
3.5L V6 ENGINE – 2B-1
V8 ENGINE – 2C-1
GENERAL ENGINE OVERHAUL PROCEDURES – 2D-1

3

COOLING, HEATING AND AIR CONDITIONING SYSTEMS – 3-1

4

FUEL AND EXHAUST SYSTEMS – 4-1

5

ENGINE ELECTRICAL SYSTEMS – 5-1

6

EMISSIONS AND ENGINE CONTROL SYSTEMS – 6-1

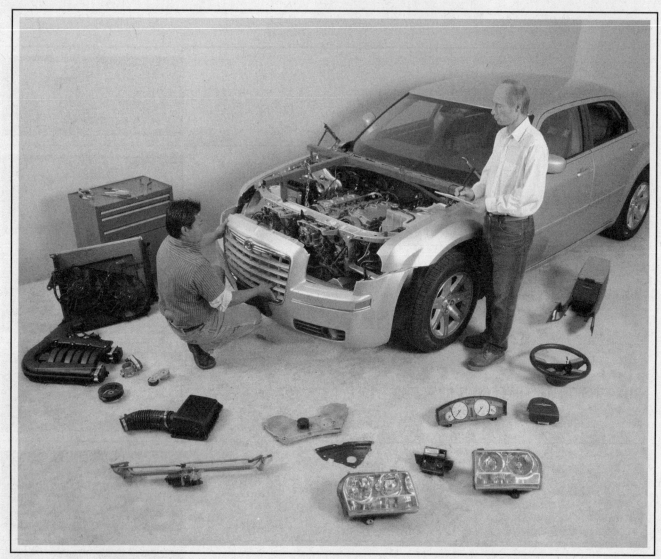

Mechanic with a 2006 Chrysler 300

ACKNOWLEDGEMENTS

Technical writers who contributed to this project include John Wegmann, Rob Maddox and Mike Stubblefield. Wiring diagrams provided exclusively for the publisher by Solution Builders.

While every attempt is made to ensure that the information in this manual is correct, no liability can be accepted by the authors or publishers for loss, damage or injury caused by any errors in, or omissions from, the information given.

About this manual

ITS PURPOSE

The purpose of this manual is to help you get the best value from your vehicle. It can do so in several ways. It can help you decide what work must be done, even if you choose to have it done by a dealer service department or a repair shop; it provides information and procedures for routine maintenance and servicing; and it offers diagnostic and repair procedures to follow when trouble occurs.

We hope you use the manual to tackle the work yourself. For many simpler jobs, doing it yourself may be quicker than arranging an appointment to get the vehicle into a shop and making the trips to leave it and pick it up. More importantly, a lot of money can be saved by avoiding the expense the shop must pass on to you to cover its labor and overhead costs. An added benefit is the sense of satisfaction and accomplishment that you feel after doing the job yourself.

USING THE MANUAL

The manual is divided into Chapters. Each Chapter is divided into numbered Sections, which are headed in bold type between horizontal lines. Each Section consists of consecutively numbered paragraphs.

At the beginning of each numbered Section you will be referred to any illustrations which apply to the procedures in that Section. The reference numbers used in illustration captions pinpoint the pertinent Section and the Step within that Section. That is, illustration 3.2 means the illustration refers to Section 3 and Step (or paragraph) 2 within that Section.

Procedures, once described in the text, are not normally repeated. When it's necessary to refer to another Chapter, the reference will be given as Chapter and Section number. Cross references given without use of the word "Chapter" apply to Sections and/or paragraphs in the same Chapter. For example, "see Section 8" means in the same Chapter.

References to the left or right side of the vehicle assume you are sitting in the driver's seat, facing forward.

Even though we have prepared this manual with extreme care, neither the publisher nor the author can accept responsibility for any errors in, or omissions from, the information given.

➡NOTE

A *Note* provides information necessary to properly complete a procedure or information which will make the procedure easier to understand.

❊❊ CAUTION

A *Caution* provides a special procedure or special steps which must be taken while completing the procedure where the Caution is found. Not heeding a Caution can result in damage to the assembly being worked on.

❊❊ WARNING

A *Warning* provides a special procedure or special steps which must be taken while completing the procedure where the Warning is found. Not heeding a Warning can result in personal injury.

Introduction

Chrysler 300 and Dodge Charger models are available in a four-door sedan body style, while Dodge Magnum models are available in a four-door wagon body style.

All models are equipped with either a 2.7L DOHC V6, 3.5L SOHC V6 or a 5.7L V8 engine.

Power from the engine is transferred through a four- or five-speed automatic transmission, then through a driveshaft and a rear differential which drives the rear wheels through a pair of driveaxles.

Suspension is a fully independent, long-arm/short arm front suspension system with upper and lower control arms, tension links and shock absorber/coil spring assemblies. A stabilizer bar controls body roll. Each steering knuckle is positioned by a series of balljoints in the ends of the upper and lower control arms and the tension links. The rear suspension consists of an independent multi-link suspension with shock absorbers, coil springs and several specialized links. Some models incorporate a stabilizer bar to control body roll.

The steering system consists of a rack-and-pinion steering gear and two adjustable tie-rods. Power assist is standard.

The brakes are disc at the front and disc at the rear, with power assist standard.

Vehicle Identification Numbers

Modifications are a continuing and unpublicized process in vehicle manufacturing. Since spare parts lists and manuals are compiled on a numerical basis, the individual vehicle numbers are necessary to correctly identify the component required.

VEHICLE IDENTIFICATION NUMBER (VIN)

This very important identification number is stamped on a plate attached to the dashboard inside the windshield on the driver's side of the vehicle (see illustration). The VIN also appears on the Vehicle Certificate of Title and Registration. It contains information such as where and when the vehicle was manufactured, the model year and the body style.

VIN ENGINE AND MODEL YEAR CODES

Two particularly important pieces of information found in the VIN are the engine code and the model year code. Counting from the left, the engine code letter designation is the 8th digit and the model year code letter designation is the 10th digit.

On the models covered by this manual the engine codes are:

R	2.7L DOHC V6
T	2.7L DOHC V6 (Magnum)
G	3.5L SOHC V6
V	3.5L SOHC V6 (Magnum)
H	5.7L Hemi V8
2	5.7L Hemi V8 (Magnum)

On the models covered by this manual the model year codes are:

5	2005
6	2006
7	2007
8	2008
9	2009
A	2010

VEHICLE CERTIFICATION LABEL

The Vehicle Certification Label is attached to the driver's side door (see illustration). Information on this label includes the name of the

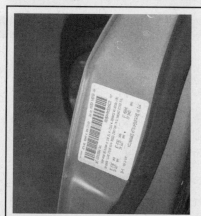

The vehicle certification label is affixed the to the driver's side door

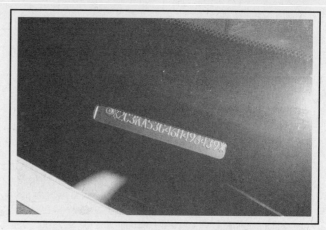

The VIN number is visible through the windshield on the driver's side

manufacturer, the month and year of production, as well as information on the options with which it is equipped. This label is especially useful for matching the color and type of paint for repair work.

ENGINE IDENTIFICATION NUMBER

Labels containing the engine code, engine number and build date can be found on the valve cover. The engine number is also stamped onto a machined pad on the external surface of the engine block.

AUTOMATIC TRANSMISSION IDENTIFICATION NUMBER

The automatic transmission ID number is affixed to a label on the left side of the case (see illustration).

VEHICLE EMISSIONS CONTROL INFORMATION LABEL

This label is found in the engine compartment. See Chapter 6 for more information on this label.

The automatic transmission identification tag is located on the left side of the transmission

Recall information

Vehicle recalls are carried out by the manufacturer in the rare event of a possible safety-related defect. The vehicle's registered owner is contacted at the address on file at the Department of Motor Vehicles and given the details of the recall. Remedial work is carried out free of charge at a dealer service department.

If you are the new owner of a used vehicle which was subject to a recall and you want to be sure that the work has been carried out, it's best to contact a dealer service department and ask about your indi-

vidual vehicle - you'll need to furnish them your Vehicle Identification Number (VIN).

The table below is based on information provided by the National Highway Traffic Safety Administration (NHTSA), the body which oversees vehicle recalls in the United States. The recall database is updated constantly. For the latest information on vehicle recalls, check the NHTSA website at www.nhtsa.gov, or call the NHTSA hotline at 1-888-327-4236.

Recall date	Recall campaign number	Model(s) affected	Concern
Jul 02, 2004	04V333000	2005 Chrysler 300, Dodge Magnum	On certain passenger vehicles, a spot welding operation for the rear floorpan reinforcement may not have been performed. This could cause the rear seat belt anchors and/or the child seat anchors to separate in certain crash conditions, which can increase the risk of injury to rear seat passengers.
Jul 02, 2004	04V334000	2005 Chrysler 300, Dodge Magnum	On certain passenger vehicles, the battery cable fasteners at the bulkhead stud may not have been properly tightened. A loose fastener can cause an instrument panel fire.
Jul 02, 2004	04V335000	2005 Chrysler 300, Dodge Magnum	On certain passenger vehicles, the front shoulder belt adjustable turning loop (ATL) bolts may not have been properly tightened. This could cause shoulder belt separation in certain crash conditions, which can increase the risk of injury to front seat occupants.
Oct 04, 2005	05V460000	2006 300/Charger/Magnum	On some vehicles with the 42RLE automatic transmission, the plug that retains the park pawl anchor shaft might be incorrectly installed. If the shaft moves out of position, the transmission might not be able to go into the Park position. If this occurs and the the parking brake is not applied, the vehicle could roll and cause a crash
May 03, 2006	06V149000	2006 300/Charger/Magnumr	On some vehicles with a 2.7L engine and an MK25E brake system, there is insufficient clearance between the rear brake lines and the Exhaust Gas Recirculation (EGR) line. Over an extended period, contact between the brake lines and EGR line might cause the brake lines to wear through, which could seriously impair braking force and potentially cause an engine fire.
Sep 06, 2006	06V341000	2007 300/Charger/Magnum	On some vehicles with automatic transmissions, the software programmed into the Powertrain Control Module (PCM) can cause a momentary lock-up of the drive wheels if the vehicle is traveling over 40 mph and the driver shifts from Drive to Neutral, then back to Drive. If the wheels lock up, loss of vehicle control could occur, which could cause a crash.
Nov 05, 2006	08V583000	2006 through 2009 Charger/Magnum	On some vehicles equipped with the police package and a column-mounted shift lever, the shift control cable might detach from the steering column mounting bracket and cause an incorrect transmission gear position display, which could allow the vehicle to move in an unexpected direction and cause a crash without warning.
Dec 22, 2006	06V493000	2007 300/Charger/Magnum	On some vehicles, the Antilock Brake System (ABS) control module software might cause the rear brakes to lock up during certain braking conditions, which could result in loss of vehicle control, which could cause a crash.
Jul 01, 2008	08V295000	2008 300/ Charger/Magnum	The torque retention crimp feature was missed during the manufacture of one lot of rear rear axle hub nuts, which could cause the nut to loosen and allow the driveaxle assembly to separate from the hub. If this happens, it could cause the vehicle to lose power and could result in a crash.
Dec 04, 2008	08V642000	2009 300/Charger	On some vehicles, the Tire Pressure Monitor (TPM) sensors might not transmit the correct tire pressure, which could prevent the driver from knowing that the tire pressure is low, which could damage the tires and might cause a crash.
Oct 29, 2009	09V420000	2009 300	On some rear-drive vehicles, no spindle nut was installed, which could result in the vehicle losing a front wheel and tire while driving, which could result in a crash.

Buying parts

Replacement parts are available from many sources, which generally fall into one of two categories - authorized dealer parts departments and independent retail auto parts stores. Our advice concerning these parts is as follows:

Retail auto parts stores: Good auto parts stores will stock frequently needed components which wear out relatively fast, such as clutch components, exhaust systems, brake parts, tune-up parts, etc. These stores often supply new or reconditioned parts on an exchange basis, which can save a considerable amount of money. Discount auto parts stores are often very good places to buy materials and parts needed for general vehicle maintenance such as oil, grease, filters, spark plugs, belts, touch-up paint, bulbs, etc. They also usually sell tools and general accessories, have convenient hours, charge lower prices and can often be found not far from home.

Authorized dealer parts department: This is the best source for parts which are unique to the vehicle and not generally available elsewhere (such as major engine parts, transmission parts, trim pieces, etc.).

Warranty information: If the vehicle is still covered under warranty, be sure that any replacement parts purchased - regardless of the source - do not invalidate the warranty!

To be sure of obtaining the correct parts, have engine and chassis numbers available and, if possible, take the old parts along for positive identification.

Maintenance techniques, tools and working facilities

MAINTENANCE TECHNIQUES

There are a number of techniques involved in maintenance and repair that will be referred to throughout this manual. Application of these techniques will enable the home mechanic to be more efficient, better organized and capable of performing the various tasks properly, which will ensure that the repair job is thorough and complete.

Fasteners

Fasteners are nuts, bolts, studs and screws used to hold two or more parts together. There are a few things to keep in mind when working with fasteners. Almost all of them use a locking device of some type, either a lockwasher, locknut, locking tab or thread adhesive. All threaded fasteners should be clean and straight, with undamaged threads and undamaged corners on the hex head where the wrench fits. Develop the habit of replacing all damaged nuts and bolts with new ones. Special locknuts with nylon or fiber inserts can only be used once. If they are removed, they lose their locking ability and must be replaced with new ones.

Rusted nuts and bolts should be treated with a penetrating fluid to ease removal and prevent breakage. Some mechanics use turpentine in a spout-type oil can, which works quite well. After applying the rust penetrant, let it work for a few minutes before trying to loosen the nut or bolt. Badly rusted fasteners may have to be chiseled or sawed off or removed with a special nut breaker, available at tool stores.

If a bolt or stud breaks off in an assembly, it can be drilled and removed with a special tool commonly available for this purpose. Most automotive machine shops can perform this task, as well as other repair procedures, such as the repair of threaded holes that have been stripped out.

Flat washers and lockwashers, when removed from an assembly, should always be replaced exactly as removed. Replace any damaged washers with new ones. Never use a lockwasher on any soft metal surface (such as aluminum), thin sheet metal or plastic.

Fastener sizes

For a number of reasons, automobile manufacturers are making wider and wider use of metric fasteners. Therefore, it is important to be able to tell the difference between standard (sometimes called U.S.

Grade 1 or 2   Grade 5   Grade 8

Bolt strength marking (standard/SAE/USS; bottom - metric)

Grade	Identification	Grade	Identification
Hex Nut Grade 5	3 Dots	Hex Nut Property Class 9	Arabic 9
Hex Nut Grade 8	6 Dots	Hex Nut Property Class 10	Arabic 10

Standard hex nut strength markings

Metric hex nut strength markings

Class 10.9   Class 9.8   Class 8.8

Metric stud strength markings

00-1 HAYNES

or SAE) and metric hardware, since they cannot be interchanged.

All bolts, whether standard or metric, are sized according to diameter, thread pitch and length. For example, a standard 1/2 - 13 x 1 bolt is 1/2 inch in diameter, has 13 threads per inch and is 1 inch long. An M12 - 1.75 x 25 metric bolt is 12 mm in diameter, has a thread pitch of 1.75 mm (the distance between threads) and is 25 mm long. The two bolts are nearly identical, and easily confused, but they are not interchangeable.

In addition to the differences in diameter, thread pitch and length, metric and standard bolts can also be distinguished by examining the bolt heads. To begin with, the distance across the flats on a standard bolt head is measured in inches, while the same dimension on a metric bolt is sized in millimeters (the same is true for nuts). As a result, a standard wrench should not be used on a metric bolt and a metric wrench should not be used on a standard bolt. Also, most standard bolts have slashes

radiating out from the center of the head to denote the grade or strength of the bolt, which is an indication of the amount of torque that can be applied to it. The greater the number of slashes, the greater the strength of the bolt. Grades 0 through 5 are commonly used on automobiles. Metric bolts have a property class (grade) number, rather than a slash, molded into their heads to indicate bolt strength. In this case, the higher the number, the stronger the bolt. Property class numbers 8.8, 9.8 and 10.9 are commonly used on automobiles.

Strength markings can also be used to distinguish standard hex nuts from metric hex nuts. Many standard nuts have dots stamped into one side, while metric nuts are marked with a number. The greater the number of dots, or the higher the number, the greater the strength of the nut.

Metric studs are also marked on their ends according to property class (grade). Larger studs are numbered (the same as metric bolts), while smaller studs carry a geometric code to denote grade.

Metric thread sizes

	Ft-lbs	Nm
M-6	6 to 9	9 to 12
M-8	14 to 21	19 to 28
M-10	28 to 40	38 to 54
M-12	50 to 71	68 to 96
M-14	80 to 140	109 to 154

Pipe thread sizes

	Ft-lbs	Nm
1/8	5 to 8	7 to 10
1/4	12 to 18	17 to 24
3/8	22 to 33	30 to 44
1/2	25 to 35	34 to 47

U.S. thread sizes

	Ft-lbs	Nm
1/4 - 20	6 to 9	9 to 12
5/16 - 18	12 to 18	17 to 24
5/16 - 24	14 to 20	19 to 27
3/8 - 16	22 to 32	30 to 43
3/8 - 24	27 to 38	37 to 51
7/16 - 14	40 to 55	55 to 74
7/16 - 20	40 to 60	55 to 81
1/2 - 13	55 to 80	75 to 108

Standard (SAE and USS) bolt dimensions/grade marks

G   Grade marks (bolt strength)
L   Length (in inches)
T   Thread pitch (number of threads per inch)
D   Nominal diameter (in inches)

Metric bolt dimensions/grade marks

P   Property class (bolt strength)
L   Length (in millimeters)
T   Thread pitch (distance between threads in millimeters)
D   Diameter

It should be noted that many fasteners, especially Grades 0 through 2, have no distinguishing marks on them. When such is the case, the only way to determine whether it is standard or metric is to measure the thread pitch or compare it to a known fastener of the same size.

Standard fasteners are often referred to as SAE, as opposed to metric. However, it should be noted that SAE technically refers to a non-metric fine thread fastener only. Coarse thread non-metric fasteners are referred to as USS sizes.

Since fasteners of the same size (both standard and metric) may have different strength ratings, be sure to reinstall any bolts, studs or nuts removed from your vehicle in their original locations. Also, when replacing a fastener with a new one, make sure that the new one has a strength rating equal to or greater than the original.

Tightening sequences and procedures

Most threaded fasteners should be tightened to a specific torque value (torque is the twisting force applied to a threaded component such as a nut or bolt). Overtightening the fastener can weaken it and cause it to break, while undertightening can cause it to eventually come loose. Bolts, screws and studs, depending on the material they are made of and their thread diameters, have specific torque values, many of which are noted in the Specifications at the end of each Chapter. Be sure to follow the torque recommendations closely. For fasteners not assigned a specific torque, a general torque value chart is presented here as a guide. These torque values are for dry (unlubricated) fasteners threaded into steel or cast iron (not aluminum). As was previously mentioned, the size and grade of a fastener determine the amount of torque that can

Micrometer set

Dial indicator set

safely be applied to it. The figures listed here are approximate for Grade 2 and Grade 3 fasteners. Higher grades can tolerate higher torque values.

Fasteners laid out in a pattern, such as cylinder head bolts, oil pan bolts, differential cover bolts, etc., must be loosened or tightened in sequence to avoid warping the component. This sequence will normally be shown in the appropriate Chapter. If a specific pattern is not given, the following procedures can be used to prevent warping.

Initially, the bolts or nuts should be assembled finger-tight only. Next, they should be tightened one full turn each, in a criss-cross or diagonal pattern. After each one has been tightened one full turn, return to the first one and tighten them all one-half turn, following the same pattern. Finally, tighten each of them one-quarter turn at a time until each fastener has been tightened to the proper torque. To loosen and remove the fasteners, the procedure would be reversed.

Component disassembly

Component disassembly should be done with care and purpose to help ensure that the parts go back together properly. Always keep track of the sequence in which parts are removed. Make note of special characteristics or marks on parts that can be installed more than one way, such as a grooved thrust washer on a shaft. It is a good idea to lay the disassembled parts out on a clean surface in the order that they were removed. It may also be helpful to make sketches or take instant photos of components before removal.

When removing fasteners from a component, keep track of their locations. Sometimes threading a bolt back in a part, or putting the washers and nut back on a stud, can prevent mix-ups later. If nuts and bolts cannot be returned to their original locations, they should be kept in a compartmented box or a series of small boxes. A cupcake or muffin tin is ideal for this purpose, since each cavity can hold the bolts and nuts from a particular area (i.e. oil pan bolts, valve cover bolts, engine mount bolts, etc.). A pan of this type is especially helpful when working on assemblies with very small parts, such as the carburetor, alternator, valve train or interior dash and trim pieces. The cavities can be marked with paint or tape to identify the contents.

Whenever wiring looms, harnesses or connectors are separated, it is a good idea to identify the two halves with numbered pieces of masking tape so they can be easily reconnected.

Gasket sealing surfaces

Throughout any vehicle, gaskets are used to seal the mating surfaces between two parts and keep lubricants, fluids, vacuum or pressure contained in an assembly.

Many times these gaskets are coated with a liquid or paste-type gasket sealing compound before assembly. Age, heat and pressure can sometimes cause the two parts to stick together so tightly that they are very difficult to separate. Often, the assembly can be loosened by striking it with a soft-face hammer near the mating surfaces. A regular hammer can be used if a block of wood is placed between the hammer and the part. Do not hammer on cast parts or parts that could be easily damaged. With any particularly stubborn part, always recheck to make sure that every fastener has been removed.

Avoid using a screwdriver or bar to pry apart an assembly, as they can easily mar the gasket sealing surfaces of the parts, which must remain smooth. If prying is absolutely necessary, use an old broom handle, but keep in mind that extra clean up will be necessary if the wood splinters.

After the parts are separated, the old gasket must be carefully scraped off and the gasket surfaces cleaned. Stubborn gasket material can be soaked with rust penetrant or treated with a special chemical to soften it so it can be easily scraped off.

❋ CAUTION:

Never use gasket removal solutions or caustic chemicals on plastic or other composite components.

A scraper can be fashioned from a piece of copper tubing by flattening and sharpening one end. Copper is recommended because it is usually softer than the surfaces to be scraped, which reduces the chance of gouging the part. Some gaskets can be removed with a wire brush, but regardless of the method used, the mating surfaces must be left clean and smooth. If for some reason the gasket surface is gouged, then a gasket sealer thick enough to fill scratches will have to be used during reassembly of the components. For most applications, a non-drying (or semi-drying) gasket sealer should be used.

Dial caliper

Hand-operated vacuum pump

Fuel pressure gauge set

Compression gauge with spark plug hole adapter

Hose removal tips

> **⁎⁎⁎ WARNING:**
>
> **If the vehicle is equipped with air conditioning, do not disconnect any of the A/C hoses without first having the system depressurized by a dealer service department or a service station.**

Hose removal precautions closely parallel gasket removal precautions. Avoid scratching or gouging the surface that the hose mates against or the connection may leak. This is especially true for radiator hoses. Because of various chemical reactions, the rubber in hoses can bond itself to the metal spigot that the hose fits over. To remove a hose, first loosen the hose clamps that secure it to the spigot. Then, with slip-joint pliers, grab the hose at the clamp and rotate it around the spigot. Work it back and forth until it is completely free, then pull it off. Silicone or other lubricants will ease removal if they can be applied between the hose and the outside of the spigot. Apply the same lubricant to the inside of the hose and the outside of the spigot to simplify installation.

As a last resort (and if the hose is to be replaced with a new one anyway), the rubber can be slit with a knife and the hose peeled from the spigot. If this must be done, be careful that the metal connection is not damaged.

If a hose clamp is broken or damaged, do not reuse it. Wire-type clamps usually weaken with age, so it is a good idea to replace them with screw-type clamps whenever a hose is removed.

TOOLS

A selection of good tools is a basic requirement for anyone who plans to maintain and repair his or her own vehicle. For the owner who has few tools, the initial investment might seem high, but when compared to the spiraling costs of professional auto maintenance and repair, it is a wise one.

To help the owner decide which tools are needed to perform the tasks detailed in this manual, the following tool lists are offered: *Maintenance and minor repair, Repair/overhaul and Special.*

The newcomer to practical mechanics should start off with the *maintenance and minor repair* tool kit, which is adequate for the simpler jobs performed on a vehicle. Then, as confidence and experience grow, the owner can tackle more difficult tasks, buying additional tools as they are needed. Eventually the basic kit will be expanded into the *repair and overhaul* tool set. Over a period of time, the experienced do-it-yourselfer will assemble a tool set complete enough for most repair and overhaul procedures and will add tools from the special category when it is felt that the expense is justified by the frequency of use.

Damper/steering wheel puller

General purpose puller

Hydraulic lifter removal tool

Valve spring compressor

Valve spring compressor

Ridge reamer

Maintenance and minor repair tool kit

The tools in this list should be considered the minimum required for performance of routine maintenance, servicing and minor repair work. We recommend the purchase of combination wrenches (box-end and open-end combined in one wrench). While more expensive than open end wrenches, they offer the advantages of both types of wrench.

Combination wrench set (1/4-inch to 1 inch or 6 mm to 19 mm)
Adjustable wrench, 8 inch
Spark plug wrench with rubber insert
Spark plug gap adjusting tool
Feeler gauge set
Brake bleeder wrench
Standard screwdriver (5/16-inch x 6 inch)
Phillips screwdriver (No. 2 x 6 inch)
Combination pliers - 6 inch
Hacksaw and assortment of blades
Tire pressure gauge
Grease gun
Oil can
Fine emery cloth
Wire brush
Battery post and cable cleaning tool
Oil filter wrench
Funnel (medium size)
Safety goggles
Jackstands (2)
Drain pan

➡**Note: If basic tune-ups are going to be part of routine maintenance, it will be necessary to purchase a good quality stroboscopic timing light and combination tachometer/dwell meter. Although they are included in the list of special tools, it is mentioned here because they are absolutely necessary for tuning most vehicles properly.**

Repair and overhaul tool set

These tools are essential for anyone who plans to perform major repairs and are in addition to those in the maintenance and minor repair tool kit. Included is a comprehensive set of sockets which, though expensive, are invaluable because of their versatility, especially when various extensions and drives are available. We recommend the 1/2-inch drive over the 3/8-inch drive. Although the larger drive is bulky and more expensive, it has the capacity of accepting a very wide range of large sockets. Ideally, however, the mechanic should have a 3/8-inch drive set and a 1/2-inch drive set.

Socket set(s)
Reversible ratchet
Extension - 10 inch
Universal joint
Torque wrench (same size drive as sockets)
Ball peen hammer - 8 ounce
Soft-face hammer (plastic/rubber)
Standard screwdriver (1/4-inch x 6 inch)
Standard screwdriver (stubby - 5/16-inch)
Phillips screwdriver (No. 3 x 8 inch)
Phillips screwdriver (stubby - No. 2)
Pliers - vise grip

Piston ring groove cleaning tool

Ring removal/installation tool

Ring compressor

Cylinder hone

Brake hold-down spring tool

Pliers - lineman's
Pliers - needle nose
Pliers - snap-ring (internal and external)
Cold chisel - 1/2-inch
Scribe
Scraper (made from flattened copper tubing)
Centerpunch
Pin punches (1/16, 1/8, 3/16-inch)
Steel rule/straightedge - 12 inch
Allen wrench set (1/8 to 3/8-inch or 4 mm to 10 mm)
A selection of files
Wire brush (large)
Jackstands (second set)
Jack (scissor or hydraulic type)

➡**Note: Another tool which is often useful is an electric drill with a chuck capacity of 3/8-inch and a set of good quality drill bits.**

Special tools

The tools in this list include those which are not used regularly, are expensive to buy, or which need to be used in accordance with their manufacturer's instructions. Unless these tools will be used frequently, it is not very economical to purchase many of them. A consideration would be to split the cost and use between yourself and a friend or friends. In addition, most of these tools can be obtained from a tool rental shop on a temporary basis.

This list primarily contains only those tools and instruments widely available to the public, and not those special tools produced by the vehicle manufacturer for distribution to dealer service departments. Occasionally, references to the manufacturer's special tools are included in the text of this manual. Generally, an alternative method of doing the job without the special tool is offered. However, sometimes there is no alternative to their use. Where this is the case, and the tool cannot be purchased or borrowed, the work should be turned over to the dealer service department or an automotive repair shop.

Valve spring compressor
Piston ring groove cleaning tool
Piston ring compressor
Piston ring installation tool
Cylinder compression gauge
Cylinder ridge reamer
Cylinder surfacing hone
Cylinder bore gauge
Micrometers and/or dial calipers
Hydraulic lifter removal tool
Balljoint separator
Universal-type puller
Impact screwdriver
Dial indicator set
Stroboscopic timing light (inductive pick-up)
Hand operated vacuum/pressure pump
Tachometer/dwell meter
Universal electrical multimeter
Cable hoist
Brake spring removal and installation tools
Floor jack

Torque angle gauge

Clutch plate alignment tool

Buying tools

For the do-it-yourselfer who is just starting to get involved in vehicle maintenance and repair, there are a number of options available when purchasing tools. If maintenance and minor repair is the extent of the work to be done, the purchase of individual tools is satisfactory. If, on the other hand, extensive work is planned, it would be a good idea to purchase a modest tool set from one of the large retail chain stores. A set can usually be bought at a substantial savings over the individual tool prices, and they often come with a tool box. As additional tools are needed, add-on sets, individual tools and a larger tool box can be purchased to expand the tool selection. Building a tool set gradually allows the cost of the tools to be spread over a longer period of time and gives the mechanic the freedom to choose only those tools that will actually be used.

Tool stores will often be the only source of some of the special tools that are needed, but regardless of where tools are bought, try to avoid cheap ones, especially when buying screwdrivers and sockets, because they won't last very long. The expense involved in replacing cheap tools will eventually be greater than the initial cost of quality tools.

Care and maintenance of tools

Good tools are expensive, so it makes sense to treat them with respect. Keep them clean and in usable condition and store them properly when not in use. Always wipe off any dirt, grease or metal chips before putting them away. Never leave tools lying around in the work area. Upon completion of a job, always check closely under the hood for tools that may have been left there so they won't get lost during a test drive.

Some tools, such as screwdrivers, pliers, wrenches and sockets, can be hung on a panel mounted on the garage or workshop wall, while others should be kept in a tool box or tray. Measuring instruments, gauges, meters, etc. must be carefully stored where they cannot be damaged by weather or impact from other tools.

When tools are used with care and stored properly, they will last a very long time. Even with the best of care, though, tools will wear out if used frequently. When a tool is damaged or worn out, replace it. Subsequent jobs will be safer and more enjoyable if you do.

HOW TO REPAIR DAMAGED THREADS

Sometimes, the internal threads of a nut or bolt hole can become stripped, usually from overtightening. Stripping threads is an all-too-

Tap and die set

common occurrence, especially when working with aluminum parts, because aluminum is so soft that it easily strips out.

Usually, external or internal threads are only partially stripped. After they've been cleaned up with a tap or die, they'll still work. Sometimes, however, threads are badly damaged. When this happens, you've got three choices:

1) Drill and tap the hole to the next suitable oversize and install a larger diameter bolt, screw or stud.
2) Drill and tap the hole to accept a threaded plug, then drill and tap the plug to the original screw size. You can also buy a plug already threaded to the original size. Then you simply drill a hole to the specified size, then run the threaded plug into the hole with a bolt and jam nut. Once the plug is fully seated, remove the jam nut and bolt.
3) The third method uses a patented thread repair kit like Heli-Coil or Slimsert. These easy-to-use kits are designed to repair damaged threads in straight-through holes and blind holes. Both are available as kits which can handle a variety of sizes and thread patterns. Drill the hole, then tap it with the special included tap. Install the Heli-Coil and the hole is back to its original diameter and thread pitch.

Regardless of which method you use, be sure to proceed calmly and carefully. A little impatience or carelessness during one of these relatively simple procedures can ruin your whole day's work and cost you a bundle if you wreck an expensive part.

WORKING FACILITIES

Not to be overlooked when discussing tools is the workshop. If anything more than routine maintenance is to be carried out, some sort of suitable work area is essential.

It is understood, and appreciated, that many home mechanics do not have a good workshop or garage available, and end up removing an engine or doing major repairs outside. It is recommended, however, that the overhaul or repair be completed under the cover of a roof.

A clean, flat workbench or table of comfortable working height is an absolute necessity. The workbench should be equipped with a vise that has a jaw opening of at least four inches.

As mentioned previously, some clean, dry storage space is also required for tools, as well as the lubricants, fluids, cleaning solvents, etc. which soon become necessary.

Sometimes waste oil and fluids, drained from the engine or cooling system during normal maintenance or repairs, present a disposal problem. To avoid pouring them on the ground or into a sewage system, pour the used fluids into large containers, seal them with caps and take them to an authorized disposal site or recycling center. Plastic jugs, such as old antifreeze containers, are ideal for this purpose.

Always keep a supply of old newspapers and clean rags available. Old towels are excellent for mopping up spills. Many mechanics use rolls of paper towels for most work because they are readily available and disposable. To help keep the area under the vehicle clean, a large cardboard box can be cut open and flattened to protect the garage or shop floor.

Whenever working over a painted surface, such as when leaning over a fender to service something under the hood, always cover it with an old blanket or bedspread to protect the finish. Vinyl covered pads, made especially for this purpose, are available at auto parts stores.

Booster battery (jump) starting

Observe the following precautions when using a booster battery to start a vehicle:

a) *Before connecting the booster battery, make sure the ignition switch is in the Off position.*
b) *Turn off the lights, heater and other electrical loads.*
c) *Your eyes should be shielded. Safety goggles are a good idea.*
d) *Make sure the booster battery is the same voltage as the dead one in the vehicle.*
e) *The two vehicles MUST NOT TOUCH each other!*
f) *Make sure the transmission is in Neutral (manual) or Park (automatic).*

g) *If the booster battery is not a maintenance-free type, remove the vent caps and lay a cloth over the vent holes.*

Connect one jumper lead between the positive (+) terminals of the two batteries (see illustration).

➡**Note: These vehicles are equipped with a remote positive terminal located on the side of the underhood fuse/relay box, to make jumper cable connection easier (see illustration).**

Connect the other jumper lead first to the negative (-) terminal of the booster battery, then to a good engine ground on the vehicle to be started.

➡**Note: These vehicles are also equipped with a remote grounding point, located on the right shock tower (near the remote positive terminal).**

Attach the lead at least 18 inches from the battery, if possible. Make sure the that the jumper leads will not contact the fan, drivebelt or other moving parts of the engine.

Start the engine using the booster battery, then, with the engine running at idle speed, disconnect the jumper cables in the reverse order of connection.

Make the booster battery cable connections in the numerical order shown (note that the negative cable of the booster battery is NOT attached to the negative terminal of the dead battery)

Remote jump starting terminals

Jacking and towing

JACKING

The jack supplied with the vehicle should only be used for changing a tire or placing jackstands under the frame. Never work under the vehicle or start the engine while this jack is being used as the only means of support.

The vehicle should be on level ground. Place the shift lever in Park, and block the wheel diagonally opposite the wheel being changed. Set the parking brake.

Remove the spare tire and jack from stowage. Remove the wheel cover and trim ring (if so equipped) with the tapered end of the lug nut wrench by inserting and twisting the handle and then prying against the back of the wheel cover. Loosen the wheel lug nuts about 1/4-to-1/2 turn each.

Place the jack so it engages the notch in the rocker panel nearest the wheel to be raised

Place the scissors-type jack under the side of the vehicle and adjust the jack height until it fits in the notch in the vertical rocker panel flange nearest the wheel to be changed. There is a front and rear jacking point on each side of the vehicle (see illustration).

Turn the jack handle clockwise until the tire clears the ground. Remove the lug nuts and pull the wheel off. Replace it with the spare.

Install the lug nuts with the beveled edges facing in. Tighten them snugly. Don't attempt to tighten them completely until the vehicle is lowered or it could slip off the jack. Turn the jack handle counterclockwise to lower the vehicle. Remove the jack and tighten the lug nuts in a diagonal pattern.

Install the cover (and trim ring, if used) and be sure it's snapped into place all the way around.

Stow the tire, jack and wrench. Unblock the wheels.

TOWING

As a general rule, the vehicle should be towed with the rear wheels off the ground. If they can't be raised, either place them on a dolly or disconnect the driveshaft from the differential. When a vehicle is towed with the rear wheels raised, the steering wheel must be clamped in the straight ahead position with a special device designed for use during towing. The ignition key must be in the OFF position, since the steering lock mechanism isn't strong enough to hold the front wheels straight while towing.

Vehicles can be towed from the front only with all four wheels on the ground, provided that speeds don't exceed 30 mph and the distance is not over 30 miles. Release the parking brake, put the transmission in Neutral and place the ignition key in the OFF position.

Equipment specifically designed for towing should be used. It should be attached to the main structural members of the vehicle, not the bumpers or brackets.

Safety is a major consideration when towing and all applicable state and local laws must be obeyed. A safety chain system must be used at all times. Remember that power steering and power brakes will not work with the engine off.

Automotive chemicals and lubricants

A number of automotive chemicals and lubricants are available for use during vehicle maintenance and repair. They include a wide variety of products ranging from cleaning solvents and degreasers to lubricants and protective sprays for rubber, plastic and vinyl.

CLEANERS

Carburetor cleaner and choke cleaner is a strong solvent for gum, varnish and carbon. Most carburetor cleaners leave a dry-type lubricant film which will not harden or gum up. Because of this film it is not recommended for use on electrical components.

Brake system cleaner is used to remove brake dust, grease and brake fluid from the brake system, where clean surfaces are absolutely necessary. It leaves no residue and often eliminates brake squeal caused by contaminants.

Electrical cleaner removes oxidation, corrosion and carbon deposits from electrical contacts, restoring full current flow. It can also be used to clean spark plugs, carburetor jets, voltage regulators and other parts where an oil-free surface is desired.

Demoisturants remove water and moisture from electrical components such as alternators, voltage regulators, electrical connectors and fuse blocks. They are non-conductive and non-corrosive.

Degreasers are heavy-duty solvents used to remove grease from the outside of the engine and from chassis components. They can be sprayed or brushed on and, depending on the type, are rinsed off either with water or solvent.

LUBRICANTS

Motor oil is the lubricant formulated for use in engines. It normally contains a wide variety of additives to prevent corrosion and reduce foaming and wear. Motor oil comes in various weights (viscosity ratings) from 0 to 50. The recommended weight of the oil depends on the season, temperature and the demands on the engine. Light oil is used in cold climates and under light load conditions. Heavy oil is used in hot climates and where high loads are encountered. Multi-viscosity oils are designed to have characteristics of both light and heavy oils and are available in a number of weights from 0W-20 to 20W-50.

Gear oil is designed to be used in differentials, manual transmissions and other areas where high-temperature lubrication is required.

Chassis and wheel bearing grease is a heavy grease used where increased loads and friction are encountered, such as for wheel bearings, ball-joints, tie-rod ends and universal joints.

High-temperature wheel bearing grease is designed to withstand the extreme temperatures encountered by wheel bearings in disc brake equipped vehicles. It usually contains molybdenum disulfide (moly), which is a dry-type lubricant.

White grease is a heavy grease for metal-to-metal applications where water is a problem. White grease stays soft under both low and high temperatures (usually from -100 to +190-degrees F), and will not wash off or dilute in the presence of water.

Assembly lube is a special extreme pressure lubricant, usually containing moly, used to lubricate high-load parts (such as main and rod bearings and cam lobes) for initial start-up of a new engine. The assembly lube lubricates the parts without being squeezed out or washed away until the engine oiling system begins to function.

Silicone lubricants are used to protect rubber, plastic, vinyl and nylon parts.

Graphite lubricants are used where oils cannot be used due to contamination problems, such as in locks. The dry graphite will lubricate metal parts while remaining uncontaminated by dirt, water, oil or acids. It is electrically conductive and will not foul electrical contacts in locks such as the ignition switch.

Moly penetrants loosen and lubricate frozen, rusted and corroded fasteners and prevent future rusting or freezing.

Heat-sink grease is a special electrically non-conductive grease that is used for mounting electronic ignition modules where it is essential that heat is transferred away from the module.

SEALANTS

RTV sealant is one of the most widely used gasket compounds. Made from silicone, RTV is air curing, it seals, bonds, waterproofs, fills surface irregularities, remains flexible, doesn't shrink, is relatively easy to remove, and is used as a supplementary sealer with almost all low and medium temperature gaskets.

Anaerobic sealant is much like RTV in that it can be used either to seal gaskets or to form gaskets by itself. It remains flexible, is solvent resistant and fills surface imperfections. The difference between an anaerobic sealant and an RTV-type sealant is in the curing. RTV cures when exposed to air, while an anaerobic sealant cures only in the absence of air. This means that an anaerobic sealant cures only after the assembly of parts, sealing them together.

Thread and pipe sealant is used for sealing hydraulic and pneumatic fittings and vacuum lines. It is usually made from a Teflon compound, and comes in a spray, a paint-on liquid and as a wrap-around tape.

CHEMICALS

Anti-seize compound prevents seizing, galling, cold welding, rust and corrosion in fasteners. High-temperature anti-seize, usually made with copper and graphite lubricants, is used for exhaust system and exhaust manifold bolts.

Anaerobic locking compounds are used to keep fasteners from vibrating or working loose and cure only after installation, in the absence of air. Medium strength locking compound is used for small nuts, bolts and screws that may be removed later. High-strength locking compound is for large nuts, bolts and studs which aren't removed on a regular basis.

Oil additives range from viscosity index improvers to chemical treatments that claim to reduce internal engine friction. It should be noted that most oil manufacturers caution against using additives with their oils.

Gas additives perform several functions, depending on their chemical makeup. They usually contain solvents that help dissolve gum and varnish that build up on carburetor, fuel injection and intake parts. They also serve to break down carbon deposits that form on the inside surfaces of the combustion chambers. Some additives contain upper cylinder lubricants for valves and piston rings, and others contain chemicals to remove condensation from the gas tank.

MISCELLANEOUS

Brake fluid is specially formulated hydraulic fluid that can withstand the heat and pressure encountered in brake systems. Care must be taken so this fluid does not come in contact with painted surfaces or plastics. An opened container should always be resealed to prevent contamination by water or dirt.

Weatherstrip adhesive is used to bond weatherstripping around doors, windows and trunk lids. It is sometimes used to attach trim pieces.

Undercoating is a petroleum-based, tar-like substance that is designed to protect metal surfaces on the underside of the vehicle from corrosion. It also acts as a sound-deadening agent by insulating the bottom of the vehicle.

Waxes and polishes are used to help protect painted and plated surfaces from the weather. Different types of paint may require the use of different types of wax and polish. Some polishes utilize a chemical or abrasive cleaner to help remove the top layer of oxidized (dull) paint on older vehicles. In recent years many non-wax polishes that contain a wide variety of chemicals such as polymers and silicones have been introduced. These non-wax polishes are usually easier to apply and last longer than conventional waxes and polishes.

CONVERSION FACTORS

LENGTH (distance)

Inches (in)	X	25.4	= Millimeters (mm)	X	0.0394	= Inches (in)
Feet (ft)	X	0.305	= Meters (m)	X	3.281	= Feet (ft)
Miles	X	1.609	= Kilometers (km)	X	0.621	= Miles

VOLUME (capacity)

Cubic inches (cu in; in^3)	X	16.387	= Cubic centimeters (cc; cm^3)	X	0.061	= Cubic inches (cu in; in^3)
Imperial pints (Imp pt)	X	0.568	= Liters (l)	X	1.76	= Imperial pints (Imp pt)
Imperial quarts (Imp qt)	X	1.137	= Liters (l)	X	0.88	= Imperial quarts (Imp qt)
Imperial quarts (Imp qt)	X	1.201	= US quarts (US qt)	X	0.833	= Imperial quarts (Imp qt)
US quarts (US qt)	X	0.946	= Liters (l)	X	1.057	= US quarts (US qt)
Imperial gallons (Imp gal)	X	4.546	= Liters (l)	X	0.22	= Imperial gallons (Imp gal)
Imperial gallons (Imp gal)	X	1.201	= US gallons (US gal)	X	0.833	= Imperial gallons (Imp gal)
US gallons (US gal)	X	3.785	= Liters (l)	X	0.264	= US gallons (US gal)

MASS (weight)

Ounces (oz)	X	28.35	= Grams (g)	X	0.035	= Ounces (oz)
Pounds (lb)	X	0.454	= Kilograms (kg)	X	2.205	= Pounds (lb)

FORCE

Ounces-force (ozf; oz)	X	0.278	= Newtons (N)	X	3.6	= Ounces-force (ozf; oz)
Pounds-force (lbf; lb)	X	4.448	= Newtons (N)	X	0.225	= Pounds-force (lbf; lb)
Newtons (N)	X	0.1	= Kilograms-force (kgf; kg)	X	9.81	= Newtons (N)

PRESSURE

Pounds-force per square inch (psi; lbf/in^2; lb/in^2)	X	0.070	= Kilograms-force per square centimeter (kgf/cm^2; kg/cm^2)	X	14.223	= Pounds-force per square inch (psi; lbf/in^2; lb/in^2)
Pounds-force per square inch (psi; lbf/in^2; lb/in^2)	X	0.068	= Atmospheres (atm)	X	14.696	= Pounds-force per square inch (psi; lbf/in^2; lb/in^2)
Pounds-force per square inch (psi; lbf/in^2; lb/in^2)	X	0.069	= Bars	X	14.5	= Pounds-force per square inch (psi; lbf/in^2; lb/in^2)
Pounds-force per square inch (psi; lbf/in^2; lb/in^2)	X	6.895	= Kilopascals (kPa)	X	0.145	= Pounds-force per square inch (psi; lbf/in^2; lb/in^2)
Kilopascals (kPa)	X	0.01	= Kilograms-force per square centimeter (kgf/cm^2; kg/cm^2)	X	98.1	= Kilopascals (kPa)

TORQUE (moment of force)

Pounds-force inches (lbf in; lb in)	X	1.152	= Kilograms-force centimeter (kgf cm; kg cm)	X	0.868	= Pounds-force inches (lbf in; lb in)
Pounds-force inches (lbf in; lb in)	X	0.113	= Newton meters (Nm)	X	8.85	= Pounds-force inches (lbf in; lb in)
Pounds-force inches (lbf in; lb in)	X	0.083	= Pounds-force feet (lbf ft; lb ft)	X	12	= Pounds-force inches (lbf in; lb in)
Pounds-force feet (lbf ft; lb ft)	X	0.138	= Kilograms-force meters (kgf m; kg m)	X	7.233	= Pounds-force feet (lbf ft; lb ft)
Pounds-force feet (lbf ft; lb ft)	X	1.356	= Newton meters (Nm)	X	0.738	= Pounds-force feet (lbf ft; lb ft)
Newton meters (Nm)	X	0.102	= Kilograms-force meters (kgf m; kg m)	X	9.804	= Newton meters (Nm)

VACUUM

Inches mercury (in. Hg)	X	3.377	= Kilopascals (kPa)	X	0.2961	= Inches mercury
Inches mercury (in. Hg)	X	25.4	= Millimeters mercury (mm Hg)	X	0.0394	= Inches mercury

POWER

Horsepower (hp)	X	745.7	= Watts (W)	X	0.0013	= Horsepower (hp)

VELOCITY (speed)

Miles per hour (miles/hr; mph)	X	1.609	= Kilometers per hour (km/hr; kph)	X	0.621	= Miles per hour (miles/hr; mph)

FUEL CONSUMPTION *

Miles per gallon, Imperial (mpg)	X	0.354	= Kilometers per liter (km/l)	X	2.825	= Miles per gallon, Imperial (mpg)
Miles per gallon, US (mpg)	X	0.425	= Kilometers per liter (km/l)	X	2.352	= Miles per gallon, US (mpg)

TEMPERATURE

Degrees Fahrenheit = (°C x 1.8) + 32   Degrees Celsius (Degrees Centigrade; °C) = (°F - 32) x 0.56

*It is common practice to convert from miles per gallon (mpg) to liters/100 kilometers (l/100km), where mpg (Imperial) x l/100 km = 282 and mpg (US) x l/100 km = 235

FRACTION/DECIMAL/MILLIMETER EQUIVALENTS

DECIMALS TO MILLIMETERS

Decimal	mm	Decimal	mm
0.001	0.0254	0.500	12.7000
0.002	0.0508	0.510	12.9540
0.003	0.0762	0.520	13.2080
0.004	0.1016	0.530	13.4620
0.005	0.1270	0.540	13.7160
0.006	0.1524	0.550	13.9700
0.007	0.1778	0.560	14.2240
0.008	0.2032	0.570	14.4780
0.009	0.2286	0.580	14.7320
0.010	0.2540	0.590	14.9860
0.020	0.5080		
0.030	0.7620		
0.040	1.0160	0.600	15.2400
0.050	1.2700	0.610	15.4940
0.060	1.5240	0.620	15.7480
0.070	1.7780	0.630	16.0020
0.080	2.0320	0.640	16.2560
0.090	2.2860	0.650	16.5100
0.100	2.5400	0.660	16.7640
0.110	2.7940	0.670	17.0180
0.120	3.0480	0.680	17.2720
0.130	3.3020	0.690	17.5260
0.140	3.5560		
0.150	3.8100		
0.160	4.0640	0.700	17.7800
0.170	4.3180	0.710	18.0340
0.180	4.5720	0.720	18.2880
0.190	4.8260	0.730	18.5420
0.200	5.0800	0.740	18.7960
0.210	5.3340	0.750	19.0500
0.220	5.5880	0.760	19.3040
0.230	5.8420	0.770	19.5580
0.240	6.0960	0.780	19.8120
0.250	6.3500	0.790	20.0660
0.260	6.6040		
0.270	6.8580	0.800	20.3200
0.280	7.1120	0.810	20.5740
0.290	7.3660	0.820	21.8280
0.300	7.6200	0.830	21.0820
0.310	7.8740	0.840	21.3360
0.320	8.1280	0.850	21.5900
0.330	8.3820	0.860	21.8440
0.340	8.6360	0.870	22.0980
0.350	8.8900	0.880	22.3520
0.360	9.1440	0.890	22.6060
0.370	9.3980		
0.380	9.6520		
0.390	9.9060	0.900	22.8600
0.400	10.1600	0.910	23.1140
0.410	10.4140	0.920	23.3680
0.420	10.6680	0.930	23.6220
0.430	10.9220	0.940	23.8760
0.440	11.1760	0.950	24.1300
0.450	11.4300	0.960	24.3840
0.460	11.6840	0.970	24.6380
0.470	11.9380	0.980	24.8920
0.480	12.1920	0.990	25.1460
0.490	12.4460	1.000	25.4000

FRACTIONS TO DECIMALS TO MILLIMETERS

Fraction	Decimal	mm	Fraction	Decimal	mm
1/64	0.0156	0.3969	33/64	0.5156	13.0969
1/32	0.0312	0.7938	17/32	0.5312	13.4938
3/64	0.0469	1.1906	35/64	0.5469	13.8906
1/16	0.0625	1.5875	9/16	0.5625	14.2875
5/64	0.0781	1.9844	37/64	0.5781	14.6844
3/32	0.0938	2.3812	19/32	0.5938	15.0812
7/64	0.1094	2.7781	39/64	0.6094	15.4781
1/8	0.1250	3.1750	5/8	0.6250	15.8750
9/64	0.1406	3.5719	41/64	0.6406	16.2719
5/32	0.1562	3.9688	21/32	0.6562	16.6688
11/64	0.1719	4.3656	43/64	0.6719	17.0656
3/16	0.1875	4.7625	11/16	0.6875	17.4625
13/64	0.2031	5.1594	45/64	0.7031	17.8594
7/32	0.2188	5.5562	23/32	0.7188	18.2562
15/64	0.2344	5.9531	47/64	0.7344	18.6531
1/4	0.2500	6.3500	3/4	0.7500	19.0500
17/64	0.2656	6.7469	49/64	0.7656	19.4469
9/32	0.2812	7.1438	25/32	0.7812	19.8438
19/64	0.2969	7.5406	51/64	0.7969	20.2406
5/16	0.3125	7.9375	13/16	0.8125	20.6375
21/64	0.3281	8.3344	53/64	0.8281	21.0344
11/32	0.3438	8.7312	27/32	0.8438	21.4312
23/64	0.3594	9.1281	55/64	0.8594	21.8281
3/8	0.3750	9.5250	7/8	0.8750	22.2250
25/64	0.3906	9.9219	57/64	0.8906	22.6219
13/32	0.4062	10.3188	29/32	0.9062	23.0188
27/64	0.4219	10.7156	59/64	0.9219	23.4156
7/16	0.4375	11.1125	15/16	0.9375	23.8125
29/64	0.4531	11.5094	61/64	0.9531	24.2094
15/32	0.4688	11.9062	31/32	0.9688	24.6062
31/64	0.4844	12.3031	63/64	0.9844	25.0031
1/2	0.5000	12.7000	1	1.0000	25.4000

Safety first!

Regardless of how enthusiastic you may be about getting on with the job at hand, take the time to ensure that your safety is not jeopardized. A moment's lack of attention can result in an accident, as can failure to observe certain simple safety precautions. The possibility of an accident will always exist, and the following points should not be considered a comprehensive list of all dangers. Rather, they are intended to make you aware of the risks and to encourage a safety conscious approach to all work you carry out on your vehicle.

ESSENTIAL DOS AND DON'TS

DON'T rely on a jack when working under the vehicle. Always use approved jackstands to support the weight of the vehicle and place them under the recommended lift or support points.

DON'T attempt to loosen extremely tight fasteners (i.e. wheel lug nuts) while the vehicle is on a jack - it may fall.

DON'T start the engine without first making sure that the transmission is in Neutral (or Park where applicable) and the parking brake is set.

DON'T remove the radiator cap from a hot cooling system - let it cool or cover it with a cloth and release the pressure gradually.

DON'T attempt to drain the engine oil until you are sure it has cooled to the point that it will not burn you.

DON'T touch any part of the engine or exhaust system until it has cooled sufficiently to avoid burns.

DON'T siphon toxic liquids such as gasoline, antifreeze and brake fluid by mouth, or allow them to remain on your skin.

DON'T inhale brake lining dust - it is potentially hazardous (see Asbestos below).

DON'T allow spilled oil or grease to remain on the floor - wipe it up before someone slips on it.

DON'T use loose fitting wrenches or other tools which may slip and cause injury.

DON'T push on wrenches when loosening or tightening nuts or bolts. Always try to pull the wrench toward you. If the situation calls for pushing the wrench away, push with an open hand to avoid scraped knuckles if the wrench should slip.

DON'T attempt to lift a heavy component alone - get someone to help you.

DON'T rush or take unsafe shortcuts to finish a job.

DON'T allow children or animals in or around the vehicle while you are working on it.

DO wear eye protection when using power tools such as a drill, sander, bench grinder, etc. and when working under a vehicle.

DO keep loose clothing and long hair well out of the way of moving parts.

DO make sure that any hoist used has a safe working load rating adequate for the job.

DO get someone to check on you periodically when working alone on a vehicle.

DO carry out work in a logical sequence and make sure that everything is correctly assembled and tightened.

DO keep chemicals and fluids tightly capped and out of the reach of children and pets.

DO remember that your vehicle's safety affects that of yourself and others. If in doubt on any point, get professional advice.

STEERING, SUSPENSION AND BRAKES

These systems are essential to driving safety, so make sure you have a qualified shop or individual check your work. Also, compressed suspension springs can cause injury if released suddenly - be sure to use a spring compressor.

AIRBAGS

Airbags are explosive devices that can CAUSE injury if they deploy while you're working on the vehicle. Follow the manufacturer's instructions to disable the airbag whenever you're working in the vicinity of airbag components.

ASBESTOS

Certain friction, insulating, sealing, and other products - such as brake linings, brake bands, clutch linings, torque converters, gaskets, etc. - may contain asbestos or other hazardous friction material. Extreme care must be taken to avoid inhalation of dust from such products, since it is hazardous to health. If in doubt, assume that they do contain asbestos.

FIRE

Remember at all times that gasoline is highly flammable. Never smoke or have any kind of open flame around when working on a vehicle. But the risk does not end there. A spark caused by an electrical short circuit, by two metal surfaces contacting each other, or even by static electricity built up in your body under certain conditions, can ignite gasoline vapors, which in a confined space are highly explosive. Do not, under any circumstances, use gasoline for cleaning parts. Use an approved safety solvent.

Always disconnect the battery ground (-) cable at the battery before working on any part of the fuel system or electrical system. Never risk spilling fuel on a hot engine or exhaust component. It is strongly recommended that a fire extinguisher suitable for use on fuel and electrical fires be kept handy in the garage or workshop at all times. Never try to extinguish a fuel or electrical fire with water.

FUMES

Certain fumes are highly toxic and can quickly cause unconsciousness and even death if inhaled to any extent. Gasoline vapor falls into this category, as do the vapors from some cleaning solvents. Any draining or pouring of such volatile fluids should be done in a well ventilated area.

When using cleaning fluids and solvents, read the instructions on the container carefully. Never use materials from unmarked containers.

Never run the engine in an enclosed space, such as a garage. Exhaust fumes contain carbon monoxide, which is extremely poisonous. If you need to run the engine, always do so in the open air, or at least have the rear of the vehicle outside the work area.

THE BATTERY

Never create a spark or allow a bare light bulb near a battery. They normally give off a certain amount of hydrogen gas, which is highly explosive.

Always disconnect the battery ground (-) cable at the battery before working on the fuel or electrical systems.

If possible, loosen the filler caps or cover when charging the battery from an external source (this does not apply to sealed or maintenance-free batteries). Do not charge at an excessive rate or the battery may burst.

Take care when adding water to a non maintenance-free battery and when carrying a battery. The electrolyte, even when diluted, is very corrosive and should not be allowed to contact clothing or skin.

Always wear eye protection when cleaning the battery to prevent the caustic deposits from entering your eyes.

HOUSEHOLD CURRENT

When using an electric power tool, inspection light, etc., which operates on household current, always make sure that the tool is correctly connected to its plug and that, where necessary, it is properly grounded. Do not use such items in damp conditions and, again, do not create a spark or apply excessive heat in the vicinity of fuel or fuel vapor.

SECONDARY IGNITION SYSTEM VOLTAGE

A severe electric shock can result from touching certain parts of the ignition system (such as the spark plug wires) when the engine is running or being cranked, particularly if components are damp or the insulation is defective. In the case of an electronic ignition system, the secondary system voltage is much higher and could prove fatal.

HYDROFLUORIC ACID

This extremely corrosive acid is formed when certain types of synthetic rubber, found in some O-rings, oil seals, fuel hoses, etc. are exposed to temperatures above 750-degrees F (400-degrees C). The rubber changes into a charred or sticky substance containing the acid. *Once formed, the acid remains dangerous for years. If it gets onto the skin, it may be necessary to amputate the limb concerned.*

When dealing with a vehicle which has suffered a fire, or with components salvaged from such a vehicle, wear protective gloves and discard them after use.

Troubleshooting

CONTENTS

Section   Symptom

Engine

1   Engine will not rotate when attempting to start
2   Engine rotates but will not start
3   Starter motor operates without turning engine
4   Engine hard to start when cold
5   Engine hard to start when hot
6   Starter motor noisy or engages roughly
7   Engine starts but stops immediately
8   Engine 'lopes' while idling or idles erratically
9   Engine misses at idle speed
10 Excessively high idle speed
11 Battery will not hold a charge
12 Alternator light stays on
13 Alternator light fails to come on when key is turned on
14 Engine misses throughout driving speed range
15 Hesitation or stumble during acceleration
16 Engine stalls
17 Engine lacks power
18 Engine backfires
19 Engine surges while holding accelerator steady
20 Pinging or knocking engine sounds when engine is under load
21 Engine diesels (continues to run) after being turned off
22 Low oil pressure
23 Excessive oil consumption
24 Excessive fuel consumption
25 Fuel odor
26 Miscellaneous engine noises
CHECK ENGINE light - See Chapter 6

Cooling system

27 Overheating
28 Overcooling
29 External coolant leakage
30 Internal coolant leakage
31 Abnormal coolant loss
32 Poor coolant circulation
33 Corrosion

Automatic transmission

34 Fluid leakage
35 General shift mechanism problems
36 Transmission will not downshift with the accelerator pedal pressed to the floor
37 Engine will start in gears other than Park or Neutral
38 Transmission slips, shifts rough, is noisy or has no drive in forward or Reverse gears

Section   Symptom

Driveshaft

39 Leaks at front of driveshaft
40 Knock or clunk when transmission is under initial load (just after transmission is put into gear)
41 Metallic grating sound consistent with vehicle speed
42 Vibration
43 Scraping noise

Rear axle and differential

44 Noise - same when in drive as when vehicle is coasting
45 Knocking sound when starting or shifting gears
46 Noise when turning
47 Vibration
48 Oil leaks

Brakes

49 Vehicle pulls to one side during braking
50 Noise (high-pitched squeal or scraping sound))
51 Excessive brake pedal travel
52 Brake pedal feels spongy when depressed
53 Excessive effort required to stop vehicle
54 Pedal travels to the floor with little resistance
55 Brake pedal pulsates during brake application
56 Brakes drag (indicated by sluggish engine performance or wheels being very hot after driving)
57 Rear brakes lock up under light brake application
58 Rear brakes lock up under heavy brake application

Suspension and steering

59 Vehicle pulls to one side
60 Shimmy, shake or vibration
61 Excessive pitching and/or rolling around corners or during braking
62 Wandering or general instability
63 Excessively stiff steering
64 Excessive play in steering
65 Lack of power assistance
66 Steering wheel fails to return to straight-ahead position
67 Steering effort not the same in both directions
68 Noisy power steering pump
69 Miscellaneous noises
70 Excessive tire wear (not specific to one area)
71 Excessive tire wear on outside edge
72 Excessive tire wear on inside edge
73 Tire tread worn in one place

ENGINE

1   Engine will not rotate when attempting to start

1   Battery terminal connections loose or corroded. Check the cable terminals at the battery; tighten cable clamp and/or clean off corrosion as necessary (see Chapter 1).

2   Battery discharged or faulty. If the cable ends are clean and tight on the battery posts, turn the key to the On position and switch on the headlights or windshield wipers. If they won't run, the battery is discharged.

3   Automatic transmission not engaged in park (P) or Neutral (N).

4   Broken, loose or disconnected wires in the starting circuit. Inspect all wires and connectors at the battery, starter solenoid and ignition switch (on steering column).

5   Starter motor pinion jammed in flywheel/driveplate ring gear. Remove the starter (Chapter 5) and inspect the pinion and ring gear (Chapter 2).

6   Starter solenoid faulty (Chapter 5).

7   Starter motor faulty (Chapter 5).

8   Ignition switch faulty (Chapter 12).

9   Engine seized. Try to turn the crankshaft with a large socket and breaker bar on the pulley bolt.

10 Starter relay faulty (Chapter 4).

11 Transmission Range (TR) sensor out of adjustment or defective (Chapter 6).

2   Engine rotates but will not start

1   Fuel tank empty.

2   Battery discharged (engine rotates slowly).

3   Battery terminal connections loose or corroded.

4   Fuel not reaching fuel injectors. Check for clogged fuel filter or lines and defective fuel pump. Also make sure the tank vent lines aren't clogged (Chapter 4).

5   Low cylinder compression. Check as described in Chapter 2.

6   Water in fuel. Drain tank and fill with new fuel.

7   Defective ignition coil(s) (Chapter 5).

8   Dirty or clogged fuel injector(s) (Chapter 4).

9   Wet or damaged ignition components (Chapters 1 and 5).

10 Worn, faulty or incorrectly gapped spark plugs (Chapter 1).

11 Broken, loose or disconnected wires in the starting circuit (see previous Section).

12 Timing belt or chain failure or wear affecting valve timing (Chapter 2).

13 Fuel injection or engine control systems failure (Chapters 4 and 6).

14 Defective MAP sensor (Chapter 6)

3   Starter motor operates without turning engine

1   Starter pinion sticking. Remove the starter (Chapter 5) and inspect.

2   Starter pinion or flywheel/driveplate teeth worn or broken. Remove the inspection cover and inspect.

4   Engine hard to start when cold

1   Battery discharged or low. Check as described in Chapter 1.

2   Fuel not reaching the fuel injectors. Check the fuel filter, lines

and fuel pump (Chapters 1 and 4).

3   Defective spark plugs (Chapter 1).

4   Defective engine coolant temperature sensor (Chapter 6).

5   Fuel injection or engine control systems malfunction (Chapters 4 and 6).

5   Engine hard to start when hot

1   Air filter dirty (Chapter 1).

2   Fuel not reaching the fuel injection (see Section 4). Check for a vapor lock situation, brought about by clogged fuel tank vent lines.

3   Bad engine ground connection.

4   Fuel injection or engine control systems malfunction (Chapters 4 and 6).

6   Starter motor noisy or engages roughly

1   Pinion or driveplate teeth worn or broken. Remove the inspection cover on the left side of the engine and inspect.

2   Starter motor mounting bolts loose or missing.

7   Engine starts but stops immediately

1   Loose or damaged wire harness connections at coil or alternator.

2   Intake manifold vacuum leaks. Make sure all mounting bolts/nuts are tight and all vacuum hoses connected to the manifold are attached properly and in good condition.

3   Insufficient fuel pressure (see Chapter 4).

4   Fuel injection or engine control systems malfunction (Chapters 4 and 6).

8   Engine 'lopes' while idling or idles erratically

1   Vacuum leaks. Check mounting bolts at the intake manifold for tightness. Make sure that all vacuum hoses are connected and in good condition. Use a stethoscope or a length of fuel hose held against your ear to listen for vacuum leaks while the engine is running. A hissing sound will be heard. A soapy water solution will also detect leaks. Check the intake manifold gasket surfaces.

2   Leaking EGR valve or plugged PCV valve (see Chapters 1 and 6).

3   Air filter clogged (Chapter 1).

4   Fuel pump not delivering sufficient fuel (Chapter 4).

5   Leaking head gasket. Perform a cylinder compression check (Chapter 2).

6   Timing chain(s) worn (Chapter 2).

7   Camshaft lobes worn (Chapter 2).

8   Valves burned or otherwise leaking (Chapter 2).

9   Ignition system not operating properly (Chapters 1 and 5).

10 Fuel injection or engine control systems malfunction (Chapters 4 and 6).

9   Engine misses at idle speed

1   Spark plugs faulty or not gapped properly (Chapter 1).

2   Faulty spark plug wires (Chapter 1).

3   Short circuits in ignition, coil or spark plug wires.

4   Sticking or faulty emissions systems (see Chapter 6).

5   Clogged fuel filter and/or foreign matter in fuel. Remove the fuel filter (Chapter 1) and inspect.

6   Vacuum leaks at intake manifold or hose connections. Check as

described in Section 8.

7 Low or uneven cylinder compression. Check as described in Chapter 2.

8 Fuel injection or engine control systems malfunction (Chapters 4 and 6).

10 Excessively high idle speed

1 Sticking throttle linkage (Chapter 4).

2 Vacuum leaks at intake manifold or hose connections. Check as described in Section 8.

3 Fuel injection or engine control systems malfunction (Chapters 4 and 6).

11 Battery will not hold a charge

1 Alternator drivebelt defective or not adjusted properly (Chapter 1).

2 Battery cables loose or corroded (Chapter 1).

3 Alternator not charging properly (Chapter 5).

4 Loose, broken or faulty wires in the charging circuit (Chapter 5).

5 Short circuit causing a continuous drain on the battery.

6 Battery defective internally.

12 Alternator light stays on

1 Fault in alternator or charging circuit (Chapter 5).

2 Alternator drivebelt defective or not properly adjusted (Chapter 1).

13 Alternator light fails to come on when key is turned on

1 Faulty bulb (Chapter 12).

2 Defective alternator (Chapter 5).

3 Fault in the printed circuit, dash wiring or bulb holder (Chapter 12).

14 Engine misses throughout driving speed range

1 Fuel filter clogged and/or impurities in the fuel system. Check fuel filter (Chapter 1) or clean system (Chapter 4).

2 Faulty or incorrectly gapped spark plugs (Chapter 1).

3 Emissions system components faulty (Chapter 6).

4 Low or uneven cylinder compression pressures. Check as described in Chapter 2.

5 Weak or faulty ignition coil(s) (Chapter 5).

6 Weak or faulty ignition system (Chapter 5).

7 Vacuum leaks at intake manifold or vacuum hoses (see Section 8).

8 Dirty or clogged fuel injector(s) (Chapter 4).

9 Leaky EGR valve (Chapter 6).

10 Fuel injection or engine control systems malfunction (Chapters 4 and 6).

15 Hesitation or stumble during acceleration

1 Ignition system not operating properly (Chapter 5).

2 Dirty or clogged fuel injector(s) (Chapter 4).

3 Low fuel pressure. Check for proper operation of the fuel pump and for restrictions in the fuel filter and lines (Chapter 4).

4 Fuel injection or engine control systems malfunction (Chapters 4 and 6).

16 Engine stalls

1 Fuel filter clogged and/or water and impurities in the fuel system (Chapter 4).

2 Emissions system components faulty (Chapter 6).

3 Faulty or incorrectly gapped spark plugs (Chapter 1).

4 Vacuum leak at the intake manifold or vacuum hoses. Check as described in Section 8.

5 Fuel injection or engine control systems malfunction (Chapters 4 and 6).

17 Engine lacks power

1 Faulty or incorrectly gapped spark plugs (Chapter 1).

2 Air filter dirty (Chapter 1).

3 Faulty ignition coil(s) (Chapter 5).

4 Brakes binding (Chapters 1 and 10).

5 Automatic transmission fluid level incorrect, causing slippage (Chapter 1).

6 Fuel filter clogged and/or impurities in the fuel system (Chapter 4).

7 EGR system not functioning properly (Chapter 6).

8 Use of sub-standard fuel. Fill tank with proper octane fuel.

9 Low or uneven cylinder compression pressures. Check as described in Chapter 2.

10 Vacuum leak at intake manifold or vacuum hoses (check as described in Section 8).

11 Dirty or clogged fuel injector(s) (Chapters 1 and 4).

12 Fuel injection or engine control systems malfunction (Chapters 4 and 6).

13 Restricted exhaust system (Chapter 4).

18 Engine backfires

1 EGR system not functioning properly (Chapter 6).

2 Vacuum leak (refer to Section 8).

3 Damaged valve springs or sticking valves.

4 Vacuum leak at the intake manifold or vacuum hoses (see Section 12).

19 Engine surges while holding accelerator steady

1 Vacuum leak at the intake manifold or vacuum hoses (see Section 8).

2 Restricted air filter (Chapter 1).

3 Fuel pump or pressure regulator defective (Chapter 4).

4 Fuel injection or engine control systems malfunction (Chapters 4 and 6).

20 Pinging or knocking engine sounds when engine is under load

1 Incorrect grade of fuel. Fill tank with fuel of the proper octane rating.

2 Carbon build-up in combustion chambers. Remove cylinder head(s) and clean combustion chambers (Chapter 2).

3 Incorrect spark plugs (Chapter 1).

4 Fuel injection or engine control systems malfunction (Chapters 4 and 6).

5 Restricted exhaust system (Chapter 4).

21 Engine diesels (continues to run) after being turned off

1 Incorrect spark plug heat range (Chapter 1).
2 Vacuum leak at the intake manifold or vacuum hoses (see Section 8).
3 Carbon build-up in combustion chambers. Remove the cylinder head(s) and clean the combustion chambers (Chapter 2).
4 Valves sticking (Chapter 2).
5 EGR system not operating properly (Chapter 6).
6 Fuel injection or engine control systems malfunction (Chapters 4 and 6).
7 Check for causes of overheating (Section 27).

22 Low oil pressure

1 Improper grade of oil.
2 Oil pump worn or damaged (Chapter 2).
3 Engine overheating (refer to Section 27).
4 Clogged oil filter (Chapter 1).
5 Clogged oil strainer (Chapter 2).
6 Oil pressure gauge not working properly (Chapter 2).

23 Excessive oil consumption

1 Loose oil drain plug.
2 Loose bolts or damaged oil pan gasket (Chapter 2).
3 Loose bolts or damaged front cover gasket (Chapter 2).
4 Front or rear crankshaft oil seal leaking (Chapter 2).
5 Loose bolts or damaged valve cover gasket (Chapter 2).
6 Loose oil filter (Chapter 1).
7 Loose or damaged oil pressure switch (Chapter 2).
8 Pistons and cylinders excessively worn (Chapter 2).
9 Piston rings not installed correctly on pistons (Chapter 2).
10 Worn or damaged piston rings (Chapter 2).
11 Intake and/or exhaust valve oil seals worn or damaged.
12 Worn valve stems or guides.
13 Worn or damaged valves/guides.
14 Faulty or incorrect PCV valve allowing too much crankcase airflow.

24 Excessive fuel consumption

1 Dirty or clogged air filter element (Chapter 1).
2 Low tire pressure or incorrect tire size (Chapter 10).
3 Inspect for binding brakes.
4 Fuel leakage. Check all connections, lines and components in the fuel system (Chapter 4).
5 Dirty or clogged fuel injectors (Chapter 4).
6 Fuel injection or engine control systems malfunction (Chapters 4 and 6).
7 Thermostat stuck open or not installed.
8 Improperly operating transmission.

25 Fuel odor

1 Fuel leakage. Check all connections, lines and components in the fuel system (Chapter 4).
2 Fuel tank overfilled. Fill only to automatic shut-off.
3 Charcoal canister in Evaporative Emissions Control system clogged (Chapter 1).
4 Vapor leaks from Evaporative Emissions Control system lines (Chapter 6).

26 Miscellaneous engine noises

1 A strong dull noise that becomes more rapid as the engine accelerates indicates worn or damaged crankshaft bearings or an unevenly worn crankshaft. To pinpoint the trouble spot, disconnect the electrical connector from one coil at a time and crank the engine over. If the noise stops, the cylinder with the disconnected coil indicates the problem area. Replace the bearing and/or service or replace the crankshaft (Chapter 2).
2 A similar (yet slightly higher pitched) noise to the crankshaft knocking described in the previous paragraph, that becomes more rapid as the engine accelerates, indicates worn or damaged connecting rod bearings (Chapter 2). The procedure for locating the problem cylinder is the same as described in Paragraph 1.
3 An overlapping metallic noise that increases in intensity as the engine speed increases, yet diminishes as the engine warms up indicates abnormal piston and cylinder wear (Chapter 2). To locate the problem cylinder, use the procedure described in Paragraph 1.
4 A rapid clicking noise that becomes faster as the engine accelerates indicates a worn piston pin or piston pin hole. This sound will happen each time the piston hits the highest and lowest points in the stroke (Chapter 2). The procedure for locating the problem piston is described in Paragraph 1.
5 A metallic clicking noise coming from the water pump indicates worn or damaged water pump bearings or pump. Replace the water pump with a new one (Chapter 3).
6 A rapid tapping sound or clicking sound that becomes faster as the engine speed increases indicates "valve tapping." This can be identified by holding one end of a section of hose to your ear and placing the other end at different spots along the valve cover. The point where the sound is loudest indicates the problem valve. If the pushrod and rocker arm components are in good shape, you likely have a collapsed valve lifter. Changing the engine oil and adding a high viscosity oil treatment will sometimes cure a stuck lifter problem. If the problem persists, the lifters, pushrods and rocker arms must be removed for inspection (see Chapter 2).
7 A steady metallic rattling or rapping sound coming from the area of the timing chain cover indicates a worn, damaged or out-of-adjustment timing chain. Service or replace the chain and related components (Chapter 2).

COOLING SYSTEM

27 Overheating

1 Insufficient coolant in system (Chapter 1).
2 Drivebelt defective or not adjusted properly (Chapter 1).
3 Radiator core blocked or dirty and restricted (Chapter 3).
4 Thermostat faulty (Chapter 3).
5 Cooling fan not functioning properly (Chapter 3).
6 Expansion tank cap not maintaining proper pressure. Have cap pressure tested by gas station or repair shop.
7 Defective water pump (Chapter 3).
8 Improper grade of engine oil.
9 Inaccurate temperature gauge (Chapter 12).

28 Overcooling

1 Thermostat faulty (Chapter 3).
2 Inaccurate temperature gauge (Chapter 12).

29 External coolant leakage

1 Deteriorated or damaged hoses. Loose clamps at hose connections (Chapter 1).
2 Water pump seals defective. If this is the case, water will drip from the weep hole in the water pump body (Chapter 3).
3 Leakage from radiator core or header tank. This will require the radiator to be replaced or professionally repaired (see Chapter 3 for removal procedures).
4 Leakage from the expansion tank or cap.
5 Engine drain plugs or water jacket freeze plugs leaking (see Chapters 1 and 2).
6 Leak from coolant temperature switch (Chapter 3).
7 Leak from damaged gaskets or small cracks (Chapter 2).

30 Internal coolant leakage

→Note: Internal coolant leaks can usually be detected by examining the oil. Check the dipstick and the underside of the engine oil filler cap for water deposits and an oil consistency like that of a milkshake.

1 Leaking cylinder head gasket. Have the system pressure tested or remove the cylinder head (Chapter 2) and inspect.
2 Cracked cylinder bore or cylinder head. Dismantle engine and inspect (Chapter 2).

31 Abnormal coolant loss

1 Overfilled cooling system (Chapter 1).
2 Coolant boiling away due to overheating (see causes in Section 27).
3 Internal or external leakage (see Sections 29 and 30).
4 Faulty expansion tank cap. Have the cap pressure tested.
5 Cooling system being pressurized by engine compression. This could be due to a cracked head or block or leaking head gasket(s). Have the system tested for the presence of combustion gas in the coolant at a shop. (Combustion leak detectors are also available at some auto parts stores.)

32 Poor coolant circulation

1 Inoperative water pump (Chapter 3).
2 Restriction in cooling system. Drain, flush and refill the system (Chapter 1). If necessary, remove the radiator (Chapter 3) and have it reverse flushed or professionally cleaned.
3 Defective drivebelt tensioner (Chapter 1).
4 Thermostat sticking (Chapter 3).
5 Insufficient coolant (Chapter 1).

33 Corrosion

1 Excessive impurities in the water. Soft, clean water is recommended. Distilled or rainwater is satisfactory.
2 Insufficient tintifreeze solution (refer to Chapter 1 for the proper ratio of water to antifreeze).

3 Infrequent flushing and draining of system. Regular flushing of the cooling system should be carried out at the specified intervals as described in (Chapter 1).

AUTOMATIC TRANSMISSION

→Note: Due to the complexity of the automatic transmission, it's difficult for the home mechanic to properly diagnose and service. For problems other than the following, the vehicle should be taken to a reputable mechanic.

34 Fluid leakage

1 Automatic transmission fluid is a deep red color, and fluid leaks should not be confused with engine oil which can easily be blown by air flow to the transmission.
2 To pinpoint a leak, first remove all built-up dirt and grime from the transmission. Degreasing agents and/or steam cleaning will achieve this. With the underside clean, drive the vehicle at low speeds so the air flow will not blow the leak far from its source. Raise the vehicle and determine where the leak is located. Common areas of leakage are:

a) *Fluid pan:* tighten mounting bolts and/or replace pan gasket as necessary (Chapter 1).
b) *Rear extension:* tighten bolts and/or replace oil seal as necessary.
c) *Filler pipe:* replace the rubber oil seal where pipe enters transmission case.
d) *Transmission oil lines:* tighten fittings where lines enter transmission case and/or replace lines.
e) *Vent pipe:* transmission overfilled and/or water in fluid (see checking procedures, Chapter 1).
f) *Vehicle speed sensor:* replace the O-ring where speed sensor enters transmission case.

35 General shift mechanism problems

Chapter 7 deals with checking and adjusting the shift cable on automatic transmissions. Common problems which may be caused by out of adjustment cable are:

a) Engine starting in gears other than P (park) or N (Neutral).
b) Indicator pointing to a gear other than the one actually engaged.
c) Vehicle moves with transmission in P (Park) position.

36 Transmission will not downshift with the accelerator pedal pressed to the floor

Since these transmissions are electronically controlled, check for any diagnostic trouble codes stored in the PCM. The actual repair will most likely have to be performed by a qualified repair shop with the proper equipment.

37 Engine will start in gears other than Park or Neutral

1 Shift cable out of adjustment (Chapter 7).
2 Defective Transmission Range (TR) sensor (42RLE transmission) or Park/Neutral Contact (NAG1 transmission) inside transmission. Check for stored trouble codes (see Chapter 6). Further diagnosis and repair should be entrusted to a professional.

38 Transmission slips, shifts rough, is noisy or has no drive in forward or Reverse gears

1 There are many probable causes for the above problems, but the home mechanic should concern himself only with one possibility: fluid level.

2 Before taking the vehicle to a shop, check the fluid level and condition as described in Chapter 1. Add fluid, if necessary, or change the fluid and filter if needed. If problems persist, have a professional diagnose the transmission.

DRIVESHAFT

➡Note: Refer to Chapter 8, unless otherwise specified, for service information.

39 Leaks at front of driveshaft

Defective transmission extension housing oil seal. See Chapter 7 for replacement procedure. As this is done, check the output shaft flange for burrs or roughness that could damage the new seal. Remove burrs with a fine file or whetstone.

40 Knock or clunk when transmission is under initial load (just after transmission is put into gear)

1 Loose or disconnected rear suspension components. Check all mounting bolts and bushings (Chapters 7 and 10).

2 Loose driveshaft bolts. Inspect all bolts and nuts and tighten them securely.

41 Metallic grating sound consistent with vehicle speed

Pronounced wear in the driveshaft center support bearing. Remove the driveshaft and have the center support bearing replaced by a driveline specialist (special tools are required).

42 Vibration

➡Note: Before blaming the driveshaft, make sure the tires are perfectly balanced and perform the following test.

1 Install a tachometer inside the vehicle to monitor engine speed as the vehicle is driven. Drive the vehicle and note the engine speed at which the vibration (roughness) is most pronounced. Now shift the transmission to a different gear and bring the engine speed to the same point.

2 If the vibration occurs at the same engine speed (rpm) regardless of which gear the transmission is in, the driveshaft is NOT at fault since the driveshaft speed varies.

3 If the vibration decreases or is eliminated when the transmission is in a different gear at the same engine speed, refer to the following probable causes:

a) *Bent or dented driveshaft. Inspect and replace as necessary.*

b) *Undercoating or built-up dirt, etc. on the driveshaft. Clean the shaft thoroughly.*

c) *Driveshaft and/or companion flange out of balance. Check for missing weights on the shaft. Remove driveshaft and reinstall 180-degrees from original position, then recheck. Have the driveshaft balanced if problem persists.*

d) *Loose driveshaft mounting bolts/nuts.*

e) *Worn transmission rear bushing (Chapter 7).*

43 Scraping noise

Make sure there is nothing, such as an exhaust heat shield, rubbing on the driveshaft.

AXLE(S) AND DIFFERENTIAL

➡Note: For differential servicing information, refer to Chapter 8, unless otherwise specified.

44 Noise - same when in drive as when vehicle is coasting

1 Road noise. No corrective action available.

2 Tire noise. Inspect tires and check tire pressures (Chapter 1).

3 Front wheel bearings worn or damaged (Chapter 10).

4 Insufficient differential oil (Chapter 1).

5 Defective differential.

45 Knocking sound when starting or shifting gears

Defective or incorrectly adjusted differential.

46 Noise when turning

Defective differential.

47 Vibration

See probable causes under Driveshaft. Proceed under the guidelines listed for the driveshaft. If the problem persists, check the rear wheel bearings by raising the rear of the vehicle and spinning the wheels by hand. Listen for evidence of rough (noisy) bearings. Remove and inspect (Chapter 8).

48 Oil leaks

1 Pinion oil seal damaged (Chapter 8).

2 Axleshaft oil seals damaged (Chapter 8).

3 Differential cover leaking. Tighten mounting bolts or replace the gasket as required.

4 Loose filler plug on differential (Chapter 1).

5 Clogged or damaged breather on differential.

BRAKES

➡Note: Before assuming a brake problem exists, make sure the tires are in good condition and inflated properly, the front end alignment is correct and the vehicle is not loaded with weight in an unequal manner. All service procedures for the brakes are included in Chapter 9, unless otherwise noted.

49 Vehicle pulls to one side during braking

1 Defective, damaged or contaminated brake pads on one side. Inspect as described in Chapter 1. Refer to Chapter 9 if replacement is required.
2 Excessive wear of brake pad material or disc on one side. Inspect and repair as necessary.
3 Loose or disconnected front suspension components. Inspect and tighten all bolts securely (Chapters 1 and 10).
4 Defective front brake caliper assembly. Remove caliper and inspect for stuck piston or damage.
5 Scored or out-of-round disc.
6 Loose brake caliper mounting bolts.

50 Noise (high-pitched squeal or scraping sound)

1 Brake pads worn out. Replace pads with new ones immediately!
2 Glazed or contaminated pads.
3 Dirty or scored disc.
4 Bent support plate.

51 Excessive brake pedal travel

1 Partial brake system failure. Inspect entire system (Chapter 1) and correct as required.
2 Insufficient fluid in master cylinder. Check (Chapter 1) and add fluid - bleed system if necessary.
3 Air in system. Bleed system.
4 Defective master cylinder.

52 Brake pedal feels spongy when depressed

1 Air in brake lines. Bleed the brake system.
2 Deteriorated rubber brake hoses. Inspect all system hoses and lines. Replace parts as necessary.
3 Master cylinder mounting nuts loose. Inspect master cylinder bolts (nuts) and tighten them securely.
4 Master cylinder faulty.
5 Incorrect brake pad clearance.
6 Clogged reservoir cap vent hole.
7 Deformed rubber brake lines.
8 Soft or swollen caliper seals.
9 Poor quality brake fluid. Bleed entire system and fill with new approved fluid.

53 Excessive effort required to stop vehicle

1 Power brake booster not operating properly.
2 Excessively worn brake pads. Check and replace if necessary.
3 One or more caliper pistons seized or sticking. Inspect and rebuild as required.

4 Brake pads contaminated with oil or grease. Inspect and replace as required.
5 Worn or damaged master cylinder or caliper assemblies. Check particularly for frozen pistons.

54 Pedal travels to the floor with little resistance

Little or no fluid in the master cylinder reservoir caused by leaking caliper piston(s) or loose, damaged or disconnected brake lines. Inspect entire system and repair as necessary.

55 Brake pedal pulsates during brake application

1 Wheel bearings damaged, worn or out of adjustment.
2 Caliper not sliding properly due to improper installation or obstructions. Remove and inspect.
3 Disc not within specifications. Check for excessive lateral runout and parallelism. Have the discs resurfaced or replace them with new ones. Also make sure that all discs are the same thickness.

56 Brakes drag (indicated by sluggish engine performance or wheels being very hot after driving)

1 Master cylinder piston seized in bore. Replace master cylinder.
2 Caliper piston seized in bore.
3 Parking brake assembly will not release.
4 Clogged or internally split brake lines.

57 Rear brakes lock up under light brake application

1 Tire pressures too high.
2 Tires excessively worn (Chapter 1).
3 Defective proportioning valve.

58 Rear brakes lock up under heavy brake application

1 Tire pressures too high.
2 Tires excessively worn (Chapter 1).
3 Front brake pads contaminated with oil, mud or water. Clean or replace the pads.
4 Front brake pads excessively worn.
5 Defective proportioning valve (models without ABS).

SUSPENSION AND STEERING

➡Note: All service procedures for the suspension and steering systems are included in Chapter 10, unless otherwise noted.

59 Vehicle pulls to one side

1 Tire pressures uneven (Chapter 1).
2 Defective tire (Chapter 1).
3 Excessive wear in suspension or steering components (Chapter 1).
4 Front end alignment incorrect.
5 Front brakes dragging. Inspect as described in Section 71.
6 Wheel bearings worn (Chapter 10).
7 Wheel lug nuts loose.

60 Shimmy, shake or vibration

1 Tire or wheel out of balance or out of round.
2 Worn wheel bearings (Chapter 10).
3 Shock absorbers and/or suspension components worn or damaged (see Chapter 10).

61 Excessive pitching and/or rolling around corners or during braking

1 Defective shock absorbers. Replace as a set.
2 Sagging springs.
3 Worn or damaged stabilizer bar or bushings.

62 Wandering or general instability

1 Improper tire pressures.
2 Incorrect front end alignment.
3 Worn or damaged steering gear or suspension components.
4 Improperly adjusted steering gear.
5 Out-of-balance wheels.
6 Loose wheel lug nuts.
7 Worn rear shock absorbers.

63 Excessively stiff steering

1 Lack of fluid in the power steering fluid reservoir, where appropriate (Chapter 1).
2 Incorrect tire pressures (Chapter 1).
3 Front end out of alignment.
4 Steering gear out of adjustment or lacking lubrication.
5 Worn or damaged steering gear.
6 Low tire pressures.
7 Worn or damaged balljoints.
8 Worn or damaged tie-rod ends.

64 Excessive play in steering

1 Worn wheel bearings (Chapter 1).
2 Excessive wear in suspension bushings (Chapter 1).
3 Steering gear worn.
4 Incorrect front end alignment.
5 Steering gear mounting bolts loose.
6 Worn or damaged tie-rod ends.

65 Lack of power assistance

1 Steering pump drivebelt faulty or tensioner defective (Chapter 1).
2 Fluid level low (Chapter 1).
3 Hoses or pipes restricting the flow. Inspect and replace parts as necessary.
4 Air in power steering system. Bleed system.
5 Defective power steering pump.

66 Steering wheel fails to return to straight-ahead position

1 Incorrect front end alignment.
2 Tire pressures low.

3 Worn or damaged balljoint.
4 Worn or damaged tie-rod end.
5 Lack of fluid in power steering pump.

67 Steering effort not the same in both directions

1 Leaks in steering gear.
2 Clogged fluid passage in steering gear.

68 Noisy power steering pump

1 Insufficient fluid in pump.
2 Clogged hoses or oil filter in pump.
3 Drivebelt faulty or tensioner defective (Chapter 1).
4 Defective pump.

69 Miscellaneous noises

1 Improper tire pressures.
2 Defective balljoint or tie-rod end.
3 Loose or worn steering gear or suspension components.
4 Defective shock absorber.
5 Defective wheel bearing.
6 Worn or damaged suspension bushings.
7 Loose wheel lug nuts.
8 Worn or damaged shock absorber mounting bushing.
9 Worn stabilizer bar bushings.
10 Incorrect rear axle endplay.
11 See also causes of noises at the rear axle and driveshaft.

70 Excessive tire wear (not specific to one area)

1 Incorrect tire pressures.
2 Tires out of balance.
3 Wheels damaged. Inspect and replace as necessary.
4 Suspension or steering components worn (Chapter 1).
5 Front end alignment incorrect.
6 Lack of proper tire rotation routine. See Routine Maintenance Schedule, Chapter 1.

71 Excessive tire wear on outside edge

1 Incorrect tire pressure.
2 Excessive speed in turns.
3 Front end alignment incorrect.

72 Excessive tire wear on inside edge

1 Incorrect tire pressure.
2 Front end alignment incorrect.

73 Tire tread worn in one place

1 Tires out of balance.
2 Damaged or buckled wheel. Inspect and replace if necessary.
3 Defective tire.

Notes

Section

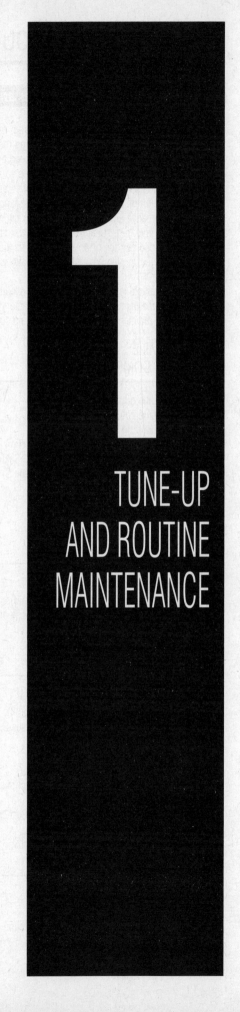

1

TUNE-UP
AND ROUTINE
MAINTENANCE

1 Chrysler 300, Dodge Charger and Magnum maintenance schedule

The maintenance intervals in this manual are provided with the assumption that you, not the dealer, will be doing the work. These are the minimum maintenance intervals recommended by the factory for vehicles that are driven daily. If you wish to keep your vehicle in peak condition at all times, you may wish to perform some of these procedures even more often. Because frequent maintenance enhances the efficiency, performance and resale value of your car, we encourage you to do so. If you drive in dusty areas, tow a trailer, idle or drive at low speeds for extended periods or drive for short distances (less than four miles) in below freezing temperatures, shorter intervals are also recommended.

When your vehicle is new, it should be serviced by a factory authorized dealer service department to protect the factory warranty. In many cases, the initial maintenance check is done at no cost to the owner.

EVERY 250 MILES OR WEEKLY, WHICHEVER COMES FIRST

Check the engine oil level (see Section 4)
Check the engine coolant level (see Section 4)
Check the brake fluid level (see Section 4)
Check the power steering fluid level (see Section 4)
Check the windshield washer fluid level (see Section 4)
Check the tires and tire pressures (see Section 5)
Check the operation of all lights
Check the horn operation

EVERY 3,000 MILES OR 3 MONTHS, WHICHEVER COMES FIRST

All items listed above, plus:
Change the engine oil and filter (see Section 6)
Check and replace, if necessary, the air filter element (Section 7)

EVERY 6,000 MILES OR 6 MONTHS, WHICHEVER COMES FIRST

All items listed above, plus:
Check the wiper blade condition (see Section 8)
Check and clean the battery and terminals (see Section 9)
Rotate the tires (see Section 10)
Check the seatbelts (see Section 11)
Inspect underhood hoses (see Section 12)
Check the cooling system hoses and connections for leaks and damage (see Section 13)
Check the exhaust pipes and hangers (see Section 14)

EVERY 15,000 MILES OR 12 MONTHS, WHICHEVER COMES FIRST

All items listed above, plus:
Check the differential lubricant (Section 4)
Replace the interior ventilation filter (see Section 15)
Check the brake system (see Section 16)*

Check the suspension, steering components and driveaxle boots (see Section 17)
Check the fuel system hoses and connections for leaks and damage (see Section 18)
Check the drivebelts and replace if necessary (see Section 19)

EVERY 30,000 MILES OR 24 MONTHS, WHICHEVER COMES FIRST

All items listed above, plus:
Replace the air filter element (see Section 7)
Change the brake fluid (see Section 20)
Replace the spark plugs (V8 engine) (see Section 21)
Check the ignition coil(s) (V8 engine) (see Section 22)
Change the differential lubricant (see Section 23)

EVERY 60,000 MILES OR 48 MONTHS, WHICHEVER COMES FIRST

All items listed above, plus:
Check and replace, if necessary, the PCV valve (see Section 24)

EVERY 90,000 MILES OR 72 MONTHS, WHICHEVER COMES FIRST

Replace the spark plugs (2.7L and 3.5L V6 engines) (see Section 21)

EVERY 60 MONTHS (REGARDLESS OF MILEAGE)

Service the cooling system (drain, flush and refill) (Section 25)

EVERY 100,000 MILES

Replace the timing belt (see Chapter 2)
Change the automatic transmission fluid and filter (Section 26)**

This item is affected by "severe" operating conditions as described below. If your vehicle is operated under "severe" conditions, perform all maintenance indicated with an asterisk (*) at 3000 mile/3 month intervals (unless otherwise specified in the schedule). Severe conditions are indicated if you mainly operate your vehicle under one or more of the following conditions:

Operating in dusty areas
Towing a trailer
Idling for extended periods and/or low speed operation
Operating in extended temperatures below freezing (32-degrees F/0-degrees C)
If more the half of your driving is at high speeds in temperatures above 90-degrees F (32-degrees C)

**If operated under one or more of the following conditions, change the or automatic transmission fluid lubricant every 30,000 miles:*

In heavy city traffic where the outside temperature regularly reaches 90-degrees F (32-degrees C) or higher
In hilly or mountainous terrain
Frequent towing of a trailer

Engine compartment layout (3.5L V6 model shown, others similar)

1	Automatic transmission fluid filler tube	5	Air filter housing	9	Windshield washer fluid reservoir
2	Brake fluid reservoir access cover	6	Engine oil filler cap	10	Remote jump start positive battery post
3	Coolant expansion tank (pressure cap)	7	Upper radiator hose	11	Underhood fuse/relay block
4	Power steering fluid reservoir	8	Engine oil dipstick		

2 Introduction

This Chapter is designed to help the home mechanic maintain the Chrysler 300, Dodge Charger and Magnum with the goals of maximum performance, economy, safety and reliability in mind.

Included is a master maintenance schedule, followed by procedures dealing specifically with each item on the schedule. Visual checks, adjustments, component replacement and other helpful items are included. Refer to the accompanying illustrations of the engine compartment and the underside of the vehicle for the locations of various components.

Servicing your vehicle in accordance with the mileage/time maintenance schedule and the step-by-step procedures will result in a planned maintenance program that should produce a long and reliable service life. Keep in mind that it's a comprehensive plan, so maintaining some items but not others at the specified intervals will not produce the same results.

As you service your vehicle, you will discover that many of the procedures can - and should - be grouped together because of the nature of the particular procedure you're performing or because of the close proximity of two otherwise unrelated components to one another.

For example, if the vehicle is raised for chassis lubrication, you should inspect the exhaust, suspension, steering and fuel systems while you're under the vehicle. When you're rotating the tires, it makes good sense to check the brakes since the wheels are already removed. Finally, let's suppose you have to borrow or rent a torque wrench. Even if you only need it to tighten the spark plugs, you might as well check the torque of as many critical fasteners as time allows.

The first step in this maintenance program is to prepare yourself before the actual work begins. Read through all the procedures you're planning to do, then gather up all the parts and tools needed. If it looks like you might run into problems during a particular job, seek advice from a mechanic or an experienced do-it-yourselfer.

Typical underside components (3.5L V6 shown, others similar)

1	Engine oil filter	3	Steering gear boot	5	Automatic transmission pan
2	Engine oil drain plug	4	Front disc brake caliper	6	Exhaust pipe

OWNER'S MANUAL AND VECI LABEL INFORMATION

Your vehicle owner's manual was written for your year and model and contains very specific information on component locations, specifications, fuse ratings, part numbers, etc. The Owner's Manual is an important resource for the do-it-yourselfer to have; if one was not supplied with your vehicle, it can generally be ordered from a dealer parts department.

Among other important information, the Vehicle Emissions Control Information (VECI) label contains specifications and procedures for

applicable tune-up adjustments and, in some instances, spark plugs. The information on this label is the exact maintenance data recommended by the manufacturer. This data often varies by intended operating altitude, local emissions regulations, month of manufacture, etc.

This Chapter contains procedural details, safety information and more ambitious maintenance intervals than you might find in manufacturer's literature. However, you may also find procedures or specifications in your Owner's Manual or VECI label that differ with what's printed here. In these cases, the Owner's Manual or VECI label can be considered correct, since it is specific to your particular vehicle.

3 Tune-up general information

The term tune-up is used in this manual to represent a combination of individual operations rather than one specific procedure.

If, from the time the vehicle is new, the routine maintenance schedule is followed closely and frequent checks are made of fluid levels and

high wear items, as suggested throughout this manual, the engine will be kept in relatively good running condition and the need for additional work will be minimized.

More likely than not, however, there will be times when the engine

Typical rear underside components

1	*Driveaxle boot*	*3*	*Fuel tank filler neck hose*	*5*	*Muffler*
2	*Rear differential*	*4*	*Rear disc brake caliper*	*6*	*Fuel tank*

is running poorly due to lack of regular maintenance. This is even more likely if a used vehicle, which has not received regular and frequent maintenance checks, is purchased. In such cases, an engine tune-up will be needed outside of the regular routine maintenance intervals.

The first step in any tune-up or diagnostic procedure to help correct a poor running engine is a cylinder compression check. A compression check (see Chapter 2D) will help determine the condition of internal engine components and should be used as a guide for tune-up and repair procedures. If, for instance, a compression check indicates serious internal engine wear, a conventional tune-up will not improve the performance of the engine and would be a waste of time and money. Because of its importance, the compression check should be done by someone with the right equipment and the knowledge to use it properly.

The following procedures are those most often needed to bring a generally poor running engine back into a proper state of tune.

MINOR TUNE-UP

Check all engine-related fluids (Section 4)
Clean, inspect and test the battery (Section 9)
Check all underhood hoses (Section 12)
Check the cooling system (Section 13)

MAJOR TUNE-UP

All items listed under Minor tune-up, plus . . .
Replace the air filter (Section 7)
Replace the spark plugs (Section 21)
Check the drivebelt (Section 19)
Replace the PCV valve (Section 24)
Check the charging system (Chapter 5)

4   Fluid level checks (every 250 miles or weekly)

1   Fluids are an essential part of the lubrication, cooling, brake and windshield washer systems. Because the fluids gradually become depleted and/or contaminated during normal operation of the vehicle, they must be periodically replenished. See *Recommended lubricants and fluids* at the end of this Chapter before adding fluid to any of the following components.

➡**Note: The vehicle must be on level ground when fluid levels are checked.**

ENGINE OIL

▶ **Refer to illustrations 4.2, 4.4 and 4.6**

2   The oil level is checked with a dipstick, which is located on the side of the engine (see illustration). The dipstick extends through a metal tube down into the oil pan.

3   The oil level should be checked before the vehicle has been driven, or about 5 minutes after the engine has been shut off. If the oil is checked immediately after driving the vehicle, some of the oil will remain in the upper part of the engine, resulting in an inaccurate read-ing on the dipstick.

4   Pull the dipstick out of the tube and wipe all the oil from the end with a clean rag or paper towel. Insert the clean dipstick all the way back into the tube and pull it out again. Note the oil at the end of the dipstick. At its highest point, the level should be between the MIN and MAX marks on the dipstick (see illustration).

5   It takes one quart of oil to raise the level from the MIN mark to the MAX mark on the dipstick. Do not allow the level to drop below the MIN mark or oil starvation may cause engine damage. Conversely, overfilling the engine (adding oil above the MAX mark) may cause oil fouled spark plugs, oil leaks or oil seal failures.

6   To add oil, remove the filler cap from the valve cover (see illus-tration). After adding oil, wait a few minutes to allow the level to stabi-lize, then pull out the dipstick and check the level again. Add more oil if required. Install the filler cap and tighten it by hand only.

7   Checking the oil level is an important preventive maintenance step. A consistently low oil level indicates oil leakage through dam-aged seals, defective gaskets or past worn rings or valve guides. If the oil looks milky in color or has water droplets in it, the cylinder head gasket(s) may be blown or the head(s) or block may be cracked. The engine should be checked immediately. The condition of the oil should also be checked. Whenever you check the oil level, slide your thumb and index finger up the dipstick before wiping off the oil. If you see small dirt or metal particles clinging to the dipstick, the oil should be changed (see Section 6).

ENGINE COOLANT

▶ **Refer to illustration 4.9**

❋❋ WARNING:

Do not allow antifreeze to come in contact with your skin or painted surfaces of the vehicle. Flush contaminated areas immediately with plenty of water. Don't store new coolant or leave old coolant lying around where it's accessible to children or pets - they're attracted by its sweet smell. Ingestion of even a small amount of coolant can be fatal! Wipe up garage floor and drip pan spills immediately. Keep antifreeze containers covered and repair cooling system leaks as soon as they're noticed.

4.2 Engine oil dipstick

4.4 At its highest point, the level should be between the MIN and MAX marks on the dipstick

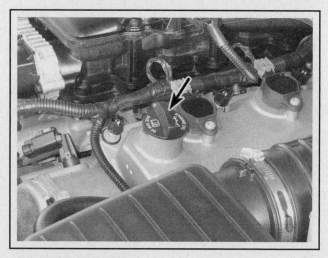

4.6 Engine oil filler cap

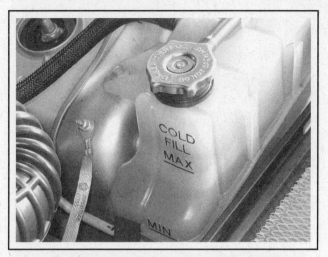

4.9 The coolant level should be at the COLD FILL RANGE mark on the expansion tank

4.14 Remove the cover to access the brake fluid reservoir

8   All vehicles covered by this manual are equipped with a pressurized coolant recovery system. A expansion tank is located in the left side of the engine compartment.

9   The coolant level in the tank should be checked regularly.

✳✳ WARNING:

Do not remove the expansion tank cap to check the coolant level when the engine is warm! The level in the tank varies with the temperature of the engine. When the engine is cold, the coolant level should be at the COLD FILL RANGE mark on the expansion tank. If it isn't, remove the cap from the tank and add a 50/50 mixture of Mopar® 5 year/100,000 mile coolant and water (see illustration).

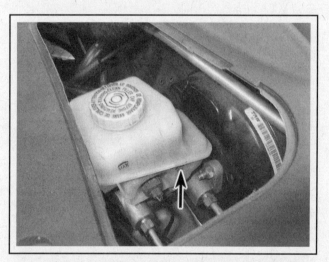

4.15 Never let the brake fluid level drop below the MIN mark

10 Drive the vehicle and recheck the coolant level. If only a small amount of coolant is required to bring the system up to the proper level, water can be used. However, repeated additions of water will dilute the antifreeze and water solution. In order to maintain the proper ratio of antifreeze and water, always top up the coolant level with the correct mixture. Don't use rust inhibitors or additives. An empty plastic milk jug or bleach bottle makes an excellent container for mixing coolant.

11 If the coolant level drops consistently, there may be a leak in the system. Inspect the radiator, hoses, filler cap, drain plugs and water pump (see Section 13). If no leaks are noted, have the expansion tank cap pressure tested by a service station.

12 If you have to remove the expansion tank cap, wait until the engine has cooled completely, then wrap a thick cloth around the cap and turn it to the first stop. If coolant or steam escapes, or if you hear a hissing noise, let the engine cool down longer, then remove the cap.

13 Check the condition of the coolant as well. It should be relatively clear. If it's brown or rust colored, the system should be drained, flushed and refilled. Even if the coolant appears to be normal, the corrosion inhibitors wear out, so it must be replaced at the specified intervals.

BRAKE FLUID

▶ **Refer to illustrations 4.14 and 4.15**

14 The brake master cylinder is located in the driver's side of the

engine compartment, near the firewall (see illustration).

15 To check the fluid level of the brake master cylinder, remove the access cover from the left cowl cover, then look at the MAX and MIN marks on the reservoir (see illustration). The level should be within the specified distance from the maximum fill line.

16 If the level is low, wipe the top of the reservoir cover with a clean rag to prevent contamination of the brake system before lifting the cover.

17 Add only the specified brake fluid to the brake reservoir (refer to *Recommended lubricants and fluids* at the end of this Chapter or to your owner's manual). Mixing different types of brake fluid can damage the system. Fill the brake master cylinder reservoir only to the MAX line.

✳✳ WARNING:

Use caution when filling either reservoir - brake fluid can harm your eyes and damage painted surfaces. Do not use brake fluid that is more than one year old or has been left open. Brake fluid absorbs moisture from the air. Excess moisture can cause a dangerous loss of braking.

4.23 Power steering reservoir

4.27 The fluid should be at the proper level, depending on whether it was checked hot or cold

18 While the reservoir cap is removed, inspect the master cylinder reservoir for contamination. If deposits, dirt particles or water droplets are present, the system should be drained and refilled.

19 After filling the reservoir to the proper level, make sure the lid is properly seated to prevent fluid leakage and/or system pressure loss.

20 The fluid in the brake master cylinder will drop slightly as the brake pads at each wheel wear down during normal operation. If the master cylinder requires repeated replenishing to keep it at the proper level, this is an indication of leakage in the brake system, which should be corrected immediately. If the brake system shows an indication of leakage, check all brake lines and connections, along with the calipers and master cylinder (see Section 16 for more information).

21 If, upon checking the brake master cylinder fluid level, you discover the reservoir empty or nearly empty, the system should be bled (see Chapter 9).

POWER STEERING FLUID

▶ **Refer to illustrations 4.23 and 4.27**

22 Check the power steering fluid level periodically to avoid steering system problems, such as damage to the pump.

✳✳ CAUTION:

DO NOT hold the steering wheel against either stop (extreme left or right turn) for more than five seconds. If you do, the power steering pump could be damaged.

---

23 The power steering reservoir, is located at the left side of the engine compartment (see illustration).

24 For the check, the front wheels should be pointed straight ahead and the engine should be off.

25 Use a clean rag to wipe off the reservoir cap and the area around the cap. This will help prevent any foreign matter from entering the reservoir during the check.

26 Twist off the cap and check the temperature of the fluid at the end of the dipstick with your finger.

27 Wipe off the fluid with a clean rag, reinsert the dipstick, then withdraw it and read the fluid level. The fluid should be at the proper level, depending on whether it was checked hot or cold (see illustration). Never allow the fluid level to drop below the lower mark on the dipstick.

28 If additional fluid is required, pour the specified type directly into the reservoir, using a funnel to prevent spills.

29 If the reservoir requires frequent fluid additions, all power steering hoses, hose connections, steering gear and the power steering pump should be carefully checked for leaks.

WINDSHIELD WASHER FLUID

▶ **Refer to illustration 4.30**

30 Fluid for the windshield washer system is stored in a plastic reservoir located at the right front of the engine compartment (see illustration).

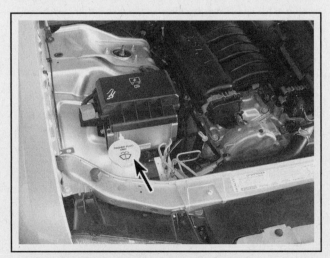

4.30 Windshield washer fluid reservoir

31 In milder climates, plain water can be used in the reservoir, but it should be kept no more than 2/3 full to allow for expansion if the water freezes. In colder climates, use windshield washer system antifreeze, available at any auto parts store, to lower the freezing point of the fluid. Mix the antifreeze with water in accordance with the manufacturer's directions on the container.

✳✳ CAUTION:

Do not use cooling system antifreeze - it will damage the vehicle's paint.

DIFFERENTIAL FLUID

▸ **Refer to illustration 4.32**

➡ **Note: It isn't necessary to check this lubricant weekly; every 15,000 miles or 12 months will be adequate.**

32 To check the fluid level, raise the vehicle and support it securely on jackstands. On the axle housing, remove the check/fill plug (see illustration). If the lubricant level is correct, it should be up to the lower edge of the hole.

33 If the differential needs more lubricant (if the level is not up to the hole), use a syringe or a gear oil pump to add more. Stop filling the differential when the lubricant begins to run out the hole.

34 Install the plug and tighten it securely. Drive the vehicle a short distance, then check for leaks.

4.32 Differential check/fill plug

---

5 Tire and tire pressure checks (every 250 miles or weekly)

▸ **Refer to illustrations 5.2, 5.3, 5.4a, 5.4b and 5.8**

1 Periodic inspection of the tires may spare you the inconvenience of being stranded with a flat tire. It can also provide you with vital information regarding possible problems in the steering and suspension systems before major damage occurs.

2 The original tires on this vehicle are equipped with 1/2-inch wide bands that will appear when tread depth reaches 1/16-inch, at which point they can be considered worn out. Tread wear can be monitored with a simple, inexpensive device known as a tread depth indicator (see illustration).

3 Note any abnormal tread wear (see illustration). Tread pattern irregularities such as cupping, flat spots and more wear on one side than the other are indications of front end alignment and/or balance problems. If any of these conditions are noted, take the vehicle to a tire shop or service station to correct the problem.

4 Look closely for cuts, punctures and embedded nails or tacks. Sometimes a tire will hold air pressure for a short time or leak down

5.2 A tire tread depth indicator should be used to monitor tire wear - they are available at auto parts stores and service stations and cost very little

UNDERINFLATION

CUPPING

Cupping may be caused by:
- Underinflation and/or mechanical irregularities such as out-of-balance condition of wheel and/or tire, and bent or damaged wheel.
- Loose or worn steering tie-rod or steering idler arm.
- Loose, damaged or worn front suspension parts.

OVERINFLATION

INCORRECT TOE-IN OR EXTREME CAMBER

FEATHERING DUE TO MISALIGNMENT

5.3 This chart will help you determine the condition of your tires, the probable cause(s) of abnormal wear and the corrective action necessary

very slowly after a nail has embedded itself in the tread. If a slow leak persists, check the valve stem core to make sure it is tight (see illustration). Examine the tread for an object that may have embedded itself in the tire or for a plug that may have begun to leak (radial tire punctures are repaired with a plug that is installed in a puncture). If a puncture is suspected, it can be easily verified by spraying a solution of soapy water onto the puncture area (see illustration). The soapy solution will bubble if there is a leak. Unless the puncture is unusually large, a tire shop or service station can usually repair the tire.

5   Carefully inspect the inner sidewall of each tire for evidence of brake fluid leakage. If you see any, inspect the brakes immediately.

6   Correct air pressure adds miles to the life span of the tires,

5.4a If a tire loses air on a steady basis, check the valve core first to make sure it's snug (special inexpensive wrenches are commonly available at auto parts stores)

5.4b If the valve core is tight, raise the corner of the vehicle with the low tire and spray a soapy water solution onto the tread as the tire is turned slowly - slow leaks will cause small bubbles to appear

5.8 To extend the life of your tires, check the air pressure at least once a week with an accurate gauge (don't forget the spare!)

improves mileage and enhances overall ride quality. Tire pressure cannot be accurately estimated by looking at a tire, especially if it's a radial. A tire pressure gauge is essential. Keep an accurate gauge in the glove compartment. The pressure gauges attached to the nozzles of air hoses at gas stations are often inaccurate.

7 Always check tire pressure when the tires are cold. Cold, in this case, means the vehicle has not been driven over a mile in the three hours preceding a tire pressure check. A pressure rise of four to eight pounds is not uncommon once the tires are warm.

8 Unscrew the valve cap protruding from the wheel or hubcap and push the gauge firmly onto the valve stem (see illustration). Note the reading on the gauge and compare the figure to the recommended tire pressure shown on the tire placard on the driver's side door. Be sure to reinstall the valve cap to keep dirt and moisture out of the valve stem mechanism. Check all four tires and, if necessary, add enough air to bring them up to the recommended pressure.

9 Don't forget to keep the spare tire inflated to the specified pressure (refer to the pressure molded into the tire sidewall).

6 Engine oil and filter change (every 3000 miles or 3 months)

▶ **Refer to illustrations 6.2, 6.7, 6.12 and 6.14**

➡**Note: Some models are equipped with an oil life indicator system that illuminates a light or message on the instrument panel when the system deems it necessary to change the oil. A number of factors are taken into consideration to determine when the oil should be considered worn out. Generally, this system will allow the vehicle to accumulate more miles between oil changes than the traditional 3000-mile interval, but we believe that frequent oil changes are cheap insurance and will prolong engine life. If you do decide not to change your oil every 3000 miles and rely on the oil life indicator instead, make sure you don't exceed 1 year or 7,500 miles before the oil is changed, regardless of what the oil life indicator shows.**

1 Frequent oil changes are the best preventive maintenance the home mechanic can give the engine, because aging oil becomes diluted and contaminated, which leads to premature engine wear.

2 Make sure you have all the necessary tools before you begin this procedure (see illustration). You should also have plenty of rags or newspapers handy for mopping up any spills.

3 Access to the underside of the vehicle is greatly improved if the vehicle can be lifted on a hoist, driven onto ramps or supported by jackstands.

❋❋ WARNING:

Do not work under a vehicle which is supported only by a bumper, hydraulic or scissors-type jack.

4 If this is your first oil change, get under the vehicle and familiarize yourself with the locations of the oil drain plug and the oil filter. The engine and exhaust components will be warm during the actual work, so try to anticipate any potential problems before the engine and accessories are hot.

5 Park the vehicle on a level spot. Start the engine and allow it to reach its normal operating temperature. Warm oil and sludge will flow out more easily. Turn off the engine when it's warmed up. Remove the filler cap from the valve cover.

6 Raise the vehicle and support it securely on jackstands.

❋❋ WARNING:

Never get beneath the vehicle when it is supported only by a jack. The jack provided with your vehicle is designed solely for raising the vehicle to remove and replace the wheels. Always use jackstands to support the vehicle when it becomes necessary to place your body underneath the vehicle.

6.2 These tools are required when changing the engine oil and filter

1 ***Drain pan*** - *It should be fairly shallow in depth, but wide in order to prevent spills*

2 ***Rubber gloves*** - *When removing the drain plug and filter, it is inevitable that you will get oil on your hands (the gloves will prevent burns)*

3 ***Breaker bar*** - *Sometimes the oil drain plug is pretty tight and a long breaker bar is needed to loosen it*

4 ***Socket*** - *To be used with the breaker bar or a ratchet (must be the correct size to fit the drain plug)*

5 ***Filter wrench*** - *This is a metal band-type wrench, which requires clearance around the filter to be effective*

6 ***Filter wrench*** - *This type fits on the bottom of the filter and can be turned with a ratchet or beaker bar (different size wrenches are available for different types of filters)*

6.7 Use a proper size box-end wrench or socket to remove the oil drain plug and avoid rounding it off

6.12 Use an oil filter wrench to remove the filter

7   Being careful not to touch the hot exhaust components, place the drain pan under the drain plug in the bottom of the pan and remove the plug (see illustration). You may want to wear gloves while unscrewing the plug the final few turns if the engine is hot.

8   Allow the old oil to drain into the pan. It may be necessary to move the pan farther under the engine as the oil flow slows to a trickle. Inspect the old oil for the presence of metal shavings and chips.

9   After all the oil has drained, wipe off the drain plug with a clean rag. Even minute metal particles clinging to the plug would immediately contaminate the new oil.

10 Clean the area around the drain plug opening, reinstall the plug and tighten it securely, but do not strip the threads.

11 Move the drain pan into position under the oil filter.

12 Loosen the oil filter (see illustration) by turning it counterclockwise with an oil filter wrench. Once the filter is loose, use your hands to unscrew it from the block. Keep the open end pointing up to prevent the oil inside the filter from spilling out.

❋❋ WARNING:

The exhaust system may still be hot, so be careful.

13 With a clean rag, wipe off the mounting surface on the block. If a residue of old oil is allowed to remain, it will smoke when the block is heated up. Also make sure that none of the old gasket remains stuck to the mounting surface. It can be removed with a scraper if necessary.

14 Compare the old filter with the new one to make sure they are the same type. Smear some clean engine oil on the rubber gasket of the new filter (see illustration).

15 Attach the new filter to the engine, following the tightening directions printed on the filter canister or packing box. Most filter manufacturers recommend against using a filter wrench due to the possibility of overtightening and damaging the seal.

16 Remove all tools, rags, etc. from under the vehicle, being careful not to spill the oil in the drain pan, then lower the vehicle.

17 Add new oil to the engine through the oil filler cap in the valve cover. Use a funnel, if necessary, to prevent oil from spilling onto the top of the engine. Pour five quarts of fresh oil into the engine. Wait a few minutes to allow the oil to drain into the pan, then check the level on the oil dipstick (see Section 4). If the oil level is at or near the FULL mark on the dipstick, install the filler cap hand tight, start the engine

and allow the new oil to circulate.

18 Allow the engine to run for about a minute. While the engine is running, look under the vehicle and check for leaks at the oil pan drain plug and around the oil filter. If either is leaking, stop the engine and tighten the plug or filter.

19 Wait a few minutes to allow the oil to trickle down into the pan, then recheck the level on the dipstick and, if necessary, add enough oil to bring the level to the FULL mark.

20 During the first few trips after an oil change, make it a point to check frequently for leaks and proper oil level.

21 The old oil drained from the engine cannot be reused in its present state and should be disposed of. Check with your local auto parts store, disposal facility or environmental agency to see if they will accept the oil for recycling. After the oil has cooled it can be drained into a container (capped plastic jugs, topped bottles, milk cartons, etc.) for transport to one of these disposal sites. Don't dispose of the oil by pouring it on the ground or down a drain!

OIL CHANGE INDICATOR - RESETTING

22 Turn the ignition key to the On position (but don't start the engine).
23 Depress the accelerator pedal three times within ten seconds.
24 Turn the ignition key off (to the Lock position).

6.14 Lubricate the oil filter gasket with clean engine oil before installing the filter on the engine

7   Air filter check and replacement (every 3000 miles or 3 months)

▶ **Refer to illustrations 7.1a and 7.1b**

1   The air filter is located inside a housing at the left (driver's) side of the engine compartment. To remove the air filter, release the tabs that secure the two halves of the air cleaner housing together, then separate the cover halves and remove the air filter element (see illustrations).

2   Inspect the outer surface of the filter element. If it is dirty, replace it. If it is only moderately dusty, it can be reused by blowing it clean from the back to the front surface with compressed air. Because it is a pleated paper type filter, it cannot be washed or oiled. If it cannot be cleaned satisfactorily with compressed air, discard and replace it. While the cover is off, be careful not to drop anything down into the housing.

✴✴ CAUTION:

Never drive the vehicle with the air cleaner removed. Excessive engine wear could result and backfiring could even cause a fire under the hood.

3   Wipe out the inside of the air cleaner housing.

4   Place the new filter into the air cleaner housing, making sure it seats properly.

5   Installation of the housing is the reverse of removal.

7.1a Release the tabs that secure the two halves of the air cleaner housing . . .

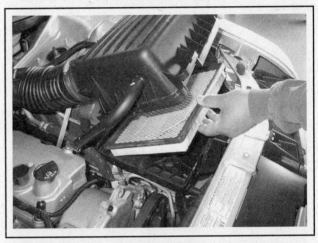

7.1b . . . then lift the air filter housing cover and remove the air filter element

8   Windshield wiper blade inspection and replacement (every 6000 miles or 6 months)

▶ **Refer to illustrations 8.5a and 8.5b**

1   The windshield wiper and blade assembly should be inspected periodically for damage, loose components and cracked or worn blade elements.

2   Road film can build up on the wiper blades and affect their efficiency, so they should be washed regularly with a mild detergent solution.

3   The action of the wiping mechanism can loosen bolts, nuts and fasteners, so they should be checked and tightened, as necessary, at the same time the wiper blades are checked.

4   If the wiper blade elements are cracked, worn or warped, or no longer clean adequately, they should be replaced with new ones.

5   Lift the arm assembly away from the glass for clearance, press the release lever, then slide the wiper blade assembly out of the hook at the end of the arm (see illustrations).

6   Attach the new wiper to the arm. Connection can be confirmed by an audible click.

8.5a To release the blade holder, push the release pin . . .

8.5b . . . and pull the wiper blade in the direction of the arrow to separate it from the arm

9 Battery check, maintenance and charging (every 6000 miles or 6 months)

▶ Refer to illustrations 9.1, 9.6a, 9.6b, 9.7a and 9.7b

✳✳ WARNING:

Certain precautions must be followed when checking and servicing the battery. Hydrogen gas, which is highly flammable, is always present in the battery cells, so keep lighted tobacco and all other open flames and sparks away from the battery. The electrolyte inside the battery is actually diluted sulfuric acid, which will cause injury if splashed on your skin or in your eyes. It will also ruin clothes and painted surfaces. When removing the battery cables, always detach the negative cable first and hook it up last!

➡Note: The battery is located in the trunk, to the right of the spare tire.

1   A routine preventive maintenance program for the battery in your vehicle is the only way to ensure quick and reliable starts. But before performing any battery maintenance, make sure that you have the proper equipment necessary to work safely around the battery (see illustration).

2   There are also several precautions that should be taken whenever battery maintenance is performed. Before servicing the battery, always turn the engine and all accessories off and disconnect the cable from the negative terminal of the battery (see Chapter 5, Section 1).

3   The battery produces hydrogen gas, which is both flammable and explosive. Never create a spark, smoke or light a match around the battery. Always charge the battery in a ventilated area.

4   Electrolyte contains poisonous and corrosive sulfuric acid. Do not allow it to get in your eyes, on your skin on your clothes. Never ingest it. Wear protective safety glasses when working near the battery. Keep children away from the battery.

5   Note the external condition of the battery. If the positive terminal and cable clamp on your vehicle's battery is equipped with a rubber

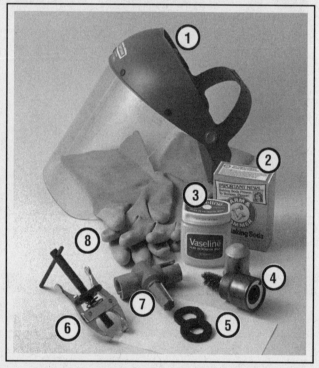

9.1 Tools and materials required for battery maintenance

1   *Face shield/safety goggles* - When removing corrosion with a brush, the acidic particles can easily fly up into your eyes
2   *Baking soda* - A solution of baking soda and water can be used to neutralize corrosion
3   *Petroleum jelly* - A layer of this on the battery posts will help prevent corrosion
4   *Battery post/cable cleaner* - This wire brush cleaning tool will remove all traces of corrosion from the battery posts and cable clamps
5   *Treated felt washers* - Placing one of these on each post, directly under the cable clamps, will help prevent corrosion
6   *Puller* - Sometimes the cable clamps are very difficult to pull off the posts, even after the nut/bolt has been completely loosened. This tool pulls the clamp straight up and off the post without damage
7   *Battery post/cable cleaner* - Here is another cleaning tool which is a slightly different version of number 4 above, but it does the same thing
8   *Rubber gloves* - Another safety item to consider when servicing the battery; remember that's acid inside the battery!

9.6a Battery terminal corrosion usually appears as light, fluffy powder

9.6b Removing a cable from the battery post with a wrench - sometimes a pair of special battery pliers are required for this procedure if corrosion has caused deterioration of the nut hex (always remove the ground (-) cable first and hook it up last!)

9.7a When cleaning the cable clamps, all corrosion must be removed

9.7b Regardless of the type of tool used to clean the battery posts, a clean, shiny surface should be the result

protector, make sure that it's not torn or damaged. It should completely cover the terminal. Look for any corroded or loose connections, cracks in the case or cover or loose hold-down clamps. Also check the entire length of each cable for cracks and frayed conductors.

6   If corrosion, which looks like white, fluffy deposits (see illustration) is evident, particularly around the terminals, the battery should be removed for cleaning. Loosen the cable clamp bolts with a wrench, being careful to remove the ground cable first, and slide them off the terminals (see illustration). Then disconnect the hold-down clamp bolt and nut, remove the clamp and lift the battery from the engine compartment.

7   Clean the cable clamps thoroughly with a battery brush or a terminal cleaner and a solution of warm water and baking soda (see illustration). Wash the terminals and the top of the battery case with the same solution but make sure that the solution doesn't get into the battery. When cleaning the cables, terminals and battery top, wear safety goggles and rubber gloves to prevent any solution from coming in contact with your eyes or hands. Wear old clothes too - even diluted, sulfuric acid splashed onto clothes will burn holes in them. If the terminals have been extensively corroded, clean them up with a terminal cleaner (see illustration). Thoroughly wash all cleaned areas with plain water.

8   Make sure that the battery tray is in good condition and the hold-down clamp fasteners are tight. If the battery is removed from the tray, make sure no parts remain in the bottom of the tray when the battery is reinstalled. When reinstalling the hold-down clamp bolts, do not overtighten them.

9   Information on removing and installing the battery can be found in Chapter 5. If you disconnected the cable(s) from the negative and/or positive battery terminals, see Chapter 5, Section 1. Information on jump starting can be found at the front of this manual.

CLEANING

10   Corrosion on the hold-down components, battery case and sur-

rounding areas can be removed with a solution of water and baking soda. Thoroughly rinse all cleaned areas with plain water.

11   Any metal parts of the vehicle damaged by corrosion should be covered with a zinc-based primer, then painted.

CHARGING

✳✳ WARNING:

When batteries are being charged, hydrogen gas, which is very explosive and flammable, is produced. Do not smoke or allow open flames near a charging or a recently charged battery. Wear eye protection when near the battery during charging. Also, make sure the charger is unplugged before connecting or disconnecting the battery from the charger.

12   Slow-rate charging is the best way to restore a battery that's discharged to the point where it will not start the engine. It's also a good way to maintain the battery charge in a vehicle that's only driven a few miles between starts. Maintaining the battery charge is particularly important in the winter when the battery must work harder to start the engine and electrical accessories that drain the battery are in greater use.

13   It's best to use a one or two-amp battery charger (sometimes called a "trickle" charger). They are the safest and put the least strain on the battery. They are also the least expensive. For a faster charge, you can use a higher amperage charger, but don't use one rated more than 1/10th the amp/hour rating of the battery. Rapid boost charges that claim to restore the power of the battery in one to two hours are hardest on the battery and can damage batteries not in good condition. This type of charging should only be used in emergency situations.

14   The average time necessary to charge a battery should be listed in the instructions that come with the charger. As a general rule, a trickle charger will charge a battery in 12 to 16 hours.

10 Tire rotation (every 6000 miles or 6 months)

▶ **Refer to illustrations 10.2a and 10.2b**

1   The tires should be rotated at the specified intervals and whenever uneven wear is noticed.

2   Refer to the accompanying illustrations for the preferred tire rotation pattern.

3   Refer to the information in *Jacking and towing* at the front of this manual for the proper procedures to follow when raising the vehicle and changing a tire. If the brakes are to be checked, don't apply the parking brake as stated. Make sure the tires are blocked to prevent the vehicle from rolling as it's raised.

4   Preferably, the entire vehicle should be raised at the same time. This can be done on a hoist or by jacking up each corner and then lowering the vehicle onto jackstands placed under the frame rails. Always use four jackstands and make sure the vehicle is safely supported.

5   After rotation, check and adjust the tire pressures as necessary. Tighten the lug nuts to the torque listed in this Chapter's Specifications.

10.2a The recommended four-tire rotation pattern for non-directional tires

10.2b The recommended four-tire rotation pattern for directional tires

11 Seat belt check (every 6000 miles or 6 months)

1   Check seat belts, buckles, latch plates and guide loops for obvious damage and signs of wear.

2   Where the seat belt receptacle bolts to the floor of the vehicle, check that the bolts are secure.

3   See if the seat belt reminder light comes on when the key is turned to the Run or Start position.

12 Underhood hose check and replacement (every 6000 miles or 6 months)

GENERAL

✳✳ CAUTION:

Replacement of air conditioning hoses must be left to a dealer service department or air conditioning shop that has the equipment to depressurize the system safely and recover the refrigerant. Never remove air conditioning components or hoses until the system has been depressurized.

1   High temperatures in the engine compartment can cause the deterioration of the rubber and plastic hoses used for engine, accessory and emission systems operation. Periodic inspection should be made for cracks, loose clamps, material hardening and leaks. Information specific to the cooling system hoses can be found in Section 13.

2   Some, but not all, hoses are secured to their fittings with clamps. Where clamps are used, check to be sure they haven't lost their tension, allowing the hose to leak. If clamps aren't used, make sure the hose has not expanded and/or hardened where it slips over the fitting, allowing it to leak.

VACUUM HOSES

3   It's quite common for vacuum hoses, especially those in the emissions system, to be color-coded or identified by colored stripes molded into them. Various systems require hoses with different wall thickness, collapse resistance and temperature resistance. When replacing hoses, be sure the new ones are made of the same material.

4   Often the only effective way to check a hose is to remove it completely from the vehicle. If more than one hose is removed, be sure to label the hoses and fittings to ensure correct installation.

5   When checking vacuum hoses, be sure to include any plastic T-fittings in the check. Inspect the fittings for cracks and the hose where it fits over the fitting for distortion, which could cause leakage.

6   A small piece of vacuum hose (1/4-inch inside diameter) can be used as a stethoscope to detect vacuum leaks. Hold one end of the hose to your ear and probe around vacuum hoses and fittings, listening for the "hissing" sound characteristic of a vacuum leak.

✳✳ WARNING:

When probing with the vacuum hose stethoscope, be very careful not to come into contact with moving engine components such as the drivebelt, cooling fan, etc.

FUEL HOSE

✳✳ WARNING:

There are certain precautions that must be taken when inspecting or servicing fuel system components. Work in a well-ventilated area and do not allow open flames (cigarettes, appliances, etc.) or bare light bulbs near the work area. Mop up any spills immediately and do not store fuel soaked rags where they could ignite. The fuel system is under high pressure, so if any fuel lines are to be disconnected, the pressure in the system must be relieved first (see Chapter 4 for more information).

7   Check all rubber fuel lines for deterioration and chafing. Check especially for cracks in areas where the hose bends and just before fittings, such as where a hose attaches to the fuel filter.

8   High quality fuel line, made specifically for high-pressure fuel injection systems, must be used for fuel line replacement. Never, under any circumstances, use unreinforced vacuum line, clear plastic tubing or water hose for fuel lines.

9   Spring-type clamps are commonly used on fuel lines. These clamps often lose their tension over a period of time, and can be "sprung" during removal. Replace all spring-type clamps with screw clamps whenever a hose is replaced.

METAL LINES

10   Sections of metal line are routed along the frame, between the fuel tank and the engine. Check carefully to be sure the line has not been bent or crimped and that cracks have not started in the line.

11   If a section of metal fuel line must be replaced, only seamless steel tubing should be used, since copper and aluminum tubing don't have the strength necessary to withstand normal engine vibration.

12   Check the metal brake lines where they enter the master cylinder and brake proportioning unit for cracks in the lines or loose fittings. Any sign of brake fluid leakage calls for an immediate and thorough inspection of the brake system.

13   Cooling system check (every 6000 miles or 6 months)

▶ **Refer to illustration 13.4**

1   Many major engine failures can be attributed to a faulty cooling system. If the vehicle is equipped with an automatic transmission, the cooling system also cools the transmission fluid and thus plays an important role in prolonging transmission life.

2   The cooling system should be checked with the engine cold. Do this before the vehicle is driven for the day or after it has been shut off for at least three hours.

3   Remove the cooling system pressure cap and thoroughly clean the cap, inside and out, with clean water. Also clean the filler neck on the radiator. All traces of corrosion should be removed. The coolant inside the radiator should be relatively transparent. If it is rust-colored, the system should be drained, flushed and refilled (see Section 25). If the coolant level is not up to the top, add additional antifreeze/coolant mixture (see Section 4).

4   Carefully check the large upper and lower radiator hoses along with the smaller diameter heater hoses that run from the engine to the firewall. Inspect each hose along its entire length, replacing any hose that is cracked, swollen or shows signs of deterioration. Cracks may become more apparent if the hose is squeezed (see illustration). Regardless of condition, it's a good idea to replace hoses with new ones every two years.

5   Make sure all hose connections are tight. A leak in the cooling system will usually show up as white or rust-colored deposits on the areas adjoining the leak. If wire-type clamps are used at the ends of the hoses, it may be a good idea to replace them with more secure screw-type clamps.

6   Use compressed air or a soft brush to remove bugs, leaves, etc. from the front of the radiator or air conditioning condenser. Be careful not to damage the delicate cooling fins or cut yourself on them.

7   Every other inspection, or at the first indication of cooling system problems, have the cap and system pressure tested. If you don't have a pressure tester, most repair shops will do this for a minimal charge.

Check for a chafed area that could fail prematurely.

Check for a soft area indicating the hose has deteriorated inside.

Overtightening the clamp on a hardened hose will damage the hose and cause a leak.

Check each hose for swelling and oil-soaked ends. Cracks and breaks can be located by squeezing the hose.

13.4   Hoses, like drivebelts, have a habit of failing at the worst possible time - to prevent the inconvenience of a blown radiator or heater hose, inspect them carefully as shown here

14 Exhaust system check (every 6000 miles or 6 months)

▶ **Refer to illustrations 14.2a and 14.2b**

1   With the engine cold (at least three hours after the vehicle has been driven), check the complete exhaust system from the manifold to the end of the tailpipe. Be careful around the catalytic converter, which may be hot even after three hours. The inspection should be done with the vehicle on a hoist to permit unrestricted access. If a hoist isn't available, raise the vehicle and support it securely on jackstands.

2   Check the exhaust pipes and connections for signs of leakage and/or corrosion indicating a potential failure. Make sure that all brackets and hangers are in good condition and tight (see illustrations).

3   Inspect the underside of the body for holes, corrosion, open seams, etc. which may allow exhaust gasses to enter the passenger compartment. Seal all body openings with silicone sealant or body putty.

4   Rattles and other noises can often be traced to the exhaust system, especially the hangers, mounts and heat shields. Try to move the pipes, mufflers and catalytic converter. If the components can come in contact with the body or suspension parts, secure the exhaust system with new brackets and hangers.

14.2a Inspect the muffler (A) for signs of deterioration, and all hangers (B)

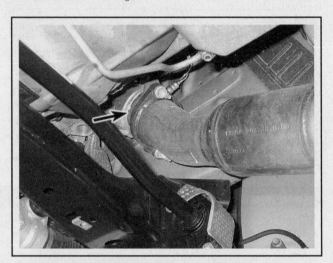

14.2b Inspect all flanged joints (arrow indicates pipe-to-manifold joint) for signs of exhaust gas leakage

15 Interior ventilation filter replacement (every 15,000 miles or 12 months)

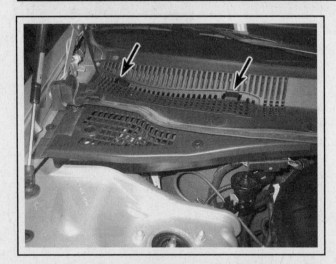

15.2 Release the two tabs to open the air inlet grille

▶ **Refer to illustration 15.2**

1   Some models are equipped with an air filtering element in the air conditioning system, located in a housing under the cowl cover.

2   Remove the air inlet grille from the cowl cover (see illustration).

3   Open the filter door by sliding it forward and down, then remove the filter. Note the direction of the arrow on the filter, indicating airflow direction.

4   Installation is the reverse of the removal procedure.

16 Brake system check (every 15,000 miles or 12 months)

❄❄ WARNING:

The dust created by the brake system is harmful to your health. Never blow it out with compressed air and don't inhale any of it. An approved filtering mask should be worn when working on the brakes. Do not, under any circumstances, use petroleum-based solvents to clean brake parts. Use brake system cleaner only!

➡Note: For detailed photographs of the brake system, refer to Chapter 9.

1 In addition to the specified intervals, the brakes should be inspected every time the wheels are removed or whenever a defect is suspected.

2 Any of the following symptoms could indicate a potential brake system defect: The vehicle pulls to one side when the brake pedal is depressed; the brakes make squealing or dragging noises when applied; brake pedal travel is excessive; the pedal pulsates; or brake fluid leaks, usually onto the inside of the tire or wheel. A brake pedal that sinks slowly to the floor, with no apparent external fluid leakage, indicates a faulty master cylinder.

➡Note: A faulty master cylinder can leak fluid into the power brake booster.

3 Loosen the wheel lug nuts.

4 Raise the vehicle and place it securely on jackstands.

5 Remove the wheels (see *Jacking and towing* at the front of this book, or your owner's manual, if necessary).

DISC BRAKES

◆ Refer to illustrations 16.7a, 16.7b and 16.9

6 There are two pads (an outer and an inner) in each caliper. The pads are visible with the wheels removed.

7 Check the pad thickness by looking at each end of the caliper and through the inspection window in the caliper body (see illustrations). If the lining material is less than the thickness listed in this Chapter's Specifications, replace the pads.

16.7a With the wheel off, check the thickness of the inner pad through the inspection hole (front disc shown, rear disc caliper similar)

➡Note: Keep in mind that the lining material is riveted or bonded to a metal backing plate and the metal portion is not included in this measurement.

8 If it is difficult to determine the exact thickness of the remaining pad material by the above method, or if you are at all concerned about the condition of the pads, remove the caliper(s), then remove the pads from the calipers for further inspection (refer to Chapter 9).

9 Once the pads are removed from the calipers, clean them with brake cleaner and re-measure them with a ruler or a vernier caliper (see illustration).

10 Measure the disc thickness with a micrometer to make sure that it still has service life remaining. If any disc is thinner than the specified minimum thickness, replace it (see Chapter 9). Even if the disc has service life remaining, check its condition. Look for scoring, gouging and burned spots. If these conditions exist, remove the disc and have it resurfaced (see Chapter 9).

11 Before installing the wheels, check all brake lines and hoses

16.7b The outer pad is more easily checked at the edge of the caliper

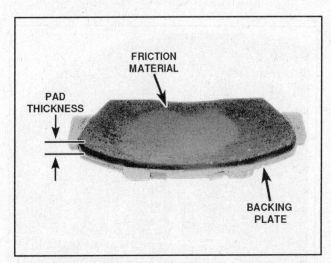

16.9 If a more precise measurement of pad thickness is necessary, remove the pads and measure the remaining friction material

for damage, wear, deformation, cracks, corrosion, leakage, bends and twists, particularly in the vicinity of the rubber hoses at the calipers. Check the clamps for tightness and the connections for leakage. Make sure that all hoses and lines are clear of sharp edges, moving parts and the exhaust system. If any of the above conditions are noted, repair, reroute or replace the lines and/or fittings as necessary (see Chapter 9).

BRAKE BOOSTER CHECK

12 Sit in the driver's seat and perform the following sequence of tests.

13 With the brake fully depressed, start the engine - the pedal should move down a little when the engine starts.

14 With the engine running, depress the brake pedal several times - the travel distance should not change.

15 Depress the brake, stop the engine and hold the pedal in for about 30 seconds - the pedal should neither sink nor rise.

16 Restart the engine, run it for about a minute and turn it off. Then firmly depress the brake several times - the pedal travel should decrease with each application.

17 If your brakes do not operate as described, the brake booster has failed. Refer to Chapter 9 for the replacement procedure.

PARKING BRAKE

18 One method of checking the parking brake is to park the vehicle on a steep hill with the parking brake set and the transmission in Neutral (be sure to stay in the vehicle for this check!). If the parking brake cannot prevent the vehicle from rolling, it's in need of adjustment (see Chapter 9).

---

17 Suspension, steering and driveaxle boot check (every 15,000 miles or 12 months)

➡**Note: The steering linkage and suspension components should be checked periodically. Worn or damaged suspension and steering linkage components can result in excessive and abnormal tire wear, poor ride quality and vehicle handling and reduced fuel economy. For detailed illustrations of the steering and suspension components, refer to Chapter 10.**

SHOCK ABSORBER CHECK

▶ **Refer to illustration 17.6**

1 Park the vehicle on level ground, turn the engine off and set the parking brake. Check the tire pressures.

2 Push down at one corner of the vehicle, then release it while noting the movement of the body. It should stop moving and come to rest in a level position within one or two bounces.

3 If the vehicle continues to move up-and-down or if it fails to return to its original position, a worn or weak shock absorber is probably the reason.

4 Repeat the above check at each of the three remaining corners of the vehicle.

5 Raise the vehicle and support it securely on jackstands.

6 Check the shock absorbers for evidence of fluid leakage (see illustration). A light film of fluid is no cause for concern. Make sure that any fluid noted is from the shocks and not from some other source. If leakage is noted, replace the shocks as a set.

7 Check the shocks to be sure that they are securely mounted and undamaged. Check the upper mounts for damage and wear. If damage or wear is noted, replace the shocks as a set (front or rear).

8 If the shocks must be replaced, refer to Chapter 10 for the procedure.

STEERING AND SUSPENSION CHECK

▶ **Refer to illustrations 17.9 and 17.11**

9 Visually inspect the steering and suspension components (front and rear) for damage and distortion. Look for damaged seals, boots and bushings and leaks of any kind. Examine the bushings where the control arms meet the chassis (see illustration).

17.9 Examine the mounting points for the upper and lower control arms on the front suspension (A, lower shown, upper not visible), the tie-rod ends (B), the balljoints (C), and the steering gear boots (D)

17.6 Check the shocks for leakage at the indicated area

17.11 With the steering wheel in the locked position and the vehicle raised, grasp the front tire as shown and try to move it back-and-forth - if any play is noted, check the steering gear mounts and tie-rod ends for looseness

10 Clean the lower end of the steering knuckle. Have an assistant grasp the lower edge of the tire and move the wheel in-and-out while you look for movement at the steering knuckle-to-control arm balljoint. If there is any movement the suspension balljoint(s) must be replaced.

11 Grasp each front tire at the front and rear edges, push in at the front, pull out at the rear and feel for play in the steering system components. If any freeplay is noted, check the idler arm and the tie-rod ends for looseness (see illustration).

12 Additional steering and suspension system information and illustrations can be found in Chapter 10.

17.14 Inspect the inner and outer driveaxle boots for loose clamps, cracks or signs of leaking lubricant

DRIVEAXLE BOOT CHECK

▶ **Refer to illustration 17.14**

13 The driveaxle boots are very important because they prevent dirt, water and foreign material from entering and damaging the constant velocity (CV) joints. Oil and grease can cause the boot material to deteriorate prematurely, so it's a good idea to wash the boots with soap and water. Because it constantly pivots back and forth following the steering action of the front hub, the outer CV boot wears out sooner and should be inspected regularly.

14 Inspect the boots for tears and cracks as well as loose clamps (see illustration). If there is any evidence of cracks or leaking lubricant, they must be replaced as described in Chapter 8.

18 Fuel system check (every 15,000 miles or 12 months)

✳✳ WARNING:

Gasoline is flammable, so take extra precautions when you work on any part of the fuel system. Don't smoke or allow open flames or bare light bulbs near the work area, and don't work in a garage where a gas-type appliance (such as a water heater or clothes dryer) is present. Since fuel is carcinogenic, wear fuel-resistant gloves when there's a possibility of being exposed to fuel, and, if you spill any fuel on your skin, rinse it off immediately with soap and water. Mop up any spills immediately and do not store fuel-soaked rags where they could ignite. When you perform any kind of work on the fuel system, wear safety glasses and have a Class B type fire extinguisher on hand. The fuel system is under constant pressure, so, before any lines are disconnected, the fuel system pressure must be relieved (see Chapter 4).

1 If you smell fuel while driving or after the vehicle has been sitting in the sun, inspect the fuel system immediately.

2 Remove the fuel filler cap and inspect it for damage and corrosion. The gasket should have an unbroken sealing imprint. If the gasket is damaged or corroded, install a new cap.

3 Inspect the fuel feed line for cracks. Make sure that the connections between the fuel lines and the fuel injection system and between the fuel lines and the in-line fuel filter are tight.

✳✳ WARNING:

Your vehicle is fuel injected, so you must relieve the fuel system pressure before servicing fuel system components. The fuel system pressure relief procedure is outlined in Chapter 4.

4 Since some components of the fuel system - the fuel tank and part of the fuel feed and return lines, for example - are underneath the vehicle, they can be inspected more easily with the vehicle raised on a hoist. If that's not possible, raise the vehicle and support it on jackstands.

5 With the vehicle raised and safely supported, inspect the fuel tank and filler neck for punctures, cracks and other damage. The connection between the filler neck and the tank is particularly critical. Sometimes a rubber filler neck will leak because of loose clamps or deteriorated rubber. Inspect all fuel tank mounting brackets and straps to be sure that the tank is securely attached to the vehicle.

※※ **WARNING:**

Do not, under any circumstances, try to repair a fuel tank (except rubber components). A welding torch or any open flame can easily cause fuel vapors inside the tank to explode.

6   Carefully check all rubber hoses and metal lines leading away from the fuel tank. Check for loose connections, deteriorated hoses, crimped lines and other damage. Repair or replace damaged sections as necessary (see Chapter 4).

19 Drivebelt check and replacement (every 15,000 miles or 12 months)

1   The drivebelt is located at the front of the engine and plays an important role in the overall operation of the vehicle and its components. Due to its function and material make-up, the drivebelt is prone to failure after a period of time and should be inspected and adjusted periodically to prevent major engine damage.
2   The vehicles covered by this manual are equipped with a single self-adjusting serpentine drivebelt, which is used to drive all of the accessory components such as the alternator, power steering pump, water pump and air conditioning compressor.

INSPECTION

▶ **Refer to illustrations 19.4 and 19.5**

3   With the engine off, open the hood and locate the drivebelt at the front of the engine. Using your fingers (and a flashlight, if necessary), move along the belts checking for cracks and separation of the belt plies. Also check for fraying and glazing, which gives the belt a shiny appearance. Both sides of each belt should be inspected, which means you will have to twist the belt to check the underside.
4   Check the ribs on the underside of the belt. They should all be the same depth, with none of the surface uneven (see illustration).
5   The tension of the belt is automatically adjusted by the belt tensioner and does not require any adjustments. Drivebelt wear can be checked visually by inspecting the wear indicator marks located on the side of the tensioner body. Locate the belt tensioner at the front of the engine, then find the tensioner operating marks (see illustration). If the indicator mark is outside the operating range, the belt should be replaced.

REPLACEMENT

▶ **Refer to illustration 19.6**

6   To replace the belt, rotate the tensioner to relieve the tension on the belt (see illustration). All models have a square hole in the tensioner arm that will accept a breaker bar or ratchet.

ACCEPTABLE

Cracks Running Across "V" Portions of Belt

1/2"

Missing Two or More Adjacent Ribs 1/2" or longer

UNACCEPTABLE

Cracks Running Parallel to "V" Portions of Belt

19.4 Here are some of the more common problems associated with drivebelts (check the belts very carefully to prevent an untimely breakdown)

19.5 Belt wear indicator marks are located on the tensioner body - when the belt reaches the maximum wear mark it must be replaced

19.6 Rotate the tensioner arm to relieve belt tension

7 Remove the belt from the auxiliary components and carefully release the tensioner.

8 Route the new belt over the various pulleys, again rotating the tensioner to allow the belt to be installed, then release the belt tensioner. Make sure the belt fits properly into the pulley grooves - it must be completely engaged.

➡**Note: Most models have a drivebelt routing decal on the upper radiator panel to help during drivebelt installation.**

9 Reconnect the battery.

TENSIONER REPLACEMENT

▶ **Refer to illustration 19.11**

10 Remove the drivebelt.

11 Remove the bolt that secures the drivebelt to the engine, then remove the tensioner (see illustration).

12 Installation is the reverse of removal. Tighten the mounting bolt to the torque listed in this Chapter's Specifications.

19.11 The drivebelt tensioner is secured by a single bolt

---

20 Brake fluid change (every 30,000 miles or 24 months)

❊❊ WARNING:

Brake fluid can harm your eyes and damage painted surfaces, so use extreme caution when handling or pouring it. Do not use brake fluid that has been standing open or is more than one year old. Brake fluid absorbs moisture from the air. Excess moisture can cause a dangerous loss of braking effectiveness.

1 At the specified intervals, the brake fluid should be drained and replaced. Since the brake fluid may drip or splash when pouring it, place plenty of rags around the master cylinder to protect any surrounding painted surfaces.

2 Before beginning work, purchase the specified brake fluid (see *Recommended lubricants and fluids* at the end of this Chapter).

3 Remove the cap from the master cylinder reservoir.

4 Using a hand suction pump or similar device, withdraw the fluid from the master cylinder reservoir.

5 Add new fluid to the master cylinder until it rises to the base of the filler neck.

6 Bleed the brake system as described in Chapter 9 at all four brakes until new and uncontaminated fluid is expelled from the bleeder screw. Be sure to maintain the fluid level in the master cylinder as you perform the bleeding process. If you allow the master cylinder to run dry, air will enter the system.

7 Refill the master cylinder with fluid and check the operation of the brakes. The pedal should feel solid when depressed, with no sponginess.

❊❊ WARNING:

Do not operate the vehicle if you are in doubt about the effectiveness of the brake system.

---

21 Spark plug check and replacement (see Maintenance schedule for intervals)

▶ **Refer to illustrations 21.2, 21.5, 21.8, 21.10, 21.11, 21.12 and 21.13**

1 The spark plugs are located in the cylinder head(s).

2 In most cases the tools necessary for spark plug replacement include a spark plug socket which fits onto a ratchet (this special socket is padded inside to protect the porcelain insulators on the new plugs and hold them in place), various extensions and a feeler gauge to check and adjust the spark plug gap (see illustration). Since these engines are equipped with an aluminum cylinder head, a torque wrench should be used when tightening the spark plugs.

3 The best approach when replacing the spark plugs is to purchase the new spark plugs beforehand, adjust them to the proper gap and then replace each plug one at a time. When buying the new spark plugs, be sure to obtain the correct plug for your specific engine. This information can be found in the Specification Section at the end of this Chapter, or on the Vehicle Emissions Control Information (VECI) label located under the hood. If differences exist between the sources, purchase the spark plug type specified on the VECI label as it was printed for your specific engine.

4 Allow the engine to cool completely before attempting to remove any of the plugs. During this cooling off time, each of the new spark plugs can be inspected for defects and the gaps can be checked.

21.2 Tools required for changing spark plugs

1 **Spark plug socket** - This will have special padding inside to protect the spark plug porcelain insulator
2 **Torque wrench** - Although not mandatory, use of this tool is the best way to ensure that the plugs are tightened properly
3 **Ratchet** - Standard hand tool to fit the plug socket
4 **Extension** - Depending on model and accessories, you may need special extensions and universal joints to reach one or more of the plugs
5 **Spark plug gap gauge** - This gauge for checking the gap comes in a variety of styles. Make sure the gap for your engine is included

5   The gap is checked by inserting the proper thickness gauge between the electrodes at the tip of the plug (see illustration). The gap between the electrodes should be as listed in this Chapter's Specifications or in your owner's manual. The wire should touch each of the electrodes. Also, at this time check for cracks in the spark plug body (if any are found, the plug must not be used).

6   Cover the fender to prevent damage to the paint. Fender covers are available from auto parts stores but an old blanket will work just fine.

7   If you're working on a V6 model, remove the upper intake manifold (see Chapter 2).

21.5 Spark plug manufacturers recommend using a wire-type gauge when checking the gap - the wire should slide between the electrodes with a slight drag

8   All models are equipped with individual ignition coils which must be removed first to access the spark plugs (see illustration).

9   If compressed air is available, use it to blow any dirt or foreign material away from the spark plug area.

✸✸ WARNING:

Wear eye protection!

The idea here is to eliminate the possibility of material falling into the cylinder through the spark plug hole as the spark plug is removed.

10 Place the spark plug socket over the plug and remove it from the engine by turning it in a counterclockwise direction (see illustration).

11 Compare the spark plug with this chart to get an indication of the overall running condition of the engine.

12 It's a good idea to lightly coat the threads of the spark plugs with an anti-seize compound (see illustration) to insure that the spark plugs do not seize in the aluminum cylinder head.

13 It's often difficult to insert spark plugs into their holes without cross-threading them. To avoid this possibility, fit a piece of rubber hose over the end of the spark plug (see illustration). The flexible

21.8 Remove the mounting bolt and the individual coil(s) to access the spark plug(s)

21.10 Use a socket and extension to unscrew the spark plugs

A **normally worn** spark plug should have light tan or gray deposits on the firing tip.

A **carbon fouled** plug, identified by soft, sooty, black deposits, may indicate an improperly tuned vehicle. Check the air cleaner, ignition components and engine control system.

An **oil fouled** spark plug indicates an engine with worn piston rings and/or bad valve seals allowing excessive oil to enter the chamber.

This spark plug has been **left in the engine too long**, as evidenced by the extreme gap. Plugs with such an extreme gap can cause misfiring and stumbling accompanied by a noticeable lack of power.

A **physically damaged** spark plug may be evidence of severe detonation in that cylinder. Watch that cylinder carefully between services, as a continued detonation will not only damage the plug, but could also damage the engine.

A **bridged or almost bridged** spark plug, identified by a build-up between the electrodes caused by excessive carbon or oil build-up on the plug.

21.11 Inspect the spark plug to determine engine running conditions

21.12 Apply a thin film of anti-seize compound to the spark plug threads to prevent damage to the cylinder head

21.13 A length of snug-fitting rubber hose will save time and prevent damaged threads when installing the spark plugs

hose acts as a universal joint to help align the plug with the plug hole. Should the plug begin to cross-thread, the hose will slip on the spark

plug, preventing thread damage. Install the spark plug and tighten it to the torque listed in this Chapter's Specifications.

14 Before pushing the ignition coil onto the end of the plug, inspect the ignition coil following the procedures outlined in Section 22.

15 Repeat the procedure for the remaining spark plugs.

22 Ignition coil check (every 30,000 miles or 24 months)

1 Clean the coils with a dampened cloth and dry them thoroughly.

2 Inspect each coil for cracks, damage and carbon tracking. Make sure the coil fits securely onto the spark plug(s). If damage exists, replace the coil.

23 Differential lubricant change (every 30,000 miles or 24 months)

23.2 Differential drain plug

▶ Refer to illustration 23.2

1   This procedure should be performed after the vehicle has been driven so the lubricant will be warm and therefore will flow out of the differential more easily. Raise the vehicle and support it securely on jackstands.

2   Remove the check/fill plug (see illustration 4.32), then remove the drain plug and drain the lubricant (see illustration).

3   Reinstall the drain plug and tighten it to the torque listed in this Chapter's Specifications.

4   Use a hand pump, syringe or funnel to fill differential housing with the specified lubricant until the lubricant level is up to the bottom of the hole.

5   Install the filler plug and tighten it to the torque listed in this Chapter's Specifications.

24 Positive Crankcase Ventilation (PCV) valve check and replacement (every 60,000 miles or 48 months)

CHECK

1   Remove the valve and shake it, listening for a rattle. If it doesn't rattle, it's clogged and must be replaced.

2   Also check the valve and hose for excessive deposits of oil and sludge.

REPLACEMENT

V6 engines

3   Detach the hose from the valve, then unscrew the valve from the upper intake manifold (2.7L engine) or the right valve cover (3.5L engine) (see illustration).

V8 engine

▶ Refer to illustration 24.4

4   To replace the valve, twist the valve and pull it out from the intake manifold, noting its installed position (see illustration).

All models

5   When purchasing a replacement PCV valve, make sure it's for your particular vehicle and engine size. Compare the old valve with the new one to make sure they're the same.

6   Inspect the rubber O-rings for damage and hardening. Replace it with a new one if necessary.

7   Install the PCV valve securely into position.

24.3 On the 3.5L V6 engine, the PCV valve is located at the rear of the right valve cover

24.4 On V8 engines, the PCV valve is located on the top of the intake manifold

25 Cooling system servicing (draining, flushing and refilling) (every 60 months)

❊❊ WARNING:

Do not allow antifreeze to come in contact with your skin or painted surfaces of the vehicle. Rinse off spills immediately with plenty of water. Antifreeze is highly toxic if ingested. Never leave antifreeze lying around in an open container or in puddles on the floor; children and pets are attracted by it's sweet smell and may drink it. Check with local authorities about disposing of used antifreeze. Many communities have collection centers which will see that antifreeze is disposed of safely.

1   Periodically, the cooling system should be drained, flushed and refilled to replenish the antifreeze mixture and prevent formation of rust and corrosion, which can impair the performance of the cooling system and cause engine damage. When the cooling system is serviced, all hoses and the expansion tank cap should be checked and replaced if necessary.

DRAINING

▶ **Refer to illustrations 25.4 and 25.5**

2   Apply the parking brake and block the wheels. If the vehicle has just been driven, wait several hours to allow the engine to cool down before beginning this procedure.

3   Once the engine is completely cool, remove the radiator cap.

4   Move a large container under the radiator drain to catch the coolant. Attach a length of hose to the drain fitting to direct the coolant into the container, then open the drain fitting (a pair of pliers may be required to turn it) (see illustration).

5   After the coolant stops flowing out of the radiator, move the container under the engine block drain plugs and allow the coolant in the block to drain (see illustration).

6   While the coolant is draining, check the condition of the radiator hoses, heater hoses and clamps (refer to Section 13 if necessary). Replace any damaged clamps or hoses.

7   Apply thread sealant to the block drain plugs. Reinstall the drain plugs and tighten them securely.

25.4 The radiator drain fitting is located at the lower corner of the radiator

FLUSHING

▶ **Refer to illustration 25.10**

8   Once the system has completely drained, remove the thermostat housing from the engine (see Chapter 3), then reinstall the housing without the thermostat. This will allow the system to be thoroughly flushed.

9   Disconnect the upper hose from the radiator.

10   Place a garden hose in the upper radiator inlet and flush the system until the water runs clear at the upper radiator hose (see illustration).

Garden Hose

Upper Hose
Expels Water

Radiator

36022-1-22.10 HAYNES

25.10 With the thermostat removed, disconnect the upper radiator hose and flush the radiator and engine block with a garden hose

25.5 The block drain plugs are generally located about one to two inches above the oil pan - there is one on each side of the engine block

25.15a Coolant bleeder valve location on the 3.5L V6 engine

25.15b Coolant bleeder plug location on the V8 engine

11 Severe cases of radiator contamination or clogging will require removing the radiator (see Chapter 3) and reverse flushing it. This involves inserting the hose in the bottom radiator outlet to allow the clean water to run against the normal flow, draining out through the top. A radiator repair shop should be consulted if further cleaning or repair is necessary.

12 When the coolant is regularly drained and the system refilled with the correct coolant mixture there should be no need to employ chemical cleaners or descalers.

REFILLING

▶ **Refer to illustrations 25.15a and 25.15b**

13 Close and tighten the radiator drain.

14 Place the heater temperature control in the maximum heat position.

15 Connect a hose to the coolant bleeder valve and direct the other end of the hose into a container.

   a) *On 2.7L V6 engines the bleeder valve is located at the front of the engine, on the water outlet.*

   b) *On 3.5L V6 engines the bleeder valve is located at the front of the intake manifold, just to the rear of where the upper radiator hose connects to the water outlet (see illustration).*

   c) *V8 engines are equipped with a plug in place of a bleeder valve (see illustration), at the front of the engine on the water outlet housing; you'll have to obtain a bleeder valve (1/4-18 npt thread) at a dealer parts department or an auto parts store and install it in place of the plug.*

16 Open the bleeder valve (be sure to do this before adding coolant).

17 Make sure to use the proper coolant listed in this Chapter's Specifications. Slowly fill the cooling system with the recommended mixture of antifreeze and water until a bubble-free stream flows from the bleeder hose, then tighten the bleeder valve.

18 Continue adding coolant to the expansion tank until the level is up to the MIN mark. Wait five minutes and recheck the coolant level, adding if necessary.

19 Install the expansion tank cap and run the engine in a well-ventilated area until the thermostat opens (coolant will begin flowing through the radiator and the upper radiator hose will become hot).

20 Turn the engine off and let it cool. Add more coolant mixture to bring the level between the MIN and MAX marks on the reservoir.

21 Squeeze the upper radiator hose to expel air, then add more coolant mixture if necessary. Install the expansion tank cap.

22 Start the engine, allow it to reach normal operating temperature and check for leaks. Also, set the heater and blower controls to the maximum setting and check to see that the heater output from the air ducts is warm. This is a good indication that all air has been purged from the cooling system.

26 Automatic transmission fluid and filter change (every 100,000 miles)

▶ **Refer to illustration 26.22a and 26.22b**

➡**Note: Before beginning this procedure, read the Note in Step 18.**

1 At the specified time intervals, the transmission fluid should be drained and replaced. Since the fluid will remain hot long after driving, perform this procedure only after everything has cooled down completely.

2 Before beginning work, purchase the specified transmission fluid (see *Recommended lubricants and fluids* at the end of this Chapter) and a new filter.

3 Other tools necessary for this job include jackstands to support the vehicle in a raised position, a drain pan capable of holding several quarts, newspapers and clean rags.

4 Raise and support the vehicle on jackstands.

5 With a drain pan in place, remove the front and side transmission pan mounting bolts.

6 Loosen the rear pan bolts one turn.

7 Carefully pry the transmission pan loose with a screwdriver, allowing the fluid to drain.

8 Remove the remaining bolts, pan and gasket. Carefully clean the gasket surface of the transmission to remove all traces of the old gasket and sealant.

9 Drain the fluid from the transmission pan, clean the pan with solvent and dry it with compressed air. Be careful not to lose the magnet.

10 Remove the filter and pry out the seal.

26.22a Automatic transmission fluid level vs. temperature chart - 42RLE transmission

11 Push a new filter seal fully into its bore, then install the new filter.

12 Make sure the gasket surface on the transmission pan is clean.

13 If you're working on a NAG1 transmission, install a new gasket. Put the pan in place against the transmission and install the bolts.

14 If you're working on a 42LE transmission, clean the pan and transmission surfaces thoroughly with lacquer thinner and apply a continuous bead of ATF-resistant RTV sealant to the pan, then bolt it in place and tighten to Specifications within five minutes.

15 Working around the pan, tighten each bolt a little at a time until the final torque figure is reached.

16 Lower the vehicle and add the specified amount of automatic transmission fluid through the filler tube and check the fluid level (see Steps 18 through 23).

17 Check under the vehicle for leaks during the first few trips.

FLUID LEVEL CHECK

▶ **Refer to illustrations 26.22a and 26.22b**

18 The manufacturer states that routine checks of the automatic transmission fluid are not necessary; this procedure should only be used when refilling the transmission after the fluid has been drained, unless an obvious leak has been detected. Low fluid level can lead to slipping or loss of drive, while overfilling can cause foaming and loss of fluid.

26.22b Automatic transmission fluid level vs. temperature chart - NAG1 transmission

➡**Note: To perform this procedure you'll have to obtain a dipstick (part number 9336), which you'll have to obtain through a dealer parts department (unlike most vehicles, a dipstick is not present in the transmission filler tube). A scan tool capable of reading the temperature of the automatic transmission fluid will also be required.**

19 With the parking brake set, start the engine, then move the shift lever through all the gear ranges, ending in Neutral. Wait at least 2 minutes.

➡**Note: The fluid level must be checked with the vehicle level and the engine running at idle.**

20 With the transmission at normal operating temperature, insert the dipstick into the filler tube and pull out again, and note the fluid level.

21 Using a scan tool capable of reading the temperature of the automatic transmission fluid, check the temperature of the automatic transmission fluid.

22 Determine the correct fluid level by using the temperature and the height of the fluid on the dipstick with the accompanying chart(s) (see illustrations).

23 If additional fluid is required, add it directly into the tube using a funnel. Add the fluid a little at a time and keep checking the level until it's correct. Once the oil level is correct, install the dipstick tube cap.

Recommended lubricants and fluids

➡Note: Listed here are manufacturer recommendations at the time this manual was written. Manufacturers occasionally upgrade their fluid and lubricant specifications, so check with your local auto parts store for current recommendations.

Engine oil type	API grade "certified for gasoline engines"
Oil viscosity	
2.7L V6 engine	5W-20
3.5L V6 engine	10W-30
5.7L Hemi engine	5W-20
Automatic transmission fluid type	Mopar® type ATF+4 or equivalent
Coolant	50/50 mixture of Mopar® 5 year/100,000 mile Formula antifreeze/coolant with HOAT (Hybrid Organic Additive Technology) and water

➡Note: Models are filled with a 50/50 mixture of Mopar® 5 year/100,000 mile coolant that shouldn't be mixed with other coolants. Always refill with the correct coolant.

Differential lubricant type	SAE 75W-140 GL-5 gear lubricant or equivalent
Brake fluid type	DOT 3 brake fluid
Power steering fluid	Mopar® type ATF+4 or equivalent
Chassis grease type	Mopar® multi-purpose lubricant NLGI Grade 2 EP, GC-LB

Capacities*

Cooling system	
2.7L V6 engine	
2006 and earlier models	9.7 quarts
2007 and later models	9.9 quarts
3.5L V6 engine	
2006 and earlier models	10.6 quarts
2007 and later models	11.1 quarts
5.7L V8 engine	14.7 quarts
Engine oil (with filter change)	
2.7L V6 engine	6 quarts
3.5L V6 engine	6 quarts
5.7L V8 engine	7 quarts
Automatic transmission (drain and refill)	
42RLE	1-1/2 quarts**
NAG1	7.4 quarts**

**Note: The best way to determine the amount of fluid to add during a routine fluid change is to measure the amount drained. It is important not to overfill the transmission.

Rear axle	
198RII	1.5 quarts
210RII	1.7 quarts
215RII	1.7 quarts

*All capacities approximate. Add as necessary to bring the appropriate levels.

Ignition system

Spark plug type
    2.7L V6 engine   RE10PMC5
    3.5L V6 engine   ZFR5LP-13G
    5.7L V8 engine   Champion - RE14MCC4
Spark plug gap
    2.7L V6 engine   0.048 inch to 0.058 inch
    3.5L V6 engine   0.048 inch to 0.058 inch
    5.7L V8 engine   0.045 inch
Firing order
    V6 engines   1-2-3-4-5-6
    V8 engine   1-8-4-3-6-5-7-2

Brakes

Disc brake pad lining thickness (minimum)   1/8 inch
Parking brake shoe lining thickness (minimum)   1/16 inch

Front

**Cylinder locations -
2.7L and 3.5L V6 engines**

FRONT

30042 -1-specs HAYNES

**Cylinder locations -
5.7L (Hemi) V8 engine**

Torque specifications   Ft-lbs (unless otherwise indicated)

➡**Note: One foot-pound (ft-lb) of torque is equivalent to 12 inch-pounds (in-lbs) of torque. Torque values below approximately 15 ft-lbs are expressed in inch-pounds, since most foot-pound torque wrenches are not accurate at these smaller values.**

Automatic transmission pan bolts
    42LE   174 in-lbs
    NAG1   70 in-lbs
Drivebelt tensioner mounting bolt   40
Engine oil drain plug   20
Differential drain/fill plug
    198RII   44
    210RII   37
    215RII   37
Spark plugs
    2.7L V6 engine   150 in-lbs
    3.5L V6 engine   20
    5.7L V8 engine   156 in-lbs
Wheel lug nuts   110

Notes

Section

1　General information
2　Repair operations possible with the engine in the vehicle
3　Top Dead Center (TDC) for number one piston - locating
4　Valve cover - removal and installation
5　Rocker arms and hydraulic lash adjusters - removal, inspection and installation
6　Timing chain and sprockets - removal, inspection and installation
7　Camshafts - removal, inspection and installation
8　Intake manifold - removal and installation
9　Exhaust manifold - removal and installation
10　Cylinder heads - removal and installation
11　Crankshaft pulley - removal and installation
12　Crankshaft front oil seal - replacement
13　Oil pan - removal and installation
14　Oil pump - removal, inspection and installation
15　Driveplate - removal and installation
16　Rear main oil seal - replacement
17　Engine mounts - check and replacement

Reference to other Chapters

CHECK ENGINE light on -See Chapter 6
Cylinder compression check - See Chapter 2D
Drivebelt check, adjustment and replacement - See Chapter 1
Engine - removal and installation - See Chapter 2D
Engine oil and filter change - See Chapter 1
Engine overhaul - general information - See Chapter 2D
Spark plug replacement - See Chapter 1
Water pump - removal and installation - See Chapter 3

2A

2.7L V6 ENGINE

1　General information

This Part of Chapter 2 is devoted to in-vehicle repair procedures for the 2.7L V6 engine. These engines utilize an aluminum block with six cylinders arranged in a "V" shape at a 60-degree angle between the two banks. The overhead camshaft aluminum cylinder heads are equipped with replaceable valve guides and seats. Stamped steel rocker arms with an integral roller bearing actuate the valves.

Information concerning engine removal and installation and engine overhaul can be found in Part D of this Chapter.

The following repair procedures are based on the assumption that the engine is installed in the vehicle. If the engine has been removed from the vehicle and mounted on a stand, many of the steps outlined in this Part of Chapter 2 will not apply.

2　Repair operations possible with the engine in the vehicle

Many major repair operations can be accomplished without removing the engine from the vehicle.

Clean the engine compartment and the exterior of the engine with some type of degreaser before any work is done. It will make the job easier and help keep dirt out of the internal areas of the engine.

Depending on the components involved, it may be helpful to remove the hood to improve access to the engine as repairs are performed (refer to Chapter 11, if necessary). Cover the fenders to prevent damage to the paint. Special pads are available, but an old bedspread or blanket will also work.

If vacuum, exhaust, oil or coolant leaks develop, indicating a need for gasket or seal replacement, the repairs can generally be made with the engine in the vehicle. The intake and exhaust manifold gaskets, oil pan gasket, crankshaft oil seals and cylinder head gaskets are all accessible with the engine in place.

Exterior engine components, such as the intake and exhaust manifolds, the oil pan, the oil pump, the water pump (see Chapter 3), the starter motor, the alternator and the fuel system components (see Chapter 4) can be removed for repair with the engine in place.

Since the cylinder heads can be removed without pulling the engine, valve component servicing can also be accomplished with the engine in the vehicle. Replacement of the camshafts, timing chains and sprockets are also possible with the engine in the vehicle.

In extreme cases caused by a lack of necessary equipment, repair or replacement of piston rings, pistons, connecting rods and rod bearings is possible with the engine in the vehicle. However, this practice is not recommended because of the cleaning and preparation work that must be done to the components involved.

3　Top Dead Center (TDC) for number one piston - locating

◆ **Refer to illustration 3.5**

1　Top Dead Center (TDC) is the highest point in the cylinder that each piston reaches as it travels up the cylinder bore. Each piston reaches TDC on the compression stroke and again on the exhaust stroke, but TDC generally refers to piston position on the compression stroke.

2　Positioning the piston(s) at TDC is an essential part of many procedures such as valve timing, camshaft and timing chain/belt sprocket removal.

3　Before beginning this procedure, be sure to place the transmission in Neutral and apply the parking brake or block the rear wheels. Also, disconnect the cable from the negative terminal of the battery, then remove the ignition coils (see Chapter 5) and the spark plugs (see Chapter 1).

4　The preferred method is to turn the crankshaft with a socket and ratchet or breaker bar attached to the bolt threaded into the front of the crankshaft. When looking at the front of the engine, normal crankshaft rotation is clockwise. Turn the bolt in a clockwise direction only.

5　Install a compression pressure gauge in the number one spark plug hole (refer to Chapter 2D). It should be a gauge with a screw-in fitting and a hose at least six inches long (see illustration).

6　Rotate the crankshaft using the method described above while observing for pressure on the compression gauge. The moment the gauge shows pressure, indicates that the number one cylinder is on the compression stroke.

7　Once the compression stroke has begun, TDC for the compression stroke of the number one cylinder is reached by bringing the piston to the top of the cylinder.

8　Insert a long dowel into the number one spark plug hole until

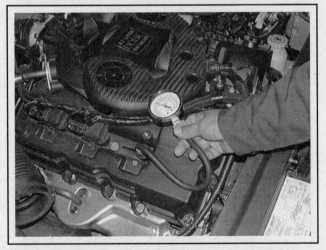

3.5　A compression gauge can be used in the number one plug hole to assist in finding TDC

it rests on top of the piston crown. Continue rotating the crankshaft slowly until the dowel levels off (piston reaches top of travel). This will be approximate TDC for number 1 piston.

9　These engines are not equipped with components (vibration damper, flywheel, timing hole, etc.) that are marked to identify the position of number 1 TDC. Therefore the only method to double-check the exact location of TDC number 1 on V8 engines is to remove the timing chain cover to access timing chain sprockets (see Section 6), or with the use of a degree wheel on the crankshaft vibration damper and a positive stop threaded into the spark plug hole, as you would use in the process of degreeing a camshaft.

10 After the No. 1 piston has been positioned at TDC on the compression stroke, TDC for any of the remaining pistons can be located by turning the crankshaft and following the firing order. Divide the crankshaft pulley into three equal sections with chalk marks at each point, each indicating 120-degrees of crankshaft rotation. Rotating the engine past TDC no. 1 to the next mark will place the engine at TDC for cylinder no. 2.

4 Valve cover - removal and installation

▶ **Refer to illustration 4.5**

REMOVAL

1 Disconnect the cable from the negative terminal of the battery (see Chapter 5, Section 1).

2 Remove the upper intake manifold (see Section 8) and cover the lower intake manifold with rags to keep out dirt.

3 Remove the ignition coils (see Chapter 5).

4 Remove the PCV hose from the grommet on the right valve cover (see Chapter 6). Remove the intake hose from the left valve cover.

5 Pull the wire harness up from the valve cover studs and remove the valve cover studs/nuts and bolts (see illustration).

6 Detach the valve cover.

➡**Note: If the cover sticks to the cylinder head, use a block of wood and a hammer to dislodge it. If the cover still won't come loose, pry on it carefully, but don't distort the sealing flange.**

INSTALLATION

7 The mating surfaces of each cylinder head and valve cover must be perfectly clean when the covers are installed. Inspect the rubber gaskets; if they're in good condition and there were no oil leaks, they can be re-used.

8 Inspect the spark plug tube seals. Replace them if they're cracked or flattened, or if the rubber has hardened. Make sure the spark plug

4.5 Valve cover mounting bolts

tube seals are in position before installing the valve cover.

9 Clean the mounting bolt threads with a die if necessary to remove any corrosion and restore damaged threads. Use a tap to clean the threaded holes in the heads.

10 Place the valve cover in position, then install the bolts. Tighten the bolts evenly, in several steps, to the torque listed in this Chapter's Specifications.

11 Complete the installation by reversing the removal procedure. Start the engine and check carefully for oil leaks.

5 Rocker arms and hydraulic lash adjusters - removal, inspection and installation

▶ **Refer to illustrations 5.5, 5.7 and 5.8**

➡**Note: A universal shaft-type valve spring compressor (available from most aftermarket specialty tool manufacturers) will be required for this procedure. The only other alternative to accomplishing this task without the use of this special tool is to remove the timing chains and the camshafts which requires major disassembly of the engine and surrounding components.**

1 Before beginning this procedure, be sure to place the transmission in Neutral and apply the parking brake or block the rear wheels. Also, disable the ignition system by disconnecting the primary electrical connectors at the ignition coils and remove the spark plugs (see Chapter 1).

2 Remove the upper intake manifold (see Section 8) and the valve cover(s) (see Section 4).

3 Rotate the engine with a socket and ratchet attached to the crankshaft pulley bolt until the cam lobe for the rocker arm to be removed is located on its base circle. Turn the crankshaft in a clockwise direction.

4 Before the rocker arms and lash adjusters are removed, arrange to label and store them, so they can be kept separate and reinstalled on the same valve they were removed from.

5 Mount the valve spring compressor on the cylinder head.

Depress the valve spring just enough to release tension on the rocker arm to be removed. Once tension on the rocker arm is relieved, the rocker arm can be removed by simply pulling it out (see illustration).

5.5 Using a shaft-type valve spring compressor, depress the valve spring just enough to remove the rocker arm

5.7 Pull the lash adjuster up and out of its bore to remove it from the cylinder head

6   If you're replacing or removing all of the rockers arms or lash adjusters, begin with cylinder number one and work on the rocker arms for one cylinder at a time. Move from cylinder-to-cylinder following the firing order sequence (see this Chapter's Specifications). Remember to keep the rocker arm and lash adjuster for each valve together so they can be reinstalled in the same locations

7   Once the rocker arms are removed, the lash adjusters can be pulled out of the cylinder head and stored with the corresponding

5.8 Inspect the rocker arms at the following locations

A   *Lash adjuster pocket*   C   *Valve stem seat*
B   *Roller*

rocker arm (see illustration).

8   Inspect each rocker arm for wear, cracks and other damage. Make sure the rollers turn freely and show no signs of wear, also check the pivot area for wear, cracks and galling (see illustration).

9   Inspect the lash adjuster contact surfaces wear or damage. Make sure the lash adjusters move up and down freely in their bores on the cylinder head without excessive side to side play.

10 Installation is the reverse of removal with the following exceptions: Always install the lash adjuster first and make sure they're at least partially full of oil before installation. This is indicated by little or no lash adjuster plunger travel.

6   Timing chain and sprockets - removal, inspection and installation

→Note 1: Special tools are necessary to complete this procedure. Read through the entire procedure and obtain the special tools before beginning work.

→Note 2: Because of work necessary to get at the timing chain and replace it, and because the water pump is in this area, it is recommended that the water pump be thoroughly inspected and replaced if necessary during this procedure (see Chapter 3).

→Note 3: The 2.7L engine utilizes three timing chains to produce proper valve timing. The primary timing chain runs around the crankshaft sprocket, the water pump and around two intake camshaft sprockets. This chain synchronizes the valve timing with the crankshaft and pistons, while two secondary timing chains run around separate intake and exhaust camshaft sprockets to synchronize the intake and exhaust camshaft events. Refer to Step 19 for primary timing chain inspection procedures prior to timing chain removal.

REMOVAL

▶ **Refer to illustrations 6.11, 6.12a, 6.12b, 6.12c, 6.14a, 6.14b, 6.16a and 6.16b**

1   Disconnect the cable from the negative terminal of the battery (see Chapter 5, Section 1).

2   Relieve the fuel system pressure (see Chapter 4) and drain the cooling system (see Chapter 1).

3   Remove the cooling fan assembly, the coolant reservoir and the radiator (see Chapter 3).

4   Remove the accessory drivebelts (see Chapter 1).

5   Remove the crankshaft pulley (see Section 11).

6   Remove the upper intake manifold (see Section 8) and the valve

covers (see Section 4).

7   Remove the spark plugs (see Chapter 1) and position the number one piston at TDC on the compression stroke (see Section 3).

8   Unbolt the air conditioning compressor and set it aside without disconnecting the lines (see Chapter 3).

9   Remove the water outlet housing from the engine block (see Chapter 3).

10 Remove the idler pulley.

11 Remove the timing chain cover (see illustration). Note that various types and sizes of bolts are used. They must be reinstalled in their

6.11 Timing chain cover retaining bolts

6.12a Make sure the mark on the crankshaft sprocket (A) aligns with the colored link on the primary timing chain and the mark on the oil pump housing (B)

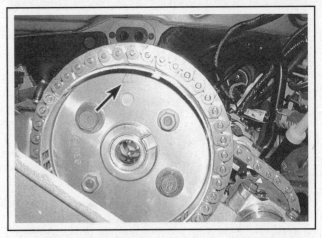

6.12b Also verify that the mark on the left camshaft sprocket is flanked by the two colored links . . .

original locations. Mark each bolt or make a sketch to help remember where they go.

12 Rotate the engine until the crankshaft sprocket timing mark is aligned with the mark on the oil pump housing and the colored links on the chain are aligned with the timing marks on the camshaft sprockets and the crankshaft sprocket (see illustrations). This position is approximately 60-degrees after TDC.

13 Remove the primary timing chain tensioner from the right cylinder head.

14 Remove the retaining bolts from the primary camshaft sprockets (see illustrations).

15 Pull the primary sprockets off the camshaft hubs one at a time, lower the sprocket(s) into the cylinder head opening until the chain can be displaced from around the sprocket, then remove the primary camshaft sprockets from the engine. Note that the left (primary) camshaft

✷✷ WARNING:

Pressure from the valve springs will make the camshafts rotate clockwise as the bolts are removed. Do not rotate the crankshaft or camshaft separately after the primary timing chain is loosened or removed as piston or valve damage may occur. The only exception to this rule is when the camshafts must be rotated counterclockwise slightly, to realign the primary camshaft sprockets with the camshafts during installation.

6.12c . . . and the marks on the right camshaft sprocket align with the colored link on the primary chain

6.14a A 3/8-inch drive extension and ratchet inserted into the end of the camshaft hub is used as leverage while the sprocket bolts are loosened - make note of the vibration damper-to-camshaft sprocket alignment hole

6.14b Left camshaft sprocket retaining bolts

6.16a Primary timing chain guide access plugs

6.16b Primary timing chain guide mounting details

1	Upper right timing chain guide mounting bolts	3	Tensioner arm pivot bolt
2	Upper left timing chain guide mounting bolts	4	Lower timing chain guide mounting bolts

sprocket is identified by the camshaft position sensor ring which is mounted on the front of the sprocket by two nuts. It is not necessary to remove the sensor ring from the sprocket during this procedure unless damage to the sensor ring or sprocket has occurred. Also note that the right (primary) camshaft sprocket is identified by a vibration damper which is mounted in front of the sprocket. Make note of the alignment holes on the damper and the right (primary) sprocket as these two components will separate as the sprocket is removed from the camshaft. Always install the damper in the same position from which it was removed.

16 Remove the access plugs from the front of the cylinder heads and detach the primary timing chain guides and tensioner arm (see illustrations).

17 Remove the primary timing chain.

➥**Note: The secondary timing chains are removed as an assembly with the camshafts and therefore covered in camshaft removal (see Section 7).**

18 If the crankshaft sprocket needs to be replaced after thorough inspection or the sprocket simply needs to be removed for other procedures such as oil pump removal, proceed to Step 36.

INSPECTION

19 Inspect the camshaft, water pump and crankshaft sprockets for wear on the teeth and keyways. Inspect the chains for cracks or excessive wear of the rollers. Inspect the facing of the chain guides and tensioner arm for excessive wear. If any of the components show signs of excessive wear they must be replaced.

INSTALLATION

▶ **Refer to illustrations 6.26 and 6.32**

20 If removed, install the crankshaft sprocket as outlined in Step 38 and 39.

21 If you purchased a new timing chain, verify that you have the correct timing chain for your vehicle by counting the number of links the chain has and comparing the new chain with the old chain. Also compare the position of the colored links in the new chain with the position of the colored links in the old chain.

22 Verify the crankshaft sprocket is still aligned with the mark on the oil pump housing (see illustration 6.12a) and install the upper chain

guides back into position on the engine (see illustration 6.16b).

23 Prepare to install the primary timing chain by aligning the left (primary) camshaft sprocket mark between the light colored links on the chain (see illustration 6.14b). Then lower the sprocket and chain assembly down through the opening in the left cylinder head and reposition the left camshaft sprocket over the camshaft hub.

24 Install the right (primary) camshaft sprocket, vibration damper and timing chain onto the engine by looping the chain around the crankshaft sprocket and aligning the light colored chain link with the mark on the crankshaft sprocket. Then place the chain around the water pump sprocket and install the right (primary) camshaft sprocket over the right camshaft hub making sure the colored links align with their respective marks on the sprockets (see illustrations 6.12a, 6.12b and 6.12c).

25 Install the lower chain guide and tensioner arm (see illustration 6.16b).

26 Use the special tool to purge the oil from the tensioner. Place the check ball end of the tensioner into the shallow end of the tool over the pin, apply hand pressure and slowly depress the tensioner until the oil

25027-2A-6.26 HAYNES

6.26 Primary timing chain tensioner - oil purging details

1	Tensioner body	3	Special tool
2	Check ball	4	Pin

6.32 With all slack removed from the left side of the chain and the colored links on the chain aligned with their respective marks on the sprockets, engage the tensioner by pushing the tensioner arm inward slightly, then release the tensioner arm to extend the tensioner

has been purged from the tensioner (see illustration).

27 After the oil has been purged, the tensioner must be reset before installation. Place the tensioner plunger into the deep end of the tool and depress the plunger until it locks into place. Once the tensioner is reset it will be about 1-1/2 inches shorter.

28 Install the reset tensioner and tighten the tensioner retaining plate bolts to the torque listed in this Chapters Specifications. Always use a new O-ring or gasket on the tensioner housing or tensioner retaining plate.

✳✳ CAUTION:

Be sure to align the tensioner retaining plate dowel pin with the hole in the cylinder head.

29 Install the camshaft sprocket retaining bolts by inserting a 3/8-inch drive extension and ratchet into the primary camshaft hub and slightly rotating the camshafts until the camshaft sprocket bolt holes align with the camshaft hub bolt holes. Perform the procedure on the right (primary) camshaft sprocket first then proceed to the left (primary) camshaft sprocket.

30 Leaving the 3/8-inch extension and ratchet inserted into the camshaft hub as leverage, tighten the camshaft sprocket bolts to the torque listed in this Chapter's Specifications.

31 Rotate the engine clockwise just enough remove any slack from the left side of the timing chain.

32 Reconfirm that the timing marks on the camshaft and crankshaft sprockets are aligned with the colored links on the chain and release the primary timing chain tensioner from its reset position (see illustration).

33 Remove all traces of old sealant from the timing chain cover and the cover bolts.

34 Apply a bead of RTV sealant to the timing chain cover gasket and

6.37 The crankshaft sprocket can be removed with a conventional three jaw puller

sealing surfaces. Place the timing cover in position on the engine and install the bolts in their original locations and tighten the bolts to the torque listed in this Chapter's Specifications.

35 The remainder of the installation is the reverse of removal. Refill the cooling system (see Chapter 1).

CRANKSHAFT SPROCKET

▶ **Refer to illustration 6.37**

36 If the crankshaft sprocket is to be removed and installed, it will require the use of several special tools, a three jaw puller, a propane torch or crankshaft sprocket installation tool and a machinist ruler or dial caliper.

37 After the primary timing chain has been removed, the crankshaft sprocket can be removed with a three jaw puller (see illustration).

38 To install the crankshaft sprocket it will be necessary to purchase a sprocket installation tool or a common household propane torch. If a sprocket installation tool is purchased follow the installation procedures outlined in the tools instructions and install the sprocket to the proper depth (see Step 39). If a propane torch is used, simply place the sprocket in a vise and heat the sprocket hub until the sprocket has expanded enough to slide over the crankshaft.

✳✳ CAUTION:

After heating the sprocket always handle the sprocket with a pair of pliers or other insulated tool to avoid serious injury and never heat an object when gasoline or other volatile chemicals are present.

39 Install the sprocket until it bottoms on the shoulder on the crankshaft. Using a machinist ruler or a caliper, make sure it has been installed completely by measuring from the end of the crankshaft to the face of the crankshaft sprocket; it should measure 1.537 inches plus-or-minus 0.020 inch (39.05 +/- 0.5 mm).

7 Camshafts - removal, inspection and installation

REMOVAL

▶ **Refer to illustrations 7.4, 7.5 and 7.6**

1   Disconnect the cable from the negative terminal of the battery (see Chapter 5, Section 1).

2   Remove the valve covers (see Section 4).

3   Remove the primary timing chain and the primary camshaft sprockets (see Section 6).

4   Remove the retaining bolts from the secondary timing chain tensioner (see illustration).

7.4 Secondary timing chain tensioner retaining bolts (right cylinder head shown, left cylinder head similar)

7.5 Verify that the camshaft bearing caps are marked to ensure correct reinstallation

5   Verify the markings on the camshaft bearing caps. The caps should be marked from 1 to 5, and with an "I" or an "E", to indicate intake or exhaust. Also verify that there are arrow marks on the caps indicating the front of the engine (see illustration). Loosen the camshaft bearing caps in two or three steps, in the reverse order of the tightening sequence (see illustration 7.19).

✳✳ CAUTION:

Keep the caps in order. They must go back in the same location they were removed from.

6   Detach the bearing caps, then remove the camshafts, secondary timing chain and the secondary tensioner as an assembly from the cylinder head. Make a note that the intake camshafts have a flanged hub at the front and the exhaust camshafts do not. Also note that the intake camshafts are installed in the cylinder head (towards the center of the engine) next to the intake manifold and the exhaust camshafts are installed (towards the sides of the engine) next to the exhaust manifolds (see illustration).

7   Remove the secondary tensioner and the timing chain from the camshafts.

8   Inspect the camshaft secondary sprockets for wear on the teeth. Inspect the chains for cracks or excessive wear of the rollers. Inspect the facing of the secondary chain tensioners for excessive wear. If any of the components show signs of excessive wear they must be replaced.

INSPECTION

▶ **Refer to illustrations 7.10, 7.11 and 7.12**

9   After the camshaft has been removed from the engine, cleaned

7.6 Camshaft installation details

A   Intake manifold location
B   Intake camshaft (left cylinder head)
C   Intake camshaft (right cylinder head)
D   Exhaust camshaft (right cylinder head)
E   Exhaust manifold

7.10 Check the diameter of each camshaft bearing journal to pinpoint excessive wear and out-of-round conditions

7.11 Measure the camshaft lobe height (greatest dimension) with a micrometer

with solvent and dried, inspect the bearing journals for uneven wear, pitting and evidence of seizure. If the camshaft journals are damaged, inspect the cylinder head and the camshaft bearing caps.

10 Measure the bearing journals with a micrometer to determine if they are excessively worn or out-of-round (see illustration). Compare the measurements with the Specifications listed in this Chapter.

11 Measure the lobe height of each cam lobe on the intake camshaft and record your measurements (see illustration). Compare the measurements for excessive variations. If the lobe heights vary more than 0.010 inch (0.254 mm), replace the camshaft. Compare the lobe height measurements on the exhaust camshaft and follow the same procedure. Do not compare intake camshaft lobe heights with exhaust camshaft lobe heights, as they are different. Only compare intake lobes with intake lobes and exhaust lobes with other exhaust lobes.

12 Check the camshaft lobes for heat discoloration, score marks, chipped areas, pitting and uneven wear (see illustration). If the lobes are in good condition and if the lobe lift variation measurements recorded earlier are within the limits, the camshaft can be reused.

INSTALLATION

▶ **Refer to illustrations 7.14, 7.17 and 7.19**

13 Install the secondary timing chain(s) over the camshaft sprockets while aligning the colored links on the chain with the marks on the secondary camshaft sprockets in a 12 o'clock position.

➡**Note: The colored links on the chain must face outward toward the front of the engine.**

14 Using a paperclip, fabricate a U-shaped tool to use as a tensioner locking pin. Then place the secondary tensioner in a vise and compress the tensioner until the U-shaped tool can be inserted into the locking holes on the tensioner. This places the tensioner in the locked position so it can be reinstalled (see illustration).

15 Once the tensioner is locked into place it can be installed back into the place between the camshafts and the secondary timing chain.

16 Apply moly-based engine assembly lubricant to the camshaft lobes and journals. Make sure the rocker arms are properly seated on their respective lash adjuster and the valve stem tip.

7.12 Check the cam lobes for pitting, excessive wear and scoring. If scoring is excessive, as shown here, replace the camshaft

7.14 Compress the secondary tensioner in a vise until a paperclip can be inserted into the secondary tensioner locking holes

Exhaust Camshaft

Intake Camshaft

7.17 Camshaft installation details

A   *Secondary timing chain colored links*
B   *Secondary camshaft sprocket marks*
C   *Tensioner locking pin*
D   *Secondary timing chain tensioner*

17 Install the camshafts, secondary tensioner and the timing chain as an assembly in their original position, with the marks on the sprockets and the colored links on the chain facing up (90-degrees from the valve cover mating surface) and inline with the cylinder bank (see illustration).

7.19 Camshaft bearing cap TIGHTENING sequence

➡**Note: When installed correctly there should be 12 timing chain pins between the intake and exhaust camshaft marks.**

18 Install the bearing caps and bolts and tighten them hand tight.
19 Tighten the bearing cap bolts in several steps, to the torque listed in this Chapter's Specifications, using the proper tightening sequence (see illustration).
20 Tighten the tensioner mounting bolts to the torque listed in this Chapter's Specifications and remove the tensioner locking pin.
21 Install the primary timing chain and camshaft sprockets (see Section 6).
22 The remainder of installation is the reverse of removal.

8   Intake manifold - removal and installation

UPPER INTAKE MANIFOLD

◆ **Refer to illustration 8.8**

1   Relieve the fuel pressure (see Chapter 4).
2   Disconnect the cable from the negative terminal of the battery (see Chapter 5, Section 1).
3   Remove the air intake duct and the air filter housing (see Chapter 4).
4   Label and disconnect the vacuum hoses and electrical connectors attached to the upper intake manifold and throttle body. Disconnect the electronic throttle control (ETC) system from the throttle body (see Chapter 4).
5   Remove the EGR pipe from the upper intake manifold (see Chapter 6).
6   Remove the upper intake manifold support brackets. Loosen the upper intake manifold bolts in the reverse order of the tightening sequence (see illustration 8.8). Remove the upper intake manifold and the foam insulator pad.
7   Clean and inspect the upper intake manifold to lower intake manifold sealing surfaces. Inspect the gaskets for tears or cracks replacing them if necessary. The gaskets can be reused if not damaged.
8   Install the upper intake manifold onto the lower intake manifold and tighten the bolts in the recommended tightening sequence (see illustration) to the torque listed in this Chapter's Specifications. The remainder of installation is the reverse of removal.

8.8 Upper intake manifold bolt TIGHTENING sequence

LOWER INTAKE MANIFOLD

◆ **Refer to illustration 8.16**

9   Remove the upper intake manifold (see Steps 1 through 6).
10 Label and detach any remaining hoses which would interfere with the removal of the lower intake manifold.

11 Remove the fuel rail and injectors from the lower intake manifold (see Chapter 4).

12 Loosen the lower intake manifold mounting bolts/nuts in 1/4-turn increments, in the reverse order of the tightening sequence, until they can be removed by hand (see illustration 8.16).

13 The manifold will probably be stuck to the cylinder heads and force may be required to break the gasket seal.

✳✳ CAUTION:

Don't pry between the manifold and the heads or damage to the gasket sealing surfaces may occur, leading to vacuum leaks.

14 Clean and inspect the lower intake manifold to cylinder head sealing surfaces. Inspect the gaskets for tears or cracks, replacing them if necessary. The gaskets can be reused if they aren't damaged.

15 Position the lower intake manifold onto the engine making sure the gaskets and manifold are aligned correctly over the cylinder heads. Install the fuel rail and injectors onto the cylinder heads and the lower manifold. Install the fuel rail retaining bolts into the manifold loosely to ensure correct gasket/manifold alignment, then install the remaining lower intake manifold bolts.

8.16 Lower intake manifold bolt TIGHTENING sequence

16 Following the recommended tightening sequence, tighten the bolts, in several steps, to the torque listed in this Chapter's Specifications (see illustration).

17 The remainder of installation is the reverse of the removal procedure. Run the engine and check for fuel, vacuum and coolant leaks.

9 Exhaust manifold - removal and installation

✳✳ WARNING:

The engine must be completely cool before beginning this procedure.

REMOVAL

▶ **Refer to illustration 9.3**

1 Disconnect the cable from the negative terminal of the battery (see Chapter 5, Section 1).

2 Block the rear wheels, set the parking brake, raise the front of the vehicle and support it securely on jackstands. Disconnect the downstream oxygen sensor connectors (see Chapter 6).

3 Remove the engine middle splash shield (see illustration).

4 Unbolt the exhaust pipes at the exhaust manifolds.

5 Lower the vehicle. Working in the engine compartment, disconnect the oxygen sensor's electrical connector. If removing the right exhaust manifold, detach the EGR pipe from the top of the manifold. If removing the left manifold, remove the air filter housing (see Chapter 4) and the engine oil dipstick tube.

6 Remove the exhaust manifold upper heat shield mounting bolts and remove the heat shields.

7 Remove the mounting bolts and detach the manifold from the cylinder head. Be sure to spray penetrating lubricant onto the bolts and threads before attempting to remove them.

INSTALLATION

8 Clean the mating surfaces to remove all traces of old gasket material, then inspect the manifold for distortion and cracks. Warpage can be checked with a precision straightedge held against the mating flange. If a feeler gauge thicker than 0.030-inch can be inserted between

the straightedge and flange surface, take the manifold to an automotive machine shop for resurfacing.

9 Place the exhaust manifold in position with a new gasket and the lower heat shields and install the mounting bolts finger tight.

➡**Note: Be sure to identify the exhaust manifold gaskets by the correct cylinder designation and the position of the exhaust ports on the gasket.**

10 Starting in the middle and working out toward the ends, tighten the mounting bolts in several increments, to the torque listed in this Chapter's Specifications.

11 Install the remaining components in the reverse order of removal.

12 Start the engine and check for exhaust leaks between the manifold and cylinder head and between the manifold and exhaust pipe.

9.3 Front engine splash shield (1) and middle engine splash shield (2) fasteners

10 Cylinder head(s) - removal and installation

✳✳ CAUTION:

The engine must be completely cool before beginning this procedure.

REMOVAL

▶ **Refer to illustration 10.5**

1   Refer to Section 6, Steps 1 through 18, and remove the primary timing chain and sprockets.

✳✳ CAUTION:

Be careful not to disturb the crankshaft from its alignment marks during the remainder of this procedure.

2   Remove the camshafts from the cylinder head (see Section 6).

3   Remove the rocker arms and hydraulic lash adjusters from the cylinder head (see Section 5). Before the rocker arms and lash adjusters are removed, arrange to label and store them, so they can be kept separate and reinstalled on the same valve from which they were removed.

4   Remove the lower intake manifold (see Section 8) and the exhaust manifold(s) (see Section 9).

5   Label and remove any remaining items attached to the cylinder head, such as coolant fittings, ground straps, cables, hoses, wires or brackets (see illustration).

6   Using a breaker bar and the appropriate sized socket, loosen the cylinder head bolts in 1/4-turn increments until they can be removed by

hand. Loosen the bolts in the reverse order of the tightening sequence (see illustration 10.19) to avoid warping or cracking the head.

7   Lift the cylinder head off the engine block with the exhaust manifold attached. If it's stuck, very carefully pry up at the transmission end, beyond the gasket surface, at a casting protrusion.

8   Remove all external components from the cylinder head to allow for thorough cleaning and inspection before having the cylinder head serviced at a qualified automotive machine shop.

INSTALLATION

▶ **Refer to illustration 10.19**

9   The mating surfaces of the cylinder head and block must be perfectly clean when the head is installed.

10   Use a gasket scraper to remove all traces of carbon and old gasket material from the cylinder head and engine block being careful not to gouge the aluminum, then clean the mating surfaces with lacquer thinner or acetone. If there's oil on the mating surfaces when the head is installed, the gasket may not seal correctly and leaks could develop. When working on the block, stuff the cylinders with clean shop rags to keep out debris. Use a vacuum cleaner to remove material that falls into the cylinders.

11   Check the block and head mating surfaces for nicks, deep scratches and other damage. If damage is slight, it can be removed with a file; if it's excessive, machining may be the only alternative.

12   Use a tap of the correct size to chase the threads in the head bolt holes, then clean the holes with compressed air - make sure that nothing remains in the holes.

✳✳ WARNING:

Wear eye protection when using compressed air!

13   Check each cylinder head bolt for stretching by laying a metal ruler or a straightedge against the threads of the bolts. If the diameter of the bolt threads has necked down anywhere in the threaded area, the bolts have exceeded the maximum amount of stretch and will need to be replaced (all of the threads must touch the straightedge).

➡ **Note: It's a good idea to replace the head bolts with new ones.**

14   Using a precision straightedge and feeler gauges, check the cylinder head for warpage. If warpage exceeds the amount listed in this Chapter's Specifications, have the heads machined at an automotive machine shop.

15   Install the components that were removed from the head.

16   Position the new cylinder head gasket over the dowel pins on the block, noting which direction on the gasket faces up.

17   Carefully set the head over the dowels on the block without disturbing the gasket.

18   Before installing the head bolts, apply a small amount of clean engine oil to the threads and hardened washers (if equipped). The chamfered side of the washers must face the bolt heads.

10.5   Remove the water outlet housing by detaching the heater supply tube retaining bolts (A), then slide the heater supply tube out of the water outlet housing and remove the water outlet housing retaining bolts (B)

19 Install the bolts in their original locations and tighten them finger tight. Then tighten all the bolts in several steps, following the proper sequence (see illustration), to the torque listed in this Chapter's Specifications.

20 Install the lash adjusters and the rocker arms in the cylinder head, then install the camshafts as described in Section 7,

21 Install the primary timing chain and sprockets as described in Section 7. The remaining installation steps are the reverse of removal.

22 Refill the cooling system and change the engine oil and filter (see Chapter 1).

23 Start the engine and check for oil and coolant leaks.

10.19 Cylinder head bolt TIGHTENING sequence

11 Crankshaft pulley - removal and installation

▶ **Refer to illustrations 11.5, 11.6 and 11.7**

1   Disconnect the cable from the negative terminal of the battery (see Chapter 5, Section 1).

2   Remove the upper radiator crossmember, the cooling fan assembly and the radiator (see Chapter 3).

3   Remove the engine splash shield (see Section 9).

4   Remove the drivebelts (see Chapter 1) and position the belt tensioner away from the crankshaft pulley.

5   Use a strap wrench around the crankshaft pulley to hold it while using a breaker bar and socket to remove the crankshaft pulley center bolt (see illustration).

6   Pull the damper off the crankshaft with a puller (see illustration).

✳✳ CAUTION:

The jaws of the puller must only contact the hub of the pulley - not the outer ring.

➡**Note:** A spacer should be placed against the end to the crankshaft nose (that fits in the pulley bore) or a long Allen-head bolt should be inserted into the crankshaft nose for the puller's tapered tip to push against to prevent damage to the crankshaft threads.

11.5 Use a strap wrench to hold the crankshaft pulley while removing the center bolt (a chain-type wrench may be used if you wrap a section of old drivebelt or rag around the crankshaft pulley first)

7   Check the surface on the pulley hub that the oil seal rides on. if the surface has been grooved from long-time contact with the seal, a press-on sleeve may be available to renew the sealing surface (see

11.6 The use of a three jaw puller will be necessary to remove the crankshaft pulley - always place the puller jaws around the pulley hub, not the outer ring

11.7 If the sealing surface of the pulley hub has a wear groove from contact with the seal, repair sleeves are available at most auto parts stores

illustration). This sleeve is pressed into place with a hammer and a block of wood and is commonly available at auto parts stores for various applications.

8   Lubricate the pulley hub with clean engine oil and reinstall the crankshaft pulley. Use a vibration damper installation tool to press the pulley onto the crankshaft.

9   Install the crankshaft pulley retaining bolt and tighten it to the torque listed in this Chapter's Specifications.

10   The remainder of installation is the reverse of the removal.

12 Crankshaft front oil seal - replacement

▶ **Refer to illustrations 12.2 and 12.4**

1   Remove the crankshaft pulley from the engine (see Section 11).

2   Carefully pry the seal out of the cover with a seal removal tool or a large screwdriver (see illustration).

✳✳ CAUTION:

Be careful not to scratch, gouge or distort the area that the seal fits into or an oil leak will develop.

3   Clean the bore to remove any old seal material and corrosion.

Position the new seal in the bore with the seal lip (usually the side with the spring) facing IN (toward the engine). A small amount of oil applied to the outer edge of the new seal will make installation easier - but don't overdo it!

4   Drive the seal into the bore with a seal driver or a large socket and hammer until it's completely seated (see illustration). Select a socket that's the same outside diameter as the seal and make sure the new seal is pressed into place until it bottoms against the cover flange.

5   Lubricate the seal lips with engine oil and reinstall the crankshaft pulley.

6   The remainder of installation is the reverse of removal. Run the engine and check for oil leaks.

12.2 Pry the seal out very carefully with a seal removal tool or screwdriver, being careful not to nick or gouge the seal bore or the crankshaft

12.4 Use a seal driver or a large socket to drive the new seal into the cover

13 Oil pan - removal and installation

REMOVAL

▶ **Refer to illustrations 13.6 and 13.8**

1   Disconnect the cable from the negative terminal of the battery (see Chapter 5, Section 1). Remove the engine oil dipstick.

2   Apply the parking brake and block the rear wheels. Raise the front of the vehicle and place it securely on jackstands. Remove the engine middle splash shield (see Section 9). Drain the engine oil and remove the oil filter (see Chapter 1).

3   Remove the intermediate shaft coupler at the steering gear (see Chapter 10) and separate the steering gear input shaft from the coupler.

4   Disconnect the power steering pressure switch and remove the power steering gear mounting bolts.

5   Remove the power steering fluid line bracket and position the power steering gear off to the side.

6   Remove the transmission-to-oil pan support brace at the rear of the pan (see illustration).

➡ **Note: The support brace must be moved to the right of the engine block and to the rear to maneuver the support brace from the engine compartment.**

7   Detach any clips securing the transmission oil cooler lines that would interfere with removal of the oil pan (see Chapter 3). Also remove the lower bolt securing the air conditioning compressor to the

13.6 Transmission-to-oil pan support brace

A Vertical bolts *B Horizontal bolts*

13.8 Insert a flathead screwdriver or small prybar on the casting protrusion at the front of the oil pan to break it loose

oil pan and the bolt securing the alternator bracket to the oil pan.

8 Remove the bolts and nuts, then carefully separate the oil pan from the block. Don't pry between the block and the pan or damage to the sealing surfaces could occur and oil leaks may develop. Instead, pry at the casting protrusion at the front of the pan (see illustration).

INSTALLATION

9 Clean the pan with solvent and remove all old sealant and gasket material from the block and pan mating surfaces. Clean the mating surfaces with lacquer thinner or acetone and make sure the bolt holes in the block are clear. Check the oil pan flange for distortion, particularly around the bolt holes.

10 Apply a bead of RTV sealant to the oil pan rail parting lines at the front cover and at the rear main oil seal retainer. Install the gasket on the block.

11 Place the oil pan in position on the block and install the nuts/bolts.

12 After the fasteners are installed, tighten them to the torque listed in this Chapter's Specifications. Starting at the center, follow a criss-cross pattern and work up to the final torque in three steps.

13 Place the transmission-to-oil pan support brace in position and install the support brace-to-oil pan bolts. Torque the bolts to 10 in-lbs. Torque the center bolts first, followed by the outer bolts. Install the support brace-to-transmission bolts. Torque the bolts to 40 ft-lbs, then re-torque the support brace-to-oil pan bolts to 40 ft-lbs (see illustration 13.6). Refer to the Specifications listed in this Chapter.

14 Install the power steering gear (see Chapter 10).

15 The remaining steps are the reverse of the removal procedure.

16 Refill the engine with oil (see Chapter 1), replace the filter, run it until normal operating temperature is reached and check for leaks.

14 Oil pump - removal, inspection and installation

➡**Note: The replacement oil pumps on early models may experience oil pressure problems because of a collapsing oil pressure relief valve and spring. These oil pumps are equipped with an expansion plug instead of the usual threaded plug to seal the oil pressure relief valve and spring inside the oil pump. Consult with a dealer parts department or other qualified automotive repair facility for the correct oil pump.**

REMOVAL

▶ **Refer to illustrations 14.3 and 14.4**

1 Refer to Section 6 and remove the primary timing chain and the crankshaft sprocket.

➡**Note: Before removing the crankshaft sprocket, verify that the crankshaft sprocket marks align with the marks on the oil pump housing and do not rotate the crankshaft from this position at any time during this procedure. This position is approximately 60 degrees after TDC.**

2 Remove the oil pan (see Section 13).

3 Remove the oil pump pick-up tube (see illustration).

14.3 Oil pump pick-up tube mounting bolts

14.4 Oil pump housing retaining bolts

14.6 Remove the screws and lift the cover off

14.9a Place a straightedge across the oil pump cover and check it for warpage with a feeler gauge

14.9b Use a micrometer or dial caliper to check the thickness and the diameter of the outer rotor

14.9c Use a micrometer or dial caliper to check the thickness of the inner rotor

4   Remove the oil pump-to-engine block bolts from the front of the engine (see illustration).

5   Gently pry the oil pump housing outward enough to clear the dowel pins on the engine block and remove it from the engine.

14.9d Check the outer rotor-to-housing clearance

INSPECTION

▶ **Refer to illustrations 14.6, 14.9a 14.9b, 14.9c, 14.9d, 14.9e and 14.9f**

6   Remove the screws holding the front cover on the oil pump housing (see illustration).

7   Clean all components with solvent, then inspect them for wear and damage.

8   Remove the oil pressure regulator cap, washer, spring and valve. Check the oil pressure relief valve sliding surface and valve spring. If either the spring or the valve is damaged, they must be replaced as a set. Small burrs can be removed with 400-grit wet sandpaper and oil.

9   Check the clearance of the following oil pump components with a feeler gauge and a micrometer or dial caliper (see illustrations) and compare the measurements to the clearance listed in this Chapter's Specifications:

a) Cover flatness
b) Outer rotor diameter and thickness
c) Inner rotor thickness
d) Outer rotor-to-body clearance
e) Inner rotor to outer rotor tip clearance

14.9e Check the clearance between the tips of the inner and outer rotors

14.9f Using a straightedge and feeler gauge, check the side clearance between the surface of the oil pump and the inner and outer rotors

f) Cover-to-inner rotor side clearance
g) Cover-to-outer rotor side clearance

If any clearance is excessive, replace the entire oil pump assembly.
10 Pack the pump with petroleum jelly to prime it. Assemble the oil pump and tighten all fasteners to the torque listed in this Chapter's Specifications. Install the oil pressure regulator valve, spring and washer, then tighten the oil pressure regulator valve cap.

INSTALLATION

11 To install the pump, turn the flats in the rotor so they align with the flats on the crankshaft.
12 Install the pump-to-block bolts and tighten them to the torque listed in this Chapter's Specifications.
13 The remainder of installation is the reverse of removal.

15 Driveplate - removal and installation

1 Raise the vehicle and support it securely on jackstands, then refer to Chapter 7 and remove the transmission.

✳✳ WARNING:

The engine must be supported from above with an engine hoist or an engine support fixture before working underneath the vehicle with the transmission removed.

2 Now would be a good time to check and replace the transmission front pump seal.

3 Use paint or a center-punch to make alignment marks on the driveplate and crankshaft to ensure correct alignment during reinstallation.
4 Remove the bolts that secure the driveplate to the crankshaft. If the crankshaft turns, jam a large screwdriver or prybar through the driveplate to keep the crankshaft from turning, then remove the mounting bolts and bolt plate.
5 Pull straight back on the driveplate to detach it from the crankshaft.
6 Installation is the reverse of removal. Be sure to align the matching paint marks. Use thread locking compound on the bolt threads and tighten them to the specified torque in a criss-cross pattern.

16 Rear main oil seal - replacement

1 All models use a one-piece rear main oil seal which is installed in a bolt-on housing. Replacing this seal requires removal of the transmission and driveplate. The rear main seal and housing are serviced as one complete assembly. This procedure will require several special tools.
2 Remove the transmission (see Chapter 7) and the oil pan (see Section 13).
3 Remove the driveplate (see Section 15).
4 Remove the rear main oil seal housing bolts and the housing.
5 Install the new oil seal housing onto the crankshaft using a spe-

cial guide tool.
6 Once the oil seal housing is attached and bolts slightly tight, install special alignment tools onto the oil pan rails.
7 While pressing the oil seal housing evenly, tighten the oil seal housing retainer bolts to the torque listed in this Chapter's Specifications. The housing must be flush with the plane of the oil pan mating surface of the engine to prevent oil leaks.
8 The remainder of installation is the reverse of the removal procedure.

17 Engine mounts - check and replacement

1 There are three powertrain mounts; left and right engine mounts attached to the engine block and to the subframe and a rear mount attached to the transmission and the subframe. Refer to Chapter 7 for check and replacement procedures for the transmission mount.

CHECK

2 During the check, the engine must be raised slightly to remove the weight from the mounts.

3 Raise the vehicle and support it securely on jackstands. Remove the front wheels and tires. Position two jacks, one under the crankshaft pulley and the other under the transmission bellhousing. Place a block of wood between the jack head and the crankshaft pulley or bellhousing, then carefully raise the engine/transmission just enough to take the weight off the mounts.

✳✳ WARNING:

DO NOT place any part of your body under the engine when it's supported only by a jack!

4 Check the mounts to see if the rubber is cracked, hardened or separated from the metal plates. Sometimes the rubber will split right down the center.

5 Check for relative movement between the mount plates and the engine or subframe (use a large screwdriver or prybar to attempt to move the mounts). If movement is noted, lower the engine and tighten the mount fasteners.

6 Rubber preservative should be applied to the mounts to slow deterioration.

REPLACEMENT

7 Disconnect the cable from the negative terminal of the battery (see Chapter 5, Section 1) then raise the vehicle and support it securely on jackstands.

8 Remove the middle engine splash shield (see Section 9).

9 Remove the nuts holding the engine mounts to the subframe.

10 Raise the engine with a jack and block of wood under the oil pan until the engine mount studs clear the engine bracket and the subframe.

11 Remove the engine mount heat shield.

12 Remove the bolts holding the engine mount to the frame.

13 Remove the engine mount and replace it with the new one. Tighten the upper bolts to the torque listed in this Chapter's Specifications.

14 Lower the engine and install the engine mount nuts and torque them to this Specifications listed in this Chapter.

Specifications

General

Firing order	1-2-3-4-5-6
Bore and stroke	3.386 x 3.091 inches
Displacement	167 cubic inches
Cylinder numbers (front to rear)	
Left bank	2-4-6
Right bank	1-3-5
Compression pressure	See Chapter 2D

Front

Cylinder identification

Cylinder head

Warpage limit	0.008 inch

Camshaft

Endplay	0.0051 to 0.0110 inch
Lobe wear limit	
Standard	0.001 inch
Service limit	0.010 inch
Camshaft bearing oil clearance	
Standard	0.0020 to 0.0035 inch
Service limit	0.0040 inch
Camshaft journal diameter	0.9441 to 0.9449 inch
Camshaft bore diameter	0.9469 to 0.9476 inch

Oil pump

Cover warpage limit	0.001 inch
Inner and outer rotor thickness	
2005	0.3731 to 0.3741 inch
2006 and later	0.3919 to 0.3929 inch
Outer rotor diameter (minimum)	3.5109 inches
Outer rotor-to-housing clearance (maximum)	0.015 inch
Inner rotor-to-outer rotor lobe clearance	0.008 inch
Oil pump housing-to-rotor side clearance	0.003 inch

Torque specifications   Ft-lbs (unless otherwise indicated)

➡**Note: One foot-pound (ft-lb) of torque is equivalent to 12 inch-pounds (in-lbs) of torque. Torque values below approximately 15 ft-lbs are expressed in inch-pounds, since most foot-pound torque wrenches are not accurate at these smaller values.**

Camshaft sprocket bolts	21
Camshaft bearing cap bolts (see illustration 7.20)	105 in-lbs
Camshaft timing chain tensioner bolts (secondary)	105 in-lbs
Crankshaft pulley bolt	125
Cylinder head bolts (in sequence - see illustration 10.19)	
Step 1 (tighten bolts 1 through 8)	35
Step 2 (tighten bolts 1 through 8)	55
Step 3 (tighten bolts 1 through 8)	55
Step 4 (tighten bolts 1 through 8)	Tighten an additional 90 degrees
Step 5 (tighten bolts 9 through 11)	21
Drivebelt tensioner	40

➡Note: One foot-pound (ft-lb) of torque is equivalent to 12 inch-pounds (in-lbs) of torque. Torque values below approximately 15 ft-lbs are expressed in inch-pounds, since most foot-pound torque wrenches are not accurate at these smaller values.

Driveplate bolts	70
Exhaust manifold bolts	200 in-lbs
Exhaust manifold heat shield bolts	105 in-lbs
Engine mount heat shield bolts	97 in-lbs
Engine mount to bracket bolts	55
Engine mount retaining nuts	55
Engine rear mount to transmission bolts	35
Idler pulley bolt	21
Intake manifold bolts	
Upper intake manifold bolts	
(see illustration 8.8)	105 in-lbs
Lower intake manifold bolts	
(see illustration 8.16)	105 in-lbs
Oil pan bolts	
6-mm bolts	105 in-lbs
6-mm nuts	105 in-lbs
8-mm bolts	21
Oil pan drain plug	20
Oil pan support brace (see illustration 13.6)	
Step 1	
Support brace-to-oil pan bolts	10 in-lbs
Support brace-to-transmission bolts	40
Step 2	
Support brace-to-oil pan bolts	40
Oil pick-up tube mounting bolts	21
Oil pump mounting bolts	21
Oil pump cover screws	105 in-lbs
Rear main oil seal retainer bolts	105 in-lbs
Timing chain cover bolts	
6 mm	105 in-lbs
10 mm	40
Timing chain guide bolts	21
Timing chain guide access plugs	15
Timing chain tensioner arm pivot bolt	21
Timing chain tensioner (primary)	105 in-lbs
Timing chain tensioner (secondary)	105 in-lbs
Transmission crossmember bolts	50
Valve cover bolts	105 in-lbs
Water outlet housing mounting bolts	105 in-lbs
Water outlet tube-to-housing bolts	30 in-lbs

2B

3.5L V6 ENGINE

Section

Reference to other Chapters

1   General information

This Part of Chapter 2 is devoted to in-vehicle repair procedures for the 3.5L V6 engine. These engines utilize an aluminum block with six cylinders arranged in a "V" shape at a 60-degree angle between the two banks. The overhead camshaft aluminum cylinder heads are equipped with replaceable valve guides and seats. Aluminum roller rockers mounted on two shafts in each cylinder head actuate the valves.

Information concerning engine removal and installation and engine block overhaul can be found in Part D of this Chapter. The following repair procedures are based on the assumption the engine is installed in the vehicle. If the engine has been removed from the vehicle and mounted on a stand, many of the steps outlined in this Part of Chapter 2 will not apply.

2   Repair operations possible with the engine in the vehicle

Many major repair operations can be accomplished without removing the engine from the vehicle.

Clean the engine compartment and the exterior of the engine with some type of degreaser before any work is done. It'll make the job easier and help keep dirt out of the internal areas of the engine.

Depending on the components involved, it may be helpful to remove the hood to improve access to the engine as repairs are performed (see Chapter 11 if necessary). Cover the fenders to prevent damage to the paint. Special pads are available, but an old bedspread or blanket will also work.

If vacuum, exhaust, oil or coolant leaks develop, indicating a need for gasket or seal replacement, the repairs can generally be done with the engine in the vehicle. The intake and exhaust manifold gaskets, timing belt cover gasket, oil pan gasket, crankshaft oil seals and cylinder head gaskets are all accessible with the engine in place.

Exterior engine components, such as the intake and exhaust manifolds, the oil pan, timing belt covers (and the oil pump), the water pump, the starter motor, the alternator and the fuel system components can be removed for repair with the engine in place.

Since the cylinder heads can be removed without pulling the engine, valve component servicing can also be accomplished with the engine in the vehicle. Replacement of the camshafts, timing belt and sprockets is also possible with the engine in the vehicle, although the cylinder head must be removed from the engine to remove the camshafts.

In extreme cases caused by a lack of necessary equipment, repair or replacement of piston rings, pistons, connecting rods and rod bearings is possible with the engine in the vehicle. However, this practice is not recommended because of the cleaning and preparation work that must be done to the components involved.

3   Top Dead Center (TDC) for number one piston - locating

This procedure is essentially the same as for the 2.7L V6 engine. Refer to Part A and follow the procedure outlined there.

4   Valve cover(s) - removal and installation

4.4 **Pull up the wire harness tabs from the valve cover grommets using a panel tool and position the harness off to the side**

REMOVAL

▶ **Refer to illustrations 4.4 and 4.5**

1   Disconnect the cable from the negative terminal of the battery (see Chapter 5, Section 1).

2   Remove the upper intake manifold (see Section 8) and cover the lower intake manifold with rags to keep out dirt.

3   Remove the ignition coils (see Chapter 5).

4   Pull up the wire harness tabs from the valve cover grommets and position the harness off to the side (see illustration).

4.5 Location of the valve cover bolts and studs - left side shown, right side similar

5   Remove the valve cover bolts (see illustration). Note the locations of the stud bolts so they can be reinstalled in their proper locations.
6   Detach the valve cover.

➡**Note: If the cover sticks to the cylinder head, use a block of wood and a hammer to dislodge it. If the cover still won't come loose, pry on it carefully, but don't distort the sealing flange.**

INSTALLATION

▸ **Refer to illustration 4.8**

7   The mating surfaces of each cylinder head and valve cover must

4.8 Install new spark plug tube seals before installing the valve cover

be perfectly clean when the covers are installed. Inspect the rubber gaskets; if they're in good condition and there were no oil leaks, they can be re-used.
8   Inspect the spark plug tube seals. Replace them if they're cracked or flattened, or if the rubber has hardened. Make sure the spark plug tube seals are in position before installing the valve cover (see illustration).
9   Clean the mounting bolt threads with a die if necessary to remove any corrosion and restore damaged threads. Use a tap to clean the threaded holes in the heads.
10 Place the valve cover and new gasket in position, then install the bolts. Tighten the bolts in several steps to the torque listed in this Chapter's Specifications.
11 Complete the installation by reversing the removal procedure. Start the engine and check carefully for oil leaks.

---

5   Rocker arm assembly and hydraulic lash adjusters- removal, inspection and installation

✳✳ CAUTION 1:

To prevent air ingestion into the lash adjusters, do not turn the rocker arm assemblies over. Keep them in an upright position.

5.3 Unscrew the rocker arm shaft bolts and lift the rocker arm assembly from the cylinder head - be sure to loosen them in the reverse order of the tightening sequence

✳✳ CAUTION 2:

When the rocker arm assemblies are placed on the bench, do not allow them to rest on the lash adjusters as the plastic retainers and the lash adjusters may become damaged.

REMOVAL

▸ **Refer to illustration 5.3**

1   Remove the valve cover(s) (see Section 4).
2   Mark the rocker arms and pedestals for identification before removing them. There are four per cylinder, two intake and two exhaust.
3   Loosen each rocker arm shaft bolt a little at a time until they are all loose enough to be removed by hand. Remove the shaft and rockers as an assembly (see illustration).

✳✳ CAUTION:

Never allow the rocker arm assembly to be placed upside down or to rest on the lash adjusters as damage may occur.

5.7 A 4 mm bolt, nut, washer and spacer can be used to extract the dowel pins from the pedestals

5.11 Rocker arm assembly TIGHTENING sequence

INSPECTION

▶ **Refer to illustration 5.7**

4   Inspect each rocker arm for wear, cracks and other damage. This engine uses aluminum rocker arms with steel roller tips and hydraulic lash adjusters. Make sure the rollers turn freely and show no signs of wear, also check the lash adjuster contact surfaces for wear or damage. Make sure the lash adjuster retaining caps hold all of the lash adjusters securely in place on the rocker arms (see illustration).

❋❋ CAUTION:

DO NOT at anytime remove the lash adjuster from the rocker arms or damage to the lash adjuster and the rocker arm will occur.

5   Check each rocker arm pivot area and shaft for wear, cracks and galling. If the rocker arms or shafts are worn or damaged, replace them with new ones.

6   Make sure the axle for the roller tip is not sticking out one side more than the other, and make sure to check for wear, cracks and galling on the hydraulic lash adjuster to valve stem tip contact surface.

7   To remove the rocker arms and pedestals from the shafts for inspection, the dowel pins from each pedestal must be pulled out. Use a 4 mm screw and nut, and a washer and spacer as a puller to extract the dowel pins from each pedestal (see illustration).

➡ **Note: New dowel pins must be installed during installation.**

INSTALLATION

▶ **Refer to illustration 5.11**

8   If the rockers arms or pedestals have been removed from the shafts for inspection, lubricate the shafts and install the rocker arms and pedestals in their marked order. Keep the intake rockers on the intake shaft, and exhaust rockers on the exhaust shaft.

❋❋ CAUTION:

The notches in the rocker arm shafts must face UP when assembled or damage to the rocker arms will occur.

9   Reinstall new dowels pins in each pedestal (they press in until they bottom out in the pedestals).

10   The rocker arm assemblies should be installed, and the bolts tightened, with the valvetrain in a "no load" situation. To accomplish this, the camshafts must be placed in a "neutral" position. Refer to Section 6 and remove the timing belt cover. Rotate the engine until the camshaft sprockets and the crankshaft sprocket are correctly aligned for TDC number 1 (see illustrations 6.7a, 6.7b and 6.7c). Tighten the right side rocker arm assembly bolts in the proper sequence to the torque listed in this Chapter's Specifications.

11   Install the left rocker arm assembly and tighten the bolts in the proper sequence (see illustration) to the torque listed in this Chapter's Specifications.

❋❋ CAUTION:

The notches in the left rocker arm shafts must face UP and towards the front of the engine. The notches in the right rocker arm shafts must face UP and towards the rear of the engine (firewall side). Improper oiling of the rocker arms and shafts will result if this procedure is not followed!

12   The remainder of installation is the reverse of the removal procedures. Start the engine and check for oil leaks.

6   Timing belt - replacement

▶ Refer to illustrations 6.6a, 6.6b, 6.7a, 6.7b, 6.7c, 6.7d, 6.8 and 6.9

❊❊ CAUTION:

Because this is an "interference" engine design, if the timing belt has broken there will be damage to the valves (and possibly the pistons) and will require removal of the cylinder heads.

➡Note: Because of work necessary to get at the timing belt and replace it, and because the water pump is driven by the timing belt, it is recommended that the water pump be replaced at the same time as the belt (see Chapter 3). The factory recommends replacing the timing belt at 100,000 miles.

1   Disconnect the cable from the negative terminal of the battery (see Chapter 5, Section 1).

2   Remove the cooling fan assembly (see Chapter 3) and the accessory drivebelt (see Chapter 1).

3   Remove the valve covers (see Section 4) and loosen the rocker arm shaft bolts (see Section 5).

4   Raise the vehicle and support it securely on jackstands. Remove the crankshaft pulley (see Section 11) and the drivebelt tensioner (see Chapter 1).

5   Remove the power steering pump mounting bolts and position the power steering pump off to the side without disconnecting the power steering system fluid lines (see Chapter 10).

6   Remove the lower timing belt cover and the upper timing belt cover from the cylinder heads (see illustrations). If the same belt is to be reinstalled, mark the direction of rotation on the belt using white paint.

7   Temporarily install the crankshaft pulley bolt and turn the crankshaft with the bolt to align the timing marks on the crankshaft and camshaft sprockets. The crankshaft sprocket arrow should line up with the TDC indicator on the oil pump cover and the camshaft sprocket marks should line up with the marks on the top of the rear covers (see illustrations).

8   Unbolt the timing belt tensioner and remove the belt (see illustration).

6.6a Location of the lower timing belt cover mounting fasteners

6.6b Location of the upper timing belt mounting fasteners

6.7a Rotate the crankshaft until the pointer on the crankshaft sprocket aligns with the TDC mark on the oil pump cover . . .

6.7b . . . the right camshaft sprocket timing mark aligns with the mark on the rear cover . . .

6.7c . . . and the left camshaft sprocket timing mark aligns with the mark on the rear cover

6.7d Overall view of the crankshaft and camshaft sprocket alignment marks on the 3.5L V6 engine

6.8 Remove the timing belt tensioner bolts, then remove the tensioner and the timing belt

9 Slowly compress the timing belt tensioner in a vise until a drill bit or Allen wrench can be inserted through the hole to lock it in (see illustration).

➡**Note: Total bleed down time of the tensioner should take approximately four to five minutes. DO NOT force tensioner to bleed down faster or damage to the tensioner may occur.**

10 Making sure that all timing marks are still aligned, start by installing the new belt at the crankshaft pulley, proceeding counter-clockwise up to the left (driver's side) camshaft sprocket. After the belt is on the left camshaft sprocket, keep tension on the belt as it is fed under the water pump pulley, over the right camshaft sprocket, and past the tensioner. If the old timing belt is being reused, be sure the directional mark made in Step 6 is pointing in the proper direction.

11 Hold the tensioner pulley against the belt and install the tensioner. Tighten the tensioner bolts to the torque listed in this Chapter's Specifications.

12 Remove the Allen key or drill bit from the tensioner, allowing it to tension the pulley on the belt. Tighten the rocker arm shaft bolts, in the proper sequence (see illustration 5.11), to the torque listed in this Chapter's Specifications.

13 Rotate the crankshaft pulley through two complete revolutions to check that the timing marks still remain aligned. If not, repeat the belt installation process.

14 The remainder of installation is the reverse of removal.

15 Start the engine and check for leaks.

6.9 Compress the plunger on the tensioner in a vise until a drill bit or Allen wrench can be inserted through the hole to retain the plunger - orient the pin in a way that won't interfere with installing the tensioner with the pin in place

➡**Note: Noise may be present upon initial start up, due to air entering the timing chain tensioner. If this situation occurs, raise the idle to 1,600 - 2,000 rpm for ten minutes to purge the air from the tensioner. This noise should last no longer than 15 minutes after initial start up.**

7 Camshafts - removal, inspection and installation

REMOVAL

1 The cylinder head(s) must be removed to withdraw the camshafts from the rear of the heads. Refer to Section 10 for cylinder head removal.

2 Remove the camshaft thrust plate and O-ring seal and withdraw the camshaft from the cylinder head, being careful not to nick the cam bearings or journals. Also remove the camshaft oil seal.

INSPECTION

▶ **Refer to illustrations 7.4, 7.5 and 7.6**

3 After the camshaft has been removed from the engine, cleaned with solvent and dried, inspect the bearing journals for uneven wear, pitting and evidence of seizure. If the camshaft journals are damaged, inspect the cylinder head also.

7.4 Check the diameter of each camshaft bearing journal to pinpoint excessive wear and out-of-round conditions

7.5 Measure the camshaft lobe height (greatest dimension) with a micrometer

7.6 Check the cam lobes for pitting, excessive wear and scoring. If scoring is excessive, as shown here, replace the camshaft

4   Measure the bearing journals with a micrometer to determine if they are excessively worn or out-of-round (see illustration). Compare the measurements with the Specifications listed in this Chapter. Use an inside micrometer to measure the journal diameters in the cylinder head. Compare the measurements with the Specifications listed in this Chapter.

5   Measure the lobe height of each cam lobe on the intake camshaft

and record your measurements (see illustration). Compare the measurements for excessive variations. Standard measurements should be 0.001 inch (0.025 mm). If the lobe heights vary more than 0.010 inch (0.254 mm), replace the camshaft. Compare the lobe height measurements on the exhaust camshaft and follow the same procedure. Do not compare intake camshaft lobe heights with exhaust camshaft lobe heights, as they are different. Only compare intake lobes with intake lobes and exhaust lobes with other exhaust lobes.

6   Check the camshaft lobes for heat discoloration, score marks, chipped areas, pitting and uneven wear (see illustration). If the lobes are in good condition and if the lobe lift variation measurements recorded earlier are within the limits, the camshaft can be reused.

INSTALLATION

▶ **Refer to illustration 7.7**

7   Lubricate the camshaft bearing journals and cam lobes with camshaft installation lube (see illustration).

8   Insert the camshaft carefully into the cylinder head, then install a new seal at the front of the head. Using a seal driver or a deep socket with an outside diameter slightly smaller than that of the seal, tap the new seal in.

9   Install the camshaft cover at the back of the head with a new O-ring.

10   The remainder of the installation is the reverse of removal and is covered in Sections 6 and 10.

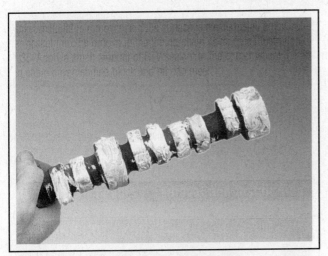

7.7 Coat both the cam lobes and the journals with camshaft installation lube before installing the camshaft

8   Intake manifold - removal and installation

UPPER INTAKE MANIFOLD

▶ **Refer to illustrations 8.6a, 8.6b, 8.7 and 8.9**

1   Relieve the fuel system pressure (see Chapter 4).

2   Disconnect the cable from the negative terminal of the battery (see Chapter 5, Section 1).

3   Remove the air filter housing (see Chapter 4).

4   Label and disconnect the hoses and electrical connectors

attached to the intake manifold and throttle body.

5   Remove the bolts securing the EGR pipe to the upper intake manifold (see Chapter 6).

6   Remove the brackets from the throttle body and the right side of the upper intake manifold (see illustrations).

7   Loosen the upper intake manifold bolts starting with the outer bolts and working to the inside bolts and remove the upper intake manifold (see illustration).

8   Clean the mounting surfaces of the lower intake manifold and the

8.6a Location of the front upper intake manifold mounting bracket mounting studs/bolts

8.6b Location of the rear upper intake manifold mounting bracket mounting studs/bolts

upper manifold. Inspect the rubber O-ring gasket for cracking, hardness or other signs of deterioration. If it's in good condition it can be reused.

9   Install the gasket into the groove in the upper intake manifold (see illustration), then install the upper intake manifold onto the lower intake manifold. Tighten the bolts, starting with the center bolts and working to the outer bolts using a circular pattern, to the torque listed in this Chapter's Specifications. The remainder of the installation is the reverse of removal.

LOWER INTAKE MANIFOLD

▶ Refer to illustrations 8.19 and 8.22

❋❋ WARNING:

Wait until the engine is completely cool before beginning this procedure.

10   Drain the cooling system (see Chapter 1).
11   Remove the upper intake manifold (see Steps 1 through 7).
12   Label and detach any remaining hoses which would interfere with the removal of the lower intake manifold

13   Remove the fuel rail and injectors from the lower intake manifold (see Chapter 4).
14   Remove the heater hoses and coolant hoses (see Chapter 3).
15   Loosen the remaining manifold mounting bolts/nuts in 1/4-turn increments until they can be removed by hand.
16   The manifold will probably be stuck to the cylinder heads and force may be required to break the gasket seal.

❋❋ CAUTION:

Don't pry between the manifold and the heads or damage to the gasket sealing surfaces may occur, leading to vacuum leaks.

17   Turn the manifold over, remove the heater supply tube and replace the O-ring with a new one.
18   Carefully use a scraper to remove all traces of old gasket material and sealant from the manifold and cylinder heads, then clean the mating surfaces with lacquer thinner or acetone.
19   Apply a bead of RTV sealant or equivalent around the front and rear cylinder head water passages before laying the new gaskets in

8.7 Lift the upper intake manifold from the engine

8.9 Install the upper intake manifold gasket, making sure it seats in the groove

8.19 Apply a bead of RTV sealant around the water passages at the ends of the heads

8.22 Lower intake manifold TIGHTENING sequence

place (see illustration).

20 Install the intake manifold gaskets on the cylinder heads and apply RTV sealant to the manifold side of the gaskets, around the water passages.

21 Position the manifold on the engine, making sure the gaskets and manifold are aligned over the ports in the cylinder heads. Install the fuel rail and injectors onto the lower manifold, then install the manifold

mounting bolts.

22 Following the recommended tightening sequence, tighten the nuts/bolts, in several steps, to the torque listed in this Chapter's Specifications (see illustration).

23 The remainder of the installation is the reverse of the removal procedure. Refill the cooling system (see Chapter 1), then run the engine and check for fuel, vacuum and coolant leaks.

9   Exhaust manifold(s) - removal and installation

✳✳ WARNING:

The engine must be completely cool before beginning this procedure.

REMOVAL

▶ **Refer to illustrations 9.2, 9.6 and 9.7**

1   Disconnect the cable from the negative terminal of the battery (see Chapter 5, Section 1).

2   Raise the front of the vehicle and support it securely on jackstands. Remove the engine splash shield (see illustration).

3   Disconnect the oxygen sensors' electrical connectors and remove the sensors (see Chapter 6).

4   Detach the exhaust pipes from the exhaust manifolds (see Chapter 4, illustration 14.4a).

5   Lower the vehicle.

9.2 Front engine splash shield (1) and middle engine splash shield (2) fasteners

9.6 Location of the upper heat shield mounting bolts/nuts

9.7 Location of the exhaust manifold mounting bolts/studs

6   Remove the exhaust manifold heat shield mounting bolts/nuts (see illustration) and remove the heat shields.

7   Remove the mounting bolts and detach the manifold from the cylinder head (see illustration).

➡**Note: Be sure to spray penetrating oil on the bolts before attempting to remove them.**

INSTALLATION

8   Clean the mating surfaces to remove all traces of old gasket material, then inspect the manifold for distortion and cracks. Warpage can be checked with a precision straightedge held against the mating flange. If a feeler gauge thicker than 0.030-inch can be inserted between the straightedge and flange surface, take the manifold to an automotive machine shop for resurfacing.

9   Place the exhaust manifold in position with a new gasket and install the mounting bolts finger tight.

➡**Note: Be sure to identify the exhaust manifold gaskets by the correct cylinder designation and the position of the exhaust ports on the gasket.**

10 Starting in the middle and working out toward the ends, tighten the mounting bolts in several increments, to the torque listed in this Chapter's Specifications.

11 Install the remaining components in the reverse order of removal.

12 Start the engine and check for exhaust leaks between the manifold and cylinder head and between the manifold and exhaust pipe.

10 Cylinder heads - removal and installation

❋❋ **WARNING:**

The engine must be completely cool before beginning this procedure.

➡**Note: Special tools are necessary to complete this procedure. Read through the entire procedure and obtain the special tools before beginning work.**

REMOVAL

▶ **Refer to illustrations 10.9a, 10.9b and 10.15**

1   Relieve the fuel system pressure (see Chapter 4). Disconnect the cable from the negative terminal of the battery (see Chapter 5, Section 1).

2   Drain the cooling system (see Chapter 1).

3   Remove the upper and lower intake manifolds (see Section 8).

4   Remove the ignition coils and the spark plugs (see Chapters 1 and 5, if necessary).

5   Detach the exhaust manifold from the cylinder head being removed (see Section 9).

6   Remove the valve cover(s) (see Section 4).

10.9a With the engine raised (or the cooling fan assembly removed), hold the camshaft sprocket with a wrench while loosening the bolt with a socket and breaker bar - these bolts are very tight

7   Remove the rocker arms and shafts (see Section 5).

8   Remove the timing belt covers, align the TDC marks and remove the timing belt (see Section 6).

10.9b The camshaft sprocket bolts are not interchangeable - the left sprocket bolt is 10 inches while the right sprocket bolt is 8-3/8 inches

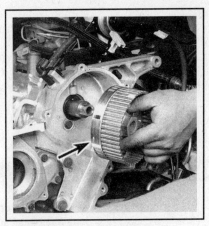

10.9c The camshaft sprockets are also not interchangeable

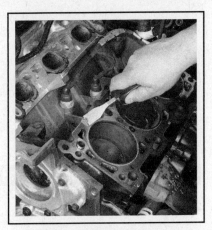

10.16 Use a putty knife or gasket scraper to remove gasket material from the cylinder head and block

25027-2B-10.23HAYNES

10.21 Cylinder head bolt tightening sequence

→Note: If the belt is to be reused, mark it's direction of rotation before removing it.

9 Hold the camshaft sprocket hex with a wrench while using a socket and breaker bar to loosen the camshaft bolt, which is under considerable torque (see illustration).

✳✳ CAUTION:

The two camshaft sprockets are not interchangeable, nor are the camshaft sprocket bolts. The left sprocket bolt is 10 inches while the right sprocket bolt is 8-3/8 inches. Always use NEW camshaft sprocket bolts.

10 Remove the camshaft thrust plate from the rear of the head and slide the camshaft back approximately 3-1/2 inches. This will allow removal of the sprocket and bolt.

11 Remove the bolts securing the rear timing belt cover to the cylinder head. Don't disturb any of the other timing belt cover bolts.

12 Using the new head gasket, outline the cylinders and bolt pattern on a piece of cardboard. Be sure to indicate the front of the engine for reference. Punch holes at the bolt locations. This cardboard holder will be used to accurately store each cylinder head bolt after they are removed from the cylinder head.

13 Loosen each of the cylinder head mounting bolts 1/4-turn at a

time until they can be removed by hand - work from bolt-to-bolt in a pattern that's the reverse of the tightening sequence (see illustration 10.21). Store the bolts in the cardboard holder as they're removed.

14 Lift the head(s) off the engine. If resistance is felt, don't pry between the head and block as damage to the mating surfaces will result. Recheck for head bolts that may have been overlooked, then use a hammer and block of wood to tap up on the head to break the gasket seal. Be careful because there are locating dowels in the block which position each head. As a last resort, pry each head up at the rear corner only and be careful not to damage anything. After removal, place the head on blocks of wood to prevent damage to the gasket surfaces.

15 If the camshaft is to be removed for examination or replacement, it must be done with the cylinder head off the engine, as it comes out the back of the cylinder head (see Section 7).

INSTALLATION

▶ Refer to illustrations 10.16 and 10.21

16 The mating surfaces of each cylinder head and block must be perfectly clean when the head is installed. Use a gasket scraper to remove all traces of carbon and old gasket material (see illustration), then clean the mating surfaces with lacquer thinner or acetone. If there's oil on the mating surfaces when the head is installed, the gasket may not seal correctly and leaks may develop. When working on the block, it's a good idea to cover the valley with shop rags to keep debris out of the engine. Use a shop rag or vacuum cleaner to remove any debris that falls into the cylinders.

17 Check the block and head mating surfaces for nicks, deep scratches and other damage. If damage is slight, it can be removed with a file; if it's excessive, machining may be the only alternative.

18 Use a tap of the correct size to chase the threads in the head bolt holes. Dirt, corrosion, sealant and damaged threads will affect torque readings. Check the cleaned head bolts for stretch by holding them next to a steel ruler. If all the threads don't touch the ruler, the bolt should be replaced.

19 Position the new gasket over the dowel pins in the block. Some gaskets are marked TOP or FRONT to ensure correct installation.

20 Make sure the camshaft is installed in the cylinder head, then carefully position the head on the block without disturbing the gasket.

21 Tighten the bolts in the recommended sequence (see illustration) to the torque listed in this Chapter's Specifications.

22 Install the rear timing belt cover-to-cylinder head bolts. Tighten the bolts to the torque listed in this Chapter's Specifications.

23 Slide the camshaft back into the cylinder head and install the camshaft sprocket and new bolt, then move the camshaft back into place. Hold the hex on the camshaft sprocket with a wrench and tighten the camshaft bolt to the torque listed in this Chapter's Specifications (see illustration 10.9a).

24 Install the camshaft thrust plate at the back of the head, using a new O-ring. Tighten the bolts to the torque listed in this Chapter's Specifications.

25 The remaining installation steps are the reverse of removal.

26 Change the oil and filter, refill the cooling system (see Chapter 1), run the engine and check for leaks.

11 Crankshaft pulley - removal and installation

▶ Refer to illustrations 11.3 and 11.4

1 Disconnect the cable from the negative terminal of the battery (see Chapter 5, Section 1). Remove the accessory drivebelts (see Chapter 1).

2 Remove the cooling fan assembly (see Chapter 3).

3 Position a large screwdriver through the crankshaft pulley to keep the crankshaft from turning and remove the pulley-to-crankshaft bolt (see illustration).

4 Pull the crankshaft pulley off the crankshaft with a puller (see illustration).

✳✳ CAUTION:

The jaws of the puller must only contact the hub of the pulley - not the outer ring.

➡**Note: A spacer that bears on the nose of the crankshaft or a long Allen-head bolt must be inserted into the crankshaft nose for the puller's tapered tip to push against. Don't allow the puller screw to bear against the crankshaft itself.**

5 To install the crankshaft pulley, slide the pulley onto the crankshaft as far as it will slide on, then use a vibration damper installation tool to press the pulley onto the crankshaft.

6 Install the crankshaft pulley retaining bolt and tighten it to the torque listed in this Chapter's Specifications.

7 The remainder of installation is the reverse of the removal.

11.3 Insert a prybar or large screwdriver through the pulley to hold it while you loosen the crankshaft pulley bolt

11.4 Use a three jaw puller to remove the crankshaft pulley. A long Allen bolt must be inserted into the crankshaft for the tool to push against

12 Crankshaft front oil seal - replacement

▶ Refer to illustrations 12.5 and 12.6

1 Remove the crankshaft pulley (see Section 11).

2 Remove the timing belt (see Section 6).

3 Use a two-bolt puller to remove the crankshaft sprocket, with the bolts threaded into the holes in the sprocket.

4 With a hammer and punch, tap the dowel pin out of the crank-

shaft. Drive the pin into the hollow, threaded area of the crankshaft snout, where it can be extracted with a small magnet.

5 Pry the old seal out with a hook-type seal tool, being very careful not to scratch the seal surface of the crankshaft (see illustration). Note how the seal is installed - the new one must be installed to the same depth and facing the same way.

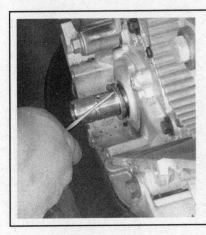

12.5 Using a hook-type seal remover, pry out the old seal

6   Lubricate the inner lip of the new seal with engine oil and drive it in with a seal driver or large deep socket and a hammer (see illustration).

7   Installation is the reverse of removal. Tap the dowel pin back into the crankshaft, with 3/64-inch extending out.

12.6 Drive the new seal in to the same depth as the old one, using a seal driver or a socket with an outside diameter the same as that of the seal

13   Oil pan - removal and installation

REMOVAL

▶ **Refer to illustrations 13.10a, 13.10b and 13.11**

1   Disconnect the cable from the negative terminal of the battery (see Chapter 5, Section 1).

2   Remove the engine oil dipstick.

3   Raise the front of the vehicle and support it securely on jackstands. Apply the parking brake and block the rear wheels to keep the vehicle from rolling off the stands.

4   Connect an engine hoist to the engine (see Chapter 2C).

5   Remove the engine splash shield (see Section 9).

6   Drain the engine oil and remove the oil filter (see Chapter 1).

7   Unbolt the engine oil cooler and set it aside (see Chapter 3).

8   Disconnect the steering intermediate shaft coupler at the steering gear (see Chapter 10).

9   Remove the steering gear mounting bolts at the subframe (see Chapter 10). Using rope or mechanics wire, tie the assembly off to the side without disconnecting the power steering fluid lines.

10   Remove the torque converter access cover, then remove the two Allen-head bolts securing the rear of the oil pan to the engine block (see illustrations).

13.10a Remove this bolt and detach the torque converter access cover . . .

13.10b . . . then remove these two oil pan bolts

11 Remove the oil pan-to-transmission bolts (see illustration).

12 Remove the engine mount nuts at the subframe (see Section 17).

13 Remove the oil pan bolts, then carefully separate the oil pan from the block. Don't pry between the block and the pan or damage to the sealing surfaces could occur and oil leaks may develop. Instead, tap the pan with a soft-face hammer to break the gasket seal.

14 Raise the engine with the hoist just enough to allow oil pan removal, then guide the pan out between the engine and the subframe.

INSTALLATION

15 Clean the pan with solvent and remove all old sealant and gasket material from the block and pan mating surfaces. Clean the mating surfaces with lacquer thinner or acetone and make sure the bolt holes in the block are clear. Check the oil pan flange for distortion, particularly around the bolt holes.

16 Apply a bead of RTV sealant to the parting lines between the engine block and the oil pump housing and then to the engine block and rear main oil seal retainer. Install the gasket on the block.

17 Place the oil pan in position on the block and install the bolts, tightening them finger-tight.

18 Lower the engine and install the engine mount nuts, tightening them to the torque listed in this Chapter's Specifications.

19 Install the oil pan-to-transmission bolts and tighten them to approximately 12 in-lbs.

20 Tighten the oil pan fasteners to the torque listed in this Chapter's Specifications. Starting at the center, follow a criss-cross pattern and

13.11 Location of the oil pan-to-transmission bolts

work up to the final torque in three steps. Don't forget the two small Allen bolts at the rear, accessible through the torque converter access opening.

21 Tighten the oil-pan-to-transmission bolts to the torque listed in this Chapter's Specifications.

22 Install the torque converter access cover.

23 The remaining steps are the reverse of the removal procedure.

24 Refill the engine with oil (see Chapter 1), replace the filter, run it until normal operating temperature is reached and check for leaks.

14 Oil pump - removal, inspection and installation

✳✳ CAUTION:

Do not remove the oil pressure relief valve, spring and plunger from the oil pump. Replace the oil pump as one complete assembly if the oil pressure relief valve is damaged.

REMOVAL

1 Remove the timing belt and crankshaft sprocket (see Sections 6 and 12).

2 Remove the oil pan (see Section 13).

3 Remove oil pump pick-up tube.

4 Remove the oil-pump-to-block bolts and pull the oil pump from the block.

INSPECTION

▶ **Refer to illustrations 14.9, 14.11, 14.12 and 14.13**

5 Unbolt the cover from the back of the oil pump housing.

6 Remove the inner and outer rotors from the oil pump body, noting their installed direction for reassembly.

14.9 Use a micrometer to check the thickness of the outer rotor

14.11 Check the outer rotor-to-housing clearance

14.12 Check the clearance between the lobes of the inner and outer rotors

14.13 Using a straightedge and feeler gauge, check the side clearance between the surface of the oil pump housing and the rotors

7   Clean all parts thoroughly in solvent and carefully inspect the rotors, pump cover and oil pump housing for nicks, scratches or burrs. Replace the assembly if it is damaged.

8   Use a straightedge and measure the oil pump cover for warpage with a feeler gauge. If it's warped more than the limit listed in this Chapter's Specifications, the pump should be replaced.

9   Measure the thickness and the diameter of the outer rotor. If either measurement is less than the value listed in this Chapter's Specifications, the pump should be replaced (see illustration).

10 Measure the thickness of the inner rotor. If the measurement is less than the value listed in this Chapter's Specifications, the pump should be replaced.

11 Insert the outer rotor into the oil pump housing and, while holding the rotor against one side of the housing with your finger, measure the clearance at the opposite side between the rotor and housing (see illustration). If the measurement is more than the maximum allowable clearance listed in this Chapter's Specifications, the pump should be replaced.

12 Install the inner rotor in the oil pump assembly and measure the clearance between the lobes on the inner and outer rotors (see illustration). If the clearance is more than the value listed in this Chapter's Specifications, the pump should be replaced.

➡**Note: Install the inner rotor with the mark facing up.**

13 Position a straightedge across the face of the oil pump assembly (see illustration). If the clearance between the pump surface and the rotors is greater than the limit listed in this Chapter's Specifications, the pump should be replaced.

INSTALLATION

14 Prime the oil pump by filling the housing with engine oil. Install the pump cover and tighten the bolts to the torque listed in this Chapter's Specifications.

15 To install the pump, place the gasket on the engine block mating surface, then turn the flats in the rotor so they align with the flats on the crankshaft and install the oil pump housing on to the engine block.

16 Install the pump-to-block bolts and tighten them to the torque listed in this Chapter's Specifications.

17 The remainder of installation is the reverse of removal.

15 Driveplate - removal and installation

This procedure is essentially the same as for the 2.7L V6 engine. Refer to Part A and follow the procedure outlined there, but use the bolt torque listed in this Chapter's Specifications.

16 Rear main oil seal - replacement

➡**Note: The rear main seal and housing are serviced as one complete assembly. This procedure will require several special tools. Read the procedure carefully before starting.**

This procedure is essentially the same as for the 2.7L V6 engine. Refer to Part A and follow the procedure outlined there, but use the bolt torque value listed in this Chapter's Specifications.

17 Engine mounts - check and replacement

▶ **Refer to illustrations 17.1a and 17.1b**

This procedure is essentially the same as for the 2.7L V6 engine.

Refer to Part A and follow the procedure and illustrations outlined there, but refer to the illustrations and use the torque values listed in this Chapter's Specifications.

17.1a Location of the left engine mount-to-subframe mounting nuts

17.1b Location of the right engine mount-to-subframe mounting nuts

Specifications

General

Firing order	1-2-3-4-5-6
Bore and stroke	3.780 x 3.189 inches
Displacement	214 cubic inches
Cylinder numbers (front to rear)	
Left bank	2-4-6
Right bank	1-3-5
Compression pressure	See Chapter 2D

Front

Cylinder identification diagram

Camshaft

Endplay	0.001 to 0.014 inch
Lobe wear limit	
Standard	0.001 inch
Service limit	0.010 inch
Camshaft journal diameter	1.6905 to 1.6913 inches
Camshaft bore diameter (inside)	1.6944 to 1.6952 inches
Camshaft bearing oil clearance	
Standard	0.003 to 0.0047 inch
Service limit	0.0059 inch

Oil pump

Cover warpage limit	0.001 inch
Inner and outer rotor thickness (minimum)	0.563 inch
Outer rotor diameter (minimum)	3.149 inch
Outer rotor-to-housing clearance (maximum)	0.015 inch
Inner rotor-to-outer rotor lobe clearance	0.008 inch
Oil pump housing-to-rotor side clearance	0.003 inch

Torque specifications   Ft-lbs (unless otherwise indicated)

➡**Note: One foot-pound (ft-lb) of torque is equivalent to 12 inch-pounds (in-lbs) of torque. Torque values below approximately 15 ft-lbs are expressed in inch-pounds, since most foot-pound torque wrenches are not accurate at these smaller values.**

Camshaft sprocket bolts*	
Step 1	75
Step 2	Tighten an additional 90-degrees
Camshaft thrust plate bolts	21
Crankshaft pulley bolt	70
Cylinder head bolts (in sequence - see illustration 10.21)	
First step	45
Second step	65
Third step	65
Fourth step	Tighten an additional 90-degrees
Drivebelt tensioner bolt	40
Driveplate-to-crankshaft bolts	70
Engine mount bracket-to-block bolts	55
Engine mount nuts	55
Exhaust manifold-to-cylinder head bolts	16.5

Torque specifications (continued) Ft-lbs (unless otherwise indicated)

➡Note: One foot-pound (ft-lb) of torque is equivalent to 12 inch-pounds (in-lbs) of torque. Torque values below approximately 15 ft-lbs are expressed in inch-pounds, since most foot-pound torque wrenches are not accurate at these smaller values.

Exhaust heat shield bolts	105 in-lbs
Exhaust pipe bolts	25
Heater supply tube mounting bolts	105 in-lbs
Intake manifold bolts	
Upper intake manifold bolts	105 in-lbs
Lower intake manifold bolts	21
Oil pan drain plug	20
Oil pan bolts	
Oil pan-to-engine block bolts	
M6 bolts	105 in-lbs
M8 bolts	21
Oil pan-to-transaxle bolts	40
Oil pump pick-up tube mounting bolt	21
Oil pump cover (plate) bolts (Torx no. 30)	105 in-lbs
Rocker arm shaft bolts	23
Timing belt cover (front and rear) bolts	
M6	105 in-lbs
M8	21
M10	40
Timing belt tensioner	21
Timing belt tensioner pulley bolt	45
Throttle body bracket-to-throttle body	105 in-lbs
Throttle body bracket-to-cylinder head	21
Rear main oil seal retainer bolts	105 in-lbs
Valve cover-to-cylinder head bolts	105 in-lbs

*Replace with new bolts

Section

Reference to other Chapters

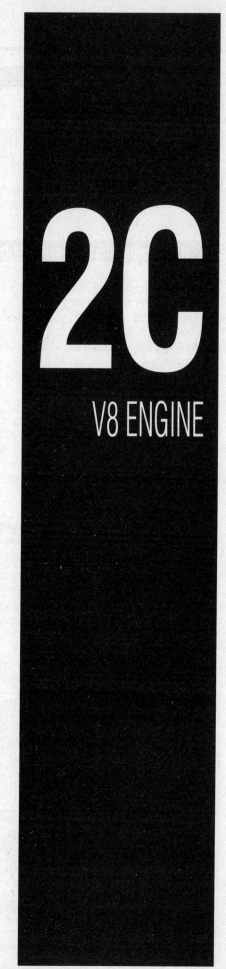

2C

V8 ENGINE

1 General information

This part of Chapter 2 is devoted to in-vehicle repair procedures for the 5.7L V8 (Hemi) engine. Information concerning engine removal and installation and engine overhaul can be found in Part D of this Chapter.

Since the repair procedures included in this Part are based on the assumption that the engine is still installed in the vehicle, if they are being used during a complete engine overhaul (with the engine already out of the vehicle and on a stand) many of the steps included here will not apply.

These V8 engines use a cast iron engine block with aluminum cylinder heads and intake manifold. The cylinder banks are positioned at a 90-degree angle with the camshaft mounted high in the engine block. The valvetrain includes roller lifters, with pushrods positioned between the camshaft and rocker arms in a nearly horizontal plane.

2 Repair operations possible with the engine in the vehicle

Many major repair operations can be accomplished without removing the engine from the vehicle.

Clean the engine compartment and the exterior of the engine with some type of pressure washer before any work is done. A clean engine will make the job easier and will help keep dirt out of the internal areas of the engine.

Depending on the components involved, it may be a good idea to remove the hood to improve access to the engine as repairs are performed (refer to Chapter 11 if necessary).

If oil or coolant leaks develop, indicating a need for gasket or seal replacement, the repairs can generally be made with the engine in the vehicle. The oil pan gasket, the cylinder head gaskets, intake and exhaust manifold gaskets, timing chain cover gaskets and the crankshaft front oil seal are all accessible with the engine in place.

Exterior engine components, such as the water pump, the starter motor, the alternator and the fuel injection components, as well as the intake and exhaust manifolds, can be removed for repair with the engine in place.

Since the cylinder heads can be removed without removing the engine, valve component servicing can also be accomplished with the engine in the vehicle.

Replacement of, repairs to or inspection of the timing chain and sprockets and the oil pump are all possible with the engine in place.

In extreme cases caused by a lack of necessary equipment, repair or replacement of piston rings, pistons, connecting rods and rod bearings is possible with the engine in the vehicle. However, this practice is not recommended because of the cleaning and preparation work that must be done to the components involved.

3 Top Dead Center (TDC) for number one piston - locating

▶ **Refer to illustrations 3.4a and 3.4b**

1 Top Dead Center (TDC) is the highest point in the cylinder that each piston reaches as it travels up-and-down when the crankshaft turns. Each piston reaches TDC on the compression stroke and again on the exhaust stroke, but TDC generally refers to piston position on the compression stroke.

2 In order to bring any piston to TDC, the crankshaft must be turned using a breaker bar and socket on the vibration damper bolt.

When looking at the front of the engine, normal crankshaft rotation is clockwise.

3 Disconnect the cable from the negative terminal of the battery (see Chapter 5, Section 1).

4 Remove one of the spark plugs from cylinder number 1, preferably the closest to the front of the engine, then thread a compression gauge into the spark plug hole (see illustration). Turn the crankshaft with a socket and breaker bar attached to the large bolt that is threaded into the vibration damper (see illustration). When compression regis-

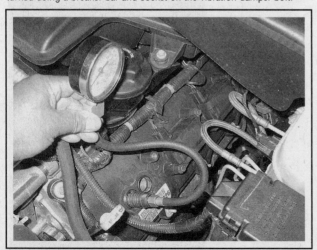

3.4a Install a compression gauge into one of the number one spark plug holes

3.4b Use a breaker bar and socket to rotate the crankshaft

ters on the gauge, the number one piston is beginning its compression stroke. Stop turning the crankshaft and remove the gauge.

5   Insert a long dowel into the number one spark plug hole until it rests on top of the piston crown. Continue rotating the crankshaft slowly until the dowel levels off (piston reaches top of travel). This will be approximate TDC for number 1 piston.

6   These engines are not equipped with components (vibration damper, flywheel, timing hole, etc.) that are marked to identify the position of number 1 TDC. Therefore the only method to pinpoint the exact position of TDC number 1 is to remove the timing chain cover to access timing chain sprockets (see Section 9), or with the use of a degree wheel on the crankshaft vibration damper and a positive stop threaded into the spark plug hole, as you would use in the process of degreeing a camshaft.

---

4   Valve covers - removal and installation

REMOVAL

▶ **Refer to illustrations 4.2, 4.4a, 4.4b, 4.6, 4.7a and 4.7b**

1   Disconnect the cable from the negative terminal of the battery (see Chapter 5, Section 1).
2   Remove the engine cover (see illustration).

3   If you're removing the left side valve cover, it may be helpful to remove the air filter housing for better access (see Chapter 4). However, it isn't mandatory.
4   Remove the harness clips from the valve cover studs (see illustrations).
5   Remove the ignition coils and, on 2005 models, the spark plug wires (see Chapter 5).
6   Remove the ground straps from the valve cover (see illustration). Be sure to mark the location of each of the ground terminals for correct installation.

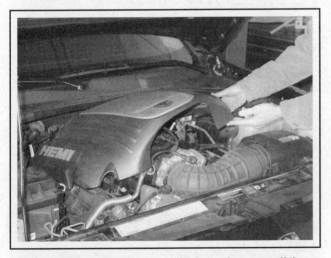

4.2 First remove the oil cap and lift the engine cover off the four support grommets

4.4b Location of the harness clips on the left side valve cover

4.4a Location of the harness clips on the right side valve cover

4.6 Remove the ground straps from the valve cover studs

4.7a Location of the valve cover mounting bolts on the right-side valve cover

7   Remove the valve cover mounting bolts (see illustrations).
8   Remove the valve cover.

➡**Note: If the cover is stuck to the head, bump the cover with a block of wood and a hammer to release it. If it still will not come loose, try to slip a flexible putty knife between the head and cover to break the seal. Don't pry at the cover-to-head joint, as damage to the sealing surface and cover flange will result and oil leaks will develop.**

4.10 If they're damaged or hardened, replace the rubber gasket and spark plug tube seals with new ones (if they're OK, they can be re-used)

4.7b Location of the valve cover mounting bolts on the left-side valve cover (two bolts hidden from view)

INSTALLATION

▶ **Refer to illustration 4.10**

9   Clean the mating surfaces of the valve cover and cylinder head. Don't use harsh chemicals or solvent on the plastic valve covers, as they could become damaged.
10 If the valve cover gasket isn't damaged or hardened, it can be re-used. If it is in need of replacement, install a new one into the valve cover perimeter and new rubber seals into the grooves in the valve cover that seal the spark plug tubes (see illustration).
11 Carefully position the cover on the head and install the bolts, making sure the bolts with the studs are in the proper locations.
12 Tighten the bolts a little at a time to the torque listed in this Chapter's Specifications. Start with the middle bolts and move to the outer bolts using a criss-cross pattern.

❋❋ **CAUTION:**

DON'T over-tighten the valve cover bolts.

13 The remaining installation steps are the reverse of removal.
14 Start the engine and check carefully for oil leaks as the engine warms up.

5   Rocker arms and pushrods - removal, inspection and installation

REMOVAL

▶ **Refer to illustrations 5.2 and 5.3**

1   Remove the valve covers from the cylinder heads (see Section 4).
2   Loosen the rocker arm shaft bolts, starting with the center bolts and working toward the outer bolts. When the bolts have been completely loosened, lift the rocker shaft assembly off the cylinder head

(see illustration).
3   Keep track of the rocker arm positions, since they must be returned to the same locations. Store each set of rocker components in such a way as to ensure that they're reinstalled in their original locations. Remove the pushrods and store them in order as well, to make sure they don't get mixed up during installation (see illustration).

➡**Note: The exhaust pushrods are slightly longer than the intake pushrods - they aren't interchangeable.**

5.2 Remove the rocker arm shaft bolts - mark each rocker arm assembly and note that the upper rocker arms are the intake and the lower rocker arms are the exhaust

INSPECTION

▸ **Refer to illustration 5.4**

✳✳ CAUTION:

If the cylinder heads have been removed and the surface milled for flatness, be sure to install correct length pushrods to compensate for the reduced distances of the rocker arms-to-camshaft dimensions. Consult with the machine shop for the correct length pushrods.

4   Check each rocker arm for wear, cracks and other damage (see illustration), especially where the pushrods and valve stems contact the rocker arm.

5   Check the rocker arm shafts and bores of the rocker arms for wear. Look for galling, stress cracks and unusual wear patterns. If the rocker arms are worn or damaged, replace them with new ones and install new shafts as well.

➥**Note: Keep in mind that there is no valve adjustment on these engines, so excessive wear or damage in the valve train can easily result in excessive valve clearance, which in turn will cause valve noise when the engine is running.**

6   Make sure the hole at the pushrod end of each rocker arm is open.

7   Inspect the pushrods for cracks and excessive wear at the ends. Roll each pushrod across a piece of plate glass to see if it's bent (if it wobbles, it's bent).

INSTALLATION

8   Lubricate the lower end of each pushrod with clean engine oil or engine assembly lube and install them in their original locations. Make sure each pushrod seats completely in the lifter socket.

9   Apply engine assembly lube to the ends of the valve stems and the upper ends of the pushrods to prevent damage to the mating surfaces on initial start-up.

10   Lubricate the rocker shafts with clean engine oil or engine assembly lube, then assemble the rocker shafts, with all of the components in their original positions. Install the rocker shafts onto the

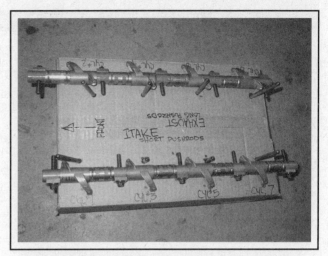

5.3 A perforated cardboard box top can be used to store the rocker arms and pushrods to ensure that they're reinstalled in their original locations - note the arrow indicating the front of the engine

cylinder heads.

11   The rocker arm shafts must be tightened starting with the center bolt, then the center right bolt, the center left bolt, the outer right bolt and finally the outer left bolt. Follow this sequence in several steps until the torque listed in this Chapter's Specifications is reached. As the bolts are tightened, make sure the pushrods seat properly in the rocker arms.

✳✳ CAUTION:

Do not continue tightening the rocker arms if the rocker arm bolts become tight before the shaft is seated or the pushrods are binding. Remove the rocker arm shafts and inspect all the components carefully before proceeding.

12   Refer to Section 4 and install the valve covers. Start the engine, listen for unusual valve train noises and check for oil leaks at the valve cover gaskets.

5.4 Rocker arm component details

A Rocker arm shaft	C Retainer
B Rocker arm	D Rocker shaft bolt

6 Intake manifold - removal and installation

REMOVAL

1 Remove the engine cover (see illustration 4.2).

2 Relieve the fuel system pressure (see Chapter 4). Disconnect the cable from the negative terminal of the battery (see Chapter 5, Section 1).

3 Remove the air filter housing and the intake air duct (see Chapter 4).

4 Remove the ignition coils and, on 2005 models, the spark plug wires (see Chapter 5).

5 Disconnect the brake booster vacuum hose, canister purge hose and the PCV hose.

6 Remove the fuel rails and injectors (see Chapter 4).

7 Remove the EGR pipe from the intake manifold (see Chapter 6).

8 Disconnect the electrical connectors from the MAP sensor (see Chapter 6) and the throttle body.

9 Starting with the outer bolts and working to the inner bolts, loosen the intake manifold bolts in 1/4-turn increments until they can be removed by hand. Follow the reverse of the tightening sequence (see illustration 6.13).

10 Remove the intake manifold. As the manifold is lifted from the engine, be sure to check for and disconnect anything still attached to the manifold.

INSTALLATION

▶ Refer to illustrations 6.11 and 6.13

✳✳ CAUTION:

The mating surfaces of the cylinder heads and intake manifold must be perfectly clean when the manifold is installed, but don't use harsh chemicals or solvent on the plastic manifold, as it could become damaged.

11 Check the O-rings on the intake manifold for damage or hardening. If they're OK, they can be re-used. If necessary, install new O-rings (see illustration).

12 Carefully set the manifold in place.

✳✳ CAUTION:

Do not disturb the rubber seals and DO NOT move the manifold fore-and-aft after it contacts the cylinder heads or the seals could be pushed out of place and the engine may develop vacuum and/or oil leaks.

6.11 Replace the intake manifold O-rings with new ones. Make sure they seat properly in their grooves

6.13 Tightening sequence for the intake manifold bolts

13 Install the intake manifold bolts and tighten them following the recommended sequence (see illustration) to the torque listed in this Chapter's Specifications.

14 The remaining installation steps are the reverse of removal. Start the engine and check carefully for vacuum leaks at the intake manifold joints.

7 Exhaust manifold(s) - removal and installation

REMOVAL

♦ Refer to illustrations 7.2, 7.6, 7.7a, and 7.7b

※ WARNING:

Allow the engine to cool completely before performing this procedure.

1   Disconnect the cable from the negative terminal of the battery (see Chapter 5, Section 1).

2   Raise the front of the vehicle and support it securely on jackstands. Remove the engine splash shield (see illustration).

3   Detach the exhaust pipes from the exhaust manifolds (see Chapter 4).

4   Connect an engine hoist to the engine (see Chapter 2D) and remove the engine mount-to-subframe fasteners (see Section 16).

5   Working from the engine compartment, disconnect the oxygen sensors electrical connectors and remove the sensors (see Chapter 6).

6   Remove the exhaust manifold heat shield mounting bolts/nuts (see illustration) and remove the heat shield.

7   Remove the bolts retaining the exhaust manifold to the cylinder head (see illustrations).

8   Raise the engine up enough to allow the exhaust manifold to be removed.

INSTALLATION

9   Clean the manifold and head gasket surfaces and check for cracks and flatness. Replace the exhaust manifold gaskets.

10 Install the exhaust manifold(s) and fasteners. Tighten the bolts/nuts to the torque listed in this Chapter's Specifications. Work from the center to the ends and approach the final torque in three steps. Install the heat shields.

11 Apply anti-seize compound to the exhaust pipe-to-exhaust manifold bolts and tighten them securely.

12 Installation is otherwise the reverse of the removal procedure.

7.2 Front engine splash shield (1) and middle engine splash shield (2) fasteners

7.6 Location of the exhaust manifold heat shield nuts on the right-side exhaust manifold

7.7a Location of the mounting bolts on the right-side exhaust manifold

7.7b Location of the mounting bolts on the left-side exhaust manifold (not all are visible in this photo)

8   Vibration damper and front oil seal - removal and installation

▶ Refer to illustrations 8.4, 8.5, 8.6 and 8.8

✳✳ WARNING:

Wait until the engine is completely cool before beginning this procedure.

1   Disconnect the cable from the negative terminal of the battery (see Chapter 5, Section 1).
2   Remove the engine drivebelt (see Chapter 1).
3   Drain the coolant (see Chapter 1), remove the upper radiator hose and remove the engine cooling fan (see Chapter 3).
4   Remove the large vibration damper-to-crankshaft bolt. To keep the crankshaft from turning, install a chain wrench or strap wrench around the circumference of the pulley. Be sure to use a piece of rubber (old drivebelt, old timing belt, etc.) under the chain wrench to protect the vibration damper from nicks or gouges (see illustration).
5   Using the proper puller (commonly available from auto parts stores), detach the vibration damper (see illustration).

8.4 A chain wrench can be used to prevent the vibration damper from turning while loosening the bolt - be sure to place a piece of drivebelt underneath the chain wrench to prevent damaging the damper

✳✳ CAUTION:

Do not use a puller with jaws that grip the outer edge of the pulley. The puller must be the type that utilizes bolts or arms to apply force to the pulley hub only. Also, the puller screw must not contact the threads in the nose of the crankshaft; it must use an adapter that allows the puller screw to apply force to the end of the crankshaft nose or a spacer must be inserted into the nose of the crankshaft to protect the threads.

6   If the seal is being removed while the cover is still attached to the engine block, carefully pry the seal out of the cover with a seal removal tool or a large screwdriver (see illustration).

✳✳ CAUTION:

Be careful not to scratch, gouge or distort the area that the seal fits into or an oil leak will develop.

7   Clean the bore to remove any old seal material and corrosion. Position the new seal in the bore with the seal lip (usually the side with the spring) facing IN (toward the engine). A small amount of oil applied to the outer edge of the new seal will make installation easier.
8   Drive the seal into the bore with a seal driver or a large socket and hammer until it's completely seated (see illustration). Select a socket that's the same outside diameter as the seal and make sure the new seal is pressed into place until it bottoms against the cover flange.
9   Check the surface of the damper that the oil seal rides on. If the surface has been grooved from long-time contact with the seal, replace the vibration damper.
10   Lubricate the seal lips with engine oil and reinstall the vibration damper, aligning the Woodruff key on the nose of the crankshaft with the keyway in the damper hub. Use a special installation tool (available at most auto parts stores) to press the vibration damper onto the crankshaft.
11   Install the vibration damper bolt and tighten it to the torque listed in this Chapter's Specifications.
12   The remainder of installation is the reverse of the removal process.
13   Refill the cooling system (see Chapter 1).

8.5 Use a three-jaw puller to remove the vibration damper from the crankshaft

8.6 Use a seal puller to remove the seal from the timing chain cover

8.8 Use a seal driver or a large socket to drive the new seal into the cover

9 Timing chain cover, chain and sprockets - removal, inspection and installation

✳✳ WARNING:

Wait until the engine is completely cool before beginning this procedure.

REMOVAL

▶ **Refer to illustrations 9.17, 9.19a, 9.19b, 9.19c, 9.20, 9.21a and 9.21b**

1 Disconnect the cable from the negative terminal of the battery (see Chapter 5, Section 1).
2 Drain the cooling system (see Chapter 1).
3 Drain the engine oil (see Chapter 1).
4 Remove the engine cover (see illustration 4.2).
5 Remove the air filter housing and the air intake duct (see Chapter 4).
6 Remove the drivebelt (see Chapter 1).

7 Remove the engine cooling fans (see Chapter 3).
8 Remove the air conditioning compressor without disconnecting the hoses (see Chapter 3). Use rope or wire to tie the compressor away from the front of the engine with the air conditioning lines attached.
9 Remove the alternator (see Chapter 5).
10 Remove the drivebelt tensioner (see Chapter 1) and the idler pulleys.
11 Remove the vibration damper (see Section 8).
12 Remove the power steering pump (see Chapter 10) and set it aside without disconnecting the power steering lines.
13 Remove the dipstick tube.
14 Remove the oil pan and the pickup tube (see Section 12).
15 Disconnect the heater hoses from the front cover.
16 Remove the water pump (see Chapter 3).
17 Remove the timing chain cover bolts (see illustration) and the front cover.
18 Remove the oil pump (see Section 13).
19 Reinstall the bolt into the end of the crankshaft and turn the crankshaft until the crankshaft sprocket timing mark is at the 6 o'clock position (with the crankshaft key at 2 o'clock) and the camshaft timing mark at the 12 o'clock position (see illustrations).
20 Retract the tensioner until the hole in the tensioner aligns with the hole in the camshaft tensioner thrust plate (see illustration). Install a

9.17 Location of the timing chain cover mounting bolts - the bolt holes marked with an (A) secure the water pump as well as the timing chain cover

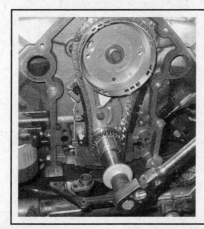

9.19a Use a breaker bar and socket to rotate the crankshaft (clockwise) to TDC number 1 position

9.19b The single colored timing chain link should align with the camshaft sprocket timing mark . . .

9.19c . . . and the two colored timing chain links (A) should straddle the crankshaft sprocket timing dot (B) - note that the keyway (C) should be at the 2 o'clock position

9.20 Use a large pair of pliers to retract the tensioner until the hole in the tensioner aligns with the hole in the bracket (thrust plate), then install a drill bit through the hole to keep it in the retracted position

9.21a Use a breaker bar and socket to prevent the crankshaft from rotating while loosening the camshaft sprocket bolt

9.21b Remove the camshaft sprocket, crankshaft sprocket and timing chain as a complete assembly

suitable size drill bit to retain the tensioner in the retracted position.

➡**Note: The timing chain tensioner is an integral component of the camshaft thrust plate. If necessary, the tensioner/thrust plate assembly must be replaced as a complete unit.**

21 Remove the camshaft sprocket bolt and remove the timing chain with the camshaft and crankshaft sprockets (see illustrations).

22 Remove the camshaft tensioner thrust plate mounting bolts (see illustration 11.9) and separate the tensioner from the engine block.

INSPECTION

23 Inspect the camshaft sprocket for damage or wear. The camshaft sprocket is a steel sprocket, but the teeth can become grooved or worn enough to cause a poor meshing of the sprocket and the chain.

➡**Note: Whenever a new timing chain is required, the entire set (chain, tensioner, camshaft and crankshaft sprockets) must be replaced as an assembly.**

24 Inspect the crankshaft sprocket for damage or wear. The crankshaft sprocket is a steel sprocket, but these teeth can also become grooved or worn enough to cause a poor meshing of the sprocket and the chain.

INSTALLATION

▶ **Refer to illustrations 9.27a, 9.27b and 9.34**

➡**Note: Always replace the timing chain as a set with the camshaft sprocket, the crankshaft sprocket and the tensioner. Never install a new timing chain onto old sprockets.**

25 Stuff a shop rag into the opening at the front of the oil pan to keep debris out of the engine, then clean off all traces of old gasket material and sealant from the engine block. Wipe the sealing surfaces with a cloth saturated with lacquer thinner or acetone.

26 If the tensioner is not compressed (retracted position), compress the tensioner until the hole aligns with the bracket hole, then insert a suitable size drill bit through both holes to keep the tensioner locked in this position (see illustration 9.20). Install the camshaft thrust plate and tighten the bolts to the torque listed in this Chapter's Specifications.

27 Assemble the timing chain and sprockets before installing them onto the engine. Loop the new chain over the camshaft sprocket with the single colored link (timing chain mark) aligned with the sprocket alignment mark (see illustration). Mesh the chain with the crankshaft sprocket, with the crankshaft sprocket alignment mark between the two

9.27a The camshaft sprocket timing mark(s) must align with the single colored timing chain link . . .

9.27b . . . and the two colored timing chain links must straddle the crankshaft sprocket mark

colored chain links (see illustration).

28 Align the sprocket with the Woodruff key in the end of the crankshaft and assemble the chain, camshaft sprocket and crankshaft sprocket onto the crankshaft and camshaft. Tap it gently into place until it is completely seated.

> ❊❊ **CAUTION:**
>
> **If resistance is encountered, do not use excessive force to hammer the sprocket onto the crankshaft. It may eventually move onto the shaft, but it may be cracked in the process and fail later, causing extensive engine damage. When the timing chain components are installed, the timing marks MUST align as shown in illustrations 9.19b and 9.19c.**

29 Apply a thread locking compound to the camshaft sprocket bolt threads and tighten the bolt to the torque listed in this Chapter's Specifications.

30 Lubricate the chain with clean engine oil.

31 Remove the drill bit from the tensioner and bracket. Make sure the tensioner has released and is pressing against the timing chain. Verify that the timing marks are still aligned properly.

32 Install the oil pump (see Section 13).

33 Install the oil pump pick-up tube to the bottom of the oil pump. Tighten the bolt to the torque listed in this Chapter's Specifications.

34 The timing chain cover rubber gasket can be re-used if it isn't damaged or hardened, but considering the amount of work that you've done to get to this point, it's a good idea to replace it. Double-check the surface of the timing chain cover and engine block. Make sure all old gasket material is removed and the surface is clean. Install a new rubber gasket into the groove in the timing chain cover (see illustration).

35 Apply a small amount of RTV sealant to the corner where the timing chain cover, engine block and oil pan meet.

9.34 Be sure to install a new rubber gasket into the timing chain cover groove

36 Install the timing chain cover on the block (see illustration 9.17) and tighten the bolts, a little at a time, until you reach the torque listed in this Chapter's Specifications.

➡**Note: Be sure to install the water pump onto the timing chain cover and tighten the timing chain cover bolts and the water pump bolts at the same time (see Chapter 3).**

37 Install the oil pan (see Section 12).

38 Lubricate the oil seal contact surface of the vibration damper hub with clean engine oil, then install the damper (see Section 8). Tighten the bolt to the torque listed in this Chapter's Specifications.

39 The remaining installation steps are the reverse of removal.

40 Add coolant and engine oil. Run the engine and check for oil and coolant leaks.

10 Cylinder head(s) - removal and installation

> ❊❊ **WARNING:**
>
> **Wait until the engine is completely cool before beginning this procedure.**

REMOVAL

1 Relieve the fuel system pressure (see Chapter 4), then disconnect the cable from the negative terminal of the battery (see Chapter 5, Section 1).

2 Drain the cooling system (see Chapter 1).

3 Remove the intake manifold (see Section 6).

4 Remove the exhaust manifold(s) from the cylinder head(s) (see Section 7).

5 Remove the valve covers (see Section 4).

6 Remove the rocker arms and pushrods (see Section 5).

> ❊❊ **CAUTION:**
>
> **Again, as mentioned in Section 5, keep all the parts in order so they are reinstalled in the same locations.**

7 Loosen the head bolts in 1/4-turn increments in a pattern opposite of the tightening sequence (see illustration 10.16) until they can be removed by hand.

➡**Note: There will be different-length head bolts for different locations, so store the bolts in order as they are removed. This will ensure that the bolts are reinstalled in their original holes.**

8 Lift the heads off the engine. If resistance is felt, do not pry between the head and block as damage to the mating surfaces will result. To dislodge the head, place a block of wood against the end of it and strike the wood block with a hammer, or lift on a casting protrusion. Store the heads on blocks of wood to prevent damage to the gasket sealing surfaces.

10.9 Make sure the cylinder head surface is perfectly clean, free from old gasket material, carbon deposits and dirt - note that the dowel is part of the cylinder head stand

10.12 A die should be used to remove sealant and corrosion from the bolt threads prior to installation

INSTALLATION

▶ **Refer to illustrations 10.9, 10.12, 10.13 and 10.16**

9 The mating surfaces of the cylinder heads and block must be perfectly clean when the heads are installed (see illustration). Gasket removal solvents are available at auto parts stores and may prove helpful.

10 Use a gasket scraper to remove all traces of carbon and old gasket material, then wipe the mating surfaces with a cloth saturated with lacquer thinner or acetone. If there is oil on the mating surfaces when the heads are installed, the gaskets may not seal correctly and leaks may develop. When working on the block, cover the lifter valley with shop rags to keep debris out of the engine. Use a vacuum cleaner to remove any debris that falls into the cylinders.

11 Check the block and head mating surfaces for nicks, deep scratches and other damage. If damage is slight, it can be removed with emery cloth. If it is excessive, machining may be the only alternative.

12 Use a tap of the correct size to chase the threads in the head bolt

holes in the block. Mount each bolt in a vise and run a die down the threads to remove corrosion and restore the threads (see illustration). Dirt, corrosion, sealant and damaged threads will affect torque readings.

13 Position the new gaskets over the dowels in the block. Be sure the letter designations for the left (L) and right (R) cylinder heads and the top gasket surface (TOP) are correctly oriented (see illustration).

14 Carefully position the heads on the block without disturbing the gaskets.

15 Before installing the head bolts, coat the threads with a small amount of engine oil.

16 Install the bolts in their original locations and tighten them finger tight. Following the recommended sequence (see illustration), tighten the bolts in several steps to the torque listed in this Chapter's Specifications.

17 The remaining installation steps are the reverse of removal.

18 Add coolant and change the engine oil and filter (see Chapter 1). Start the engine and check for proper operation and coolant or oil leaks.

10.13 Make sure the head gaskets are installed on the correct cylinder banks, and the TOP marking is facing up

10.16 Cylinder head bolt tightening sequence

11 Camshaft and lifters - removal, inspection and installation

✳✳ WARNING:

Wait until the engine is completely cool before beginning this procedure.

➡**Note: These engines are equipped with a Multiple Displacement System (MDS) that uses a specialized camshaft. Replace the camshaft ONLY with a camshaft compatible with the MDS design. Refer to Chapter 6 for a description of the MDS system.**

REMOVAL

◆ **Refer to illustrations 11.6, 11.7a, 11.7b and 11.9**

1 Relieve the fuel system pressure (see Chapter 4), then disconnect the cable from the negative terminal of the battery (see Chapter 5, Section 1).

2 Drain the cooling system (see Chapter 1).

11.6 Each lifter rail is secured by one bolt

3 Remove the timing chain cover, the timing chain and the sprockets (see Section 9).

4 Remove the cylinder heads (see Section 10).

5 Remove the radiator (see Chapter 3).

6 Remove the lifter rail mounting bolts (see illustration).

7 Remove the lifters from the lifter bores in the engine block (see illustration). Carefully place them in the correct location in the lifter rail. Each lifter must be installed into the same lifter bore and in the same direction (roller rotation) (see illustration). Be sure to mark each lifter and lifter rail with a felt pen to designate the cylinder number and the type of lifter (intake or exhaust). There are several ways to extract the lifters from the bores. A special tool designed to grip and remove lifters is manufactured by many tool companies and is widely available, but it may not be required in every case. On newer engines without a lot of varnish buildup, the lifters can often be removed with a small magnet or even with your fingers. A machinist's scribe with a bent end can be used to pull the lifters out by positioning the point under the retainer ring inside the top of each lifter.

✳✳ CAUTION:

Do not use pliers to remove the lifters unless you intend to replace them with new ones (along with the camshaft). The pliers will damage the precision machined and hardened lifters, rendering them useless. Do not attempt to withdraw the camshaft with the lifters in place.

8 Before removing the camshaft, check the endplay. Mount a dial indicator so that it contacts the nose of the camshaft. Pry the camshaft forward and back using a long screwdriver with the tip taped to prevent damage to the camshaft. Record the movement of the dial indicator and compare the reading to the value given in this Chapter's Specifications. If the endplay is excessive, the camshaft must be replaced.

9 Unbolt and remove the camshaft thrust plate (see illustration).

10 Thread a long bolt into the camshaft sprocket bolt hole to use as a handle when removing the camshaft from the block. Carefully pull the

11.7a Remove the lifters from the lifter bores and install them into the lifter rail - each lifter must be installed into the same lifter bore and in the same direction (roller rotation)

11.7b Install the lifters into the lifter rail and make sure the lifters are marked in their original positions with number designations for the cylinders and letter designations for the valve each one operates (intake or exhaust)

11.9 Location of the camshaft thrust plate mounting bolts

11.12 Check the diameter of each camshaft bearing journal to pinpoint excessive wear and out-of-round conditions

11.13 Measure the camshaft lobe height (greatest dimension) with a micrometer

camshaft out. Support the cam near the block so the lobes do not nick or gouge the bearings as it is withdrawn.

INSPECTION

▶ **Refer to illustrations 11.12, 11.13, 11.14 and 11.18**

11 After the camshaft has been removed from the engine, cleaned with solvent and dried, inspect the bearing journals for uneven wear, pitting and evidence of seizure. If the journals are damaged, the bearing inserts in the block are probably damaged as well. Both the camshaft and bearings will have to be replaced.

➡**Note: Camshaft bearing replacement requires special tools and expertise that place it beyond the scope of the average home mechanic. The tools for bearing removal and installation are available at stores that carry automotive tools, possibly even found at a tool rental business. It is advisable though, if bearings are bad and the procedure is beyond your ability, remove the engine block and take it to an automotive machine shop to ensure that the job is done correctly.**

12 Measure the bearing journals with a micrometer to determine if they are excessively worn or out-of-round (see illustration).

13 Measure the lobe height of each cam lobe on the intake camshaft and record your measurements (see illustration). Compare the measurements for excessive variations. If the lobe heights vary more than 0.005 inch (0.125 mm), replace the camshaft. Compare the lobe height measurements on the exhaust camshaft and follow the same procedure. Do not compare intake camshaft lobe heights with exhaust camshaft lobe heights, as they are different. Only compare intake lobes with intake lobes and exhaust lobes with other exhaust lobes.

14 Check the camshaft lobes for heat discoloration, score marks, chipped areas, pitting and uneven wear (see illustration). If the lobes are in good condition and if the lobe lift variation measurements recorded earlier are within the limits, the camshaft can be reused.

15 Clean the lifters with solvent and dry them thoroughly without mixing them up.

16 Check each lifter wall, pushrod seat and foot for scuffing, score marks and uneven wear. If the lifter walls are damaged or worn (which is not very likely), inspect the lifter bores in the engine block as well. If the pushrod seats are worn, check the pushrod ends.

17 If new lifters are being installed, a new camshaft must also be installed. If a new camshaft is installed, then use new lifters as well.

Never install used lifters unless the original camshaft is used and the lifters can be installed in their original locations.

18 Check the rollers carefully for wear and damage and make sure they turn freely without excessive play (see illustration).

INSTALLATION

▶ **Refer to illustration 11.19**

19 Lubricate the camshaft bearing journals and cam lobes with camshaft installation lube (see illustration).

20 Slide the camshaft slowly and gently into the engine. Support the cam near the block and be careful not to scrape or nick the bearings. Only install the camshaft far enough to install the camshaft thrust plate. Pushing it in too far could dislodge the camshaft plug at the rear of the engine, causing an oil leak. Tighten the camshaft thrust plate mounting bolts to the torque listed in this Chapter's Specifications.

21 Install the timing chain and sprockets (see Section 9). Align the timing marks on the crankshaft and camshaft sprockets.

22 Lubricate the lifters with clean engine oil and install them in the block. If the original lifters are being reinstalled, be sure to return them to their original locations, and with the numbers facing UP (exactly as they were removed). Install the lifter rail and mounting bolts. Tighten the lifter rail mounting bolts to the torque listed in this Chapter's Specifications.

➡**Note: Each lifter rail should be numbered and coincide with the correct cylinder numbers.**

23 The remaining installation steps are the reverse of removal.

24 Change the oil and install a new oil filter (see Chapter 1). Fill the cooling system with the proper type of coolant (see Chapter 1).

25 Start the engine and check for oil pressure and leaks.

❈❈ CAUTION:

Do not run the engine above a fast idle until all the hydraulic lifters have filled with oil and become quiet again.

26 If a new camshaft and lifters have been installed, the engine should be brought to operating temperature and run at a fast idle for 15 to 20 minutes to "break in" the new components. Change the oil and filter again after 500 miles of operation.

11.14 Check the cam lobes for pitting, excessive wear and scoring. If scoring is excessive, as shown here, replace the camshaft

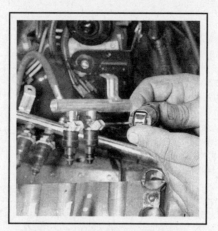

11.18 The roller on the roller lifters must turn freely - check for wear and excessive play as well

11.19 Be sure to apply camshaft installation lube to the cam lobes and bearing journals before installing the camshaft

12 Oil pan - removal and installation

✳✳ WARNING:

Wait until the engine is completely cool before beginning this procedure.

REMOVAL

◆ **Refer to illustration 12.10**

1 Disconnect the cable from the negative terminal of the battery (see Chapter 5, Section 1).

2 Drain the cooling system (see Chapter 1).

3 Raise the vehicle and support it securely on jackstands (see Chapter 1).

4 Drain the engine oil and replace the oil filter (see Chapter 1). Remove the engine oil dipstick.

5 Remove the engine splash shield (see illustration 7.2). Disconnect the exhaust pipes from the exhaust manifolds (see Chapter 4).

12.10 Location of the transmission-to-oil pan mounting bolts

6 Remove the engine cooling fans and shroud (see Chapter 3).

7 Remove the power steering gear from the crossmember (see Chapter 10). Do not disconnect the intermediate shaft coupler or the tie rod ends. Also, do not disconnect the power steering fluid lines from the power steering gear. Position the power steering gear assembly down and away from the engine.

8 Connect an engine hoist to the engine (see Chapter 2D).

9 Remove the left and right side engine mount-to-subframe nuts and studs (see Section 16), then raise the engine slightly.

10 Remove all of the oil pan bolts (see illustration), then lower the pan from the engine. The pan will probably stick to the engine, so strike the pan with a rubber mallet until it breaks the gasket seal.

✳✳ CAUTION:

Before using force on the oil pan, be sure all the bolts have been removed. Carefully slide the oil pan out, to the rear.

➡**Note: The M10 horizontal bolts are slightly longer in length than the other M10 vertical bolts. Be sure to mark the longer bolts and reinstall them in the correct locations.**

11 Remove the windage tray from the engine block.

➡**Note: The windage tray and gasket assembly must be replaced with new parts whenever the oil pan is removed from the engine block.**

INSTALLATION

◆ **Refer to illustration 12.19**

12 Install a new gasket and windage tray.

13 Wash out the oil pan with solvent.

14 Thoroughly clean the mounting surfaces of the oil pan and engine block of old gasket material and sealer. If the oil pan is distorted at the bolt-hole areas, straighten the flange by supporting it from below on a 1x4 wood block and tapping the bolt holes with the rounded end of a ball-peen hammer. Wipe the gasket surfaces clean with a rag

soaked in lacquer thinner or acetone.

15 Apply some RTV sealant to the corners where the timing chain cover meets the block and at the rear where the rear main oil seal retainer meets the block. Then attach the one-piece oil pan gasket to the engine block with contact-cement-type gasket adhesive.

16 Make sure the alignment studs are installed in the correct locations in the engine block.

17 Lift the pan into position, slipping it over the alignment studs and being careful not to disturb the gasket, install several bolts finger tight.

18 Check that the gasket isn't sticking out anywhere around the block's perimeter. When all the bolts are in place, install the oil pan nuts onto the studs.

19 Following the correct torque sequence (see illustration), tighten the fasteners to the torque listed in this Chapter's Specifications.

20 The remainder of the installation procedure is the reverse of removal.

21 Add the proper type and quantity of oil, change the oil filter, and refill the cooling system (see Chapter 1), start the engine and check for leaks before placing the vehicle back in service.

12.19 Oil pan bolt tightening sequence

13 Oil pump - removal and installation

✳✳ WARNING:

Wait until the engine is completely cool before beginning this procedure.

✳✳ CAUTION:

The oil pressure relief valve must not be removed from the oil pump housing on this engine. If the oil pressure relief valve is removed from the housing, the entire oil pump assembly must be replaced with a new unit.

13.5 Location of the oil pump pick-up tube retainer bolt (A) and the oil pump mounting bolts (B)

➡Note: The oil pump on the V8 engine is available only as a complete unit.

REMOVAL

▶ **Refer to illustration 13.5**

1 Disconnect the cable from the negative terminal of the battery (see Chapter 5, Section 1).

2 Drain the cooling system (see Chapter 1).

3 Remove the timing chain cover (see Section 9).

4 Remove the oil pan (see Section 12).

5 Remove the bolt from the pick-up tube assembly and lower it away from the oil pump (see illustration).

6 Remove the oil pump mounting bolts and detach the pump from the engine block.

INSTALLATION

7 Position the pump on the engine. Make sure the pump rotor is aligned with the crankshaft drive. Install the oil pump mounting bolts and tighten them to the torque listed in this Chapter's Specifications.

8 Install a new O-ring onto the oil pump pick-up tube, connect the tube to the pump and tighten the bolt to the torque listed in this Chapter's Specifications.

9 The remainder of installation is the reverse of removal.

10 Fill the crankcase with the proper type and quantity of engine oil, change the oil filter and refill the cooling system (see Chapter 1).

11 Run the engine and check for oil pressure and leaks.

14 Driveplate - removal and installation

This procedure is essentially the same as for the 2.7L V6 engine. Refer to Part A and follow the procedure outlined there, but refer to the torque Specifications listed in this Chapter.

15 Rear main oil seal - replacement

▶ **Refer to illustrations 15.4 and 15.5**

1   V8 engines use a one-piece rear main oil seal which is installed in a bolt-on housing. Replacing this seal requires removal of the transmission, torque converter and driveplate. Refer to Chapter 7 for the transmission removal procedures.

2   The seal can be removed by prying it out of the housing by inserting a screwdriver, being careful not to nick the crankshaft surface. Wrap the screwdriver tip with tape to avoid damage. Be sure to note how far it's recessed into the housing bore before removal so the new seal can be installed to the same depth. Preferably, a seal installation tool is needed to press the new seal back into place. If the proper seal installation tool is unavailable, use a large socket, section of pipe or a blunt tool and carefully drive the new seal into place. The lip is stiff so carefully work it onto the seal journal of the crankshaft. Don't rush it or you may damage the seal.

3   The rear main seal housing can also be removed to change the seal, but whenever the housing is removed from the block the oil pan must be removed (see Section 12). Install a new rear main oil seal and gasket.

4   If the housing is removed, place it on two blocks of wood and use a small punch to drive out the old seal (see illustration).

5   Clean the housing thoroughly, then apply a thin coat of engine oil to the new seal. Set the seal squarely into the recess of the housing, then, using a piece of wood and a hammer, press the seal into place (see illustration).

6   Carefully slide the seal over the crankshaft and bolt the seal housing to the block. Be sure to use a new gasket.

7   The remainder of installation is the reverse of the removal procedure.

15.4 Place the rear main oil seal housing on two blocks of wood and use a small punch to drive out the old seal

15.5 Use a block of wood to drive the oil seal squarely into the housing

16 Engine mounts - check and replacement

1   There are three powertrain mounts; left and right engine mounts attached to the engine block and to the subframe and a rear mount attached to the transmission and the frame. Refer to Chapter 7 for check and replacement procedures for the transmission mount.

CHECK

2   During the check, the engine must be raised slightly to remove the weight from the mounts.

3   Raise the vehicle and support it securely on jackstands, then position a jack under the engine oil pan. Place a large wood block between the jack head and the oil pan, then carefully raise the engine just enough to take the weight off the mounts.

❋❋ WARNING:

DO NOT place any part of your body under the engine when it's supported only by a jack!

4   Check the mount insulators to see if the rubber is cracked, hardened or separated from the metal in the center of the mount.

5   Check for relative movement between the mount and the engine or subframe. Use a large screwdriver or prybar to attempt to move the mounts.

6   If movement is noted, lower the engine and tighten the mount fasteners.

REPLACEMENT

▶ **Refer to illustrations 16.9**

7   Disconnect the cable from the negative terminal of the battery (see Chapter 5, Section 1). Raise the vehicle and support it securely on jackstands (if not already done). Position a jack under the engine oil pan. Place a large wood block between the jack head and the oil pan.

8   If you're removing the right side engine mount, remove the alternator support bracket (see Chapter 5).

9   Remove the engine mount-to-subframe nuts (see illustration) and raise the engine with the jack.

10 Remove the mount-to-engine bracket bolts.

11 Install the new mount, making sure it is correctly positioned in the bracket. Install the fasteners and tighten them securely.

16.9 Location of the subframe-to-engine mount nuts - one bolt hidden from view

Specifications

General

Firing order	1-8-4-3-6-5-7-2
Bore and stroke	3.92 x 3.58 inches
Displacement	5.7L (345 cubic inches)
Cylinder numbers (front-to-rear)	
Left (driver's) side	1-3-5-7
Right side	2-4-6-8
Compression pressure	See Chapter 2D

Cylinder locations on the 5.7L Hemi V8 engine

Camshaft

Journal diameters	
No. 1	2.290 inches
No. 2	2.280 inches
No. 3	2.260 inches
No. 4	2.240 inches
No. 5	1.720 inches
Journal oil clearance	
No. 1, 3 and 5	0.0015 to 0.0030 inch
No. 2 and 4	0.0019 to 0.0035 inch
Endplay	0.0031 to 0.0114 inch

Torque specifications   Ft-lbs (unless otherwise indicated)

➥**Note: One foot-pound (ft-lb) of torque is equivalent to 12 inch-pounds (in-lbs) of torque. Torque values below approximately 15 ft-lbs are expressed in inch-pounds, since most foot-pound torque wrenches are not accurate at these smaller values.**

Camshaft sprocket bolt	90
Camshaft thrust plate bolts	21
Cylinder head bolts (see illustration 10.16)	
Step 1	
Large bolts	25
Small bolts	15
Step 2	
Large bolts	40
Small bolts	15
Step 3	
Large bolts	Tighten an additional 90 degrees
Small bolts	25
Drivebelt tensioner mounting bolt	40
Drivebelt pulley mounting bolt	40
Driveplate bolts	70
Exhaust manifold bolts/nuts	18
Exhaust manifold heat shield nuts	70 in-lbs
Exhaust pipe flange nuts	25
Intake manifold bolts	105 in-lbs
Oil pan bolts (see illustration 12.19)	
Step 1 Small bolts	44 in-lbs
Step 2 Large bolts	39
Step 3 Small bolts	105 in-lbs
Oil pump pick-up tube bolts	21
Oil pump mounting bolts	21
Rear main seal retainer bolts	132 in-lbs
Rocker arm bolts	195 in-lbs
Rocker arm lifter rail bolts	106 in-lbs
Timing chain cover bolts	21
Valve cover nuts/studs	70 in-lbs
Vibration damper-to-crankshaft bolt	129
Water pump-to-timing chain cover bolts	21

Notes

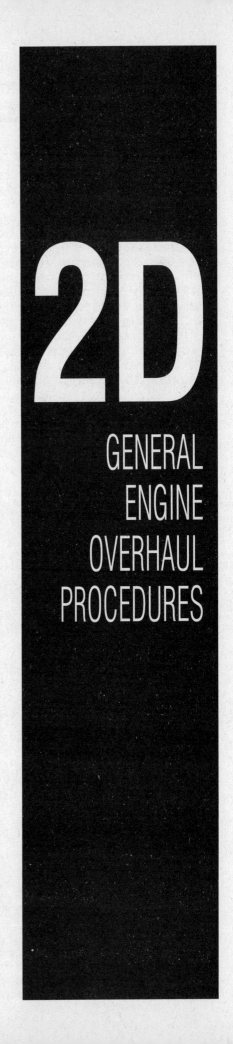

2D

GENERAL ENGINE OVERHAUL PROCEDURES

Section

Reference to other Chapters

1 General information - engine overhaul

▶ **Refer to illustrations 1.1, 1.2, 1.3, 1.4, 1.5 and 1.6**

Included in this portion of Chapter 2 are general information and diagnostic testing procedures for determining the overall mechanical condition of your engine.

The information ranges from advice concerning preparation for an overhaul and the purchase of replacement parts and/or components to detailed, step-by-step procedures covering removal and installation.

The following Sections have been written to help you determine whether your engine needs to be overhauled and how to remove and install it once you've determined it needs to be rebuilt. For information concerning in-vehicle engine repair, see Chapter 2A, 2B or 2C.

The Specifications included in this Part are general in nature and include only those necessary for testing the oil pressure and engine compression, and bottom-end torque specifications. Refer to Chapter 2A, 2B or 2C for additional engine Specifications.

It's not always easy to determine when, or if, an engine should be completely overhauled, because a number of factors must be considered.

High mileage is not necessarily an indication that an overhaul is needed, while low mileage doesn't preclude the need for an overhaul. Frequency of servicing is probably the most important consideration. An engine that's had regular and frequent oil and filter changes, as well as other required maintenance, will most likely give many thousands of miles of reliable service. Conversely, a neglected engine may require an overhaul very early in its service life.

Excessive oil consumption is an indication that piston rings, valve seals and/or valve guides are in need of attention. Make sure that oil leaks aren't responsible before deciding that the rings and/or guides are bad. Perform a cylinder compression check to determine the extent of the work required (see Section 3). Also, check the vacuum readings under various conditions (see Section 4).

Check the oil pressure with a gauge installed in place of the oil pressure sending unit and compare it to this Chapter's Specifications (see Section 2). If it's extremely low, the bearings and/or oil pump are probably worn out.

Loss of power, rough running, knocking or metallic engine noises, excessive valve train noise and high fuel consumption rates may also point to the need for an overhaul, especially if they're all present at the same time. If a complete tune-up doesn't remedy the situation, major mechanical work is the only solution.

An engine overhaul involves restoring the internal parts to the specifications of a new engine. During an overhaul, the piston rings are replaced and the cylinder walls are reconditioned (rebored and/or honed) (see illustrations 1.1 and 1.2). If a rebore is done by an automotive machine shop, new oversize pistons will also be

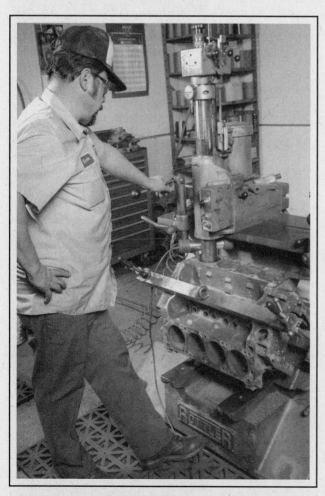

1.1 An engine block being bored. An engine rebuilder will use special machinery to recondition the cylinder bores

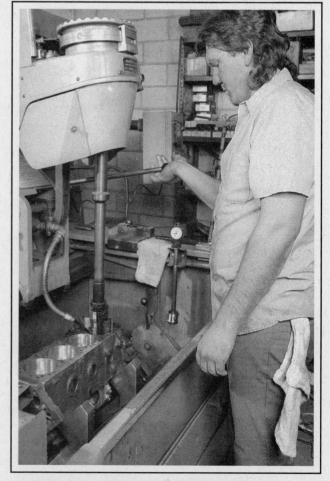

1.2 If the cylinders are bored, the machine shop will normally hone the engine on a machine like this

installed. The main bearings, connecting rod bearings and camshaft bearings are generally replaced with new ones and, if necessary, the crankshaft may be reground to restore the journals (see illustration 1.3). Generally, the valves are serviced as well, since they're usually in less-than-perfect condition at this point. While the engine is being overhauled, other components, such as the starter and alternator, can be rebuilt as well. The end result should be similar to a new engine that will give many trouble free miles.

➡ **Note: Critical cooling system components such as the hoses, drivebelts, thermostat and water pump should be replaced with new parts when an engine is overhauled. The radiator should be checked carefully to ensure that it isn't clogged or leaking (see Chapter 3). If you purchase a rebuilt engine or short block, some rebuilders will not warranty their engines unless the radiator has been professionally flushed. Also, we don't recommend overhauling the oil pump - always install a new one when an engine is rebuilt.**

Overhauling the internal components on today's engines is a difficult and time-consuming task which requires a significant amount of specialty tools and is best left to a professional engine rebuilder (see illustrations 1.4, 1.5 and 1.6). A competent engine rebuilder will handle the inspection of your old parts and offer advice concerning the reconditioning or replacement of the original engine, never purchase parts or have machine work done on other components until the block has been thoroughly inspected by a professional machine shop. As a general rule, time is the primary cost of an overhaul, especially since the vehicle may be tied up for a minimum of two weeks or more. Be

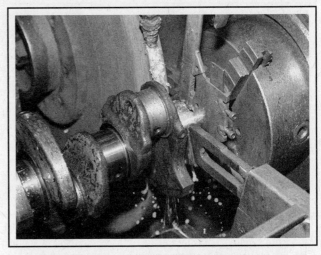

1.3 A crankshaft having a main bearing journal ground

aware that some engine builders only have the capability to rebuild the engine you bring them while other rebuilders have a large inventory of rebuilt exchange engines in stock. Also be aware that many machine shops could take as much as two weeks time to completely rebuild your engine depending on shop workload. Sometimes it makes more sense to simply exchange your engine for another engine that's already rebuilt to save time.

1.4 A machinist checks for a bent connecting rod, using specialized equipment

1.5 A bore gauge being used to check the main bearing bore

1.6 Uneven piston wear like this indicates a bent connecting rod

2 Oil pressure check

▸ **Refer to illustrations 2.2a, 2.2b, 2.2c and 2.3**

1   Low engine oil pressure can be a sign of an engine in need of rebuilding. A "low oil pressure" indicator (often called an "idiot light") is not a test of the oiling system. Such indicators only come on when the oil pressure is dangerously low. Even a factory oil pressure gauge in the instrument panel is only a relative indication, although much better for driver information than a warning light. A better test is with a mechanical (not electrical) oil pressure gauge.

2   Locate the oil pressure indicator sending unit on the engine block. The oil pressure sending unit is located in various locations depending upon engine type:

a) *On 2.7L V6 engines, the oil pressure sending unit is located on the right-rear side of the engine block (see illustration).*
b) *On 3.5L V6 engines, the oil pressure sending unit is located on the left side of the timing chain cover (see illustration).*
c) *On 5.7L V8 engines, the oil pressure sending unit is located on the oil filter housing above the oil filter (see illustration).*

2.2a On the 2.7L V6 engine, the oil pressure sending unit is located on the left-rear side of the engine block

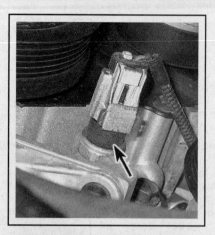

2.2b On the 3.5L V6 engine, the oil pressure sending unit is located on the left front side of the timing chain cover

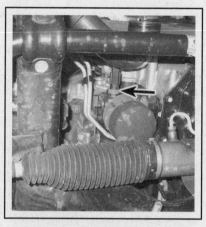

2.2c On the V8 engine, the oil pressure sending unit is located right above the oil filter

3   Unscrew and remove the oil pressure sending unit, then screw in the hose for your oil pressure gauge (see illustration). If necessary, install an adapter fitting. Use Teflon tape or thread sealant on the threads of the adapter and/or the fitting on the end of your gauge's hose.

4   Connect an accurate tachometer to the engine, according to the tachometer manufacturer's instructions.

5   Check the oil pressure with the engine running (normal operating temperature) at the specified engine speed, and compare it to this Chapter's Specifications. If it's extremely low, the bearings and/or oil pump are probably worn out.

2.3 Install an oil pressure gauge after removing the oil pressure sending unit - V8 engine shown

3   Cylinder compression check

▶ **Refer to illustration 3.6**

1   A compression check will tell you what mechanical condition the upper end of your engine (pistons, rings, valves, head gaskets) is in. Specifically, it can tell you if the compression is down due to leakage caused by worn piston rings, defective valves and seats or a blown head gasket.

➡**Note: The engine must be at normal operating temperature and the battery must be fully charged for this check.**

2   Begin by cleaning the area around the spark plugs before you remove them (compressed air should be used, if available). The idea is to prevent dirt from getting into the cylinders as the compression check is being done.

3   Remove the ignition coil assemblies (see Chapter 5). Also disable the fuel pump by removing the fuel pump relay (see Chapter 4, Section 2).

4   If you're working on a V8 engine, remove one spark plug from each cylinder; on all other engines, remove all of the spark plugs (see Chapter 1).

5   Block the throttle wide open.

6   Install a compression gauge in the spark plug hole (see illustration).

7   Crank the engine over at least seven compression strokes and watch the gauge. The compression should build up quickly in a healthy engine. Low compression on the first stroke, followed by gradually increasing pressure on successive strokes, indicates worn piston rings. A low compression reading on the first stroke, which doesn't build up during successive strokes, indicates leaking valves or a blown head gasket (a cracked head could also be the cause). Deposits on the undersides of the valve heads can also cause low compression. Record the highest gauge reading obtained.

8   Repeat the procedure for the remaining cylinders and compare the results to this Chapter's Specifications.

9   Add some engine oil (about three squirts from a plunger-type oil

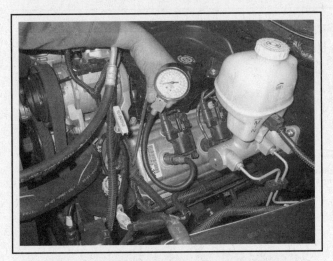

3.6 Use a compression gauge with a threaded fitting for the spark plug hole, not the type that requires hand pressure to maintain the seal

can) to each cylinder, through the spark plug hole, and repeat the test.

10 If the compression increases after the oil is added, the piston rings are definitely worn. If the compression doesn't increase significantly, the leakage is occurring at the valves or head gasket. Leakage past the valves may be caused by burned valve seats and/or faces or warped, cracked or bent valves.

11 If two adjacent cylinders have equally low compression, there's a strong possibility that the head gasket between them is blown. The appearance of coolant in the combustion chambers or the crankcase would verify this condition.

12 If one cylinder is slightly lower than the others, and the engine has a slightly rough idle, a worn lobe on the camshaft could be the cause.

13 If the compression is unusually high, the combustion chambers are probably coated with carbon deposits. If that's the case, the cylinder head(s) should be removed and decarbonized.

14 If compression is way down or varies greatly between cylinders, it would be a good idea to have a leak-down test performed by an automotive repair shop. This test will pinpoint exactly where the leakage is occurring and how severe it is.

4   Vacuum gauge diagnostic checks

▶ **Refer to illustrations 4.4 and 4.6**

A vacuum gauge provides inexpensive but valuable information about what is going on in the engine. You can check for worn rings or cylinder walls, leaking head or intake manifold gaskets, incorrect carburetor adjustments, restricted exhaust, stuck or burned valves, weak valve springs, improper ignition or valve timing and ignition problems.

Unfortunately, vacuum gauge readings are easy to misinterpret, so they should be used in conjunction with other tests to confirm the diagnosis.

Both the absolute readings and the rate of needle movement are important for accurate interpretation. Most gauges measure vacuum in inches of mercury (in-Hg). The following references to vacuum assume the diagnosis is being performed at sea level. As elevation increases (or atmospheric pressure decreases), the reading will decrease. For every

1,000 foot increase in elevation above approximately 2,000 feet, the gauge readings will decrease about one inch of mercury.

Connect the vacuum gauge directly to the intake manifold vacuum, not to ported (throttle body) vacuum (see illustration). Some models are equipped with a vacuum fitting built into the brake booster vacuum hose grommet at the brake booster. Other models are equipped with a vacuum hose fitting on the intake manifold. Use a T-fitting to access the vacuum signal. Be sure no hoses are left disconnected during the test or false readings will result.

Before you begin the test, allow the engine to warm up completely. Block the wheels and set the parking brake. With the transmission in Park, start the engine and allow it to run at normal idle speed.

✳✳ WARNING:

Keep your hands and the vacuum gauge clear of the fans.

Read the vacuum gauge; an average, healthy engine should normally produce about 17 to 22 in-Hg with a fairly steady needle (see illustration). Refer to the following vacuum gauge readings and what they indicate about the engine's condition:

1   A low, steady reading usually indicates a leaking gasket between the intake manifold and cylinder head(s) or throttle body, a leaky vacuum hose, late ignition timing or incorrect camshaft timing. Check ignition timing with a timing light and eliminate all other possible causes, utilizing the tests provided in this Chapter before you remove the timing chain cover to check the timing marks.

2   If the reading is three to eight inches below normal and it fluctuates at that low reading, suspect an intake manifold gasket leak at an intake port or a faulty fuel injector.

3   If the needle has regular drops of about two-to-four inches at a steady rate, the valves are probably leaking. Perform a compression check or leak-down test to confirm this.

4   An irregular drop or down-flick of the needle can be caused by a

4.4 A simple vacuum gauge can be handy in diagnosing engine condition and performance

Low, steady reading   Low, fluctuating needle   Regular drops

Irregular drops   Rapid vibration

Large fluctuation   Slow fluctuation

STD-O-OBR HAYNES

4.6 Typical vacuum gauge readings

sticking valve or an ignition misfire. Perform a compression check or leak-down test and read the spark plugs.

5   A rapid vibration of about four in-Hg vibration at idle combined with exhaust smoke indicates worn valve guides. Perform a leak-down test to confirm this. If the rapid vibration occurs with an increase in engine speed, check for a leaking intake manifold gasket or head gasket, weak valve springs, burned valves or ignition misfire.

6   A slight fluctuation, say one inch up and down, may mean ignition problems. Check all the usual tune-up items and, if necessary, run the engine on an ignition analyzer.

7   If there is a large fluctuation, perform a compression or leak-down test to look for a weak or dead cylinder or a blown head gasket.

8   If the needle moves slowly through a wide range, check for a clogged PCV system, incorrect idle fuel mixture, throttle body or intake manifold gasket leaks.

9   Check for a slow return after revving the engine by quickly snapping the throttle open until the engine reaches about 2,500 rpm and let it shut. Normally the reading should drop to near zero, rise above normal idle reading (about 5 in-Hg over) and then return to the previous idle reading. If the vacuum returns slowly and doesn't peak when the throttle is snapped shut, the rings may be worn. If there is a long delay, look for a restricted exhaust system (often the muffler or catalytic converter). An easy way to check this is to temporarily disconnect the exhaust ahead of the suspected part and redo the test.

5 Engine rebuilding alternatives

The do-it-yourselfer is faced with a number of options when purchasing a rebuilt engine. The major considerations are cost, warranty, parts availability and the time required for the rebuilder to complete the project. The decision to replace the engine block, piston/connecting rod assemblies and crankshaft depends on the final inspection results of your engine. Only then can you make a cost effective decision whether to have your engine overhauled or simply purchase an exchange engine for your vehicle.

Some of the rebuilding alternatives include:

Individual parts - If the inspection procedures reveal that the engine block and most engine components are in reusable condition, purchasing individual parts and having a rebuilder rebuild your engine may be the most economical alternative. The block, crankshaft and piston/connecting rod assemblies should all be inspected carefully by a machine shop first.

Short block - A short block consists of an engine block with a crankshaft and piston/connecting rod assemblies already installed. All new bearings are incorporated and all clearances will be correct. The existing camshafts, valve train components, cylinder head and external parts can be bolted to the short block with little or no machine shop work necessary.

Long block - A long block consists of a short block plus an oil pump, oil pan, cylinder head, valve cover, camshaft and valve train components, timing sprockets and chain or gears and timing cover. All components are installed with new bearings, seals and gaskets incorporated throughout. The installation of manifolds and external parts is all that's necessary.

Low mileage used engines - Some companies now offer low mileage used engines which is a very cost effective way to get your vehicle up and running again. These engines often come from vehicles which have been in totaled in accidents or come from other countries which have a higher vehicle turn over rate. A low mileage used engine also usually has a similar warranty like the newly remanufactured engines.

Give careful thought to which alternative is best for you and discuss the situation with local automotive machine shops, auto parts dealers and experienced rebuilders before ordering or purchasing replacement parts.

6 Engine removal - methods and precautions

▶ **Refer to illustrations 6.1, 6.2, 6.3 and 6.4**

If you've decided that an engine must be removed for overhaul or major repair work, several preliminary steps should be taken. Read all removal and installation procedures carefully prior to committing to this job. These engines are removed by lowering the engine to the floor, along with the transmission, and then raising the vehicle sufficiently to slide the assembly out; this will require a vehicle hoist as well as an engine hoist.

Locating a suitable place to work is extremely important. Adequate work space, along with storage space for the vehicle, will be needed. If a shop or garage isn't available, at the very least a flat, level, clean work surface made of concrete or asphalt is required.

Cleaning the engine compartment and engine before beginning the removal procedure will help keep tools clean and organized (see illustrations 6.1 and 6.2).

An engine hoist will also be necessary. Make sure the hoist is rated in excess of the combined weight of the engine and transmission. Safety is of primary importance, considering the potential hazards involved in removing the engine from the vehicle.

If you're a novice at engine removal, get at least one helper. One person cannot easily do all the things you need to do to remove a big heavy engine and transmission assembly from the engine compartment. Also helpful is to seek advice and assistance from someone who's experienced in engine removal.

6.1 After tightly wrapping water-vulnerable components, use a spray cleaner on everything, with particular concentration on the greasiest areas, usually around the valve cover and lower edges of the block. If one section dries out, apply more cleaner

6.2 Depending on how dirty the engine is, let the cleaner soak in according to the directions and then hose off the grime and cleaner. Get the rinse water down into every area you can get at; then dry important components with a hair dryer or paper towels

6.3 Get an engine stand sturdy enough to firmly support the engine while you're working on it. Stay away from three-wheeled models; they have a tendency to tip over more easily, so get a four-wheeled unit

6.4 An engine support fixture installed on a 3.5L V6 engine

Plan the operation ahead of time. Arrange for or obtain all of the tools and equipment you'll need prior to beginning the job (see illustration 6.3). Some of the equipment necessary to perform engine removal and installation safely and with relative ease are (in addition to a vehicle hoist and an engine hoist) a heavy duty floor jack (preferably fitted with a transmission jack head adapter), complete sets of wrenches and sockets as described in the front of this manual, wooden blocks, plenty

of rags and cleaning solvent for mopping up spilled oil, coolant and gasoline.

Another tool that supports the engine while the engine mounts are removed from the chassis and engine is the engine support fixture (see illustration). The engine support fixture can set the height of the engine for many other types of repair procedures such as transmission removal, power steering gear removal, subframe removal, etc.

Plan for the vehicle to be out of use for quite a while. A machine shop can do the work that is beyond the scope of the home mechanic. Machine shops often have a busy schedule, so before removing the engine, consult the shop for an estimate of how long it will take to rebuild or repair the components that may need work.

7 Engine - removal and installation

❊❊ WARNING 1:

Gasoline is extremely flammable, so take extra precautions when you work on any part of the fuel system. Don't smoke or allow open flames or bare light bulbs near the work area, and don't work in a garage where a gas-type appliance (such as a water heater or clothes dryer) is present. Since gasoline is carcinogenic, wear fuel-resistant gloves when there's a possibility of being exposed to fuel, and, if you spill any fuel on your skin, rinse it off immediately with soap and water. Mop up any spills immediately and do not store fuel-soaked rags where they could ignite. The fuel system is under constant pressure, so, if any fuel lines are to be disconnected, the fuel pressure in the system must be relieved first (see Chapter 4 for more information). When you perform any kind of work on the fuel system, wear safety glasses and have a Class B type fire extinguisher on hand.

❊❊ WARNING 2:

The air conditioning system is under high pressure. Do not loosen any hose fittings or remove any components until after the system has been discharged. Air conditioning refrigerant must be properly discharged into an EPA-approved recovery/recycling unit at a dealer service department or an automotive air conditioning repair facility. Always wear eye protection when disconnecting air conditioning system fittings.

❊❊ WARNING 3:

The engine must be completely cool before beginning this procedure.

REMOVAL

▶ **Refer to illustrations 7.13, 7.17, 7.35, 7.38 and 7.39**

1 If you're working on a V6 model, have the air conditioning system discharged by an automotive air conditioning technician.

2 Relieve the fuel system pressure (see Chapter 4).

3 Disconnect the cable from the negative terminal of the battery (see Chapter 5, Section 1).

4 Remove the hood (see Chapter 11).

5 Remove the cowl cover (see Chapter 11) and the strut support brace.

6 Remove the air filter housing and the intake air duct (see Chapter 4).

7 Remove the drivebelt (see Chapter 1).

8 Remove the alternator (see Chapter 5).

9 Remove the power steering pump, without disconnecting the hoses, and tie it out of the way (see Chapter 10).

10 Remove the PCV hose (see Chapter 6).

7.13 Label both ends of each wire or vacuum connection before disconnecting them

11 Remove the intake manifold (V8 models, see Chapter 2C) or the upper intake manifold (V6 models see Chapter 2A or 2B).

12 Remove the fuel rail (see Chapter 4).

13 Label and disconnect all wires and ground straps from the engine (see illustration). Masking tape and/or a touch-up paint applicator work well for marking items.

➡**Note: Take instant photos or sketch the locations of components and brackets to help with reassembly.**

14 Label and remove all vacuum lines between the engine and the firewall (or other components in the engine compartment).

15 Remove the engine oil dipstick tube.

16 Raise the vehicle and support it securely on jackstands.

17 Remove the engine splash shields (see illustration).

18 Drain the cooling system (see Chapter 1).

19 On 3.5L V6 engines, disconnect the hoses from the engine oil cooler.

20 Detach the transmission cooler lines from the engine brackets and the transmission (see Chapter 7).

21 Disconnect the engine block heater, if equipped.

22 Disconnect the oxygen sensors and the crankshaft position sensor connector (see Chapter 6).

23 If you're working on a V6 model, disconnect the intermediate shaft coupler from the steering gear (see Chapter 10).

24 Remove the starter (see Chapter 5).

25 Drain the engine oil (see Chapter 1).

26 Disconnect the oxygen sensor connectors (see Chapter 6) and separate the exhaust pipes from the exhaust manifolds (see Chapter 4).

27 On 2.7L V6 engines, remove the oil pan-to-transmission brace (see Chapter 2A).

28 Remove the torque converter-to-driveplate bolts (see Chapter 7).

7.35 On 3.5L V6 engines, attach the chain to the front timing belt cover and to the engine block at the rear of the engine near the EGR pipe

7.17 Front engine splash shield (1) and middle engine splash shield (2) fasteners

29 On 2.7L V6 engines, remove the power steering gear mounting bolts, lower the assembly without disconnecting the power steering fluid lines, then secure the assembly using rope (see Chapter 10).

30 Remove the engine mount-to-subframe fasteners (see Chapter 2A, 2B or 2C).

31 Remove the transmission-to-engine mounting bolts that are accessible from below.

32 Lower the vehicle.

33 Remove the engine cooling fans (see Chapter 3).

34 Remove the radiator hoses and heater hoses (see Chapter 3).

35 Support the engine from above with a hoist. Attach the chain hoist to the engine lifting brackets (see illustration). If no brackets are present, you'll have to fasten the chains to some substantial part of the engine - one that is strong enough to take the weight, but in a location that will provide good balance. If you're attaching the chain to a stud on the engine, or are using a bolt passing through the chain and into a threaded hole, place a washer between the nut or bolt head and the chain, and tighten the nut or bolt securely.

36 Support the transmission with a floor jack. Place a block of wood on the jack head to protect the transmission.

37 Remove the transmission-to-engine mounting bolts that are accessible from above.

7.38 Remove the mounting nut and ground strap, then remove the transmission-to-engine stud

38 Remove the ground strap from the upper right side of the transmission, if equipped (see illustration).

39 Remove the harness bracket at the top of the transmission bellhousing (see illustration).

40 Check to make sure everything is disconnected, then lift the engine out of the vehicle. The engine will probably need to be tilted and/or maneuvered as it's lifted out, so have an assistant handy.

✳✳ WARNING:

Do not place any part of your body under the engine when it is supported only by a hoist or other lifting device.

✳✳ CAUTION:

Be careful not to let the engine contact the radiator.

41 Remove the driveplate and mount the engine on an engine stand or set the engine on the floor and support it so it doesn't tip over. Then disconnect the engine hoist.

INSTALLATION

42 Installation is the reverse of the removal procedure, noting the following points:

   a) *Check the engine mounts. If they're worn or damaged, replace them (see Chapter 2A, 2B or 2C).*

   b) *Inspect the front transmission fluid seal and bearing (see Chapter 7).*

   c) *Tighten the transmission-to-engine bolts and the torque converter-to-driveplate bolts to the torque listed in the Chapter 7 Specifications.*

7.39 Remove the two mounting nuts and bracket, separate the wiring harness from the assembly and remove the two transmission-to-engine studs

✳✳ CAUTION:

Don't use the transmission-to-engine bolts to force the transmission and engine together!

   d) *Add coolant, oil, power steering and transmission fluid as needed (see Chapter 1).*

   e) *Run the engine and check for proper operation and leaks. Shut off the engine and recheck the fluid levels.*

8   Engine overhaul - disassembly sequence

1 It's much easier to remove the external components if it's mounted on a portable engine stand. A stand can often be rented quite cheaply from an equipment rental yard. Before the engine is mounted on a stand, the driveplate should be removed from the engine.

2 If a stand isn't available, it's possible to remove the external engine components with it blocked up on the floor. Be extra careful not to tip or drop the engine when working without a stand.

3 If you're going to obtain a rebuilt engine, all external components must come off first, to be transferred to the replacement engine. These components include:

   Driveplate
   Ignition system components
   Emissions-related components
   Engine mounts and mount brackets
   Engine rear cover (spacer plate between driveplate and engine block)
   Intake/exhaust manifolds

   Fuel injection components
   Oil filter
   Spark plug wires and spark plugs
   Thermostat and housing assembly
   Water pump

➡**Note: When removing the external components from the engine, pay close attention to details that may be helpful or important during installation. Note the installed position of gaskets, seals, spacers, pins, brackets, washers, bolts and other small items.**

4 If you're going to obtain a short block (assembled engine block, crankshaft, pistons and connecting rods), then remove the timing chain, cylinder head, oil pan, oil pump pick-up tube, oil pump and water pump from your engine so that you can turn in your old short block to the rebuilder as a core. See *Engine rebuilding alternatives* for additional information regarding the different possibilities to be considered.

9   Pistons and connecting rods - removal and installation

REMOVAL

▶ **Refer to illustrations 9.1, 9.3 and 9.4**

➡**Note: Prior to removing the piston/connecting rod assemblies, remove the cylinder head and oil pan (see Chapter 2A, 2B or 2C).**

1   Use your fingernail to feel if a ridge has formed at the upper limit of ring travel (about 1/4-inch down from the top of each cylinder). If carbon deposits or cylinder wear have produced ridges, they must be completely removed with a special tool (see illustration). Follow the manufacturer's instructions provided with the tool. Failure to remove the ridges before attempting to remove the piston/connecting rod assemblies may result in piston breakage.

2   After the cylinder ridges have been removed, turn the engine so the crankshaft is facing up.

3   Before the main bearing cap assembly and connecting rods are removed, check the connecting rod endplay with feeler gauges. Slide them between the first connecting rod and the crankshaft throw until the play is removed (see illustration). Repeat this procedure for each connecting rod. The endplay is equal to the thickness of the feeler

gauge(s). Check with an automotive machine shop for the endplay service limit (a typical endplay should measure between 0.005 to 0.015 inch [0.127 to 0.396 mm]). If the play exceeds the service limit, new connecting rods will be required. If new rods (or a new crankshaft) are installed, the endplay may fall under the minimum allowable. If it does, the rods will have to be machined to restore it. If necessary, consult an automotive machine shop for advice.

4   Check the connecting rods and caps for identification marks. If they aren't plainly marked, use paint or marker (see illustration) to clearly identify each rod and cap (1, 2, 3, etc., depending on the cylinder they're associated with). Do not interchange the rod caps. Install the exact same rod cap onto the same connecting rod.

✲✲ CAUTION:

Do not use a punch and hammer to mark the connecting rods or they may be damaged.

5   Loosen each of the connecting rod cap bolts 1/4-turn at a time until they can be removed by hand.

➡**Note: New connecting rod cap bolts must be used when reassembling the engine, but save the old bolts for use when checking the connecting rod bearing oil clearance.**

6   Remove the number one connecting rod cap and bearing insert. Don't drop the bearing insert out of the cap.

7   Remove the bearing insert and push the connecting rod/piston assembly out through the top of the engine. Use a wooden or plastic hammer handle to push on the upper bearing surface in the connecting rod. If resistance is felt, double-check to make sure that all of the ridge was removed from the cylinder.

8   Repeat the procedure for the remaining cylinders.

9   After removal, reassemble the connecting rod caps and bearing inserts in their respective connecting rods and install the cap bolts finger tight. Leaving the old bearing inserts in place until reassembly will help prevent the connecting rod bearing surfaces from being accidentally nicked or gouged.

10   The pistons and connecting rods are now ready for inspection and overhaul at an automotive machine shop.

9.1 If there's a ridge at the top of the cylinder(s), use a ridge reamer to remove the raised material (ridge) from the top of the cylinders before you try to remove the piston(s)

9.3 Checking the connecting rod endplay (side clearance)

9.4 If the connecting rods or caps are not marked, use permanent ink or paint to mark the caps to the rods by cylinder number (for example, this would be number 4 cylinder connecting rod)

ENGINE BEARING ANALYSIS

Debris

Babbitt bearing embedded with debris from machinings

Microscopic detail of debris

Microscopic detail of gouges

Overplated copper alloy bearing gouged by cast iron debris

Aluminum bearing embedded with glass beads

Microscopic detail of glass beads

Damaged lining caused by dirt left on the bearing back

Misassembly

Result of a lower half assembled as an upper - blocking the oil flow

Excessive oil clearance is indicated by a short contact arc

Polished and oil-stained backs are a result of a poor fit in the housing bore

Result of a wrong, reversed, or shifted cap

Overloading

Damage from excessive idling which resulted in an oil film unable to support the load imposed

Damaged upper connecting rod bearings caused by engine lugging; the lower main bearings (not shown) were similarly affected

The damage shown in these upper and lower connecting rod bearings was caused by engine operation at a higher-than-rated speed under load

Misalignment

A warped crankshaft caused this pattern of severe wear in the center, diminishing toward the ends

A poorly finished crankshaft caused the equally spaced scoring shown

A tapered housing bore caused the damage along one edge of this pair

A bent connecting rod led to the damage in the "V" pattern

Lubrication

Result of dry start: The bearings on the left, farthest from the oil pump, show more damage

Result of a low oil supply or oil starvation

Severe wear as a result of inadequate oil clearance

Corrosion

Microscopic detail of corrosion

Corrosion is an acid attack on the bearing lining generally caused by inadequate maintenance, extremely hot or cold operation, or inferior oils or fuels

Microscopic detail of cavitation

Example of cavitation - a surface erosion caused by pressure changes in the oil film

Damage from excessive thrust or insufficient axial clearance

Bearing affected by oil dilution caused by excessive blow-by or a rich mixture

9.13 Install the piston ring into the cylinder then push it down into position using a piston so the ring will be square in the cylinder

9.14 With the ring square in the cylinder, measure the ring end gap with a feeler gauge

9.15 If the ring end gap is too small, clamp a file in a vise as shown and file the piston ring ends - be sure to remove all raised material

PISTON RING INSTALLATION

▶ **Refer to illustrations 9.13, 9.14, 9.15, 9.19a, 9.19b and 9.22**

11 Before installing the new piston rings, the ring end gaps must be checked. It's assumed that the piston ring side clearance has been checked and verified correct.

12 Lay out the piston/connecting rod assemblies and the new ring sets so the ring sets will be matched with the same piston and cylinder during the end gap measurement and engine assembly.

13 Insert the top (number one) ring into the first cylinder and square it up with the cylinder walls by pushing it in with the top of the piston (see illustration). The ring should be near the bottom of the cylinder, at the lower limit of ring travel.

14 To measure the end gap, slip feeler gauges between the ends of the ring until a gauge equal to the gap width is found (see illustration). The feeler gauge should slide between the ring ends with a slight amount of drag. A typical ring gap should fall between 0.010 and 0.020 inch [0.25 to 0.50 mm] for compression rings and up to 0.030 inch [0.76 mm] for the oil ring steel rails. If the gap is larger or smaller than specified, double-check to make sure you have the correct rings before proceeding.

15 If the gap is too small, it must be enlarged or the ring ends may come in contact with each other during engine operation, which can

cause serious damage to the engine. If necessary, increase the end gaps by filing the ring ends very carefully with a fine file. Mount the file in a vise equipped with soft jaws, slip the ring over the file with the ends contacting the file face and slowly move the ring to remove material from the ends. When performing this operation, file only by pushing the ring from the outside end of the file towards the vise (see illustration).

16 Excess end gap isn't critical unless it's greater than 0.040 inch (1.01 mm). Again, double-check to make sure you have the correct ring type.

17 Repeat the procedure for each ring that will be installed in the first cylinder and for each ring in the remaining cylinders. Remember to keep rings, pistons and cylinders matched up.

18 Once the ring end gaps have been checked/corrected, the rings can be installed on the pistons.

19 The oil control ring (lowest one on the piston) is usually installed first. It's composed of three separate components. Slip the spacer/expander into the groove (see illustration). If an anti-rotation tang is used, make sure it's inserted into the drilled hole in the ring groove. Next, install the lower side rail in the same manner (see illustration). Don't use a piston ring installation tool on the oil ring side rails, as they may be damaged. Instead, place one end of the side rail into the groove between the spacer/expander and the ring land, hold it firmly in

9.19a Installing the spacer/expander in the oil ring groove

9.19b DO NOT use a piston ring installation tool when installing the oil ring side rails

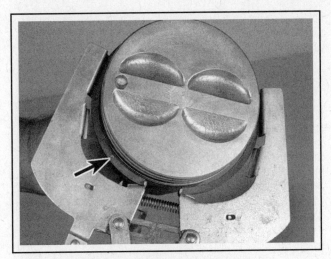

9.22 Use a piston ring installation tool to install the compression rings - on some engines the number two compression ring has a directional mark that must face toward the top of the piston

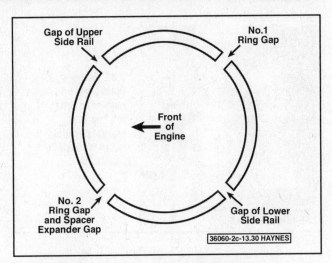

9.30 Position the piston ring end gaps as shown

place and slide a finger around the piston while pushing the rail into the groove. Finally, install the upper side rail.

20 After the three oil ring components have been installed, check to make sure that both the upper and lower side rails can be rotated smoothly inside the ring grooves.

21 The number two (middle) ring is installed next. It's usually stamped with a mark which must face up, toward the top of the piston. Do not mix up the top and middle rings, as they have different cross-sections.

➡**Note: Always follow the instructions printed on the ring package or box - different manufacturers may require different approaches.**

22 Use a piston ring installation tool and make sure the identification mark is facing the top of the piston, then slip the ring into the middle groove on the piston (see illustration). Don't expand the ring any more than necessary to slide it over the piston.

➡**Note: Be careful not to confuse the number one and number two rings.**

23 Install the number one (top) ring in the same manner.

24 Repeat the procedure for the remaining pistons and rings.

INSTALLATION

25 Before installing the piston/connecting rod assemblies, the cylinder walls must be perfectly clean, the top edge of each cylinder bore must be chamfered, and the crankshaft must be in place.

26 Remove the cap from the end of the number one connecting rod (refer to the marks made during removal). Remove the original bearing inserts and wipe the bearing surfaces of the connecting rod and cap with a clean, lint-free cloth. They must be kept spotlessly clean.

Connecting rod bearing oil clearance check

▸ **Refer to illustrations 9.30, 9.35, 9.37 and 9.41**

27 Clean the back side of the new upper bearing insert, then lay it in place in the connecting rod.

28 Make sure the tab on the bearing fits into the recess in the rod. Don't hammer the bearing insert into place and be very careful not to nick or gouge the bearing face. Don't lubricate the bearing at this time.

29 Clean the back side of the other bearing insert and install it in the

rod cap. Again, make sure the tab on the bearing fits into the recess in the cap, and don't apply any lubricant. It's critically important that the mating surfaces of the bearing and connecting rod are perfectly clean and oil free when they're assembled.

30 Position the piston ring gaps at the intervals around the piston as shown (see illustration).

31 Lubricate the piston and rings with clean engine oil and attach a piston ring compressor to the piston. Leave the skirt protruding about 1/4-inch to guide the piston into the cylinder. The rings must be compressed until they're flush with the piston.

32 Rotate the crankshaft until the number one connecting rod journal is at BDC (bottom dead center) and apply a liberal coat of engine oil to the cylinder walls. Refer to the TDC locating procedure in Chapter 2A, 2B or 2C for additional information.

33 With the "front" mark (letter F or arrow) on the piston facing the front (timing chain/timing belt end) of the engine, gently insert the piston/connecting rod assembly into the number one cylinder bore and rest the bottom edge of the ring compressor on the engine block.

➡**Note: Some engines have a letter "F" marking on the side of the piston near the wrist pin, others have an arrow, an "F" or a dimple or groove on the top of the piston. All of these are marks that indicate the front of the piston.**

34 Tap the top edge of the ring compressor to make sure it's contacting the block around its entire circumference.

35 Gently tap on the top of the piston with the end of a wooden or plastic hammer handle (see illustration) while guiding the end of the connecting rod into place on the crankshaft journal. The piston rings

9.35 Use a plastic or wooden hammer handle to push the piston into the cylinder

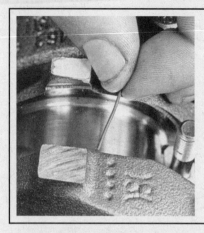

9.37 Place Plastigage on each connecting rod bearing journal parallel to the crankshaft centerline

may try to pop out of the ring compressor just before entering the cylinder bore, so keep some downward pressure on the ring compressor. Work slowly, and if any resistance is felt as the piston enters the cylinder, stop immediately. Find out what's hanging up and fix it before proceeding. Do not, for any reason, force the piston into the cylinder - you might break a ring and/or the piston.

36 Once the piston/connecting rod assembly is installed, the connecting rod bearing oil clearance must be checked before the rod cap is permanently installed.

37 Cut a piece of the appropriate size Plastigage slightly shorter than the width of the connecting rod bearing and lay it in place on the number one connecting rod journal, parallel with the journal axis (see illustration).

38 Clean the connecting rod cap bearing face and install the rod cap. Make sure the mating mark on the cap is on the same side as the mark on the connecting rod (see illustration 9.4).

39 Install the old rod bolts, at this time, and tighten them to the torque listed in this Chapter's Specifications.

➡**Note: Use a thin-wall socket to avoid erroneous torque readings that can result if the socket is wedged between the rod cap and the bolt or nut. If the socket tends to wedge itself between the fastener and the cap, lift up on it slightly until it no longer contacts the cap. DO NOT rotate the crankshaft at any time during this operation.**

40 Remove the fasteners and detach the rod cap, being very careful

not to disturb the Plastigage. Discard the cap bolts at this time as they cannot be reused.

➡**Note: You MUST use new connecting rod bolts.**

41 Compare the width of the crushed Plastigage to the scale printed on the Plastigage envelope to obtain the oil clearance (see illustration). The connecting rod bearing oil clearance is usually about 0.001 to 0.002 inch. Consult an automotive machine shop for the clearance specified for the rod bearings on your engine.

42 If the clearance is not as specified, the bearing inserts may be the wrong size (which means different ones will be required). Before deciding that different inserts are needed, make sure that no dirt or oil was between the bearing inserts and the connecting rod or cap when the clearance was measured. Also, recheck the journal diameter. If the Plastigage was wider at one end than the other, the journal may be tapered. If the clearance still exceeds the limit specified, the bearing will have to be replaced with an undersize bearing.

✳✳ CAUTION:

When installing a new crankshaft always use a standard size bearing.

Final installation

43 Carefully scrape all traces of the Plastigage material off the rod journal and/or bearing face. Be very careful not to scratch the bearing - use your fingernail or the edge of a plastic card.

44 Make sure the bearing faces are perfectly clean, then apply a uniform layer of clean moly-base grease or engine assembly lube to both of them. You'll have to push the piston into the cylinder to expose the face of the bearing insert in the connecting rod.

45 Slide the connecting rod back into place on the journal, install the rod cap, install the bolts and tighten them to the torque listed in this Chapter's Specifications.

✳✳ CAUTION:

Install new connecting rod cap bolts. Do NOT reuse old bolts - they have stretched and cannot be reused.

46 Repeat the entire procedure for the remaining pistons/connecting rods.

47 The important points to remember are:
  a) Keep the back sides of the bearing inserts and the insides of the connecting rods and caps perfectly clean when assembling them.
  b) Make sure you have the correct piston/rod assembly for each cylinder.
  c) The mark on the piston must face the front (timing chain end) of the engine.
  d) Lubricate the cylinder walls liberally with clean oil.
  e) Lubricate the bearing faces when installing the rod caps after the oil clearance has been checked.

48 After all the piston/connecting rod assemblies have been correctly installed, rotate the crankshaft a number of times by hand to check for any obvious binding.

49 As a final step, check the connecting rod endplay again. If it was correct before disassembly and the original crankshaft and rods were reinstalled, it should still be correct. If new rods or a new crankshaft were installed, the endplay may be inadequate. If so, the rods will have to be removed and taken to an automotive machine shop for resizing.

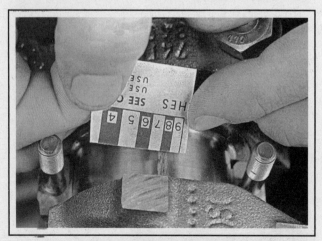

9.41 Use the scale on the Plastigage package to determine the bearing oil clearance - be sure to measure the widest part of the Plastigage and use the correct scale; it comes with both standard and metric scales

10 Crankshaft - removal and installation

REMOVAL

▶ **Refer to illustrations 10.1 and 10.3**

➡**Note: The crankshaft can be removed only after the engine has been removed from the vehicle. It's assumed that the driveplate, crankshaft pulley, timing chain/belt, oil pan, oil pump, oil filter and piston/connecting rod assemblies have already been removed. The rear main oil seal retainer must be unbolted and separated from the block before proceeding with crankshaft removal.**

1 Before the crankshaft is removed, measure the endplay. Mount a dial indicator with the indicator in line with the crankshaft and touching the end of the crankshaft (see illustration).

2 Pry the crankshaft all the way to the rear and zero the dial indicator. Next, pry the crankshaft to the front as far as possible and check the reading on the dial indicator. The distance traveled is the endplay. A typical crankshaft endplay will fall between 0.003 to 0.010 inch (0.076 to 0.254 mm). If it is greater than that, check the crankshaft thrust washer/bearing assembly surfaces for wear after it's removed. If no wear is evident, new main bearings should correct the endplay. Refer to Step 14 for the location of the thrust washer/bearing assembly on each engine.

3 If a dial indicator isn't available, feeler gauges can be used. Gently pry the crankshaft all the way to the front of the engine. Slip feeler gauges between the crankshaft and the front face of the thrust bearing or washer to determine the clearance (see illustration).

4 Loosen the main bearing cap bolts 1/4-turn at a time each, until they can be removed by hand.

➡**Note: The main bearing caps on the V8 engine are each secured by four bolts, two of which are accessed from the sides of the engine block.**

5 Gently tap the main bearing caps with a soft-face hammer around the perimeter of the assembly. Pull the main bearing cap assembly straight up and off the cylinder block. Try not to drop the bearing inserts if they come out with the assembly.

6 Carefully lift the crankshaft out of the engine. It may be a good idea to have an assistant available, since the crankshaft is quite heavy and awkward to handle. With the bearing inserts in place inside the engine block and main bearing caps, reinstall the main bearing cap assembly onto the engine block and tighten the bolts finger tight. Make sure you install the main bearing cap assembly with the arrow facing the front of the engine.

INSTALLATION

7 Crankshaft installation is the first step in engine reassembly. It's assumed at this point that the engine block and crankshaft have been cleaned, inspected and repaired or reconditioned.

8 Position the engine block with the bottom facing up.

9 Remove the mounting bolts and lift off the main bearing cap assembly.

10 If they're still in place, remove the original bearing inserts from the block and from the main bearing cap assembly. Wipe the bearing surfaces of the block and main bearing cap assembly with a clean, lint-free cloth. They must be kept spotlessly clean. This is critical for determining the correct bearing oil clearance.

MAIN BEARING OIL CLEARANCE CHECK

▶ **Refer to illustrations 10.14a, 10.14b, 10.17, 10.19a, 19.19b and 10.21**

11 Without mixing them up, clean the back sides of the new upper main bearing inserts (with grooves and oil holes) and lay one in each main bearing saddle in the block. Each upper bearing has an oil groove and oil hole in it.

☀ CAUTION:

The oil holes in the block must line up with the oil holes in the upper bearing inserts.

Clean the back sides of the lower main bearing inserts and lay them in the corresponding location in the main bearing cap. Make sure the tab on the bearing insert fits into the recess in the block or main bearing cap. The upper bearings with the oil holes are installed into the engine block while the lower bearings without the oil holes are installed in the caps.

10.1 Checking crankshaft endplay with a dial indicator

10.3 Checking crankshaft endplay with feeler gauges at the thrust bearing journal

10.14a Thrust washer identification

※※ **CAUTION:**

Do not hammer the bearing insert into place and don't nick or gouge the bearing faces. DO NOT apply any lubrication at this time.

12 Clean the faces of the bearing inserts in the block and the crankshaft main bearing journals with a clean, lint-free cloth.

13 Check or clean the oil holes in the crankshaft, as any dirt here can go only one way - straight through the new bearings.

14 Once you're certain the crankshaft is clean, carefully lay it in position in the cylinder block. Locate the thrust washers (see illustrations).

a) On 2.7L V6 engines, the thrust washers are located on the number 3 main journal.

b) On 3.5L V6 engines, the thrust washers are located on the number 2 main journal.

c) On V8 engines, the thrust washers are located on the number 3 main journal.

The thrust washers must be installed in the correct journal (counting from the front of the engine).

➡Note: Install the thrust washers with the groove in the thrust washer facing the crankshaft with the smooth sides facing the main bearing saddle.

10.14b Insert the thrust washer into the machined surface between the crankshaft and the upper bearing saddle, then rotate it down into the block until it's flush with the parting line on the main bearing saddle - make sure the oil grooves on the thrust washer face the crankshaft

15 Before the crankshaft can be permanently installed, the main bearing oil clearance must be checked.

16 Cut several strips of the appropriate size of Plastigage. They must be slightly shorter than the width of the main bearing journal.

17 Place one piece on each crankshaft main bearing journal, parallel with the journal axis as shown (see illustration).

18 Clean the faces of the bearing inserts in the main bearing caps. Hold the bearing inserts in place and install the inserts onto the crankshaft and cylinder block. DO NOT disturb the Plastigage. Make sure you install the main bearing cap with the arrow facing the front (timing chain/timing belt end) of the engine.

19 Apply clean engine oil to all bolt threads prior to installation, then install all bolts finger-tight. Tighten main bearing cap bolts in the sequence shown (see illustrations) progressing in steps, to the torque listed in this Chapter's Specifications. DO NOT rotate the crankshaft at any time during this operation.

20 Remove the bolts in the reverse order of the tightening sequence and carefully lift the main bearing cap assembly straight up and off the block. Do not disturb the Plastigage or rotate the crankshaft. If the main

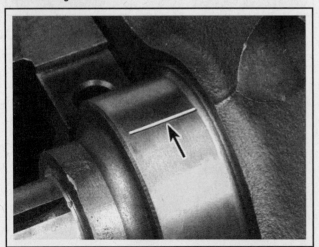

10.17 Place the Plastigage onto the crankshaft bearing journal as shown

10.19a Main bearing cap bolt tightening sequence on the V6 engine

Front of Engine

30042-2E-10.19c HAYNES

10.19b Main bearing cap and crossbolt tightening sequence on the V8 engine

10.21 Use the scale on the Plastigage package to determine the bearing oil clearance - be sure to measure the widest part of the Plastigage and use the correct scale; it comes with both standard and metric scales

bearing cap assembly is difficult to remove, tap it gently from side-to-side with a soft-face hammer to loosen it.

21 Compare the width of the crushed Plastigage on each journal to the scale printed on the Plastigage envelope to determine the main bearing oil clearance (see illustration). A typical main bearing oil clearance should fall between 0.0015 and 0.0023-inch. Check with an automotive machine shop for the clearance for your engine.

22 If the clearance is not as specified, the bearing inserts may be the wrong size (which means different ones will be required). Before deciding if different inserts are needed, make sure that no dirt or oil was between the bearing inserts and the cap assembly or block when the clearance was measured. If the Plastigage was wider at one end than the other, the crankshaft journal may be tapered. If the clearance still exceeds the limit specified, the bearing insert(s) will have to be replaced with an undersize bearing insert(s).

✳✳ CAUTION:

When installing a new crankshaft always install a standard bearing insert set.

23 Carefully scrape all traces of the Plastigage material off the main bearing journals and/or the bearing insert faces. Be sure to remove all residue from the oil holes. Use your fingernail or the edge of a plastic card - don't nick or scratch the bearing faces.

FINAL INSTALLATION

24 Carefully lift the crankshaft out of the cylinder block.

25 Clean the bearing insert faces in the cylinder block, then apply a thin, uniform layer of moly-base grease or engine assembly lube to each of the bearing surfaces. Be sure to coat the thrust faces as well as the journal face of the thrust washers.

➡Note: Install the thrust washers after the crankshaft has been installed.

26 Make sure the crankshaft journals are clean, then lay the crankshaft back in place in the cylinder block.

27 Clean the bearing insert faces and then apply the same lubricant to them. Clean the engine block thoroughly. The surfaces must be free of oil residue. Install the thrust washers.

28 Install each main bearing cap onto the crankshaft and cylinder block. On the 5.7L V8 engine, make sure the arrow on each main bearing cap faces the front of the engine.

29 Prior to installation, apply clean engine oil to all bolt threads wiping off any excess, then install all bolts finger-tight.

30 Tighten the main bearing cap bolts to the torque listed in this Chapter's Specifications (in the proper sequence) (see illustrations 10.19a and 10.19b).

31 Recheck crankshaft endplay with a feeler gauge or a dial indicator. The endplay should be correct if the crankshaft thrust faces aren't worn or damaged and if new bearings have been installed.

32 Rotate the crankshaft a number of times by hand to check for any obvious binding. It should rotate with a running torque of 50 in-lbs or less. If the running torque is too high, identify and correct the problem at this time.

33 Install the new rear main oil seal (see Chapter 2A, 2B or 2C).

11 Engine overhaul - reassembly sequence

1   Before beginning engine reassembly, make sure you have all the necessary new parts, gaskets and seals as well as the following items on hand:

Common hand tools
A 1/2-inch drive torque wrench
New engine oil
Gasket sealant
Thread locking compound

2   If you obtained a short block it will be necessary to install the cylinder head, the oil pump and pick-up tube, the oil pan, the water pump, the timing chain and timing cover, and the valve cover (see Chapter 2A, 2B or 2C). In order to save time and avoid problems, the external components must be installed in the following general order:

Thermostat and housing cover
Water pump
Intake and exhaust manifolds
Fuel injection components
Emission control components
Spark plugs
Ignition coils
Oil filter
Engine mounts and mount brackets
Driveplate

12 Initial start-up and break-in after overhaul

✳✳ WARNING:

Have a fire extinguisher handy when starting the engine for the first time.

1   Once the engine has been installed in the vehicle, double-check the engine oil and coolant levels.

2   With the spark plugs out of the engine and the ignition system and fuel pump disabled, crank the engine until oil pressure registers on the gauge or the light goes out.

3   Install the spark plugs and ignition coils, and reinstall the fuel pump relay.

4   Start the engine. It may take a few moments for the fuel system to build up pressure, but the engine should start without a great deal of effort.

5   After the engine starts, it should be allowed to warm up to normal operating temperature. While the engine is warming up, make a thorough check for fuel, oil and coolant leaks.

6   Shut the engine off and recheck the engine oil and coolant levels.

7   Drive the vehicle to an area with minimum traffic, accelerate from 30 to 50 mph, then allow the vehicle to slow to 30 mph with the throttle closed. Repeat the procedure 10 or 12 times. This will load the piston rings and cause them to seat properly against the cylinder walls. Check again for oil and coolant leaks.

8   Drive the vehicle gently for the first 500 miles (no sustained high speeds) and keep a constant check on the oil level. It is not unusual for an engine to use oil during the break-in period.

9   At approximately 500 to 600 miles, change the oil and filter.

10 For the next few hundred miles, drive the vehicle normally. Do not pamper it or abuse it.

11 After 2,000 miles, change the oil and filter again and consider the engine broken in.

Specifications

General

Displacement

2.7L V6 engine	167 cubic inches
3.5L V6 engine	214 cubic inches
V8 engine	345 cubic inches

Bore and stroke

2.7L V6 engine	3.386 x 3.091 inches
3.5L V6 engine	3.780 x 3.189 inches
V8 engine	3.92 x 3.58 inches

Cylinder compression pressure

V6 engines

Minimum	170 psi
Maximum variation between cylinders	40 psi
V8 engine	Not available, but pressure should not vary more than 40 psi between cylinders

Oil pump pressure

V6 engines

Minimum pressure at curb idle	5 psi
Operating pressure	45 to 105 psi at 3,000 rpm

V8 engine

Minimum pressure at curb idle	4 psi
Operating pressure	25 to 110 psi at 3,000 rpm

Torque specifications   Ft-lbs (unless otherwise indicated)

Connecting rod cap bolts

V6 engines

Step 1	20
Step 2	Tighten an additional 90-degrees

V8 engine

Step 1	15
Step 2	Tighten an additional 90-degrees

Connecting rod cap bolts

Main bearing cap bolts

V6 engines (see illustration 10.19a)

Inner main bearing cap bolts

Step 1	15
Step 2	Tighten an additional 90-degrees

Outer main (windage tray) bearing cap bolts

Step 1	20
Step 2	Tighten an additional 90-degrees
Main bearing cap cross bolts	21

V8 engine* (see illustration 10.19b)

Step 1, bolts 1 through 10	20
Step 2, bolts 1 through 10	Tighten an additional 90-degrees
Step 3, crossbolts 11 through 20	21
Step 4, crossbolts 11 through 20	21 (re-check)

Install a new washer/seal onto each crossbolt before tightening. First, install main bearing bolts and main bearing crossbolts all finger tight. Next tighten the main bearing bolts completely (Steps 1 and 2) before tightening the crossbolts

GLOSSARY

B

Backlash - The amount of play between two parts. Usually refers to how much one gear can be moved back and forth without moving gear with which it's meshed.

Bearing Caps - The caps held in place by nuts or bolts which, in turn, hold the bearing surface. This space is for lubricating oil to enter.

Bearing clearance - The amount of space left between shaft and bearing surface. This space is for lubricating oil to enter.

Bearing crush - The additional height which is purposely manufactured into each bearing half to ensure complete contact of the bearing back with the housing bore when the engine is assembled.

Bearing knock - The noise created by movement of a part in a loose or worn bearing.

Blueprinting - Dismantling an engine and reassembling it to EXACT specifications.

Bore - An engine cylinder, or any cylindrical hole; also used to describe the process of enlarging or accurately refinishing a hole with a cutting tool, as to bore an engine cylinder. The bore size is the diameter of the hole.

Boring - Renewing the cylinders by cutting them out to a specified size. A boring bar is used to make the cut.

Bottom end - A term which refers collectively to the engine block, crankshaft, main bearings and the big ends of the connecting rods.

Break-in - The period of operation between installation of new or rebuilt parts and time in which parts are worn to the correct fit. Driving at reduced and varying speed for a specified mileage to permit parts to wear to the correct fit.

Bushing - A one-piece sleeve placed in a bore to serve as a bearing surface for shaft, piston pin, etc. Usually replaceable.

C

Camshaft - The shaft in the engine, on which a series of lobes are located for operating the valve mechanisms. The camshaft is driven by gears or sprockets and a timing chain. Usually referred to simply as the cam.

Carbon - Hard, or soft, black deposits found in combustion chamber, on plugs, under rings, on and under valve heads.

Cast iron - An alloy of iron and more than two percent carbon, used for engine blocks and heads because it's relatively inexpensive and easy to mold into complex shapes.

Chamfer - To bevel across (or a bevel on) the sharp edge of an object.

Chase - To repair damaged threads with a tap or die.

Combustion chamber - The space between the piston and the cylinder head, with the piston at top dead center, in which air-fuel mixture is burned.

Compression ratio - The relationship between cylinder volume (clearance volume) when the piston is at top dead center and cylinder volume when the piston is at bottom dead center.

Connecting rod - The rod that connects the crank on the crankshaft with the piston. Sometimes called a con rod.

Connecting rod cap - The part of the connecting rod assembly that attaches the rod to the crankpin.

Core plug - Soft metal plug used to plug the casting holes for the coolant passages in the block.

Crankcase - The lower part of the engine in which the crankshaft rotates; includes the lower section of the cylinder block and the oil pan.

Crank kit - A reground or reconditioned crankshaft and new main and connecting rod bearings.

Crankpin - The part of a crankshaft to which a connecting rod is attached.

Crankshaft - The main rotating member, or shaft, running the length of the crankcase, with offset throws to which the connecting rods are attached; changes the reciprocating motion of the pistons into rotating motion.

Cylinder sleeve - A replaceable sleeve, or liner, pressed into the cylinder block to form the cylinder bore.

D

Deburring - Removing the burrs (rough edges or areas) from a bearing.

Deglazer - A tool, rotated by an electric motor, used to remove glaze from cylinder walls so a new set of rings will seat.

E

Endplay - The amount of lengthwise movement between two parts. As applied to a crankshaft, the distance that the crankshaft can move forward and back in the cylinder block.

F

Face - A machinist's term that refers to removing metal from the end of a shaft or the face of a larger part, such as a flywheel.

Fatigue - A breakdown of material through a large number of loading and unloading cycles. The first signs are cracks followed shortly by breaks.

Feeler gauge - A thin strip of hardened steel, ground to an exact thickness, used to check clearances between parts.

Free height - The unloaded length or height of a spring.

Freeplay - The looseness in a linkage, or an assembly of parts, between the initial application of force and actual movement. Usually perceived as slop or slight delay.

Freeze plug - See Core plug.

G

Gallery - A large passage in the block that forms a reservoir for engine oil pressure.

Glaze - The very smooth, glassy finish that develops on cylinder walls while an engine is in service.

H

Heli-Coil - A rethreading device used when threads are worn or damaged. The device is installed in a retapped hole to reduce the thread size to the original size.

I

Installed height - The spring's measured length or height, as installed on the cylinder head. Installed height is measured from the spring seat to the underside of the spring retainer.

J

Journal - The surface of a rotating shaft which turns in a bearing.

K

Keeper - The split lock that holds the valve spring retainer in position on the valve stem.

Key - A small piece of metal inserted into matching grooves machined into two parts fitted together - such as a gear pressed onto a shaft - which prevents slippage between the two parts.

Knock - The heavy metallic engine sound, produced in the combustion chamber as a result of abnormal combustion - usually detonation. Knock is usually caused by a loose or worn bearing. Also referred to as detonation, pinging and spark knock. Connecting rod or main bearing knocks are created by too much oil clearance or insufficient lubrication.

L

Lands - The portions of metal between the piston ring grooves.

Lapping the valves - Grinding a valve face and its seat together with lapping compound.

Lash - The amount of free motion in a gear train, between gears, or in a mechanical assembly, that occurs before movement can begin. Usually refers to the lash in a valve train.

Lifter - The part that rides against the cam to transfer motion to the rest of the valve train.

M

Machining - The process of using a machine to remove metal from a metal part.

Main bearings - The plain, or babbitt, bearings that support the crankshaft.

Main bearing caps - The cast iron caps, bolted to the bottom of the block, that support the main bearings.

O

O.D. - Outside diameter.

Oil gallery - A pipe or drilled passageway in the engine used to carry engine oil from one area to another.

Oil ring - The lower ring, or rings, of a piston; designed to prevent excessive amounts of oil from working up the cylinder walls and into the combustion chamber. Also called an oil-control ring.

Oil seal - A seal which keeps oil from leaking out of a compartment. Usually refers to a dynamic seal around a rotating shaft or other moving part.

O-ring - A type of sealing ring made of a special rubberlike material; in use, the O-ring is compressed into a groove to provide the sealing action.

Overhaul - To completely disassemble a unit, clean and inspect all parts, reassemble it with the original or new parts and make all adjustments necessary for proper operation.

P

Pilot bearing - A small bearing installed in the center of the flywheel (or the rear end of the crankshaft) to support the front end of the input shaft of the transmission.

Pip mark - A little dot or indentation which indicates the top side of a compression ring.

Piston - The cylindrical part, attached to the connecting rod, that moves up and down in the cylinder as the crankshaft rotates. When the fuel charge is fired, the piston transfers the force of the explosion to the connecting rod, then to the crankshaft.

Piston pin (or wrist pin) - The cylindrical and usually hollow steel pin that passes through the piston. The piston pin fastens the piston to the upper end of the connecting rod.

Piston ring - The split ring fitted to the groove in a piston. The ring contacts the sides of the ring groove and also rubs against the cylinder wall, thus sealing space between piston and wall. There are two types of rings: Compression rings seal the compression pressure in the combustion chamber; oil rings scrape excessive oil off the cylinder wall.

Piston ring groove - The slots or grooves cut in piston heads to hold piston rings in position.

Piston skirt - The portion of the piston below the rings and the piston pin hole.

Plastigage - A thin strip of plastic thread, available in different sizes, used for measuring clearances. For example, a strip of plastigage is laid across a bearing journal and mashed as parts are assembled. Then parts are disassembled and the width of the strip is measured to determine clearance between journal and bearing. Commonly used to measure crankshaft main-bearing and connecting rod bearing clearances.

Press-fit - A tight fit between two parts that requires pressure to force the parts together. Also referred to as drive, or force, fit.

Prussian blue - A blue pigment; in solution, useful in determining the area of contact between two surfaces. Prussian blue is commonly used to determine the width and location of the contact area between the valve face and the valve seat.

R

Race (bearing) - The inner or outer ring that provides a contact surface for balls or rollers in bearing.

Ream - To size, enlarge or smooth a hole by using a round cutting tool with fluted edges.

Ring job - The process of reconditioning the cylinders and installing new rings.

Runout - Wobble. The amount a shaft rotates out-of-true.

S

Saddle - The upper main bearing seat.

Scored - Scratched or grooved, as a cylinder wall may be scored by abrasive particles moved up and down by the piston rings.

Scuffing - A type of wear in which there's a transfer of material between parts moving against each other; shows up as pits or grooves in the mating surfaces.

Seat - The surface upon which another part rests or seats. For example, the valve seat is the matched surface upon which the valve face rests. Also used to refer to wearing into a good fit; for example, piston rings seat after a few miles of driving.

Short block - An engine block complete with crankshaft and piston and, usually, camshaft assemblies.

Static balance - The balance of an object while it's stationary.

Step - The wear on the lower portion of a ring land caused by excessive side and back-clearance. The height of the step indicates the ring's extra side clearance and the length of the step projecting from the back wall of the groove represents the ring's back clearance.

Stroke - The distance the piston moves when traveling from top dead center to bottom dead center, or from bottom dead center to top dead center.

Stud - A metal rod with threads on both ends.

T

Tang - A lip on the end of a plain bearing used to align the bearing during assembly.

Tap - To cut threads in a hole. Also refers to the fluted tool used to cut threads.

Taper - A gradual reduction in the width of a shaft or hole; in an engine cylinder, taper usually takes the form of uneven wear, more pronounced at the top than at the bottom.

Throws - The offset portions of the crankshaft to which the connecting rods are affixed.

Thrust bearing - The main bearing that has thrust faces to prevent excessive end-play, or forward and backward movement of the crankshaft.

Thrust washer - A bronze or hardened steel washer placed between two moving parts. The washer prevents longitudinal movement and provides a bearing surface for thrust surfaces of parts.

Tolerance - The amount of variation permitted from an exact size of measurement. Actual amount from smallest acceptable dimension to largest acceptable dimension.

U

Umbrella - An oil deflector placed near the valve tip to throw oil from the valve stem area.

Undercut - A machined groove below the normal surface.

Undersize bearings - Smaller diameter bearings used with re-ground crankshaft journals.

V

Valve grinding - Refacing a valve in a valve-refacing machine.

Valve train - The valve-operating mechanism of an engine; includes all components from the camshaft to the valve.

Vibration damper - A cylindrical weight attached to the front of the crankshaft to minimize torsional vibration (the twist-untwist actions of the crankshaft caused by the cylinder firing impulses). Also called a harmonic balancer.

W

Water jacket - The spaces around the cylinders, between the inner and outer shells of the cylinder block or head, through which coolant circulates.

Web - A supporting structure across a cavity.

Woodruff key - A key with a radiused backside (viewed from the side).

Notes

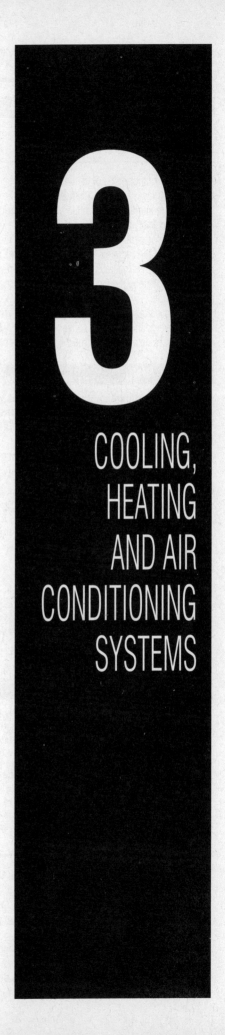

3

COOLING, HEATING AND AIR CONDITIONING SYSTEMS

Section

Reference to other Chapters

1 General information

ENGINE COOLING SYSTEM

The main components of the cooling system consist of a radiator, an expansion tank, a pressure cap (located on the expansion tank), a thermostat, temperature-controlled electric cooling fans and a belt or chain-driven water pump.

The radiator cooling fans are mounted in a housing/shroud at the engine side of the radiator. It is designed to come on when the engine reaches a certain temperature, and shut off again when the engine cools down some, thereby keeping the engine in the desired operating-temperature range.

The expansion tank functions somewhat differently than a conventional recovery tank. It is pressurized and equipped with a pressure cap on top and it's designed to purge air from the coolant.

✳✳ WARNING:

Unlike a conventional coolant recovery tank, the pressure cap on the expansion tank should never be opened after the engine has warmed up, because of the danger of severe burns caused by steam or scalding coolant.

Coolant circulates through the cylinder block and heads around the combustion chambers and valve seats, flows out of the cylinder head into the radiator and heater core.

When the engine is cold, the thermostat restricts the circulation of coolant to the radiator. When the minimum operating temperature is reached, the thermostat begins to open, allowing coolant to flow through the radiator.

All vehicles covered in this manual are equipped with a transmission oil cooler that is integrated with the air conditioning condenser mounted to the radiator. Hot transmission fluid is directed to the cooler by lines and hoses. Once cooled, the fluid is directed back to the transmission.

HEATING SYSTEM

The heating system consists of a blower fan and a heater core located in an air conditioning and heater housing under the dash with hoses connecting the heater core to the engine cooling system. Hot engine coolant is circulated through the heater core. When the heater is activated, a flap door opens in the housing and directs warm air to the passenger compartment. A fan switch on the heater/air conditioning control activates the blower motor, which creates the flow of warm air into the cab.

AIR CONDITIONING SYSTEM

The air conditioning system consists of a condenser (mounted in front of the radiator), an evaporator (mounted adjacent to the heater core under the dash), a compressor (mounted on the engine), a receiver-drier (mounted to the condenser) and the plumbing that connects all of these components.

A blower fan forces the warmer air of the passenger compartment through an evaporator core (sort of a radiator-in-reverse), transferring the heat from the air to the refrigerant. The liquid refrigerant boils off into low-pressure vapor, taking the heat with it when it leaves the evaporator.

2 Antifreeze/coolant - general information

▶ Refer to illustration 2.3

✳✳ WARNING:

Do not allow antifreeze to come in contact with your skin or painted surfaces of the vehicle. Rinse off spills immediately with plenty of water. Antifreeze is highly toxic if ingested. Never leave antifreeze lying around in an open container or in puddles on the floor; children and pets are attracted by its sweet smell and may drink it. Check with local authorities about disposing of used antifreeze. Many communities have collection centers which will see that antifreeze is disposed of safely. Never dump used antifreeze on the ground or pour it into drains. Keep antifreeze containers covered and repair leaks in your cooling system as soon as they are noticed.

These models use only Mopar 5 year/100,000 mile coolant or equivalent with a hybrid organic acid technology (HOAT) type antifreeze. Never mix different types or colors of coolants or damage to the cooling system can occur. Refer to the Specifications listed in Chapter 1 for the correct type of coolant.

Before adding antifreeze, check all hose connections, because antifreeze tends to leak through very minute openings. Engines don't normally consume coolant, so if the level goes down, find the cause and correct it.

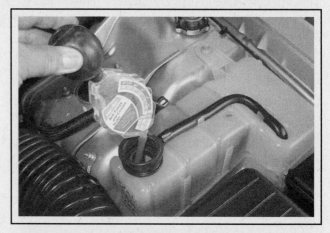

2.3 An inexpensive hydrometer can be used to test the condition of your coolant

The exact mixture of antifreeze-to-water which you should use depends on the manufacturer's recommendation. Consult the mixture ratio chart on the antifreeze container before adding coolant. Hydrometers are available at most auto parts stores to test the coolant (see illustration).

3   Thermostat - check and replacement

❋❋ WARNING:

Do not remove the radiator or expansion tank cap, drain the coolant or replace the thermostat until the engine has cooled completely.

➡Note: On V6 engines, the thermostat is located on the lower left side of the engine and connected to large diameter coolant hose. On V8 engines, the thermostat is located at the top front area of the engine at the intake manifold and connected to a large diameter coolant hose.

CHECK

1   Before assuming the thermostat is to blame for a cooling system problem, check the coolant level, drivebelt tension (see Chapter 1) and temperature gauge operation.

2   If the engine seems to be taking a long time to warm up (based on heater output or temperature gauge operation), the thermostat is probably stuck open. Replace the thermostat with a new one.

➡Note: It is very likely that a diagnostic trouble code (DTC) will be stored in the memory of the Powertrain Control Module (PCM) if the thermostat has failed. Refer to Chapter 6 for more information regarding DTCs.

3   If the engine runs hot, use your hand to check the temperature of the radiator hose that leads from the thermostat to the radiator. If the hose isn't hot, but the engine is, the thermostat is probably stuck closed, preventing the coolant inside the engine from escaping to the radiator. Replace the thermostat.

❋❋ CAUTION:

Don't drive the vehicle without a thermostat. On some models the computer may stay in open-loop, potentially causing oil sludge, and excessive exhaust emissions/fuel consumption.

4   If the inlet radiator hose is hot, it means that the coolant is flowing and the thermostat is open. Consult the *Troubleshooting* section at the front of this manual for cooling system diagnosis.

REPLACEMENT

5   Disconnect the cable from the negative battery terminal (see Chapter 5, Section 1).

6   Drain the cooling system (see Chapter 1). If the coolant is relatively new or in good condition, save it and reuse it (see Section 2).

7   Remove the air cleaner housing (see Chapter 4).

➡Note: Skip this step for 5.7L V8 engine (Hemi) models.

8   Squeeze the tabs on the hose clamp to loosen it from the hose(s), then reposition the clamp several inches back up the hose. Detach the hose(s) from the thermostat housing.

➡Note: Special hose clamp pliers are available at most auto parts stores. If the hose is stuck, grasp it near the end with a pair of adjustable pliers and twist it to break the seal, then pull it off. If the hose is old or deteriorated, cut it off and install a new one.

9   If the outer surface of the thermostat housing that mates with the hose is deteriorated (corroded, pitted, etc.) it may be damaged further

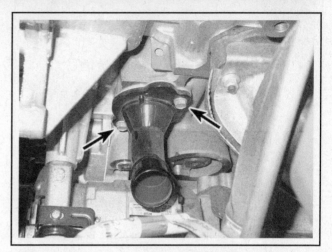

3.16 The thermostat housing cover fasteners on the 3.5L V6 engine - other models are similar

by hose removal. If it is, the thermostat housing (or housing cover) will have to be replaced.

2.7L V6 engines

10   Loosen the bolt at the starter motor that holds the small heater tube bracket that leads to the thermostat housing.

11   Remove the heater tube flange mounting nuts from the thermostat housing, disconnect the tube and move it aside.

12   Remove the thermostat housing cover fasteners and remove the housing. Note the position of the thermostat and where the small valve is located, because it must be installed in the same position.

13   Remove the thermostat and discard the O-ring seal on the housing. If the housing is stuck, tap it with a soft-face hammer to jar it loose. Be prepared for some coolant to spill as the gasket seal is broken.

14   Note how the thermostat is installed (which end is facing up, or out, and the position of the air bleed "jiggle valve," if equipped).

3.5L V6 engines

▶ **Refer to illustrations 3.16, 3.17a and 3.17b**

15   Disconnect the electrical connectors from the nearby engine oil and power steering pressure switches.

➡Note: It may be necessary to raise the front of the vehicle on 3.5L engine models for access to the thermostat and surrounding components.

16   Remove the thermostat housing cover mounting fasteners (see illustration).

17   Remove the thermostat housing cover and thermostat. The thermostat will come out with the housing cover if it is the original one installed.

➡Note: The original thermostat is 'staked' or 'swaged' into place and the housing and thermostat are keyed so that the thermostat fits into the housing in one position when placed in the right direction (with the large spring towards the engine) (see illustration). The distorted metal on the housing must be carefully removed for the replacement thermostat to fit properly (see illustration). There is no need to stake or swage the replacement thermostat.

18   Remove the gasket from the engine block and discard it.

3.17a Thermostat mounting details on a 3.5L V6 engine:

1 Swaged area of thermostat housing
2 Key for thermostat and housing

5.7L V8 (Hemi) engines

19 Remove the thermostat housing cover fasteners and remove the cover.

20 Remove the thermostat and seal.

➡**Note: The seal and thermostat are serviced as an assembly.**

All models

21 Clean all mating surfaces before beginning any reassembly.

22 Install a new gasket or seal, as applicable.

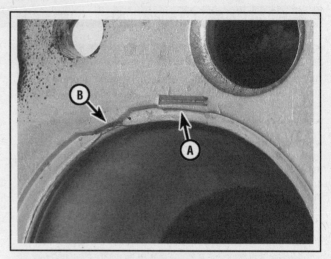

3.17b Remove the distorted metal from the swaged area of the housing (A) so the replacement thermostat will fit correctly; but leave the housing/thermostat key as shown (B)

23 The remainder of installation is the reverse of removal. Make sure that the replacement thermostat is installed in the same direction and position as the one removed. Tighten the thermostat housing cover bolts to the torque listed in this Chapter's Specifications.

24 Reattach the hose(s) to the housing cover and fitting(s), then tighten the hose clamp(s) securely.

25 Refill the cooling system (see Chapter 1).

26 Start the engine and allow it to reach normal operating temperature, then check for leaks and proper thermostat operation.

4 Engine cooling fans - check and component replacement

❄❄ WARNING:

To avoid possible injury or damage, DO NOT operate the engine with a damaged fan. Do not attempt to repair fan blades - replace a damaged fan with a new one.

CHECK

▶ **Refer to illustrations 4.2 and 4.3**

1 These models are equipped with two cooling fans mounted side-by-side behind the radiator. The PCM (Powertrain Control Module - engine computer) and three relays are used to operate the fans at Low or High speeds depending on engine needs and other conditions. The fans are protected by fuses inside the engine compartment's fuse/relay box.

2 If the engine is overheating and neither of the cooling fans operate, check the fuses for the fans. Locate the fuses in the engine compartment fuse/relay box (see illustration). Remove the fuse(s) and check them for continuity (see Chapter 12).

3 If the fuses test good, check each cooling fan motor by unplugging the fan motor electrical connector and applying battery power directly to the motor terminals with fused jumper wires (see illustration). When done correctly, the fan should come on. If a fan motor

4.2 The cooling fan fuses (A) and relays (B) are located in the fuse/relay box in the engine compartment

doesn't work, replace the motor.

4 If the fan motors are okay but are still not coming on when the engine gets hot, the fan relays might be defective. Locate the relays in the engine compartment's fuse/relay box (see illustration 4.2). You can

4.3 To test either fan motor, disconnect the electrical connector and use jumper wires to connect the fan directly to the battery (B) and ground (A) - if the fan still doesn't work, replace the motor

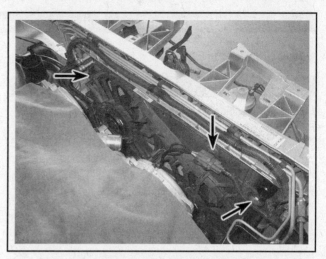

4.9 The location of the main cooling fan electrical connector and the fan assembly mounting fasteners

4.12 The (reverse threaded) fan blade mounting nut (A) and the fan motor mounting fasteners (B) (one fastener is hidden from view)

4.14 A fan assembly lower mount at the radiator

pull each relay out and test them individually (see Chapter 12).

➡**Note: Relays are used to control a circuit by turning it on and off in response to a signal from the PCM. The control circuits themselves are fairly complex, and checking them should be left to a dealer service department. It's also likely that a failure in one of these circuits will result in setting a Diagnostic Trouble Code (DTC) in the PCM which will require a scan tool to retrieve. For more information on DTC retrieval, see Chapter 6.**

5   If the fuses, motors and relays are functional, check all wiring and connections to the fan motors. If no obvious problems are found, have the cooling fan system and circuit diagnosed by a dealer service department or repair shop with the proper diagnostic equipment.

COMPONENT REPLACEMENT

▸ **Refer to illustrations 4.9, 4.12 and 4.14**

✳✳ WARNING:

Wail until the engine is completely cool before beginning this procedure.

6   Disconnect the cable from the negative battery terminal (see Chapter 5, Section 1), then disconnect the cooling fan electrical connector.

7   Partially drain the cooling system (see Chapter 1).

8   Remove the upper radiator hose (see Section 6).

9   Disconnect the cooling fan electrical connector (see illustration).

10   Remove the cooling fan shroud assembly mounting fasteners (see illustration 4.9).

11   Remove the cooling fan assembly by pulling it straight up and out of the engine compartment.

12   If you are replacing a motor, remove the fan blade mounting nut to separate it from the motor.

➡**Note: The nut for the fan blade is reverse threaded; turning the nut clockwise will remove it (see illustration).**

13   Remove the mounting fasteners for the motor and separate it from the shroud assembly.

14   Installation is the reverse of removal. Be sure to engage the bottom of the fan assembly with the plastic mounts that hold it to the bottom of the radiator (see illustration).

5 Coolant expansion tank - removal and installation

▸ Refer to illustration 5.2

❊ WARNING:

Wait until the engine is completely cool before beginning this procedure.

1   Drain the cooling system (see Chapter 1). If the coolant is relatively new and still in good condition, it can be saved and reused.

➡ **Note: Be careful to clean up any spilled coolant as stated in the Warning at the beginning of Section 2.**

2   Disconnect the expansion tank hoses by sliding the hose clamp away with pliers and then removing the hose from the tank fitting (see illustration).

3   Remove the expansion tank mounting fasteners (see illustration 5.2).

4   Clean out the tank with soapy water and a brush to remove any deposits inside. Inspect the tank carefully for cracks. If you find a crack, replace the tank.

5   Installation is the reverse of removal. Refill the cooling system with the proper concentration of antifreeze (see Chapter 1).

5.2 The expansion tank mounting fasteners (A) and hoses (B)

6 Radiator - removal and installation

❊ WARNING:

Wait until the engine is completely cool before beginning this procedure.

REMOVAL

▸ **Refer to illustrations 6.3, 6.4, 6.8, 6.9, 6.10 and 6.13**

1   Disconnect the cable from the negative battery terminal (see Chapter 5, Section 1).

2   Drain the cooling system (see Chapter 1). If the coolant is rela-

tively new or in good condition, save it and reuse it.

3   Remove the upper radiator hose (see illustration).

4   Remove the plastic panels between the radiator support and the top front of the front cover (see illustration).

5   Remove the cooling fan assembly (see Section 4).

6   Raise the front of the vehicle and support it securely on jackstands.

7   Remove the lower engine splash shield (see Chapter 2).

8   Remove the lower radiator hose (see illustration).

9   Remove the lower mounting fasteners that attach the air conditioning condenser to the radiator (see illustration).

10 Remove the radiator mounting brackets from the radiator support (see illustration).

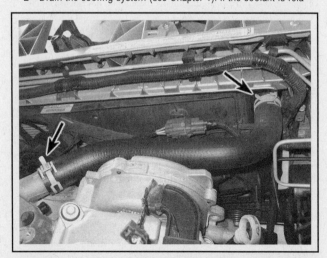

6.3 Location of the upper radiator hose and clamps (3.5L V6 engine shown, others similar)

6.4 Pull up on the panels to release them from their retaining clips

6.8 Location of the lower radiator hose clamp (3.5L V6 engine shown, others similar)

6.9 The location of the air conditioning condenser mounting fasteners (front bumper cover and air deflectors removed for clarity)

✱✱ CAUTION:

Use hand tools on the mounting bolts because they may be treated with thread locking compound.

11 Remove the upper mounting fasteners for the air conditioning condenser and carefully separate the condenser from the radiator (see illustration 6.9).

➡**Note: It may be necessary to remove the fasteners for the plastic air deflectors and move them aside to gain access to the upper condenser fasteners.**

12 Tilt the radiator towards the engine and lift it from the engine compartment. Be careful not to damage the air-flow seals on the top and bottom of the radiator, spill coolant on the vehicle or scratch the paint.

13 Whenever the radiator is removed from the vehicle, make note of the location of all rubber mounting bushings and their condition (see illustration). If they're cracked, hardened or otherwise deteriorated, replace them.

INSTALLATION

14 With the radiator removed, it can be inspected for leaks and damage. If it needs repair, have a radiator shop or dealer service department perform the work, as special tools and techniques are required.

15 Bugs and dirt can be removed from the front of the radiator with a garden hose, followed by compressed air and a soft brush. Don't bend the cooling fins as this is done. When blowing out the core, direct the hose or air line from the engine side out only.

16 Inspect the radiator mounts for deterioration and make sure there's nothing in them when the radiator is installed.

17 Installation is the reverse of the removal procedure. Tighten the fasteners to the torque listed in this Chapter's Specifications.

18 Fill the cooling system with the proper mixture of antifreeze and water (see Chapter 1).

19 Start the engine and check for leaks. Allow the engine to reach normal operating temperature and recheck the coolant level; add more if required.

6.10 The mounting fastener for a radiator mounting bracket (left side shown)

6.13 A mounting bushing for the radiator (right side shown)

7 Water pump - check

1   A failure in the water pump can cause serious engine damage due to overheating.

2   If a failure occurs at the pump seal, it's common for coolant to leak from around that area.

3   On V6 engines, the water pump is driven by a timing belt or chain and is located at the front of the engine, but covered. On 3.5L V6 engines, if you notice coolant under the front of the vehicle, look at the bottom of the lower timing belt cover (behind the crankshaft pulley). Coolant leaks in this area usually indicate a failing water pump seal. On 2.7L V6 engine models, a failed seal may direct fluid to the "valley" of the motor and eventually leak out the back side of the engine. In this case, suspect water pump failure before other major engine leaks first.

4   On the 5.7L V8 engine, the water pump is externally mounted and weep holes may be visible. Using a flashlight, look for traces of coolant residue or dried coolant tracks around the weep hole(s). If the seal has leaked, it should be very apparent.

5   If the water pump is making noise, the impeller shaft bearing most likely has worn out. On V8 models, this can sometimes be confirmed by removing the drivebelt and wiggling the water pump drive pulley. Don't mistake drivebelt slippage, which causes a squealing sound, for water pump bearing failure.

6   A quick water pump performance check is to put the heater on. If the pump is failing, it may not be able to efficiently circulate hot water all the way to the heater core as it should.

8 Water pump - removal and installation

❋❋ WARNING:

Wait until the engine is completely cool before beginning this procedure.

REMOVAL

1   Disconnect the cable from the negative battery terminal (see Chapter 5, Section 1).

2   Drain the cooling system (see Chapter 1). If the coolant is relatively new or in good condition, save it and reuse it.

3   Remove the engine cooling fan assembly (see Section 4).

4   Remove the drivebelt (see Chapter 1).

2.7L V6 engines

5   Remove the timing chain and guides (see Chapter 2).

3.5L V6 engines

6   Remove the timing belt (see Chapter 2B).

5.7L V8 engines

7   Remove the thermostat (see Section 3).

8   Detach the radiator hose from the water pump. If a hose sticks, grasp it near the end with a pair of adjustable pliers and twist it to break the seal, then pull it off. If the hose is deteriorated, cut it off and install a new one upon reassembly.

9   Remove the idler pulley for the drivebelt located on the lower left of the water pump.

All engines

▸ **Refer to illustrations 8.10a and 8.10b**

10 Remove the bolts and detach the water pump from the engine. Note the locations of the various lengths and different types of bolts as they're removed to ensure correct installation (see illustrations).

8.10a Remove the timing chain guide mounting bolts (A) and then the water pump mounting bolts (B) on the 2.7L V6 engine

8.10b The water pump mounting bolt locations on a 3.5L V6 engine

INSTALLATION

▶ **Refer to illustration 8.15**

11 Clean the bolt threads and the threaded holes in the engine to remove corrosion and sealant.

12 Compare the new pump to the old one to make sure they're identical. If the old pump is being reused, check the impeller blades on the backside for corrosion. If any fins are missing or badly corroded, replace the pump with a new one.

13 Remove all traces of old gasket material or the O-ring seal from the engine and water pump (if the same one is to be installed).

14 Clean the engine and water pump mating surfaces with lacquer thinner or acetone.

15 On water pumps equipped with an O-ring seal, apply a thin coat of RTV sealant to the new water pump O-ring and position it in the groove on the back of the water pump (see illustration).

8.15 In this example, the O-ring is seated completely in its groove (2.7L V6 shown)

❋❋ CAUTION:

Make sure the O-ring is correctly seated in the water pump groove to avoid a coolant leak.

16 On water pumps equipped with a gasket, apply a thin film of RTV sealant to the gasket mating surface of the new pump, and position the gasket on the pump. Apply a thin film of RTV sealant to the engine-side of the gasket and slip a couple of bolts through the pump mounting holes to hold the gasket in place.

17 Carefully attach the pump and O-ring/gasket (as applicable) to the engine and thread the bolts into the holes finger tight.

18 With all the bolts in place, tighten them in a criss-cross pattern, a little at a time, to the torque listed in this Chapter's Specifications. Turn the water pump by hand to make sure it rotates freely.

19 Connect the hoses to the water pump (if applicable) and reinstall all parts removed for access to the pump.

20 Refill the cooling system (see Chapter 1). Run the engine and check for leaks.

---

9 Coolant temperature sending unit - check and replacement

CHECK

1 The coolant temperature indicator system consists of a warning light or a temperature gauge on the dash and a coolant temperature sending unit mounted on the engine. On the models covered by this manual, the Engine Coolant Temperature (ECT) sensor, which is an information sensor for the Powertrain Control Module (PCM), also functions as the coolant temperature sending unit (see Chapter 6).

2 If an overheating indication occurs, check the coolant level in the system and then make sure all connectors in the wiring harness between the sending unit and the indicator light or gauge are tight.

3 When the ignition switch is turned to START and the starter motor is turning, the indicator light (if equipped) should come on. This doesn't mean the engine is overheated; it just means that the bulb is good.

4 If the light doesn't come on when the ignition key is turned to START, the bulb might be burned out, the ignition switch might be faulty or the circuit might be open.

5 As soon as the engine starts, the indicator light should go out and remain off, unless the engine overheats. If the light doesn't go out, refer to Chapter 6 and check for any stored trouble codes in the Powertrain Control Module (PCM).

6 If the engine tends to overheat easily, check the coolant to make sure it's the proper type and concentration (see Chapter 1).

REPLACEMENT

7 See Chapter 6 for the ECT sensor replacement procedure.

---

10 Blower motor resistor and blower motor - replacement

❋❋ WARNING:

The models covered by this manual are equipped with a Supplemental Restraint System (SRS), more commonly known as airbags. Always disarm the airbag system before working in the vicinity of any airbag system component to avoid the possibility of accidental deployment of the airbag, which could cause personal injury (see Chapter 12). Do not use a memory saving device to preserve the PCM's memory when working on or near airbag system components.

BLOWER MOTOR RESISTOR

▶ **Refer to illustration 10.4**

➡**Note: Models with automatic temperature control utilize a power module instead of a blower motor resistor. It mounts the same as a blower motor resistor and is replaced in the same manner.**

1 Disconnect the cable from the negative battery terminal (see Chapter 5, Section 1).

10.4 The blower motor resistor electrical connector (A) and mounting fasteners (B) - the power module is similar

2   Remove the lower instrument panel insulator (see Chapter 11).
3   Disconnect the electrical connector(s) from the blower motor resistor or power module (see illustration).
4   Remove the mounting screws and remove it from the housing.
5   Installation is the reverse of removal.

BLOWER MOTOR

▶ **Refer to illustration 10.8**

6   Disconnect the cable from the negative battery terminal (see

10.8 Remove the electrical connector (A) and the mounting screws (B) for the blower motor assembly - one fastener hidden from view

Chapter 5, Section 1).
7   Remove the lower instrument panel insulator (see Chapter 11).
8   Disconnect the electrical connector from the blower motor, then remove the mounting screws and lower the blower motor out of the housing (see illustration).
9   If either the fan or motor is damaged, the entire unit must be replaced as an assembly.
10 Installation is the reverse of removal.

11 Heater/air conditioning control assembly - removal and installation

▶ **Refer to illustrations 11.3 and 11.4**

❊❊ WARNING:

The models covered by this manual are equipped with a Supplemental Restraint System (SRS), more commonly known as airbags. Always disarm the airbag system before working in the

vicinity of any airbag system component to avoid the possibility of accidental deployment of the airbag, which could cause personal injury (see Chapter 12). Do not use a memory saving device to preserve the PCM's memory when working on or near airbag system components.

1   Disconnect the cable from the negative battery terminal (see

11.3 Heater/air conditioning control assembly electrical connectors (manual shown - automatic is similar)

11.4 Heater/air conditioning control assembly mounting screws

Chapter 5, Section 1).

2   Detach the instrument panel center bezel (see Chapter 11).

3   Disconnect the electrical connectors for the assembly (see illustration).

4   Remove the mounting screws and detach the air conditioning and heater control assembly from the bezel (see illustration).

5   Installation is the reverse of the removal procedure.

→**Note: The control assembly may need calibration if replaced with a new one. This must be performed at a dealer service department or a qualified repair shop with the appropriate scan tool.**

12 Heater core - removal and installation

☀☀ WARNING 1:

The models covered by this manual are equipped with a Supplemental Restraint System (SRS), more commonly known as airbags. Always disarm the airbag system before working in the vicinity of any airbag system component to avoid the possibility of accidental deployment of the airbag, which could cause personal injury (see Chapter 12). Do not use a memory saving device to preserve the PCM's memory when working on or near airbag system components.

☀☀ WARNING 2:

Wait until the engine is completely cool before beginning this procedure.

REMOVAL

▶ **Refer to illustration 12.3, 12.5, 12.6, 12.7 and 12.9**

1   Disconnect the cable from the negative battery terminal (see Chapter 5, Section 1).

2   Drain the cooling system (see Chapter 1).

12.3 Slide the clamps away and detach the hoses from the heater core at the firewall in the engine compartment

3   Disconnect the heater hoses at the heater core in the engine compartment at the firewall (see illustration). Tape or plug all openings.

4   Remove the lower instrument panel insulator (see Chapter 11).

5   Remove the blend door actuator from the heater/air conditioning housing located just above the heater core (see illustration).

6   Remove the two fasteners that hold the heater core tubes to the heater/air conditioning housing and then remove the flange from the housing (see illustration).

7   Place towels underneath the heater core tubes and fittings, cut

12.5 Blend door actuator mounting details and heater core fittings:

1   *Blend door actuator mounting fasteners (one hidden - vicinity shown)*

2   *Blend door actuator electrical connector*

3   *Heater core tube fittings (the shrink tubing must be cut away to remove the fitting retainer clips)*

12.6 Remove the two fasteners that hold the heater core tube flange to the heater/air conditioning housing (one hidden - vicinity shown)

12.7 On a similar design, one heater core tube fitting retainer clip is installed (A) and the other has been removed (B) by pulling it off the fitting

12.9 The location of the heater core retainer screw

INSTALLATION

11 Before installing the heater core, make sure all foam seals are in place.

12 Carefully slide the heater core into the housing.

13 Reinstall the remaining components in the reverse order of removal.

14 Refill the cooling system (see Chapter 1) and reconnect the battery (see Chapter 5).

15 Start the engine and check for any leaks and for proper heater operation.

the rubber shrink tubing from around the fittings (if equipped) and then remove the retaining clips from the fittings (see illustration 12.5 and the accompanying illustration).

8   Pull the heater core tubes directly out of the heater core and from the firewall and set them aside. Cover or plug the heater core openings.

9   Remove the retainer screw and retainer holding the heater core in the heater/air conditioning housing (see illustration).

10 Pull the heater core out of the heater/air conditioning housing being careful not to damage any of the seals.

13 Air conditioning and heating system - check and maintenance

AIR CONDITIONING SYSTEM

◆ Refer to illustration 13.1

※※ WARNING:

The air conditioning system is under high pressure. Do not loosen any hose fittings or remove any components until after the system has been discharged. Air conditioning refrigerant must be properly discharged into an EPA-approved recovery/recycling unit at a dealer service department or an automotive air conditioning repair facility. Always wear eye protection when disconnecting air conditioning system fittings.

※※ CAUTION 1:

All models covered by this manual use environmentally friendly R-134a. This refrigerant (and its appropriate refrigerant oils) are not compatible with R-12 refrigerant system components and must never be mixed or the components will be damaged.

※※ CAUTION 2:

When replacing entire components, additional refrigerant oil should be added equal to the amount that is removed with the component being replaced. Be sure to read the can before adding any oil to the system, to make sure it is compatible with the R-134a system.

1   The following maintenance checks should be performed on a regular basis to ensure that the air conditioning continues to operate at peak efficiency.

   a) *Inspect the condition of the drivebelt. If it is worn or deteriorated, replace it (see Chapter 1).*
   b) *Inspect the system hoses. Look for cracks, bubbles, hardening and deterioration. Inspect the hoses and all fittings for oil bubbles or seepage. If there is any evidence of wear, damage or leakage, replace the hose(s).*
   c) *Inspect the condenser fins for leaves, bugs and any other foreign material that may have embedded itself in the fins. Use a "fin comb" or compressed air to remove debris from the condenser.*

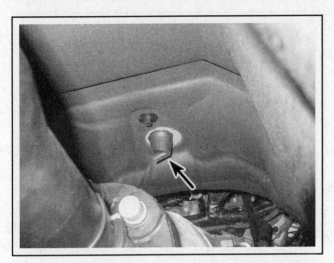

13.1 Check the evaporator housing drain tube (just above the transmission) for blockage

13.9 When feeling the pipes going to and from the evaporator, the larger-diameter pipe (A) should feel much cooler than the smaller-diameter one (B, which may even be hot)

d) *Make sure the system has the correct refrigerant charge.*

e) *If you hear water sloshing around in the dash area or have water dripping on the carpet, check the evaporator housing drain tube (see illustration) and insert a piece of wire into the opening to check for blockage.*

2   It's a good idea to operate the system for about 10 minutes at least once a month, particularly during the winter. Long-term non-use can cause hardening, and subsequent failure, of the seals.

3   Leaks in the air conditioning system are best spotted when the system is brought up to temperature and pressure, by running the engine with the air conditioning ON for five minutes. Shut the engine off and inspect the air conditioning hoses and connections. Traces of oil usually indicate refrigerant leaks.

4   Because of the complexity of the air conditioning system and the special equipment necessary to service it, in-depth troubleshooting and repairs are not included in this manual. However, simple checks and component replacement procedures are provided in this Chapter.

5   If the air conditioning system doesn't operate at all, check the fuse panel and the air conditioning relay, located in the relay box in the engine compartment (see Chapter 12).

6   The most common cause of poor cooling is simply a low system refrigerant charge. If a noticeable drop in cool air output occurs, the following quick check will help you determine if the refrigerant level is low.

Checking the refrigerant charge

▶ **Refer to illustration 13.9**

7   Warm the engine up to normal operating temperature.

8   Place the air conditioning temperature selector at the coldest setting and put the blower at the highest setting. Open the doors (to make sure the air conditioning system doesn't cycle off as soon as it cools the passenger compartment).

9   With the compressor engaged, the clutch will make an audible click and the center of the clutch will rotate. Feel the pipes going to and from the evaporator (see illustration); the small diameter pipe should be warm and the large diameter pipe should feel cool.

10 If the larger-diameter pipe isn't considerably cooler, the system charge is probably low. The earliest warning that a system is low on refrigerant is the air temperature coming out of the ducts inside the vehicle. If the air isn't as cold as it used to be, the system probably needs a charge.

11 Further inspection or testing of the system requires special tools and techniques and is beyond the scope of this manual.

Adding refrigerant

▶ **Refer to illustrations 13.12, 13.15 and 13.18**

12 Buy an automotive charging kit at an auto parts store. A charging kit includes a can of refrigerant, a tap valve and a short section of hose that can be attached between the tap valve and the system low side service valve (see illustration).

13.12 A basic charging kit for 134a systems is available at most auto parts stores - it must say 134a (not R-12) and so must the can of refrigerant

> ❄❄ **CAUTION:**
>
> **Although the system will hold more than one can of refrigerant, don't add more than one can (you could overfill the system). If more refrigerant than that is required, the system should be evacuated and leak tested.**

13.15 Add refrigerant to the system at the low-pressure port

13 Hook up the charging kit by following the manufacturer's instructions.

☀☀ WARNING:

DO NOT attempt hook the charging kit hose to the system high pressure side! The fittings on the charging kit are designed to fit only on the low pressure side of the system.

14 Back off the valve handle on the charging kit and screw the kit onto the refrigerant can, making sure first that the O-ring or rubber seal inside the threaded portion of the kit is in place.

☀☀ WARNING:

Wear protective eyewear when dealing with pressurized refrigerant cans.

15 Remove the dust cap from the low-side charging port and attach the quick-connect fitting on the kit hose (see illustration).

16 Warm up the engine and turn on the air conditioner. Keep the charging kit hose away from the fan and other moving parts. The charging process requires the compressor to be running.

17 Turn the valve handle on the kit until the stem pierces the can, then back the handle out to release the refrigerant. You should be able to hear the rush of gas. Add refrigerant to the low side of the system until both the accumulator surface and the evaporator inlet pipe feel about the same temperature. Allow stabilization time between each addition.

18 If you have an accurate thermometer, you can place it in the center air conditioning duct inside the vehicle (see illustration) and keep track of the outlet air temperature. A charged system that is working properly should cool to approximately 40-degrees F. If the ambient (outside) air temperature is very high, say 110-degrees F, or if the relative humidity is high, the duct air temperature may be as high as 60- to 70-degrees F, but generally the air conditioning is 30 to 50-degrees F cooler than the ambient air.

19 When the can is empty, turn the valve handle to the closed position and release the connection from the low-side port. Replace the dust cap.

20 Remove the charging kit from the can and store the kit for future

13.18 If you have an accurate thermometer, you can place it in the center air conditioning duct inside the vehicle

use with the piercing valve in the UP position to prevent inadvertently piercing the can on the next use.

Eliminating air conditioning odors

▶ **Refer to Illustration 13.24**

21 Unpleasant odors that often develop in air conditioning systems are caused by the growth of a fungus, usually on the surface of the evaporator core. The warm, humid environment there is a perfect breeding ground for mildew to develop.

22 The evaporator core on most vehicles Is difficult to access, and factory dealerships have a lengthy, expensive process for eliminating the fungus by opening up the evaporator case and using a powerful disinfectant and rinse on the core until the fungus is gone. You can service your own system at home, but it takes something much stronger than basic household germ-killers or deodorizers.

23 Aerosol disinfectants for automotive air conditioning systems are available in most auto parts stores, but remember when shopping for them that the most effective treatments are also the most expensive. The basic procedure for using these sprays is to start by running the system in the Recirculating mode for ten minutes with the blower on its highest speed. Use the highest heat mode to dry out the system - keep the compressor from engaging by disconnecting the wiring connector at the compressor (see Section 14).

24 Make sure that the disinfectant can comes with a long spray hose. Work the nozzle through the opening in the heater/air conditioning recirculation housing so that it protrudes inside and points toward the evaporator housing (towards the center of the instrument panel) (see illustration) and then spray according to the manufacturer's recommendations. Try to cover the whole surface of the evaporator core, by aiming the spray up, down and sideways. Follow the manufacturer's recommendations for the length of spray and waiting time between applications.

25 Once the evaporator has been cleaned, the best way to prevent the mildew from coming back again is to make sure your evaporator housing drain tube is clear (see illustration 13.1).

HEATING SYSTEM

26 If the carpet under the heater core is damp, or if antifreeze vapor or steam is coming through the vents, the heater core is leaking.

13.24 To disinfect the evaporator housing, insert the nozzle of the disinfectant can through the opening in the recirculation housing and point it toward the evaporator core (which is toward the left of the opening) - glove box removed for access

Remove it (see Section 12) and install a new unit (most radiator shops will not repair a leaking heater core).

27 If the air coming out of the heater vents isn't hot, the problem could stem from any of the following causes:

a) The thermostat is stuck open, preventing the engine coolant from warming up enough to carry heat to the heater core. Replace the thermostat (see Section 3).

b) There is a blockage in the system, preventing the flow of coolant through the heater core. Feel both heater hoses at the firewall. They should be hot. If one of them is cold, there is an obstruction in one of the hoses or in the heater core. Detach the hoses and back flush the heater core with a water hose. If the heater core is clear but circulation is still restricted, remove the two hoses and flush them out with a water hose.

c) If flushing fails to remove the blockage from the heater core, the core must be replaced (see Section 12).

14 Air conditioning compressor - removal and installation

▶ Refer to illustration 14.5

❋❋ WARNING:

The air conditioning system is under high pressure. Do not loosen any hose fittings or remove any components until after the system has been discharged. Air conditioning refrigerant must be properly discharged into an EPA-approved recovery/recycling unit at a dealer service department or an automotive air conditioning repair facility. Always wear eye protection when disconnecting air conditioning system fittings.

➡**Note: The receiver-drier (see Section 15) should be replaced whenever the compressor is replaced due to an internal failure.**

1 Have the air conditioning system discharged by an automotive air conditioning technician.

2 Disconnect the cable from the negative battery terminal (see Chapter 5, Section 1).

3 Remove the air filter housing (see Chapter 4).

4 Remove the drivebelt (see Chapter 1). Also, removing the power steering pump and positioning it aside (without disconnecting the hoses) will make access to the compressor easier. See Chapter 10 for the power steering pump removal procedure.

5 Disconnect the compressor clutch electrical connector (see illustration).

6 Disconnect the refrigerant lines from the compressor. Plug the open fittings to prevent entry of dirt and moisture and discard the O-ring seals).

7 Raise the front of the vehicle and support it securely on jackstands.

➡**Note: On V8 models, this step is not necessary.**

8 Remove the front engine splash shield (see Chapter 2).

➡**Note: On V8 models, this step is not necessary.**

14.5 Air conditioning compressor details (3.5L V6 engine shown, others similar. Also, some components are removed for clarity)

1 *Compressor clutch electrical connector*
2 *High pressure line (discharge) fitting*
3 *Low pressure line (suction) fitting*
4 *Mounting fastener (some aren't visible in this photo)*

9 Unbolt the mounting fasteners and carefully remove the compressor from the vehicle.

➡**Note: The compressor mounting fasteners also secure a transmission oil cooler line bracket. Be careful not to damage these lines as the compressor is removed.**

10 If a new compressor is being installed, follow the directions with the compressor regarding the draining of excess oil prior to installation.

→Note: Any replacement compressor used must be designated as compatible with R-134a refrigerant.

11 The clutch may have to be transferred from the original to the new compressor.

12 Installation is the reverse of removal. Replace all O-rings with new ones specifically made for air conditioning system use and compatible with R-134a refrigerant. Lubricate them with refrigerant oil. Any refrigerant oil added must also be compatible with R-134a refrigerant.

13 Have the system evacuated, recharged and leak-tested by the shop that discharged it.

15 Air conditioning receiver-drier - removal and installation

▶ **Refer to illustration 15.4**

❋❋ **WARNING:**

The air conditioning system is under high pressure. Do not loosen any hose fittings or remove any components until after the system has been discharged. Air conditioning refrigerant must be properly discharged into an EPA-approved recovery/recycling unit at a dealer service department or an automotive air conditioning repair facility. Always wear eye protection when disconnecting air conditioning system fittings.

1   Have the air conditioning system discharged by an automotive air conditioning technician.

2   Disconnect the cable from the negative battery terminal (see Chapter 5, Section 1).

3   Remove the front bumper cover (see Chapter 11).

4   Remove the receiver-drier mounting fastener (see illustration).

5   Pull the receiver-drier directly up and out of the fitting for the condenser (see illustration15.4). Remove the O-ring seals and discard them.

6   Plug all open fittings to prevent entry of dirt and moisture.

7   Using new O-ring seals, install the receiver-drier into the fitting at the condenser. If a new receiver-drier is being installed, add 1 oz (30 ml) of new refrigerant oil (a type designated as compatible with R-134a refrigerant) to the new unit.

15.4 Air conditioning receiver-drier mounting details:

1	Receiver-drier	3	Condenser fitting
2	Mounting fastener		

8   The remainder of installation is the reverse of removal.

9   Take the vehicle back to the shop that discharged it. Have the air conditioning system evacuated, charged and leak tested.

16 Air conditioning condenser - removal and installation

▶ **Refer to illustration 16.7**

❋❋ **WARNING:**

The air conditioning system is under high pressure. Do not loosen any hose fittings or remove any components until after the system has been discharged. Air conditioning refrigerant must be properly discharged into an EPA-approved recovery/recycling unit at a dealer service department or an automotive air conditioning repair facility. Always wear eye protection when disconnecting air conditioning system fittings.

→Note: The receiver-drier (see Section 15) should be replaced whenever the condenser is replaced.

1   Have the air conditioning system discharged by an automotive air conditioning technician.

2   Disconnect the cable from the negative battery terminal (see Chapter 5, Section 1).

3   Remove the front bumper cover (see Chapter 11).

4   Remove the plastic air deflectors on each side of the condenser.

16.7 The location of the refrigerant line fittings on the condenser

5   Disconnect the transmission oil cooler lines from the condenser.

6   Remove the mounting fasteners for the power steering oil cooler (at the front of the condenser) and move the cooler aside.

7   Disconnect the refrigerant lines from the condenser (see illustration). Plug the lines and fittings to prevent the entry of moisture and contaminants. Discard the O-ring seals.

8   Remove the fasteners that mount the condenser to the radiator and lower the condenser from the vehicle (see illustration 6.7).

9   If the original condenser will be reinstalled, store it with the line fittings on top to prevent oil from draining out.

10 If a new condenser is being installed, pour 1 oz (30 ml) of the appropriate refrigerant oil into it prior to installation.

11 Install new R-134a compatible O-ring seals onto the refrigerant line fittings.

12 Reinstall the components in the reverse order of removal.

13 Have the system evacuated, recharged and leak-tested by the shop that discharged it.

17 Air conditioning pressure switch - replacement

▶ Refer to illustration 17.2

➡Note: It is not necessary to discharge the air conditioning system in order to replace the pressure switch (a Schrader valve is present in the fitting under the switch).

1   Disconnect the cable from the negative battery terminal (see Chapter 5, Section 1).

2   Unplug the electrical connector from the air conditioning pressure switch (see illustration).

3   Unscrew the pressure switch from the line. Be careful not to damage the refrigerant line. Discard the O-ring seal.

4   Lubricate a new R-134a compatible O-ring seal with the appropriate refrigerant oil and place it into position.

5   Screw the new switch onto the refrigerant line valve until hand tight, and then tighten it securely.

6   Reconnect the electrical connector and the battery cable.

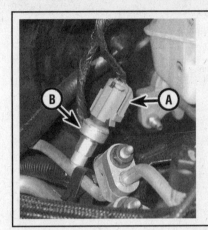

17.2 Unplug the electrical connector (A), then unscrew the switch (B)

18 Air conditioning expansion valve - removal and installation

▶ Refer to illustrations 18.3 and 18.4

❊❊ WARNING:

The air conditioning system is under high pressure. Do not loosen any hose fittings or remove any components until after the system has been discharged. Air conditioning refrigerant must be properly discharged into an EPA-approved recovery/recycling unit at a dealer service department or an automotive air conditioning repair facility. Always wear eye protection when disconnecting air conditioning system fittings.

1   Have the air conditioning system discharged by an automotive air conditioning technician.

2   Disconnect the cable from the negative battery terminal (see Chapter 5, Section 1).

3   Remove the bracket that secures the refrigerant lines to the left shock tower (see illustration).

4   Disconnect the refrigerant lines at the firewall by removing the nut that secures the line fitting to the expansion valve (see illustration).

18.3 Refrigerant line bracket at the left shock tower

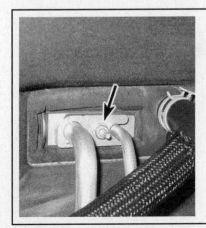

18.4 Remove the refrigerant line fitting nut and fittings to get to the expansion valve mounting fasteners

Cap or plug the line openings to prevent any dirt or moisture from entering the system.

5 Remove the two exposed mounting screws that secure the expansion valve.

6 Detach the expansion valve from the evaporator fitting and discard the O-rings.

7 Installation is the reverse of removal.

➡**Note: Use new R-134a compatible O-rings during reassembly.**

8 Have the system evacuated, recharged and leak-tested by the shop that discharged it.

19 Engine oil cooler - removal and installation

▸ **Refer to illustration 19.4**

❄❄ **WARNING:**

The engine must be completely cool before beginning this procedure.

19.4 Engine oil cooler mounting details (3.5L V6 engine shown)

A   Hose clamps   B   Mounting bolt

1 Raise the front of the vehicle and support it securely on jackstands.

2 Drain the cooling system (see Chapter 1).

3 Remove the engine oil filter (see Chapter 1).

4 Squeeze the hose clamps and slide them back on the hoses, then detach the hoses from the oil cooler (see illustration). Be prepared for coolant spillage.

5 Using a large hex bit, unscrew the bolt from the center of the oil cooler, then detach the cooler from the engine.

6 Installation is the reverse of removal, noting the following points:

a) Clean the mating surfaces and use a new gasket.

b) When installing the cooler, align the cutout on the cooler with the tab on the oil pan.

c) Tighten the bolt to the torque listed in this Chapter's Specifications. When tightening the bolt, hold the oil cooler to prevent it from turning.

d) Install a new oil filter, refill the cooling system, and check the oil level, adding as necessary (see Chapter 1).

Specifications

General

Coolant capacity	See Chapter 1
Drivebelt tension	See Chapter 1
Radiator/expansion tank cap pressure rating	16 to 20 psi

Torque specifications   Ft-lbs (unless otherwise indicated)

→**Note: One foot-pound (ft-lb) of torque is equivalent to 12 inch-pounds (in-lbs) of torque. Torque values below approximately 15 ft-lbs are expressed in inch-pounds, since most foot-pound torque wrenches are not accurate at these smaller values.**

Engine oil cooler mounting bolt	
3.5L V6 engine	45
5.7L V8 engine	41
Radiator bracket mounting bolts	106 in-lbs
Thermostat housing bolts	
2.7L V6 engines	53 in-lbs
3.5L V6 engines	105 in-lbs
5.7L V8 (Hemi) engines	112 in-lbs
Water pump mounting bolts	
2.7L and 3.5L V6 engines	105 in-lbs
5.7L V8 (Hemi) engines	20

Notes

Section

Reference to other Chapters

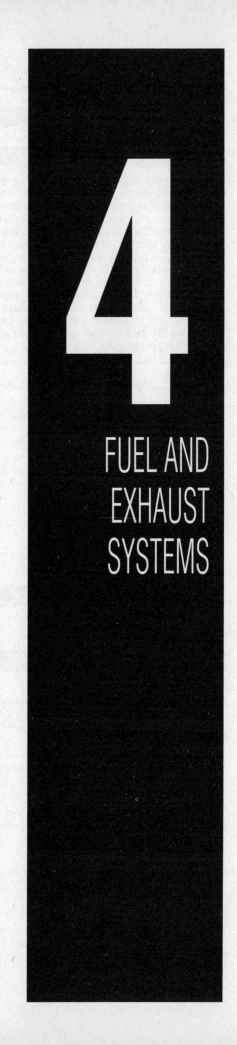

4

FUEL AND EXHAUST SYSTEMS

1   General information

All models covered by this manual are equipped with a sequential multi-port fuel injection system. This type of fuel injection system uses timed impulses to sequentially inject the fuel directly into the intake ports of each cylinder in the same sequence as the firing order. The Powertrain Control Module (PCM) controls the injectors. The PCM monitors various engine parameters and delivers the exact amount of fuel, in firing order sequence, into the intake ports. For more information about the fuel injection system, see Section 10.

The fuel pump module consists of the fuel inlet strainer, the pump and the fuel pressure regulator. The fuel pump module is located inside the left part of the fuel tank, and can be accessed by removing the rear seat cushion, an access cover and a locking ring on top of the tank. The fuel level sending unit and fuel filter module, which is located in the right part of the fuel tank, has its own access cover and is accessed in the same manner. Neither of these modules is serviceable. You can replace the fuel level sensor separately from the filter, but if anything malfunctions on the fuel pump module (pump or pressure regulator) you must replace the entire unit.

There are two fuel filters. One is the nylon mesh fuel "sock" or strainer at the lower (inlet) end of the fuel pump module, which is mounted in the roof of the fuel tank and protrudes down into the fuel inside. The main fuel filter is located in the right part of the fuel tank with the fuel level sensor. No external fuel filters are used on any of the vehicles covered by this manual. The fuel filters are extended-life parts and do not need to be replaced at scheduled maintenance intervals. They should only be replaced if diagnostic testing indicates the need to do so.

The exhaust system consists of the two exhaust manifolds, a pair of catalytic converters, an exhaust pipe and a muffler. All of these components are replaceable. For further information regarding the catalytic converters, refer to Chapter 6.

2   Fuel pressure relief procedure

▶ **Refer to illustration 2.2**

1   Remove the fuel filler cap (this will relieve any pressure that has built-up in the tank).

2   The fuel pump relay is located in the rear fuse and relay box, which is located in the trunk under the spare tire access panel. Open the cover of the fuse and relay box and remove the fuel pump relay (see illustration).

3   Turn the ignition key to START and crank over the engine for several seconds. It will either start momentarily and immediately stall, or it won't start at all.

4   Turn the ignition key to the OFF position.

5   Disconnect the cable from the negative battery terminal before beginning work on the fuel system (see Chapter 5, Section 1).

6   Install the fuel pump relay.

7   After all work on the fuel system has been completed, the CHECK ENGINE light or Malfunction Indicator Light (MIL) might come on during operation because the engine was cranked with the fuel pump relay unplugged. The light will likely go out after a period of normal operation. If it does not go out, refer to Chapter 6.

2.2 The fuel pump fuse (A) and the fuel pump relay (B) are located in the fuse and relay box in the trunk

3 Fuel pump/fuel pressure - check

PRELIMINARY CHECK

1   The fuel pump is located inside the fuel tank, which muffles its sound when the engine is running. But you can actually hear the fuel pump. Turn the ignition key to ON (not START) and listen carefully for the soft whirring sound made by the fuel pump as it's briefly turned on by the PCM to pressurize the fuel system prior to starting the engine. You will only hear a soft whirring sound for a second or two, but that sound tells you that the pump is working. If you can't hear the pump from inside the vehicle, remove the fuel filler cap and have an assistant turn the ignition switch to ON while you listen for the sound of the pump. If the pump does not come on when the ignition key is turned to ON, check the fuel pump fuse and relay, both of which are located in the fuse and relay box in the trunk (see illustration 2.2). If the fuse and relay are okay, check the wiring back to the fuel pump (see Section 5 if you need help locating the fuel pump electrical connector). If the fuse, relay and wiring are okay, the fuel pump is probably defective. If the pump runs continuously with the ignition key in its ON position, the Powertrain Control Module (PCM) is probably defective. Have the PCM checked by a dealer service department or other qualified repair shop.

PRESSURE CHECK

▶ **Refer to illustrations 3.3 and 3.4**

➡**Note: In order to perform the fuel pressure test, you will need a fuel pressure gauge capable of measuring high fuel pressure. You'll also need the right fittings or adapters to attach it to the fuel rail.**

2   Relieve the fuel system pressure (see Section 2).

3   For this check, you'll need to obtain a fuel pressure gauge with a hose and an adapter suitable for tee-ing it into the fuel system between the fuel supply line quick-connect fitting and the fuel rail inlet pipe (see illustration).

4   Disconnect the fuel supply line quick-connect fitting from the fuel rail inlet pipe and tee in your fuel pressure gauge (see illustration).

➡**Note: You must work in a very confined space to carry out a fuel pressure test. The fuel rail inlet pipe is difficult to reach on some engines because it's located behind and below the intake manifold, near the firewall. The accompanying illustration depicts a typical hook-up (on a 3.5L V6 engine) with the intake manifold removed for clarity. But you can't, of course, remove the intake manifold and still operate the engine. On some models you can make a little bit of working room by removing the cowl covers (see Chapter 11).**

5   Start the engine and check the pressure on the gauge, comparing your reading with the pressure listed in this Chapter's Specifications.

6   If the fuel pressure is not within specifications, check the following:

3.3 A typical fuel pressure gauge, with hoses and fittings suitable for tee-ing into the fuel system between the fuel delivery line and the fuel rail

3.4 Fuel gauge connection details (3.5L V6 engine shown, other engines similar; intake manifold removed for clarity)

A   *Fuel feed line fitting*
B   *Fuel rail*
C   *Tee fitting*
D   *Quick-connect fitting attached to fuel rail*

a) *If the pressure is lower than specified, check for a restriction in the fuel system. Two likely suspects are the fuel inlet strainer at the base of the fuel pump/fuel level sensor module in the left fuel tank compartment and the main fuel filter in the right fuel tank compartment (see Section 6).*

➡**Note: Neither of these components can be inspected or replaced separately.**

b) *If the fuel pressure is higher than specified, replace the fuel pressure regulator, which is part of the left fuel pump/fuel level sensor module (see Section 6).*

4   Fuel lines and fittings - repair and replacement

✳✳ WARNING:

Gasoline is extremely flammable, so take extra precautions when you work on any part of the fuel system. See the Warning in Section 2.

1   Always relieve the fuel pressure before servicing fuel lines or fittings on fuel-injected vehicles (see Section 2).

2   The fuel supply line connects the fuel tank to the fuel rail on the engine. Be sure to inspect the fuel and the Evaporative Emission Control (EVAP) system lines for leaks, kinks and dents whenever you're servicing something underneath the vehicle. All of these lines are secured to the vehicle underbody by plastic clips. To disengage fuel and EVAP lines from these clips, simply pry the clip down and pull out the lines from above.

3   Whenever you're working under the vehicle, be sure to inspect all fuel and EVAP lines for leaks, kinks, dents and other damage. Always replace a damaged fuel line or EVAP line immediately. Leaking fuel and EVAP lines will result in loss of fuel and excessive air pollution (leaking raw fuel emits unburned hydrocarbon vapors into the atmosphere).

4   If you find signs of dirt in the lines during disassembly, disconnect all lines and blow them out with compressed air. If the fuel lines are particularly dirty, you might also have to replace the fuel pump module and the fuel filter module (see Sections 5 and 6). (Neither the inlet strainer at the inlet end of the pump nor the main fuel filter can be inspected for contamination.)

STEEL TUBING

5   Because fuel lines used on fuel-injected vehicles are under fairly high pressure, it is critical that they be replaced with lines of equivalent specification. If you have to replace a steel line, make sure that you use steel tubing that meets the manufacturer's specifications. Don't use copper or aluminum tubing to replace steel tubing. These materials cannot withstand normal vehicle vibration.

6   Some steel fuel lines have threaded fittings. When loosening these fittings to service or replace components:

 a) *Use a backup wrench on the stationary portion of the fitting while loosening and tightening the fitting nuts.*

 b) *If you're going to replace one of these fittings, use original equipment parts or parts that meet original equipment standards.*

PLASTIC TUBING

7   If you ever have to replace a plastic line, use only the original equipment plastic tubing.

✳✳ CAUTION:

When removing or installing plastic fuel line tubing, be careful not to bend or twist it too much, which can damage it. And damaged fuel lines MUST be replaced! Also, be aware that the plastic fuel tubing is NOT heat resistant, so keep it away from excessive heat. Nor is it acid-proof, so don't wipe it off with a shop rag that has been used to wipe off battery electrolyte. If you accidentally spill or wipe electrolyte on plastic fuel or emissions tubing, replace the tubing.

FLEXIBLE HOSES

✳✳ WARNING:

Use only original equipment replacement hoses or their equivalent. Unapproved hoses might fail when subjected to the high operating pressures of the fuel system.

8   Don't route fuel hoses within four inches of exhaust system components or within ten inches of a catalytic converter.

9   Make sure that no flexible hoses are installed directly against the vehicle, particularly in places where there is any vibration. If allowed to touch some vibrating part of the vehicle, a hose can easily become chafed and it might start leaking. A good rule of thumb is to maintain a minimum of 1/4-inch clearance around a hose (or metal line) to prevent contact with the vehicle underbody.

FUEL LINE AND EVAP LINE QUICK-CONNECT FITTINGS

✳✳ WARNING:

ALWAYS relieve the fuel system pressure (see Section 2) before disconnecting a fuel line fitting.

10 The vehicles covered in this manual use several kinds of fuel line quick-connect fittings for connections at the fuel pump, the EVAP canister and the fuel rail. The procedure for releasing each type of fuel line fitting is different. But a few rules of thumb apply to all fittings:

 a) *ALWAYS relieve the fuel system pressure (see Section 2) before disconnecting a fuel line fitting.*

 b) *Inspect the fitting for dirt. If the fitting is dirty, clean it off before disassembling it. The seals in the fitting will stick to the fuel line as they age. Twist the fitting on the line, then push and pull the fitting until it moves freely.*

 c) *Always disconnect all fuel line fittings from a fuel system component before removing the component.*

 d) *When disconnecting a quick-connect fitting, inspect the condition of the retainer before reconnecting the fitting. The best strategy with respect to retainers is to simply replace the retainer every time that you disconnect the fitting.*

 e) *When you disconnect a fitting with an O-ring inside, inspect the O-ring before reconnecting the fitting. To avoid leaks (and fires!) make VERY SURE that the O-ring is good condition. Even better, simply replace it.*

 f) *In most cases, the fitting itself is a non-removable part of the fuel line, so you might have to replace an entire fuel line if a fitting is damaged or defective.*

Two-button type fitting

▶ **Refer to illustration 4.11**

11 This type of fitting has a pair of push buttons located on opposite sides of the fitting (see illustration). No special tools are needed to disconnect a two-button fitting. Simply press on both buttons and pull the fitting off the fuel line or fuel component to which it's connected.

4.11 Some quick-connect fittings have two buttons (one on each side of the fitting) that must be depressed to release the fitting. No tools are necessary

12 To reconnect a two-button fitting, push the fitting onto the fuel line or fuel system component until the raised "stop" on the fuel line or component is fully seated against the back of the fitting, then keep pushing until you feel a "click." Verify that the fitting is correctly reconnected by trying to pull the fuel line or component and the fitting in opposite directions.

Pinch-type fitting

13 Instead of push buttons, this type of fitting has two "finger tabs." Again, no special tools are needed to disconnect it. Simply pinch both tabs together and pull the fitting off the fuel line or fuel component to which it's connected.

14 To reconnect a pinch-type fitting, push it onto the fuel line or fuel component until the raised "stop" on the fuel line or component is fully seated against the back of the fitting. Then keep pushing until you feel a click. Verify that the fitting is correctly reconnected by trying to pull the fuel line or component and the fitting in opposite directions.

Single-tab type fitting

▶ **Refer to illustration 4.15**

15 This type of fitting is locked into place by a single removable pull-tab (see illustration). The only tool you might need to disconnect it is a small screwdriver. To disconnect the fitting, squeeze the legs of the

4.15 To disconnect a single-tab type fitting, squeeze the legs of the tab together, pull up the tab and pull the fitting and fuel line or fuel component apart. Discard the old tab and substitute a new one for reassembly

tab together, pull up the tab (pry it up with a small screwdriver if necessary) and pull the fitting off the fuel line or fuel component to which it's connected. Remove and discard the old pull-tab, then install a new tab before reconnecting the fitting.

16 To reconnect a single-tab type fitting, install a new pull tab (but don't push it down into its locked position), push the fitting onto the fuel line or fuel component until the raised "stop" on the fuel line or component is seated against the back of the fitting, then keep pushing until you feel a click. When the fitting is fully seated, push the new tab down until it locks into place. Verify that the fitting is locked by firmly pulling the fuel line or component and the fitting in opposite directions.

Two-tab type fitting

▶ **Refer to illustrations 4.17a, 4.17b and 4.18**

17 This type of fitting is one of the more common ones used. It uses a plastic retainer with two release tabs protruding from opposite sides of the fitting. To disconnect it, depress both release tabs with your fingers, then pull the fitting off the fuel line or fuel component (see illustration).

4.17a To disconnect a two-tab type fitting, depress both tabs with your fingers then pull the fuel line and the fitting apart (the plastic retainer comes off with the fuel line)

4.17b Inspect the O-ring inside the fitting. If it's cracked, torn, deteriorated or otherwise damaged in any way, replace it

4.18 Before reconnecting a two-tab type fitting, be sure to position the plastic retainer correctly:

A   *Plastic retainer release tabs*
B   *Plastic retainer locking tabs (must be aligned with "window" in fitting)*
C   *Raised stop (must be visible through opening in plastic retainer)*
D   *Fitting "window" (must be aligned with locking tabs on plastic retainer)*

❋❋ CAUTION:

Do NOT use a tool, such a pair of pliers, to squeeze the tabs together. Using anything besides your fingers might damage the plastic retainer. The retainer will remain on the fuel line or fuel component and the O-ring (see illustration) will remain inside the fitting. Inspect the condition of the O-ring. If it's cracked, torn, deteriorated or otherwise damaged in any way, replace it.

---

18 To reconnect a two-tab type fitting, make sure that the retainer is correctly positioned on the fuel line or component, with the locking tabs of the retainer aligned with the "windows" in the fitting (see illustration). When everything's correctly aligned, push the fitting onto the fuel line or fuel component until the raised stop on the fuel line or fuel component seats against the back of the fitting, then keep pushing until you feel a click. Verify that the fitting is locked into place by firmly pulling the fuel line or component and the fitting in opposite directions.

Plastic retainer ring type fitting

▸ **Refer to illustration 4.19**

19 This type of fitting has a round plastic retainer ring, usually black in color, located inside the fitting. To disconnect a plastic retainer ring type fitting, push the fitting body toward the fuel line or fuel system component to which it's connected while firmly pushing the plastic retainer ring into the fitting, then while holding the retainer in its depressed position, pull the fuel line or fuel component out of the fitting (see illustration). When disconnecting a plastic retainer type fitting, make sure that the plastic retainer ring is pressed squarely into the fitting body. If the retainer becomes cocked in the fitting body it will be difficult or impossible to disconnect the fuel line or fuel system component from the fitting. One way to ensure that the retainer is depressed squarely into the fitting body is to depress the shoulder of the retainer with the flat face of an open-end wrench. After disconnecting the fuel line or fuel system component from the fitting, the plastic retainer ring will remain with quick-connect fitting connector body. Inspect the con-

4.19 To disconnect a plastic retainer type fitting, push the plastic retainer ring and fitting body together and pull the line from the fitting. To reconnect, push the line into the fitting until you feel a click

dition of the fitting body, the plastic retainer ring and the end of the fuel line or fuel system component for damage. Replace any damaged parts.

20 To reconnect a plastic retainer type fitting, push the fitting onto the fuel line or fuel system component until the raised stop on the fuel line or fuel component rests against the back of the fitting, then continue pushing until you feel a click. Verify that the two halves of the fitting are locked together by firmly pulling the fuel line and the fitting in opposite directions.

Metal collar type fittings with latch clips

▸ **Refer to illustrations 4.21, 4.22a, 4.22b and 4.23**

➡**Note 1: You'll find these fittings at the connections between the fuel supply and return lines and the fuel rail.**

➡**Note 2: You'll need a special tool, available at most auto parts stores, to disconnect these fittings.**

21 To remove a latch clip, pull or pry the end of the latch off the fuel

4.21 To remove a latch clip from a metal collar fitting, pull or pry the end of the clip off the fuel line, then disengage the other end from the female side of the fitting

4.22a To release the locking fingers inside a metal collar type fitting, insert a special fuel line disconnection tool into the female side of the fitting until it releases the locking fingers . . .

4.22b . . . then pull the two halves of the fitting apart

4.23 Inspect the old O-ring inside the female side of the metal collar fitting. If it's cracked, torn or otherwise deteriorated, replace it

line, then disengage the other end of the latch from the female end of the metal collar fitting (see illustration).

22 To disconnect a metal collar fitting (with either type of latch clip), release the locking fingers inside the fitting by inserting a special fuel line disconnection tool (available at most auto parts stores) into the metal collar (see illustration). With the special tool still inserted, disconnect the metal collar from the fuel line or from the fuel system component (see illustration).

23 Inspect the O-ring inside the metal collar fitting (see illustration). If it's dried out, cracked, torn or otherwise deteriorated, replace it.

24 Apply a few drops of clean engine oil to the end of the fuel line or fuel system component, push the fitting onto the fuel line or component until the locking fingers snap into place. Verify that the fitting is correctly connected by pulling the fuel line or component and the fitting in opposite directions.

25 Install the latch clip until it snaps into position.

---

5 Fuel pump/fuel level sensor and fuel filter/fuel level sensor modules - removal and installation

FUEL PUMP/FUEL LEVEL SENSOR MODULE

▶ Refer to illustrations 5.5, 5.6, 5.7, 5.9, 5.10, 5.11, 5.13, 5.14, 5.15 and 5.16

❋❋ WARNING:

See the Warning in Section 1.

➡Note: The fuel pump/fuel level sensor module is located in the left compartment of the fuel tank. This module includes the fuel pump inlet strainer, the pump and a fuel level sensor. This section covers the removal and installation of the complete module, which is removed as a complete assembly. You can replace any of these components separately (see Section 6).

1 Relieve the fuel system pressure (see Section 2).
2 Disconnect the cable from the negative battery terminal (see Chapter 5, Section 1).

3 Drain the fuel tank to under 5/8-full with a hose routed through the fuel filler neck hose. Use a hard nylon tube with a 30-degree cut on the end to push open the check valve in the fuel filler neck.

❋❋ WARNING:

Do NOT start the siphoning action by mouth! Use a siphoning kit (available at most auto parts stores).

4 Remove the rear seat cushion (see Chapter 11).
5 Pull back the foam pad covering the fuel pump/fuel level sensor module or the pad covering the fuel filter/fuel level sensor module (see illustration).
6 Pull off the plastic access cover (see illustration). The wiring harness between the grommet in the access cover and the electrical connector for the fuel pump and fuel level sensor is short, so be careful.
7 Disconnect the electrical connector from the terminal on top of the fuel pump/fuel level sensor module mounting flange (see illustration) and place the harness safely out of the way.

5.5 Peel back this foam pad (A) to gain access to the fuel pump/fuel level sensor module (B). Peel back this foam pad (C) to access the fuel filter/fuel pressure regulator/fuel level sensor module (D)

5.7 . . . then depress this release tab and disconnect the electrical connector

5.9 To loosen the lock-ring, tap it counterclockwise with a hammer and a brass drift (using a steel drift can be dangerous because it might cause a spark)

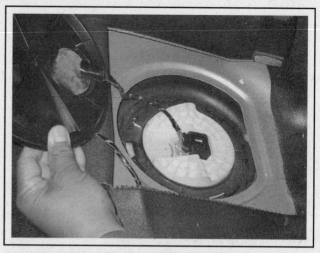

5.6 Carefully lift off the plastic access cover . . .

8   To prevent dirt from entering the fuel tank, clean the area surrounding the mounting flange for the fuel pump/fuel level sensor module.

9   Using a hammer and a brass drift, tap on the lock-ring to turn it counterclockwise (see illustration). When the lock-ring is loose, unscrew it.

✳✳ WARNING:

Do NOT use a steel drift to loosen the lock-ring. Doing so could produce sparks, which could ignite fuel vapors from the tank.

10 Before removing the fuel pump/fuel level sensor module, note the square tab on the edge of the mounting flange, which faces forward (see illustration). The flange must be oriented just like this when you install the fuel pump/fuel level sensor module.

11 Lift up the mounting flange for the fuel pump/fuel level sensor module and disconnect the two electrical connectors (see illustration) for the fuel level sensors and the fuel pump.

12 If the lower half of the module (the fuel pump part) is still submerged in gasoline, drain the rest of the fuel from the left fuel tank. Lift

5.10 Note how the square tab on the mounting flange faces forward. When you install the fuel pump/fuel level sensor module, make sure that the square tab is oriented just like this

5.11 Lift up the mounting flange for the fuel pump/fuel level sensor module and disconnect these two electrical connectors

up the fuel pump module far enough to insert a siphon hose into the tank and siphon out as much gas as possible.

13 Disconnect the fuel supply line fitting from the outlet pipe on top of the fuel pump (see illustration).

14 Disconnect the two return lines from the fuel pump module (see illustration).

15 To drain the residual fuel from the reservoir inside the fuel pump module, reach through the opening and tilt the fuel pump module on its side to allow the fuel to drain out the top of the module (see illustration).

16 Carefully remove the fuel pump/fuel level sensor module from the fuel tank (see illustration). Tilt the pump/sensor module as necessary to protect the fuel level sensor float arm from damage.

5.13 To disconnect the fuel supply line quick-connect fitting from the outlet pipe on top of the fuel pump, depress this release tab and pull off the fitting

5.14 To disconnect the fuel return lines from the fuel pump module, simply lift them up and pop them loose from these retaining tangs (these two lines connect the fuel filter/fuel pressure regulator in the right fuel tank compartment to the fuel pump module)

17 If you want to replace the fuel pump module or the fuel level sensor, refer to Section 6.

18 Installation is the reverse of removal.

5.15 To drain the residual fuel from the reservoir inside the fuel pump module, reach through the opening and tilt the fuel pump module on its side to allow the fuel to drain out the top of the module

5.16 To remove the fuel pump/fuel level sensor module from the fuel tank, angle it as shown to protect the fuel level sensor float arm from damage

5.20 To access the fuel filter/fuel pressure regulator/fuel level sensor module, remove this plastic access cover

5.21 To disconnect the quick-connect fitting for the fuel supply line, squeeze these two tabs with a pair of needle nose pliers and pull off the fitting

5.25 Carefully lift the fuel filter/fuel pressure regulator/fuel level sensor out of the fuel tank. Be careful not to snap the fuel return lines or the electrical wiring harnesses

FUEL FILTER/FUEL PRESSURE REGULATOR/FUEL LEVEL SENSOR MODULE

▶ Refer to illustrations 5.20, 5.21 and 5.25

❈❈ **WARNING:**

See the Warning in Section 1.

➡**Note: The fuel filter/fuel level sensor module is located in the right compartment of the fuel tank. This module includes the fuel filter, the fuel pressure regulator and a fuel level sensor. This Section covers the removal and installation of the complete module, which is removed as a complete assembly. You can replace either of these two components separately (see Section 6).**

19 Remove the fuel pump/fuel level sensor module from the left fuel tank compartment (see Steps 1 through 16).

20 Pull off the plastic access cover (see illustration).

21 Disconnect the fuel supply line quick-connect fitting (see illustration).

22 To prevent dirt from entering the fuel tank, clean the area surrounding the mounting flange for the fuel filter/fuel pressure regulator/

fuel level sensor module.

23 Using a hammer and a brass drift, tap on the lock-ring to turn it counterclockwise (see illustration 5.9). When the lock-ring is loose, unscrew it.

❈❈ **WARNING:**

Do NOT use a steel drift to loosen the lock-ring. Doing so could produce sparks, which could ignite fuel vapors from the tank.

24 Before removing the fuel filter/fuel pressure regulator/fuel level sensor module, note the square tab on the circumference of the mounting flange, which faces forward (see illustration 5.10). The flange must be oriented just like this when you install the fuel filter/fuel pressure regulator/fuel level sensor module.

25 Lift up the mounting flange for the fuel filter/fuel pressure regulator/fuel level sensor module and carefully remove the module (see illustration). The electrical harness and fuel return lines, which you have already disconnected from the fuel pump/fuel level sensor module, are permanently attached to the module that you're removing, so make sure that they don't get caught on anything.

26 If you want to replace the fuel filter, the fuel pressure regulator or the fuel level sensor, refer to Section 6.

27 Installation is the reverse of removal.

---

6   Fuel pump/fuel level sensor module and fuel filter/fuel pressure regulator/fuel level sensor module - component replacement

LEFT FUEL LEVEL SENSOR AND FUEL PUMP MODULE

▶ Refer to illustrations 6.2 and 6.3

1   Remove the fuel pump/fuel level sensor module (see Section 5).

2   Carefully cut the wiring harness clip (see illustration) and disen-

gage the fuel level sensor wires from the clip.

3   Loosen the two retaining clips (see illustration) and pull the fuel level sensor out of the fuel pump module.

4   You can replace the fuel level sensor unit or the fuel pump module. No further disassembly of the pump module is possible.

5   Installation is the reverse of removal.

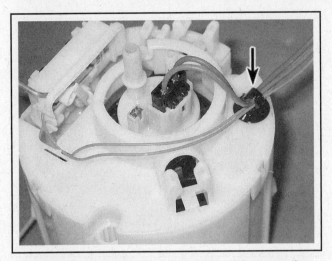

6.2 Carefully cut this wiring harness clip and disengage the fuel level sensor leads

6.3 To remove the left fuel level sensor from the fuel pump module, pry these two black clips loose and pull the sensor straight up

6.7 To detach the fuel level sensor from the fuel filter module, spread these four locking tangs away from the module and pull off the sensor

RIGHT FUEL LEVEL SENSOR, FUEL PRESSURE REGULATOR AND FUEL FILTER MODULE

▶ **Refer to illustrations 6.7, 6.8, 6.10, 6.11 and 6.14**

6 Remove the fuel filter/fuel pressure regulator/fuel level sensor module (see Section 5).

7 Detach the fuel level sensor from the fuel filter module (see illustration).

8 Carefully cut the two wire ties that secure the wiring to the fuel return lines, disconnect the two ground wires from the fuel filter module (see illustration) and remove the fuel level sensor.

9 If you're just replacing the fuel pressure regulator, this is as far as you need to go. Installation is the reverse of removal.

10 To remove the fuel pressure regulator from the fuel filter module, pull out the retaining clip (see illustration).

11 Inspect the condition of the fuel pressure regulator O-rings (see illustration).

6.8 To remove the fuel level sensor from the fuel filter module, cut the two wire ties (1), then disconnect the ground wires from the ground terminal (2) at the check valve and from the ground terminal (3) at the fuel pressure regulator

6.10 To remove the fuel pressure regulator from the fuel filter module, pry off this retainer clip with a screwdriver

6.11 Inspect the condition of these two O-rings (you might find the smaller O-ring here, on the regulator, or it might be in the recess for the regulator in the underside of the fuel filter module)

12 If you're just replacing the fuel pressure regulator, this is as far as you need to go. Installation is the reverse of removal.

13 If you're replacing the fuel filter module, remove the ground ring (see illustration 6.14) from the recess for the fuel pressure regulator.

6.14 The arrow indicates the notch in which the ground ring terminal must be seated when installing the ring (the terminal has been moved out of the notch and offset a little so that you can see the notch)

14 When installing the ground ring in the new fuel filter module, make sure that the ground ring terminal is seated correctly in the notch (see illustration).

15 Installation is otherwise the reverse of removal.

7 Fuel tank - removal and installation

► **Refer to illustrations 7.9, 7.10, 7.11, 7.12, 7.13 and 7.14**

❊❊ **WARNING:**

See the Warning in Section 1.

1 Relieve the fuel system pressure (see Section 2).

2 Disconnect the cable from the negative battery terminal (see Chapter 5, Section 1).

3 Drain as much fuel out of the tank through the fuel filler neck tube as you can. Use a hard nylon tube with a 30-degree cut on the end to push open the check valve in the fuel filler neck (see illustration 5.3).

❊❊ **WARNING:**

Never start the siphoning action by mouth!

4 Remove the lower cushion from the back seat (see Chapter 11).

7.9 In the left rear wheel well, disconnect the quick-connect fitting for the fuel filler neck vent line. If you're unfamiliar with quick-connect fittings, refer to Section 4

7.10 In the right rear wheel well, disconnect the quick-connect fitting for the EVAP vent line. If you're unfamiliar with quick-connect fittings, refer to Section 4

7.11 Also in the right rear wheel well, disconnect the EVAP line quick-connect fitting. If you're unfamiliar with quick-connect fittings, refer to Section 4

7.12 Disconnect the fuel supply quick-connect fitting. If you're unfamiliar with quick-connect fittings, refer to Section 4

7.13 To detach the under-body splash shields, remove the two nuts at the front and the bolt in the middle, then pull the splash shield down to disengage the locator pins at the rear (left side shown)

7.14 To disconnect the fuel filler neck hose, loosen the screws for the hose clamps (A) and pull off the hose. To detach the left half of the fuel tank, remove the strap bolts (B) and remove the strap (right-side straps similar)

5   Remove the foam pad covering the access covers for the fuel pump/fuel level sensor module and the fuel filter/fuel pressure regulator/fuel level sensor (see illustration 5.5).

6   Remove the access cover for the fuel pump/fuel level sensor module (see illustration 5.6).

7   Disconnect the electrical connector from the fuel pump/fuel level sensor module (see illustration 5.7).

8   Loosen the rear wheel lug nuts. Raise the vehicle and place it securely on jackstands. Remove the rear wheels.

9   Disconnect the quick-connect fitting (see illustration) for the filler neck vent line in the left rear wheel well.

10   Disconnect the quick-connect fitting (see illustration) for the vent line quick-connect fitting in the right rear wheel well.

11   Disconnect the EVAP line quick-connect fitting (see illustration), which is also located in the right rear wheel well.

12   Disconnect the fuel supply line quick-connect fitting (see illustration).

13   Remove the under-body splash shields (see illustration).

14   Loosen the hose clamps for the fuel filler neck hose (see illustration) and disconnect the fuel filler neck pipe from the filler neck hose.

15   Remove the exhaust pipe(s) (see Section 14) and the driveshaft (see Chapter 8).

16   Support the fuel tank.

17   Remove the fuel tank retaining strap bolts and remove both retaining straps.

18   Carefully lower the fuel tank just far enough to pull the fuel tank filler neck vent line through the gap between the floorpan and the left end of the rear suspension crossmember. Pull the EVAP vent line through the gap between the floorpan and the right end of the suspension crossmember. Then make a final check of the upper part of the tank for anything else that still needs to be disconnected. When you have verified that EVERYTHING is disconnected, slowly lower the fuel tank.

19   Installation is the reverse of removal, noting the following points:

a)   *If you're replacing the fuel tank, remove all components from the old fuel tank and install them on the new tank. If you need help with the fuel pump/fuel level sensor module and the fuel filter/fuel pressure regulator/fuel level sensor module, refer to Sections 5 and 6. If you need help with the EVAP lines, refer to Chapter 6.*

b)   *Tighten the fuel tank strap bolts securely.*

8 Fuel tank cleaning and repair - general information

1   The fuel tank installed in the vehicles covered by this manual is not repairable. If it becomes damaged, it must be replaced.

2   Cleaning the fuel tank (due to fuel contamination) should be performed by a professional with the proper training to carry out this critical and potentially dangerous work. Even after cleaning and flush-

ing, explosive fumes may remain inside the fuel tank.

3   If the fuel tank is removed from the vehicle, it should not be placed in an area where sparks or open flames could ignite the fumes coming out of the tank. Be especially careful inside a garage where a gas-type appliance is located.

9 Air filter housing and air intake duct - removal and installation

2.7L AND 3.5L V6 MODELS

➡**Note: The accompanying photos depict the air intake duct and air filter housing used on 3.5L models. However, the air intake duct and air filter housing used on 2.7L models are quite similar.**

9.1 Air intake duct details (3.5L engine shown, 2.7L engine similar)

1   Intake Air Temperature (IAT) sensor electrical connector
2   Hose clamps

9.6 Before removing the air filter housing, disconnect the Positive Crankcase Ventilation (PCV) fresh air inlet hose (1) from the air filter housing cover, then remove the filter housing retaining bolt (2)

Air intake duct

▶ **Refer to illustration 9.1**

1   Disconnect the electrical connector from the Intake Air Temperature (IAT) sensor (see illustration).

2   Loosen the hose clamp screws and remove the air intake duct.

3   Inspect the condition of the air intake duct. Look for cracks, tears, deterioration and other damage. If the air intake duct is damaged in any way, replace it. A leaking air intake duct will allow the introduction of "false air" (unmetered air) into the air intake manifold, which will cause the air/fuel mixture to become excessively lean. A lean air/fuel mixture can cause rough running at idle, and even misfires if the leak is big enough.

4   Installation is the reverse of removal.

Air filter housing

▶ **Refer to illustrations 9.6 and 9.8**

➡**Note: The following procedure is for replacing the air filter housing, not for replacing the air filter element. If you want to replace the air filter element, refer to Chapter 1.**

5   Disconnect the air intake duct from the air filter housing (see illustration 9.1).

6   Disconnect the Positive Crankcase Ventilation (PCV) fresh air inlet hose from the air filter housing (see illustration).

7   Remove the air filter housing retaining bolt (see illustration 9.6) and remove the housing by lifting it straight up. The air filter housing is positioned by a single locator pin inserted into a hole in the fender and by a large inlet pipe on the bottom of the housing that fits over the outlet pipe of the air resonator box.

8   Inspect the condition of the rubber insulator that covers the locator pin (see illustration). If it's cracked, torn, deteriorated or otherwise damaged, replace it.

9.8 Inspect the condition of the rubber insulator covering this locator pin and replace it if it's damaged or deteriorated (V6 models)

9.12 To remove the air resonator box, remove the filter housing from the vehicle, remove the retaining bolt (1), then pull the two locator pins (2) out of their holes in the lower radiator support bracket

9 Installation is the reverse of removal. Make sure that the air filter housing locator pin is aligned with its mounting hole in the fender and that the inlet pipe on the bottom of the filter housing fits over the outlet pipe of the air resonator box, then install the filter housing retaining bolt.

Air resonator box

▶ **Refer to illustration 9.12**

10 Raise the front of the vehicle and place it securely on jackstands.
11 Remove the front engine splash shield (see Chapter 2).
12 Remove the air resonator box mounting bolt (see illustration).
13 Pull the two locator pins out of their mounting holes in the lower radiator support bracket and remove the resonator.
14 Inspect the condition of the rubber insulators covering the two locator pins. If either insulator is cracked, deteriorated or otherwise damaged, replace it.
15 Installation is the reverse of removal.

5.7L V8 ENGINE

Air intake duct

▶ **Refer to illustration 9.17**

16 Remove the engine cover (see *Intake manifold - removal and*

9.23 To detach the air filter housing from a V8 model, remove the retaining bolt

9.17 Air intake duct details (V8 engine)

1 *Intake Air Temperature (IAT) sensor electrical connector*
2 *Hose clamps*

installation in Chapter 2C).
17 Disconnect the electrical connector from the Intake Air Temperature (IAT) sensor (see illustration).
18 Loosen the hose clamp screws and remove the air intake duct.
19 Inspect the condition of the air intake duct. Look for cracks, tears, deterioration and other damage. If the air intake duct is damaged in any way, replace it. A leaking air intake duct will allow the introduction of "false air" (unmetered air) into the air intake manifold, which will cause the air/fuel mixture to become excessively lean. A lean air/fuel mixture can cause rough running at idle, and even misfires if the leak is big enough.
20 Installation is the reverse of removal.

Air filter housing

▶ **Refer to illustrations 9.23 and 9.24**

21 Disconnect the air intake duct from the air filter housing (see illustration 9.17).
22 Disconnect the Positive Crankcase Ventilation (PCV) fresh air inlet hose from the air filter housing.
23 Remove the air filter housing retaining bolt (see illustration) and remove the housing by lifting it straight up. The air filter housing is positioned by a pair of locator pins inserted into holes in the fender and by a large inlet pipe on the bottom of the housing that fits over the outlet pipe of the air resonator box.

9.24 Inspect the condition of the rubber insulators covering the two locator pins and replace them if they're damaged or deteriorated (V8 models)

24 Inspect the condition of the rubber insulators covering the locator pins (see illustration). If they're cracked, torn, deteriorated or otherwise damaged, replace them.

25 Installation is the reverse of removal. Make sure that the air filter housing locator pins are aligned with three mounting holes in the fender and that the inlet pipe on the bottom of the filter housing fits

over the outlet pipe of the air resonator box, then install the filter housing retaining bolt.

Air Resonator box

26 See Steps 10 through 15.

10 Fuel injection system - general information

The fuel injection systems used on all vehicles covered by this manual are the "sequential multiport" type. This means that there is a fuel injector in each intake port, and that these fuel injectors inject fuel into the intake ports in the cylinder firing order. The injectors are turned on and off by the Powertrain Control Module (PCM). When the engine is running, the PCM constantly monitors engine operating conditions with an array of information sensors, calculates the correct amount of fuel, then varies the interval of time during which the injectors are open. Sequential multiport systems provide much better control of the air/fuel mixture ratio than earlier fuel injection systems, and are therefore able to produce more power, better mileage and lower emissions.

The fuel injection system uses the PCM and an array of information sensors to determine and deliver the correct air/fuel ratio under all operating conditions. The fuel injection system consists of three sub-systems: air induction, electronic control and fuel delivery. The fuel injection system is also closely interrelated with PCM-controlled emission control systems. (For additional information about the PCM, the information sensors and the emission control systems, refer to Chapter 6.)

AIR INDUCTION SYSTEM

The air induction system consists of the air resonator box, the air filter housing, the air intake duct, the throttle body and the intake manifold. The throttle body contains a throttle plate that regulates the amount of air entering the intake manifold. The throttle plate is opened and closed response to input from the Accelerator Pedal Position Sensor (APPS); there is no accelerator cable. When you depress the accelerator pedal, the APPS measures the angle of the pedal and sends a voltage signal to the Powertrain Control Module (PCM) that's proportional to the pedal angle. The PCM processes this input, then commands a solenoid motor inside the throttle body to open or close the throttle plate accordingly.

The Manifold Absolute Pressure (MAP) sensor, which is located on the intake manifold, measures intake manifold pressure and vacuum and generates a variable voltage signal that's proportional to the pressure or vacuum. The PCM uses this data to calculate the load on the engine.

The Intake Air Temperature (IAT) sensor, which is located on the air intake duct, relays a voltage signal to the PCM that varies in accordance with the temperature of the incoming air. The PCM uses this data to calculate how rich or lean the air/fuel mixture should be.

All of the air induction components (air resonator box, air filter housing, air intake duct and throttle body) are covered in this Chapter, except for the intake manifold, which is covered in Chapter 2, and the information sensors, which are covered in Chapter 6.

There is no Idle Air Control (IAC) valve on these engines. When the engine is idling, the PCM maintains the correct idle speed by regulating the amount of air that bypasses the (closed) throttle plate. The idle speed is controlled by the PCM in response to the running conditions

of the engine (cold or warm running, power steering pressure high or low, air conditioning system on or off, etc.). As the PCM receives data from the information sensors (vehicle speed, coolant temperature, air conditioning and/or power steering load, etc.) it adjusts the idle according to the demands of the engine and driver. The idle control system consists of the PCM, the throttle plate solenoid motor inside the throttle body, and several information sensors, including the Engine Coolant Temperature (ECT) sensor, the Intake Air Temperature (IAT) sensor and the Manifold Absolute Pressure (MAP) sensor.

ELECTRONIC CONTROL SYSTEM

For more information about the electronic control system, including the PCM, its information sensors and output actuators, refer to Chapter 6.

FUEL DELIVERY SYSTEM

The fuel delivery system consists of the fuel pump/fuel level sensor module, the fuel filter/fuel pressure regulator/fuel level sensor module, the fuel rail and fuel injectors, and the hoses, lines and pipes that carry fuel between all of these components. This is a returnless system; there is no fuel return line from the fuel rail back to the fuel tank. For more information about the fuel lines and the various types of fittings used on different models, refer to Section 4.

The fuel pump is an in-tank design. It's accessible by removing the rear seat cushion and an access plate in the floor. Because of the "tunnel" in the fuel tank for the driveshaft, the tank is essentially divided into two tanks, although it's a one-piece assembly. There are two fuel level sensors, one for each side of the tank. Each fuel level sensor is integrated into one of the modules. The fuel level sensors are actually information sensors for the Powertrain Control Module (PCM) but their replacement involves removing one of the module and removing the fuel level sensor, so their replacement procedures are in this Chapter (see Sections 5 and 6).

The fuel pump/fuel level sensor module is located in the left half of the tank. Fuel is drawn through a "sock" (or strainer) at the pump inlet, then pumped out the upper end of the pump, through the outlet hose and through the main fuel filter, which is located in the other (right) half of the fuel tank.

The fuel filter/pressure regulator/fuel level sensor module, which is located in the right half of the tank, is also accessible by removing the rear seat cushion and an access plate in the floor. The fuel filter and fuel pressure regulator are connected to the fuel pump by a pair of lines that ensure that the two sides of the fuel tank contain an equal amount of fuel.

The fuel pressure regulator is an integral part of the fuel filter. The regulator, which is mounted in the underside of the fuel filter housing, maintains the fuel pressure within the specified operating range. When the operating pressure exceeds the specified operating range, the pressure regulator opens and sends the excess fuel back into the fuel tank (there is no return fuel line from the fuel rail back to the tank). After the fuel has been filtered, it's pumped through a fuel supply line to the fuel rail on the engine.

The fuel rail, which is bolted to the intake manifold, functions as a reservoir for pressurized fuel so that there's always enough fuel available for acceleration and high speed operation. The upper end of each injector is inserted into the fuel rail and the lower end of each injector is inserted into the intake manifold. The upper and lower ends of each injector are sealed by O-rings.

Each fuel injector is a solenoid-actuated, pintle-type design consisting of a solenoid, plunger, ball or needle valve, and housing. When the engine is running, there is always voltage on the "hot" side of each injector terminal. Injector "drivers" inside the PCM turn the injectors on and off by switching their ground paths on and off. When the ground path for an injector is closed by the PCM, current flows through the solenoid coil, the ball or needle valve raises and pressurized fuel inside the injector housing squirts out the nozzle into the intake port directly above the intake valve(s). The quantity of fuel injected each time an injector opens is determined by its "pulse width," which is the interval of time during which the valve is open.

11 Fuel injection system - check

▶ **Refer to illustrations 11.7 and 11.8**

➡**Note: The following procedure is based on the assumption that the fuel pressure is adequate (see Section 3).**

1   Inspect all electrical connectors that are related to the system. Check the ground wire connections on the intake manifold for tightness. Loose connectors and poor grounds can cause many problems that resemble more serious malfunctions.

2   Verify that the battery is fully charged, as the control unit and sensors depend on an accurate supply of voltage in order to properly meter the fuel.

3   Inspect the air filter element (see Chapter 1). A dirty or partially blocked filter will severely impede performance and economy.

4   Check the related fuses. If a blown fuse is found, replace it and see if it blows again. If it does, search for a grounded wire in the harness.

5   Inspect the condition of all vacuum hoses connected to the intake manifold.

6   Remove the air intake duct and air resonator box (if equipped) and inspect the mouth of the throttle body for dirt, carbon or other residue build-up. If it's dirty, wipe it clean with a shop towel.

7   With the engine running, place an automotive stethoscope against each injector, one at a time, and listen for a clicking sound, indicating operation (see illustration). If you don't have a stethoscope, place the tip of a screwdriver against the injector and listen through the handle.

8   If an injector doesn't make a clicking sound, disconnect the electrical connector and measure the resistance of that injector (see illustration), then measure the resistance of the other injectors and compare the resistance of all six or eight injectors.

   a) *If the resistance of the silent injector is well outside the range of indicated resistance for the other injectors, the injector is defective.*

   b) *If the indicated resistance of all the injectors is within the same range, the Powertrain Control Module (PCM) or the injector wiring harness could be the cause of the injector not operating.*

9   Any further testing of the fuel injection system should be performed at a dealer service department or some other qualified repair shop.

10 For more information about the engine control system, refer to Chapter 6.

11.7 Use a stethoscope to determine if the injectors are working properly - they should make a steady clicking sound that rises and falls with engine speed changes

11.8 If you discover an injector that doesn't appear to be operating, measure the resistance of all of the injectors and compare them

12 Throttle body - removal and installation

2.7L AND 3.5L V6 ENGINES

▶ **Refer to illustrations 12.3, 12.4, 12.5 and 12.6**

→**Note: The accompanying photos depict the throttle body on a 3.5L V6, but the throttle body unit on a 2.7L engine is virtually identical.**

1   Disconnect the cable from the negative terminal of the battery (see Chapter 5, Section 1).

2   Remove the air intake duct (see Section 9).

3   Disconnect the electrical connector from the throttle body (see illustration).

4   On 3.5L models, remove the two nuts that attach the intake manifold bracket to the throttle body (see illustration), then remove the two lower bolts that attach the bracket to the cylinder head and remove the bracket.

5   Remove the four mounting bolts (see illustration) and remove the throttle body.

6   Remove the throttle body O-ring (see illustration) and inspect it for cracks, tears and deterioration. If it's damaged, replace it.

7   Wipe off the gasket mating surfaces of the throttle body and the intake manifold.

✳✳ CAUTION:

Do NOT use spray carburetor cleaners or silicone lubricants on any part of the throttle body.

8   Installation is the reverse of removal. Be sure to tighten the throttle body mounting bolts to the torque listed in this Chapter's Specifications. If a Diagnostic Trouble Code (DTC) is set, take the vehicle to a dealer and have the service department use a factory scan tool to re-learn parameters.

12.3 To disconnect the electrical connector from the throttle body, slide the lock (1) toward the harness, then depress the release tab (2) and pull off the connector (3.5L engine shown, 2.7L similar)

12.4 To remove the intake manifold bracket from a 3.5L V6 engine, remove the two upper nuts that attach the bracket to the throttle body and the two lower bolts that attach it to the cylinder head

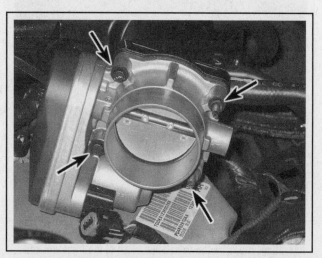

12.5 To remove the throttle body, remove these four bolts (3.5L engine shown, 2.7L similar)

12.6 Remove the throttle body O-ring and inspect it for cracks, tears and deterioration. If it's damaged, replace it

12.10 Loosen the hose clamp screw (1) and disconnect the air intake duct from the throttle body. Then slide the lock (2) toward the harness, depress the release tab (3) and pull off the connector

V8 ENGINE

▶ **Refer to illustrations 12.10 and 12.12**

9   Disconnect the cable from the negative terminal of the battery (see Chapter 5, Section 1).

10   Disconnect the air intake duct from the throttle body (see illustration).

11   Disconnect the electrical connector from the throttle body.

12   Remove the four throttle body mounting bolts (see illustration) and remove the throttle body.

13   Remove the throttle body's O-ring type gasket (see illustration 12.6) inspect it for cracks, tears and deterioration. If it's damaged,

12.12 To remove the throttle body from a V8 engine, remove these four bolts

replace it.

14   Wipe off the gasket mating surfaces of the throttle body and the intake manifold.

> ✳✳ **CAUTION:**
>
> **Do NOT use spray carburetor cleaners or silicone lubricants on any part of the throttle body.**

15   Installation is the reverse of removal. Be sure to tighten the throttle body mounting bolts to the torque listed in this Chapter's Specifications. If a Diagnostic Trouble Code (DTC) is set, take the vehicle to a dealer and have the service department use a factory scan tool to re-learn parameters.

13   Fuel rail and injectors - removal and installation

> ✳✳ **WARNING 1:**
>
> **See the Warning in Section 1.**

> ✳✳ **WARNING 2:**
>
> **The engine must be completely cool before beginning this procedure.**

2.7L AND 3.5L V6 ENGINES

▶ **Refer to illustrations 13.6a, 13.6b, 13.7, 13.9, 13.10, 13.11a, 13.11b, 13.11c and 13.12**

➡ **Note: You'll need to obtain a special fuel line disconnection tool, available at auto parts stores or from automotive tool manufacturers, to disconnect the metal-collar type fitting that connects the fuel supply line to the fuel rail.**

1   Remove the fuel tank filler neck cap to relieve any pressure inside the fuel tank. Then relieve the fuel system pressure (see Section 2).

2   Disconnect the cable from the negative terminal of the battery (see Chapter 5, Section 1).

3   Remove the air intake duct (see Section 9).

4   Disconnect the electrical connector from the throttle body and, on 3.5L V6 engines, remove the intake manifold bracket that's bolted between the cylinder head and the throttle body (see Section 12).

5   Remove the upper intake manifold (2.7L engines, see Chapter 2A; 3.5L engines, see Chapter 2B).

➡ **Note: It's not necessary to remove the throttle body to remove the upper intake manifold.**

6   Disconnect the fuel supply line from the fuel rail (see illustrations).

➡ **Note: You will need a special tool to disconnect this metal-collar type of quick-connect fitting. There are several versions of this tool. You can find these tools at your local auto parts store.**

7   Disconnect the electrical connectors from the fuel injectors (see

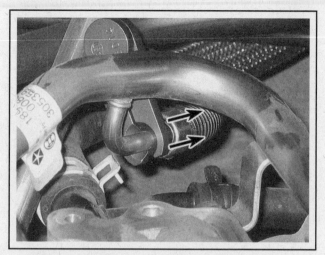

13.6a To disconnect the quick-connect fitting for the fuel supply line, insert the tool over the fitting, then push it into the female side of the fitting to disengage the wire spring inside . . .

illustration) and set the injector harness aside.

➡**Note: Each connector should be numbered with the corresponding cylinder number. If the number tag is obscured or missing, renumber the connectors. Also, the injector harness includes leads for other components, such as the ignition coils, but don't disconnect anything else unless it's necessary to do so in order to place the harness out of the way.**

8   Clean any debris from around the injectors so that it doesn't fall into the injector holes when you remove the fuel rail and injector assembly.

9   Remove the fuel rail mounting nuts/bolts (see illustration).

10 Gently rock the fuel rail and injectors to loosen the injectors and remove the fuel rail and fuel injectors as a single assembly (see illustration).

✳✳ CAUTION:

Do not attempt to separate the left and right fuel rails. Both sides are serviced together as an assembly.

13.9 To detach the fuel rail from the engine, remove these four mounting bolts (3.5L V6 engine shown, 2.7L V6 similar)

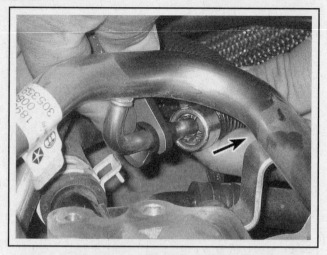

13.6b . . . and pull the female side of the fitting off the fuel supply pipe

13.7 To disconnect the electrical connector from an injector, slide the lock up (away from the injector, toward the harness), then depress the release tab and pull off the connector

13.10 Using a gentle rocking motion, wiggle the injectors free and lift the fuel rail and injectors out of the engine compartment as a single assembly

13.11a Using a screwdriver or pliers, remove the injector retaining clip . . .

11 Remove the injectors from the fuel rail, then remove and discard the O-rings (see illustrations).

➡Note: Whether you're replacing an injector or a leaking O-ring, it's a good idea to remove all the injectors from the fuel rail and replace all the O-rings.

12 Coat the new O-rings with clean engine oil and install them on the injector(s), then install the injector retaining clip and insert each injector into its corresponding bore in the fuel rail until the retainer clip snaps into place (see illustration).

13 Clean the injector bores on the intake manifold.

14 Guide the injectors/fuel rail assembly into the injector bores on the intake manifold. Make sure the injectors are fully seated, then tighten the fuel rail mounting bolts securely

15 The remainder of installation is the reverse of removal. After installing the fuel rail and injectors, turn the ignition switch to ON, but don't operate the starter. This activates the fuel pump for about two seconds, which builds up fuel pressure in the fuel lines and the fuel rail. Repeat this step two or three times, then check the fuel lines, fuel rail and injectors for fuel leakage.

13.11b . . . and withdraw the injector from the fuel rail

13.11c Carefully remove the O-rings from the injectors

V8 ENGINE

▶ **Refer to illustrations 13.19 and 13.20**

➡Note: You'll need to obtain a special fuel line disconnection tool, available at auto parts stores or from automotive tool manufacturers, to disconnect the metal-collar type fitting that connects the fuel supply line to the fuel rail.

13.12 Injector installation details

A *Flat part of retainer aligned with . . .*
B *. . . flat part of flange on fuel rail*
C *Slots in retainer will engage with . . .*
D *. . . semi-circular flanges when injector is pushed into pipe*

13.19 To disconnect the fuel supply line from the fuel rail on V8 engines, you'll need a tool like the one shown in illustrations 13.6a and 13.6b to disconnect the metal collar type quick-connect fitting (refer to Section 4 if you're unfamiliar with this type of fitting)

16 Remove the fuel tank filler neck cap to relieve any pressure inside the fuel tank. Then relieve the fuel system pressure (see Section 2).

17 Disconnect the cable from the negative terminal of the battery (see Chapter 5, Section 1).

18 Remove the air intake duct (see Section 9).

19 Disconnect the fuel supply line fitting (see illustration) from the right fuel rail. If you're unfamiliar with this metal-collar type quick-connect fitting, refer to Section 4 or to Step 6 above.

➡**Note: You will need a special tool to disconnect this metal collar type of quick-connect fitting. There are several versions of this tool. You can find these tools at your local auto parts store.**

20 Disconnect the electrical connectors from all eight fuel injectors (see illustration).

21 Remove the fuel rail mounting bolts.

22 Starting with the left side of the fuel rail, carefully pull on the injectors while wiggling them from side to side at the same time until all four injectors start to clear their mounting holes. Then go the right side and repeat this step. Go back and forth between the two sides of the engine, gradually working the injectors out of their mounting holes, until all eight injectors are free. When all of the injectors are free, remove the fuel rail and injectors as a single assembly (see illustration).

23 To remove an injector from the fuel rail, remove the injector retainer clip and pull the injector out of the fuel rail (see illustrations 13.11a and 13.11b).

➡**Note: Whether you're replacing an injector or a leaking O-ring, it's a good idea to remove all the injectors from the fuel rail and replace all the O-rings.**

24 Remove the O-rings from the injector (see illustration 13.11c), discard them and install new O-rings. Be sure to lubricate the new O-

13.20 Disconnect the electrical connectors (1) from all eight fuel injectors (see illustration 13.7 for disconnection technique). Remove the mounting bolts (2) to remove the fuel rail (left fuel rail shown, right rail identical)

rings with clean engine oil before installing the injectors into the fuel rail (see illustration 13.12).

25 Installation is the reverse of removal. Be sure to tighten the fuel rail mounting bolts securely. After installing the fuel rail and injectors, turn the ignition switch to ON, but don't operate the starter. This activates the fuel pump for about two seconds, which builds up fuel pressure in the fuel lines and the fuel rail. Repeat this step two or three times, then check the fuel lines, fuel rail and injectors for fuel leakage.

14 Exhaust system servicing - general information

▸ Refer to illustrations 14.1a, 14.1b, 14.4a and 14.4b

✳✳ **WARNING:**

The vehicle's exhaust system generates very high temperatures and must be allowed to cool down completely before touching any of the components. Be especially careful around the catalytic converter, which stays hot longer than other exhaust components.

1 The exhaust system consists of the exhaust manifolds, the exhaust pipes, the catalytic converter(s), the muffler, the tailpipe, various exhaust heat shields and all connecting flanges and clamps. The exhaust system is isolated from the vehicle body and from chassis components by a series of rubber hangers (see illustrations). Inspect these hangers periodically for cracks or other signs of deterioration, and replace them as necessary. Some exhaust components are also supported by brackets bolted to the underside of the vehicle. Make sure that these brackets are tightly fastened to the exhaust system and to the vehicle and that they're neither cracked nor corroded.

2 Conduct regular inspections of the exhaust system to keep it safe and quiet. Look for any damaged or bent parts, open seams, holes, loose connections, excessive corrosion or other defects which could allow exhaust fumes to enter the vehicle. Do not repair deteriorated exhaust system components; replace them with new parts.

14.1a Inspect the exhaust system rubber hangers for damage. These are typical exhaust hangers for the intermediate exhaust pipe and pre-muffler

3 If the exhaust system components are extremely corroded, or rusted together, you'll need welding equipment and a cutting torch to remove them. The convenient strategy at this point is to have a muffler repair shop remove the corroded sections with a cutting torch. If you

14.1b Typical exhaust hangers for the main muffler

14.4a Be sure to apply penetrating oil to exhaust system fasteners before attempting to loosen them

14.4b Nuts and bolts on clamps used to secure slip joints are also subjected heat, water, mud and grime, so they should be sprayed with penetrating oil as well

want to save money by doing it yourself, but you don't have a welding outfit and cutting torch, simply cut off the old components with a hacksaw. If you have compressed air, there are special pneumatic cutting chisels (available from specialty tool manufacturers) that can also be used. If you decide to tackle the job at home, be sure to wear safety goggles to protect your eyes from metal chips and wear work gloves to protect your hands.

4   Replacement of exhaust system components is basically a matter of removing the heat shields, disconnecting the component and installing a new one. The heat shields and exhaust system hangers must be reinstalled in the original locations or damage could result. Due to the high temperatures and exposed locations of the exhaust system components, rust and corrosion can seize parts together. Penetrating oils are available to help loosen frozen fasteners. However, in some cases it may be necessary to cut the pieces apart with a hacksaw or cutting torch. (Only persons experienced in this work should employ this latter method.) Here are some simple guidelines to follow when repairing the exhaust system:

a) *Work from the back to the front when removing exhaust system components.*

b) *Apply penetrating oil to the exhaust system component fasteners (see illustrations) to make them easier to remove.*

c) *While you're waiting for the penetrant to loosen up the exhaust system fasteners, always disconnect the electrical connector for the downstream oxygen sensor and remove the sensor before removing the exhaust pipe section that includes the catalytic converter.*

c) *Use new gaskets, hangers and clamps when installing exhaust systems components.*

d) *Apply anti-seize compound to the threads of all exhaust system fasteners during reassembly.*

e) *Be sure to allow sufficient clearance between newly installed parts and all points on the underbody to avoid overheating the floor pan and possibly damaging the interior carpet and insulation. Pay particularly close attention to the catalytic converter and heat shield.*

Specifications

General

Fuel pressure	53 to 63 psi

Torque specifications

Throttle body mounting bolts (all engines)	105 in-lbs

Section

Reference to other Chapters

5

ENGINE ELECTRICAL SYSTEMS

1   General information

1   The engine electrical systems include all ignition, charging and starting components. Because of their engine-related functions, these components are discussed separately from chassis electrical devices such as the lights, the instruments, etc. (which are included in Chapter 12).

2   Always observe the following precautions when working on the electrical systems:

a) *Be extremely careful when servicing engine electrical components. They are easily damaged if checked, connected or handled improperly.*

b) *Never leave the ignition switch on for long periods of time with the engine off.*

c) *Don't disconnect the battery cables while the engine is running.*

d) *Maintain correct polarity when connecting a battery cable from another vehicle during jump-starting.*

e) *Always disconnect the negative cable first and hook it up last or the battery may be shorted by the tool being used to loosen the cable clamps.*

3   It's also a good idea to review the safety-related information regarding the engine electrical systems located in the *Safety First!* Section near the front of this manual before beginning any operation included in this Chapter.

BATTERY RECONNECTION PROCEDURES

4   Anytime that you disconnect the battery, you must carry out the following procedures after reconnecting the battery.

Front window auto-up system

5   If the vehicle is equipped with the front window auto-up system, the door module must be recalibrated after reconnecting the battery:

a) *Turn the ignition key to the RUN position.*

b) *Depress the power window switch for the left (driver side) front door window until the window reaches its fully-closed position and stops, and keep depressing the power window switch for at least two more seconds after the window stops.*

c) *Depress the power window switch for the left (driver side) front door window until the window reaches its fully-open position and stops, and keep depressing the power window switch for at least two more seconds after the window stops.*

d) *Again, depress the power window switch for the left (driver side) front door window until the window reaches its fully-closed position and stops, and keep depressing the power window switch for at least two more seconds after the window stops.*

e) *Repeat Steps b, c and d for the right (passenger side) front door window.*

f) *Verify that the windows are correctly calibrated by operating the express down and up features. If the windows are still not correctly calibrated, repeat this procedure until they are. If you're unable to calibrate the auto-up system using this procedure, have the system diagnosed and calibrated by a dealer service department.*

Electronic Stability Program (ESP)

6   If the vehicle is equipped with ESP, the Steering Angle Sensor (SAS) must be recalibrated after reconnecting the battery, or after reconnecting any Anti-Lock Brake (ABS) component (the ABS system is part of the ESP). If the SAS is not recalibrated after reconnecting the battery or reconnecting an ABS component, the ESP/SAS indicator lamp will turn on after five ignition cycles, indicating the need for recalibration.

➡**Note: The following procedure does not apply to 2007 models, on which the SAS must be recalibrated with a factory scan tool. If the SAS is not recalibrated immediately after reconnecting the battery or reconnecting an ABS component, the ESP/SAS indicator lamp will flash continuously until the SAS is recalibrated, though it won't set any Diagnostic Trouble Codes (DTCs).**

a) *Start the engine.*

b) *Center the steering wheel.*

c) *Turn the steering wheel all the way to the left until it stops, then turn the wheel all the way to the right until it stops.*

d) *Center the steering wheel.*

e) *Stop the engine.*

2   Battery - emergency jump starting

Refer to the *Booster battery (jump) starting* procedure at the front of this manual.

3   Battery - check, removal and installation

✳✳ WARNING:

Hydrogen gas is produced by the battery, so keep open flames and lighted cigarettes away from it at all times. Always wear eye protection when working around a battery. Rinse off spilled electrolyte immediately with large amounts of water.

✳✳ CAUTION:

Always disconnect the negative cable first and hook it up last or you might accidentally short the battery with the tool that you're using to loosen the cable clamps.

CHECK

◆ **Refer to illustrations 3.2 and 3.3**

1   To check the battery state of charge, look at the indicator eye (if equipped) on top of the battery. The eye is the top of a hydrometer that's built into the battery. If the indicator eye is green, the battery is 75 to 100 percent charged. If the indicator eye is black, the battery is 0 to 75 percent charged. If the indicator eye is clear (or bright), the battery electrolyte level is low. All factory-installed batteries are the maintenance-free type, i.e. the cell caps cannot be removed, so no water can be added. If the indicator eye is clear on a maintenance-free battery,

3.2 To test the open circuit voltage of the battery, connect a voltmeter to the battery terminals. A fully charged battery should have at least 12.4 volts

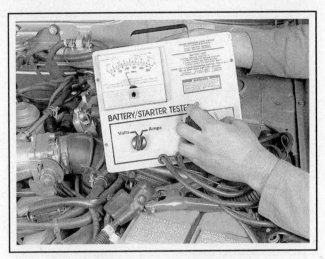

3.3 Connect a battery load tester to the battery and check the battery condition under load following the tool manufacturer's instructions

replace the battery. If the maintenance-free battery has been replaced by a low-maintenance battery with removable cell caps, remove the caps and add enough water to bring it up to the correct level (which should be marked on the outside of the battery case. (If there are no MINIMUM and MAXIMUM lines on the battery case, add enough water to each cell so that the plates are fully immersed).

➡**Note: A low-electrolyte/low-water condition is often a symptom of overcharging, so check the alternator charging voltage (see Section 9) and, if necessary, replace the alternator. Otherwise, the same condition will reoccur.**

2   Perform an open-voltage circuit test using a voltmeter (see illustration).

➡**Note: To obtain an accurate voltage measurement, you must first remove the battery's surface charge. To remove the surface**

3.5 When disconnecting the battery cables, always disconnect the cable from the negative terminal (1) first, then disconnect the cable from the positive terminal (2)

charge, turn on the high beams for ten seconds, then turn them off and let the vehicle stand for two minutes. With the engine and all accessories off, touch the negative probe of the voltmeter to the negative terminal of the battery and the positive probe to the positive terminal of the battery. The battery voltage should be 12.4 volts or more. If the battery is less than the specified voltage, charge the battery before proceeding to the next test. Do not proceed with the battery load test unless the battery charge is correct.

3   Perform a battery load test. An accurate check of the battery condition can only be performed with a battery load tester (available at most auto parts stores). This test evaluates the ability of the battery to operate the starter and other accessories during periods of heavy amperage draw (load). The tool increases the load demand (amperage draw) on the battery. Connect a battery load-testing tool to the terminals (see illustration). Load test the battery according to the tool manufacturer's instructions. Typically a load of 50-percent of the cold cranking amperage rating is applied during the test. The cold cranking amperage rating can usually be found on the battery label. Maintain the load on the battery for a maximum of 15 seconds. The battery voltage should not drop below 9.6 volts during the test. If the battery condition is weak or defective, the tool will indicate this condition immediately.

➡**Note: Cold temperatures will cause the voltage readings to drop slightly. Follow the chart given in the tool manufacturer's instructions to compensate for cold climates. Minimum load voltage for freezing temperatures (32-degrees F) should be approximately 9.1 volts.**

REPLACEMENT

Battery

▸ **Refer to illustrations 3.5 and 3.6**

4   Remove the spare tire access cover.

5   Disconnect the cable from the negative battery terminal (see illustration), then disconnect the cable from the positive terminal.

3.6 To remove the battery, loosen the retention strap buckle (1), disconnect the vent tube (2), remove the hold-down bolt (3) and remove the hold-down clamp (4)

6 Remove the battery retention strap (see illustration).
7 Disconnect the vent tube from the battery.
8 Remove the battery hold-down bolt and hold-down clamp.
9 Lift out the battery. Be careful - it's heavy.

3.16 To detach the battery tray, remove these four bolts

3.15 To detach the Power Distribution Center (rear fuse and relay box) from the battery tray, disengage these two tabs with a couple of small screwdrivers

➡**Note: Battery straps and handlers are available at most auto parts stores for a reasonable price. They make it easier to remove and carry the battery.**

10 While the battery is out, inspect the tray for corrosion deposits. Clean the battery tray, then use a baking soda/water solution to neutralize any deposits to prevent further oxidation. If the metal around the tray is corroded, too, clean it as well and spray the area with a rust-inhibiting paint.
11 If corrosion has leaked down past the battery tray, remove the tray (see Step 14) for further cleaning.
12 If you're replacing the battery, make sure you get an identical unit, with the same dimensions, amperage rating, cold cranking rating, etc.
13 Installation is the reverse of removal.

Battery tray

▶ **Refer to illustrations 3.15 and 3.16**

14 Remove the battery (see Steps 4 through 9).
15 Detach the Power Distribution Center (rear fuse and relay box) from the battery tray (see illustration).
16 Remove the battery tray mounting bolts (see illustration) and remove the battery tray.
17 Installation is the reverse of removal.

4   Battery cables - check, general information and replacement

CHECK

1 Periodically inspect the entire length of each battery cable for damage, cracked or burned insulation and corrosion. Poor battery cable connections can cause starting problems and decreased engine performance.
2 Check the cable-to-terminal connections at the ends of the cables for cracks, loose wire strands and corrosion. The presence of white, fluffy deposits under the insulation at the cable terminal connection is a sign that the cable is corroded and should be replaced. Check the terminals for distortion, missing mounting bolts and corrosion.

GENERAL INFORMATION

3 When removing the cables, always disconnect the cable from the negative battery terminal first and hook it up last to prevent the battery from being accidentally shorted by the tool you're using to loosen the cable clamps. Even if you're only replacing the cable for the positive terminal, be sure to disconnect the cable from the negative battery terminal first.
4 When buying new battery cables, take the old cables with you. It is critical that you replace the old cables with identical replacement cables. Battery cables have characteristics that make them easy to iden-

4.10 To disconnect the positive battery cable from the rear fuse and relay box, remove this nut

tify: positive cables are usually red and larger in cross-section; ground cables are usually black and smaller in cross-section.

   5   Clean the threads of the solenoid terminals and/or ground terminals with a wire brush to remove rust and corrosion. Apply a light coat of battery terminal corrosion inhibitor or petroleum jelly to the threads to prevent future corrosion.

   6   Attach the cable to the solenoid or ground connection and tighten the mounting nut/bolt securely.

   7   Before connecting a new cable to the battery, make sure that it reaches the battery post without having to be stretched.

   8   Connect the positive cable first, followed by the negative cable.

REPLACEMENT

Positive battery cables

Interior cable

▶ **Refer to illustrations 4.10, 4.11a, 4.11b and 4.14**

➡**Note: Because the battery is located in the trunk, the interior positive battery cable is longer than the typical positive cable in a vehicle with a battery located in the engine compartment. The cable is routed from the battery in the trunk, under the right end of the rear seat, along the right side of the floor, to a terminal located at the right front corner of the passenger compartment, under the right end of the instrument panel. This cable is not easy to replace, because you will have to remove the front passenger seat, the back seat cushion, the right front and right rear door sill trim plates, the right B-pillar trim panel and the carpeting.**

4.11b To disengage the positive battery cable from this cable guide, just pull it up and out of the clips

4.11a To disengage the positive battery cable from this clamp, carefully pry off the upper half of the clamp at the indicated points with a small screwdriver (the upper half of the clamp is pushed onto a pair of threaded studs)

   9   Disconnect the ground cable, then the positive cable, from the negative battery terminal (see Section 3).

   10 Disconnect the positive cable from the rear fuse and relay box (see illustration).

   11 Trace the positive battery cable forward and disengage it from the harness clamp and guide that secure it to the floor (see illustrations).

   12 Working inside the vehicle, remove the front passenger seat, the rear seat cushion, the right front and right rear door sill trim plates, the right B-pillar trim panel and the right kick panel (see Chapter 11). Then peel back the carpeting on the right side to expose the positive battery cable.

   13 Note the routing of the cable before removing it. Make a sketch if necessary. From the right front corner of the trunk floor, the positive battery cable is routed under the right end of the rear seat back into the vehicle interior, then it's routed along the right side of the floor, adjacent to the sill area. At the right front corner of the passenger compartment, the cable is routed up the firewall to an insulated terminal under the right end of the instrument panel, near the right kick panel area.

   14 Disengage the cable from all clips inside the vehicle (see illustration).

4.14 The positive battery cable (A) enters the vehicle interior under the right rear end of the rear seat back, then dives down to the right side of the floor and travels along the right sill area. Along the way the cable is secured by a series of clips like this one in the rear seat area. To disengage the cable from each clip, simply pull it straight up

4.19 Open this cap (1) and remove the nut (2) that secures the engine compartment positive battery cable to the terminal, then pull out the cable clip (3). After you have disconnected the cable from the three clips across the back of the engine (see next illustration) and from the starter solenoid terminal, pull the cable out through the grommet (4). While the cable is out, inspect this grommet to make sure that it's in good shape

15 Remove the protective cap from the forward cable terminal on the firewall and disconnect the cable from the terminal.

16 Installation is the reverse of removal.

Engine compartment cable

▶ **Refer to illustrations 4.19, 4.21 and 4.22**

➥**Note: The engine compartment positive battery cable is routed from a terminal inside the right front wheel well, through a rubber grommet into the engine compartment, across the back of the engine to the left side of the engine compartment, where it turns forward to the starter solenoid.**

17 Loosen the right front wheel lug nuts. Raise the vehicle and place it securely on jackstands. Remove the right front wheel.

18 Remove the splash shield from the right front wheel well (see Chapter 11).

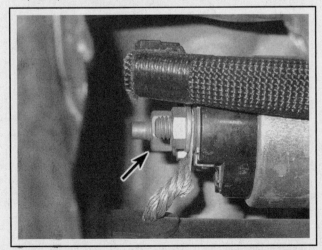

4.22 To disconnect the positive battery cable from the starter solenoid terminal, remove this nut

4.21 There are three clips that secure the engine compartment positive battery cable to a plate at the back of the engine. Here are two of those clips (right clip not visible in this photo) on a 3.5L V6. To detach the cable clips from the plate, simply pull them out

19 Open the cap and remove the nut that secures the engine compartment cable to the bulkhead terminal (see illustration).

20 Trace the routing of the cable from the wheel well through the rubber grommet into the engine compartment, across the back of the engine and to the starter motor solenoid. Carefully note the cable routing because you must use this same route when installing the new cable. Make a sketch if necessary.

21 Three retaining clips secure the cable where it's routed across the back of the engine. On V6 engines, these clips are mounted on a short plate located right above the top of the transmission bellhousing (see illustration). On V8 engines, the plate for the clips is mounted in the same location above the bellhousing, but it's much wider and semi-circular in shape, so that it fits tightly against the top of the bellhousing. To disengage the three cable clips, simply pull them out of their mounting holes in the plate.

22 Disconnect the positive battery cable from the starter solenoid terminal (see illustration).

23 Remove the cable.

24 Before installing a new cable, inspect the condition of the grommet (see illustration 4.19). Make sure that it's not cracked, torn or otherwise deteriorated. If it's damaged, replace it. Also, if any of the locator clips (see illustration 4.21) across the back of the engine are damaged, replace them.

25 Installation is the reverse of removal.

Ground cables

Ground cable in trunk

▶ **Refer to illustration 4.27**

➥**Note: There is one short ground cable in the trunk. It's routed from the negative terminal to a terminal right behind the battery tray.**

26 Disconnect the ground cable from the negative battery terminal (see Section 3).

27 Remove the nut that secures the ground cable to the stud terminal right next to the battery tray (see illustration).

28 Installation is the reverse of removal.

4.27 To disconnect the battery ground cable in the trunk, remove this nut

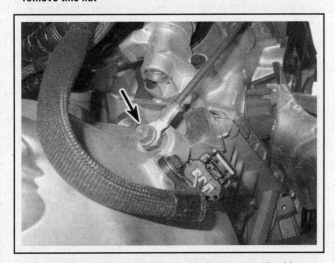

4.32 To disconnect the engine compartment ground cable from the transmission bellhousing, remove this nut (3.5L V6 shown, other engines similar)

4.30 To disconnect the upper end of the engine compartment ground cable, remove this nut (A). The other nut (B) secures one end of another ground cable that is integrated into a large engine compartment harness

Ground cables in engine compartment

▶ Refer to illustrations 4.30 and 4.32

➡Note: There are two ground cables in the engine compartment, but only one of them is separately replaceable. Its upper end is connected to the right strut tower and the lower end is connected to the upper right part of the transmission bellhousing. The other ground cable is also connected to the right strut tower, but it's routed through a large engine compartment harness. If this cable becomes damaged, the best course of action to take is to splice a new section of cable (or cable end) to it.

29 Disconnect the ground cable from the negative battery terminal (see Section 3).

30 Disconnect the ground cable from the right strut tower (see illustration).

31 Raise the vehicle and place it securely on jackstands.

32 Disconnect the ground cable from the upper right part of the transmission bellhousing (see illustration).

33 Installation is the reverse of removal.

5 Ignition system - general information

All engines are equipped with a distributorless ignition system. The ignition system consists of the battery, the ignition coils, the spark plugs, the knock sensor (two on V8 models, the Camshaft Position (CMP) sensor, the Crankshaft Position (CKP) sensor, the Manifold Absolute Pressure (MAP) sensor, the Throttle Position (TP) sensor and the Powertrain Control Module (PCM). (For more information about the CMP sensor, CKP sensor, knock sensors, MAP sensor, TP sensor and PCM, refer to Chapter 6.) The PCM controls the base ignition timing and the ignition timing advance on all engines. The base ignition timing is not adjustable on any model.

The PCM controls the ignition system by opening and closing the ignition coil ground circuit. The computerized ignition system provides complete control of the ignition timing by determining the optimum timing in response to engine speed, coolant temperature, throttle position and vacuum pressure in the intake manifold. These parameters are relayed to the PCM by the camshaft position sensor, crankshaft

position sensor, throttle position sensor, coolant temperature sensor and manifold absolute pressure sensor. The PCM and the crankshaft position sensor are very important components of the ignition system. The ignition system will not operate and the engine will not start if the PCM or the crankshaft position sensor are defective. Refer to Chapter 6 for additional information on the various sensors.

On 2005 V8 engines, there are eight ignition coils, each with two secondary terminals, eight spark plug wires and 16 spark plugs, i.e. two sparks per cylinder. Each coil is located on top of and connected directly to one spark plug, and fires a plug in the companion cylinder on the other cylinder bank via a second high-tension terminal and a spark plug wire. The spark plug wire routing looks complicated, but the corresponding spark plug/coil number is displayed on the each plug wire: 1/6, 2/3, 4/7 and 5/8. On these engines, each coil fires two spark plugs, one at the cylinder directly below the coil and, simultaneously, one plug at the "companion cylinder" for that cylinder. Cylinders one and six are companion cylinders, as are cylinders two and three, four and seven, and five and eight.

All other engines use a coil-over-plug system, which consists of an individual coil above, and connected directly to, each spark plug (V6 engines), or a coil above and connected directly to each pair of plugs (2006 and 2007 V8 engines). There are no spark plug wires on any of these engines.

On all engines, the Automatic Shut Down (ASD) relays supply battery voltage to the ignition coil primary circuits. The PCM fires the coils in firing order sequence by turning the ground paths for their primary circuits on and off.

6 Ignition system - check

▶ Refer to illustrations 6.5a, 6.5b, 6.5c and 6.5d

❋❋ WARNING 1:

Because of the high voltage generated by the ignition system, extreme care should be taken whenever an operation is performed involving ignition components. This not only includes the ignition coil, but also related components and test equipment.

❋❋ WARNING 2:

The following procedure requires the engine to be cranked during testing. When cranking the engine, make sure that no meter lead, loose clothing, long hair, etc. come in contact with any moving parts (drivebelt, cooling fan, etc.).

1 Before proceeding with the ignition system, check the following items:

  a) *Make sure the battery cable clamps, where they connect to the battery, are clean and tight.*
  b) *Test the condition of the battery (see Section 3). If it does not pass all the tests, replace it with a new battery.*
  c) *Check the ignition system wiring and connections for tightness, damage, corrosion or any other signs of a bad connection.*
  d) *Check the related fuses inside the engine compartment fuse and relay box (see Chapter 12). If they're burned, determine the cause and repair the circuit.*

2 If the engine turns over but won't start or has a severe misfire, perform the following steps using a calibrated ignition tester to make sure there is sufficient secondary ignition voltage to fire the spark plugs.

3 Disable the fuel system by removing the fuel pump relay, which is located in the rear fuse and relay box, in the trunk (see Chapter 4).

4 Remove the ignition coil (see Section 7) to test for spark to the plug(s) that it fires.

➡Note: On V8 engines, you'll have to simultaneously test for spark at both coil high-tension terminals, so you'll need two testers.

5 Hook up the calibrated ignition system tester(s) (available at most auto parts stores) to the boot(s) underneath the coils (see illustrations). Note whether the bulb within the tester body flashes.

6 If the tester flashes during cranking, sufficient voltage is reaching the plug to fire it. Repeat this test for each spark plug (or both plugs at each cylinder on Hemis) to verify that all the coils are OK.

7 If no flashes occur during cranking at any one cylinder, inspect the primary wire connection at the coil that isn't functioning. Make sure that it's clean and tight.

8 If the coil is operating but a cylinder still has a misfire condition, the plug(s) might be fouled. So remove and inspect the plug(s) (see Chapter 1), then retest.

9 If no sparks or intermittent sparks occur during cranking at all cylinders, the Powertrain Control Module (PCM) might be defective. Have the PCM checked out by a dealer service department or other qualified repair shop (testing the PCM is beyond the scope of the do-it-

6.5b **To use an ignition tester on a 2005 V8 engine, you'll need to test for spark twice at each cylinder. First, disconnect the plug wire coming from the companion cylinder's coil, connect it to the tester, connect the other end of the tester to the spark plug and crank over the engine. If there's enough power to fire the plug, the tester will flash. If the plug wire is putting out a healthy spark, remove the tester and reconnect the plug wire . . .**

6.5a **To use a calibrated ignition tester on a V6 model, remove an ignition coil, then connect the tester to the coil and the spark plug. Crank over the engine; if there's enough power to fire the plug, the tester will flash**

6.5c . . . then remove the ignition coil (see Section 7), connect the tester to the spark plug boot, connect the other end of the tester to the spark plug and crank over the engine again

6.5d To test the spark on a 2006 or 2007 V8 engine, you'll need two calibrated spark testers - one for each spark plug. Detach the ignition coil from the valve cover, then connect the testers to the coil and spark plugs and crank over the engine. If there's enough power to fire the plugs, the testers will flash

yourselfer because it requires expensive special tools). Any additional testing of the ignition system must be done by a dealer service department or by an independent repair shop with the right tools.

7 Ignition coil - check and replacement

CHECK

1   If a coil seems to be misfiring or not firing at all, or is causing the Powertrain Control Module (PCM) to set a Diagnostic Trouble Code (DTC) that indicates a misfire, try swapping it with an adjacent coil. If the suspect coil was causing a DTC for one cylinder, it will likely set the same DTC when it's installed above another cylinder. If this is the case, the coil is probably defective because it's unlikely that the harnesses for two adjacent ignition coils would both be defective. At any rate, no fur-

7.3 To remove an ignition coil from a V6 engine, depress the release tab on top of the electrical connector (1) and disconnect the connector, remove the coil mounting screw (2), then grasp the coil firmly and pull it off the spark plug (3.5L V6 shown, 2.7L V6 similar)

ther testing is possible at home. If you're not sure whether you should replace the coil at this point, consult a dealer service department or other qualified repair shop.

REPLACEMENT

V6 engines

▶ **Refer to illustration 7.3**

2   If you want to remove the rear ignition coil on the left cylinder head on a 2.7L V6, remove the air intake duct (see *Air filter housing - removal and installation* in Chapter 4). If you want to remove the rear ignition coil on the left cylinder head on a 3.5L V6, remove the upper intake manifold (see Chapter 2B). If you want to remove any of the three coils on the right cylinder head on either engine, remove the upper intake manifold (2.7L V6, see Chapter 2A; 3.5L V6, see Chapter 2B).

3   Disconnect the electrical connector from the coil (see Illustration).

4   Remove the ignition coil mounting screw and remove the coil.

5   Installation is the reverse of removal.

V8 engine

2005 models

▶ **Refer to illustration 7.7**

6   Remove the engine cover (see Chapter 2C).

7   Disconnect the electrical connector and the spark plug wire boot for the companion cylinder from the ignition coil (see illustration).

8   Remove the coil mounting bolts. To remove the coil, carefully pull it up with a twisting motion to disengage the rubber spark plug boots from the plugs.

9   While the coil is removed, inspect the condition of the rubber spark plug boot. If it's cracked, torn or deteriorated, replace it. Also

7.7 To remove an ignition coil from a 2005 V8 engine, push the slide lock (A) sideways to unlock the electrical connector, depress the release tab (B) and disconnect the connector, disconnect the spark plug wire boot (C) for the companion cylinder and remove the two coil mounting bolts (D)

7.12 To remove an ignition coil from a 2006 and later V8 engine, disconnect the electrical connector (1), then remove the two coil mounting bolts (2)

inspect the condition of the spark plug wire connected to the coil (see Chapter 1).

10 Installation is the reverse of removal.

2006 and later models

▶ Refer to illustration 7.12

11 Remove the engine cover (see Chapter 2C).

12 Disconnect the electrical connector from the ignition coil (see illustration).

13 Remove the coil mounting bolts. To remove the coil, carefully pull it up with a twisting motion to disengage the rubber spark plug boots from the plugs.

14 While the coil is removed, inspect the condition of the rubber spark plug boots. If they're cracked, torn or deteriorated, replace them.

15 Installation is the reverse of removal.

8   Charging system - general information and precautions

The charging system consists of the alternator; the Electronic Voltage Regulator (EVR), the ignition switch, the battery, an ambient air temperature sensor, a voltage gauge, a charge indicator light and the wiring between all the components. The charging system supplies electrical power for the ignition system, the lights, the radio, etc. The alternator is driven by a serpentine drivebelt at the front of the engine.

The ignition switch turns the charging system on and off. The system remains on as long as the engine is running and the Automatic Shut Down (ASD) relay is energized. When the PCM grounds the ASD control circuit, it energizes the ASD relay, which supplies voltage to the alternator field terminal (GEN SOURCE +) on the alternator. The EVR's field control circuit inside the PCM regulates the current output of the alternator (there is no external voltage regulator). The field control circuit is connected in series with the second rotor field terminal and ground.

The ambient air temperature sensor, which is mounted on the bumper, monitors the air temperature. The PCM uses the signal from the ambient air temperature sensor and data from monitored line voltage to vary the battery-charging rate. It does so by cycling the alternator's ground path, which controls the strength of the rotor's magnetic field. The PCM regulates the alternator's current output accordingly. System voltage is higher when the engine is cold and is gradually reduced to a lower voltage as the temperature increases.

When the engine is running, the voltage gauge on the instrument cluster indicates electrical system voltage. The indicator needle should be within the normal range if the battery is charged. If the needle moves

outside the normal range and stays there during normal driving, inspect the charging system (see Section 9). If the voltage gauge is defective, replace the instrument cluster (see Chapter 12). The voltage gauge cannot be serviced separately from the cluster.

The charging system doesn't ordinarily require periodic maintenance. However, you should inspect the drivebelt, the battery, the charging system wiring harness and all connections at the intervals outlined in Chapter 1. Be very careful when making electrical circuit connections to the alternator or the charging system circuit and note the following:

a) *When reconnecting wires to the alternator from the battery, be sure to note the polarity.*

b) *Before using arc-welding equipment to repair any part of the vehicle, disconnect the wires from the alternator and the battery terminals.*

c) *Never start the engine with a battery charger connected.*

d) *Always disconnect both battery cables before using a battery charger.*

e) *The alternator is turned by an engine drivebelt, which could cause serious injury if your hands, hair or clothes become entangled in it with the engine running.*

f) *Because the alternator is connected directly to the battery, it could arc or cause a fire if overloaded or shorted out.*

g) *Wrap a plastic bag over the alternator and secure it with rubber bands before steam-cleaning the engine.*

9 Charging system - check

▸ Refer to illustration 9.3

➡Note: These vehicles are equipped with an On-Board Diagnostic-II (OBD-II) system that is useful for detecting charging system problems because it can provide you with the Diagnostic Trouble Code (DTC) that will indicate the general nature of the problem. Refer to Chapter 6 for a list of the DTCs used by the Powertrain Control Module (PCM) on these vehicles and for the procedure you'll need to use to obtain DTCs.

1 If a malfunction occurs in the charging circuit, do not immediately assume that the alternator is causing the problem. First check the following items:

   a) *The battery cables where they connect to the battery. Make sure the connections are clean and tight.*
   b) *The battery electrolyte specific gravity (by observing the charge indicator on the battery). If it is low, charge the battery.*
   c) *Inspect the external alternator wiring and connections.*
   d) *Check the drivebelt condition and tension (see Chapter 1).*
   e) *Check the alternator mounting bolts for tightness.*
   f) *Run the engine and check the alternator for abnormal noise.*

2 Using a voltmeter, check the battery voltage with the engine off (see illustration 3.2). It should be at least 12.0 volts with a fully charged battery.

3 Start the engine and check the battery voltage again (see illustration). It should now be at least 13 volts, but should not read more than 15 volts.

9.3 To test the charging voltage of the battery, connect a voltmeter to the battery terminals. A healthy battery should have at least 13 volts, but not more than 15 volts

4 If the indicated voltage reading is less or more than the specified charging voltage, have the charging system checked at a dealer service department or other properly equipped repair facility. The voltage regulator on these models is contained within the PCM and it cannot be adjusted, removed or tampered with in any way.

10 Alternator - removal and installation

➡Note 1: If you are replacing the alternator, take the old one with you when purchasing a replacement unit. Make sure the new/rebuilt unit looks identical to the old alternator. Look at the terminals - they should be the same in number, size and location as the terminals on the old alternator. Finally, look at the identification numbers - they will be stamped into the housing or printed on a tag attached to the housing. Make sure the numbers are the same on both alternators.

10.8 Remove the upper alternator mounting bolt (A) and the support bracket bolt (B) and remove the support bracket (C) (3.5L V6 engine)

➡Note 2: Many new and remanufactured alternators do not have a pulley installed, so you may have to switch the pulley from the old unit to the new/rebuilt one. When buying an alternator, find out the shop's policy regarding pulleys; some shops will perform this service free of charge.

2.7L V6 ENGINE

1 Disconnect the cable from the negative terminal of the battery (see Section 3).

2 Remove the drivebelt (see Chapter 1).

3 Disconnect the battery cable from the B+ output terminal and disconnect the field wire electrical connector from the field terminal.

4 Remove the upper mounting bolt and the two lower mounting bolts and remove the alternator.

5 Installation is the reverse of removal. When you're done, check the charging voltage (see Section 9) to verify that the alternator is operating correctly.

3.5L V6 ENGINE

▸ Refer to illustrations 10.8, 10.11 and 10.12

6 Disconnect the cable from the negative terminal of the battery (see Section 3).

7 Remove the drivebelt (see Chapter 1).

8 Remove the upper mounting bolt and the support bracket bolt (see illustration) and remove the support bracket.

10.11 Remove the nut from the battery (B+) output terminal stud (A) and disconnect the battery cable from the stud, then disconnect the electrical connector (B) for the field terminals (3.5L V6 engine)

9   Raise the front of the vehicle and place it securely on jackstands.

10 Remove the middle engine splash shield (see Chapter 2B).

11 Disconnect the battery cable from the B+ output terminal and disconnect the field wire electrical connector from the field terminal (see illustration).

12 Remove the lower alternator mounting bolts (see illustration) and remove the alternator.

13 Installation is the reverse of removal. When you're done, check the charging voltage (see Section 9) to verify that the alternator is operating correctly.

V8 ENGINE

▶ **Refer to illustrations 10.18 and 10.19**

➡**Note: The alternator is located on the right side of the engine block.**

14 Disconnect the cable from the negative terminal of the battery (see Section 3).

15 Remove the drivebelt (see Chapter 1).

16 Raise the front of the vehicle and place it securely on jackstands.

17 Unsnap the plastic insulator cap from the B+ output terminal, remove the battery cable retaining nut from the B+ output terminal and disconnect the battery cable from the B+ output terminal. Then disconnect the field wire electrical connector from the field terminal.

18 Working underneath the engine, remove the alternator support bracket nut and bolt (see illustration) and remove the support bracket.

19 Remove the upper mounting bolt (see illustration) and the lower mounting bolt (see illustration 10.18) and remove the alternator.

20 Installation is the reverse of removal. When you're done, check the charging voltage (see Section 9) to verify that the alternator is operating correctly.

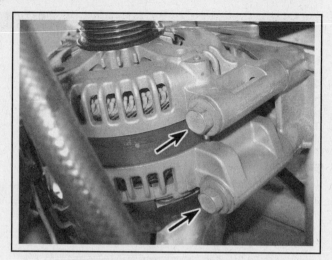

10.12 To detach the alternator from a 3.5L V6 engine, remove these two lower mounting bolts

10.18 To detach the lower part of the alternator from a V8 engine, first remove this bolt (A), then remove the nut (not shown) at the rear end of the support bracket (B) and remove the support bracket, then remove the lower alternator mounting bolt (C)

10.19 To detach the upper part of the alternator from a V8 engine, remove this bolt

11 Starting system - general description and precautions

GENERAL DESCRIPTION

The starting system consists of the starter relay, the starter motor and starter solenoid assembly, the battery, the battery cables, the ignition switch and key lock cylinder, the Transmission Range (TR) sensor and the wiring connecting these components. All starter motors are located on the lower part of the engine, near the transmission bellhousing, where they can engage the ring gear on the driveplate.

The starting system has two separate circuits: A low-amperage control circuit, which operates on less than 20 amps, and a high-amperage supply circuit that delivers up to 300 amps to the starter motor. The low-amp control circuit includes the ignition switch, the Transmission Range (TR) sensor (formerly known as the Park/Neutral Position, or PNP, switch), the starter relay, the coil inside the starter solenoid and the wire harness connecting these components. The high-amperage supply circuit consists of the battery, the battery cables, the contact disc in the starter solenoid and the starter motor itself.

The TR sensor is installed in series between the starter relay ground terminal and ground. The TR sensor is normally open to prevent the starter relay from being energized unless the shift lever is in the NEUTRAL or PARK position. When the ignition switch is turned to START, battery voltage is supplied through the low-amperage control circuit to the battery terminal of the starter relay coil if the shift lever is in the NEUTRAL or PARK position. If it isn't, the starter circuit remains open and the engine won't start.

When the starter relay coil is energized, the normally-open relay contacts close and connect the relay common supply terminal to the relay's normally-open terminal. The closed relay contacts energize the windings of the starter solenoid pull-in coil, which pulls in the solenoid plunger, which pulls the shift lever in the starter motor, which engages the starter's overrunning clutch and pinion gear with the starter's ring gear. As the solenoid plunger reaches the end of its travel, the solenoid contact disc completes the high-current starter supply circuit and energizes the solenoid plunger hold-in coil. Current flows from the solenoid battery terminal to the starter motor and energizes the starter.

The starter motors used on the vehicles covered in this manual are not rebuildable because no parts are available. They're sold as complete new or remanufactured assemblies. If any part of the starter motor fails, including the starter solenoid, the entire assembly must be replaced.

PRECAUTIONS

Always observe the following precautions when working on the starting system:

a) *Excessive cranking of the starter motor can overheat it and cause serious damage. Never operate the starter motor for more than 15 seconds at a time without pausing to allow it to cool for at least two minutes.*

b) *The starter is connected directly to the battery and could arc or cause a fire if mishandled, overloaded or shorted.*

c) *Always detach the cable(s) from the negative terminal of the battery before working on the starting system.*

12 Starter motor and circuit - check

▶ **Refer to illustrations 12.3 and 12.4**

1 If a malfunction occurs in the starting circuit, do not immediately assume that the starter is causing the problem. First, check the following items:

a) *Make sure the battery cable clamps, where they connect to the battery, are clean and tight.*

b) *Check the condition of the battery cables (see Section 4). Replace any defective battery cables with new parts.*

c) *Test the condition of the battery (see Section 3). If it does not pass all the tests, replace it with a new battery.*

d) *Check the starter motor wiring and connections.*

e) *Check the starter motor mounting bolts for tightness.*

f) *Check the related fuses in the engine compartment fuse box (see Chapter 12). If they're blown, determine the cause and repair the circuit.*

g) *Check the ignition switch circuit for correct operation (see the Wiring Diagrams at the end of Chapter 12).*

h) *Check the starter relay (see the Wiring Diagrams at the end of Chapter 12).*

i) *The Transmission Range (TR) sensor must operate correctly to provide battery voltage to the starter solenoid. But on these vehicles you cannot adjust or check the TR sensor, so if everything else is working correctly, the TR sensor might be the problem, but it will have to be checked by a dealer service department or by a competent automatic transmission shop.*

2 If the starter does not activate when the ignition switch is turned to the start position, check for battery voltage to the starter solenoid. This will determine if the solenoid is receiving the correct voltage from the ignition switch. Connect a 12-volt test light or a voltmeter to the starter solenoid positive terminal. While an assistant turns the ignition switch to the start position, observe the test light or voltmeter. The test light should shine brightly or battery voltage should be indicated on the voltmeter. If voltage is not available to the starter solenoid, refer to the wiring diagrams in Chapter 12 and check the fuses and starter relay in series with the starting system. If voltage is available but there is no movement from the starter motor, remove the starter from the engine (see Section 13) and bench test the starter (see Step 4).

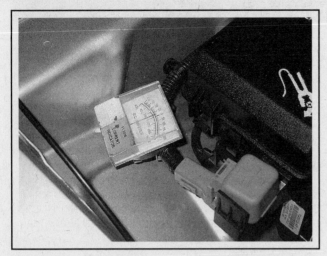

12.3 Use an inductive ammeter to measure starter current draw

12.4 Starter motor bench-testing details

3   If the starter turns over slowly, check the starter cranking voltage and the current draw from the battery. This test must be performed with the starter assembly on the engine. Crank the engine over (for 10 seconds or less) and observe the battery voltage. It should not drop below 9.6 volts. Also, observe the current draw with an ammeter (see illustration). Typically a starter should not exceed 160 amps. If the starter motor amperage draw is excessive, have it tested by a dealer service department or other qualified repair shop. There are several conditions that may affect the starter cranking potential. The battery must be in good condition and the battery cold-cranking rating must not be under-rated for the particular application. Be sure to check the battery specifications carefully. The battery terminals and cables must be clean and not corroded. Also, in cases of extreme cold temperatures, make sure the battery and/or engine block is warmed before performing the tests.

4   If the starter is receiving voltage but does not activate, remove and check the starter motor assembly on the bench (see illustration).

Most likely the solenoid is defective. In some rare cases, the engine may be seized so be sure to try and rotate the crankshaft pulley (see Chapter 2) before proceeding. With the starter assembly mounted in a vise on the bench, install one jumper cable from the positive terminal of a test battery to the B+ terminal on the starter. Install another jumper cable from the negative terminal of the battery to the body of the starter. Install a starter switch and apply battery voltage to the solenoid S terminal (for 10 seconds or less) and observe the solenoid plunger, shift lever and overrunning clutch extend and rotate the pinion drive. If the pinion drive extends but does not rotate, the solenoid is operating but the starter motor is defective. If there is no movement but the solenoid clicks, the solenoid and/or the starter motor is defective. If the solenoid plunger extends and rotates the pinion drive, the starter assembly is operating properly.

13   Starter motor - removal and installation

V6 ENGINES

▶ **Refer to illustrations 13.5 and 13.6**

1   Disconnect the cable from the negative terminal of the battery.
2   Raise the vehicle and support it securely on jackstands.
3   Remove the middle engine splash shield (see Chapter 2B).
4   Remove the bolt that secures the intermediate steering shaft to the lower steering coupling shaft and separate the two shafts (see *Steering column - removal and installation* in Chapter 10).
5   Remove the nut that secures the battery cable to the terminal stud on the starter solenoid, disconnect the cable from the terminal stud and disconnect the electrical connector from the spade terminal on the solenoid (see illustration).

13.5 Disconnect the electrical connector from the spade terminal on the solenoid (A), then remove the nut (B) and disconnect the battery cable from the terminal stud on the solenoid (starter motor on 3.5L V6 shown, starter on 2.7L similar)

13.6 To remove the starter motor, remove these three bolts and the oil cooler line clip (A) (3.5L V6 engine shown, 2.7L V6 similar)

6   Remove the three starter mounting bolts and the oil cooler line clip (see illustration).

7   To remove the starter, pull it forward and down, work it up over the exhaust pipe, then work it past the disconnected steering shafts.

8   Installation is the reverse of removal. Don't forget to reattach the oil cooler line clip to the middle starter mounting bolt.

V8 ENGINE

▶ **Refer to illustrations 13.10 and 13.12**

9   Disconnect the cable from the negative terminal of the battery. Raise the vehicle and support it securely on jackstands.

10   Remove the three starter motor mounting bolts (see illustration).

11   Move the starter motor assembly forward far enough for the pinion gear to clear the starter hole and the driveplate ring gear, then tilt the starter downward so that you can reach the electrical terminals on the solenoid.

12   Disconnect the battery cable and electrical connector from the terminals on the starter motor solenoid (see illustration) and remove the starter motor.

13   Installation is the reverse of removal.

13.10 To detach the starter motor from the engine and transmission bellhousing on a V8, remove these three mounting bolts and the ground cable terminal from the upper bolt (A)

13.12 After unbolting the starter motor and moving it forward, remove the battery cable-to-solenoid nut (A) and disconnect the battery cable from the solenoid terminal, then disconnect the electrical connector (B) from the solenoid

Specifications

General

Battery voltage
    Engine off   At least 12.0 volts
    Engine running   13.5 to 15 volts
Firing order
    V6 engine   1-2-3-4-5-6
    V8 engines   1-8-4-3-6-5-7-2

Section

Reference to other Chapters

CHECK ENGINE light on - See Section 2

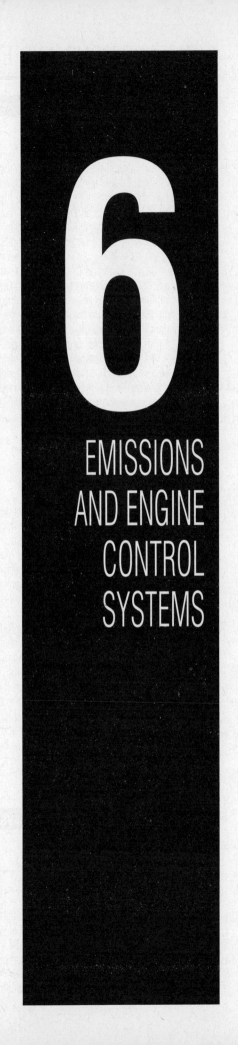

6

EMISSIONS
AND ENGINE
CONTROL
SYSTEMS

1 General information

▶ **Refer to illustration 1.7**

To prevent pollution of the atmosphere from incompletely burned and evaporating gases, and to maintain good driveability and fuel economy, a number of emission control systems are incorporated on the vehicles covered in this manual. These emission control systems and their components are an integral part of the engine management system. The engine management system also includes all the government mandated diagnostic features of the second generation of on-board diagnostics, which is known as On-Board Diagnostics II (OBD-II).

At the center of the engine management and OBD-II systems is the on-board computer, which is known as the Powertrain Control Module (PCM). Using a variety of information sensors, the PCM monitors all of the important engine operating parameters (temperature, speed, load, etc.). It also uses an array of output actuators - such as the ignition coils, the fuel injectors, the Idle Air Control (IAC) motor, the Torque Converter Clutch (TCC) and various solenoids and relays - to respond to and alter these parameters as necessary to maintain optimal performance, economy and emissions. The principal emission control systems used on the vehicles covered in this manual include the:

Catalytic converters
Evaporative Emission Control (EVAP) system
Exhaust Gas Recirculation (EGR) system
Positive Crankcase Ventilation (PCV) system
Torque Converter Clutch (TCC) system

The Sections in this Chapter include general descriptions and component replacement procedures for most of the information sensors and output actuators, as well as the important components that are part of the systems listed above. Refer to Chapter 4 for more information on the air induction, fuel delivery and injection systems and exhaust systems, and to Chapter 5 for information on the ignition system. Refer to Chapter 1 for any scheduled maintenance for emission-related systems and components.

The procedures in this Chapter are intended to be practical, affordable and within the capabilities of the home mechanic. The diagnosis of most engine and emission control functions and driveability problems requires specialized tools, equipment and training. When servicing emission devices or systems becomes too difficult or requires special test equipment, consult a dealer service department.

Although engine and emission control systems are very sophisticated on late-model vehicles, you can do most of the regular maintenance and some servicing at home with common tune-up and hand tools and relatively inexpensive digital multimeters. Because of the

1.7 The Vehicle Emission Control Information (VECI) label, located in the engine compartment, contains information on the emission devices installed on your vehicle and a vacuum hose routing schematic

Federally mandated extended warranty that covers the emission control system, check with a dealer about warranty coverage before working on any emission-related systems. After the warranty has expired, you might want to perform some of the component replacement procedures in this Chapter to save money. Remember that the most frequent cause of emission and driveability problems is a loose electrical connector or a broken wire or vacuum hose, so before jumping to conclusions the first thing you should always do is to inspect all electrical connections, electrical wiring and vacuum hoses related to a system.

Pay close attention to any special precautions given in this Chapter. Remember that illustrations of various system components might not exactly match the component installed on the vehicle on which you're working because of changes made by the manufacturer during production or from year to year.

A Vehicle Emission Control Information (VECI) label (see illustration) is located in the engine compartment. This label contains emission-control and engine tune-up specifications and adjustment information. It also includes a vacuum hose routing diagram for emission-control components. When servicing the engine or emission systems, always check the VECI label in your vehicle. If any information in this manual contradicts what you read on the VECI label on your vehicle, always defer to the information on the VECI label.

2 On-Board Diagnostic (OBD) system and Diagnostic Trouble Codes (DTCs)

SCAN TOOL INFORMATION

▶ **Refer to illustrations 2.1 and 2.2**

1   Hand-held scanners are handy for analyzing the engine management systems used on late-model vehicles. Because extracting the Diagnostic Trouble Codes (DTCs) from an engine management system is now the first step in troubleshooting many computer-controlled systems and components, even the most basic generic code readers are capable of accessing a computer's DTCs (see illustration). More power-

ful scan tools can also perform many of the diagnostics once associated with expensive factory scan tools. If you're planning to obtain a generic scan tool for your vehicle, make sure that it's compatible with OBD-II systems. If you don't plan to purchase a code reader or scan tool and don't have access to one, you can have the codes extracted by a dealer service department or by an independent repair shop.

2   With the advent of the Federally mandated emission control system known as On-Board Diagnostics-II (OBD-II), specially designed scanners were developed. Several tool manufacturers have released OBD-II scan tools for the home mechanic (see illustration).

2.1 Simple code readers are an economical way to extract trouble codes when the CHECK ENGINE light comes on

➡**Note: An aftermarket generic scanner should work with any model covered by this manual. Before purchasing a generic scan tool, verify that it will work properly with the OBD-II system you want to scan. If necessary, of course, you can always have the codes extracted by a dealer service department or an independent repair shop with a professional scan tool. Some auto parts stores even provide this service.**

OBD-II SYSTEM

3   All vehicles covered by this manual are equipped with the OBD-II system. This system consists of the on-board computer, known as the Powertrain Control Module (PCM) and information sensors that monitor various functions of the engine and send a constant stream of data to the PCM during engine operation. Unlike earlier on-board diagnostics systems, the OBD-II system doesn't just monitor everything, store Diagnostic Trouble Codes (DTCs) and illuminate a Check Engine light or Malfunction Indicator Light (MIL) when there's a problem. (This warning light was referred to as the "Check Engine" light prior to OBD-II, and many do-it-yourselfers and professional technicians still use this term. However, its name was changed to "Malfunction Indicator Light," or simply "MIL," as part of the Society of Automotive Engineers' standard terminology that was introduced in 1996 to encourage all manufacturers to use the same terms when referring to the same components.)

4   The PCM is the "brain" of the electronically controlled OBD-II system. It receives data from a number of information sensors and switches. Based on the data that it receives from the sensors, the PCM constantly alters engine operating conditions to optimize driveability, performance, emissions and fuel economy. It does so by turning on and off and by controlling various output actuators such as relays, solenoids, valves and other devices. The PCM can only be accessed with an OBD-II scan tool plugged into the 16-pin Data Link Connector (DLC), which is located underneath the driver's end of the dashboard, near the steering column.

5   If your vehicle is still under warranty, virtually every fuel, ignition and emission control component in the OBD-II system is covered by a Federally mandated emissions warranty that is longer than the warranty covering the rest of the vehicle. Vehicles sold in California and in some other states have even longer emissions warranties than other states. Read your owner's manual for the terms of the warranty protecting the emission-control systems on your vehicle. It isn't a good idea to "do-

2.2 Scanners like these from Actron and AutoXray are powerful diagnostic aids - they can tell you just about anything that you want to know about your engine management system

it-yourself" at home while the vehicle emission systems are still under warranty because owner-induced damage to the PCM, the sensors and/or the control devices might VOID this warranty. So as long as the emission systems are still under warranty, take the vehicle to a dealer service department if there's a problem.

INFORMATION SENSORS

6   Accelerator Pedal Position Sensor (APPS) - The APPS is located at the upper end of and is an integral component of the accelerator pedal assembly. The APPS provides the PCM with a variable voltage signal that's proportional to the position (angle) of the accelerator pedal. The PCM uses this data to control the position of the throttle plate inside the electronically controlled throttle body.

7   **Ambient temperature sensor** - The ambient temperature sensor, which is located on the bumper, monitors the ambient temperature. The Powertrain Control Module (PCM) uses this data, along with data from monitored line voltage, to control the battery's charging rate. The PCM keeps system voltage at a higher level in colder temperatures and at a lower level in warmer temperatures.

8   **Camshaft Position (CMP) sensor** - The CMP sensor is a Hall effect switching device (the manufacturer calls it a "sync signal generator"), which produces a square-wave (high voltage-low voltage) signal that the PCM uses to monitor the position of the camshaft. The CMP sensor is positioned adjacent to the circumference of a "tone wheel" mounted on the front end of the camshaft. The tone wheel has notches machined into it. When the engine is operating, the CMP sensor receives a 5-volt signal from the PCM, then switches back and forth from a high (5-volt) to a low (0.3-volt) signal every time one of the notches in the tone wheel passes by it. This data enables the PCM to determine the position of the camshaft (and therefore the valve train) so that it can time the firing sequence of the fuel injectors. The PCM also uses the signal from the CMP sensor and the signal from the Crankshaft Position (CKP) sensor to distinguish between fuel injection and spark timing.

On 2.7L V6 engines the CMP sensor is located on the front end of the left cylinder head. On 3.5L V6 engines, the CMP sensor is located on top and at the outer side of the front end of the left cylinder head. On V8 engines the CMP sensor is located on the upper front part of the timing chain cover.

9 **Crankshaft Position (CKP) sensor** - Like the CMP sensor, the CKP sensor is also a Hall effect device (see the explanation for how a Hall effect device works in the CMP sensor description above). And like the CMP sensor, the CKP sensor uses a "tone wheel" with notches machined into it to "flip" the CKP sensor's output from 0.3 volt to 5 volts every time a notch passes by it. The PCM uses data from the CKP sensor to calculate engine speed and crankshaft position, which enables it to synchronize ignition timing with fuel injector timing, to control spark knock and to detect misfires.

On 2.7L and 3.5L V6 engines the CKP sensor is located on the right side of the transmission bellhousing. On V8 engines, the CKP sensor is located on the right rear side of the block. You'll have to raise the front of the vehicle to access the CKP sensor on all engines.

10 **Engine Coolant Temperature (ECT) sensor** - The ECT sensor is a Negative Temperature Coefficient (NTC) "thermistor" (temperature-sensitive variable resistor). In an NTC-type thermistor, the resistance of the thermistor decreases as the coolant temperature increases, so the voltage output of the ECT sensor increases. Conversely, the resistance of the thermistor increases as the coolant temperature decreases, so the voltage of the ECT sensor decreases. The PCM uses this variable voltage signal to calculate the temperature of the engine coolant. The ECT sensor tells the PCM when the engine is sufficiently warmed up to go into closed-loop operation and helps the PCM control the air/fuel mixture ratio and ignition timing.

On 2.7L V6 engines the ECT sensor is located at the front of the intake manifold, on the coolant outlet tube from the coolant outlet housing. On 3.5L V6 engines, the ECT sensor is located at the front of the engine, on the front end of the lower intake manifold. On V8 engines, the ECT sensor is located on the front of the engine block, below the air conditioning compressor.

11 **Intake Air Temperature (IAT) sensor** - The IAT sensor is a Negative Temperature Coefficient (NTC) "thermistor" (temperature-sensitive variable resistor) that monitors the temperature of the air entering the engine and sends a variable voltage signal to the PCM. (See the explanation for how an NTC-type thermistor works in the ECT sensor description above.) The voltage signal from the IAT sensor is one of the parameters used by the PCM to determine injector pulse-width (the duration of each injector's "on-time") and to adjust spark timing (to prevent spark knock). On all engines the IAT sensor is located on the air intake duct.

12 **Knock Sensor (KS)** - The Knock Sensor (KS) is a "piezoelectric" crystal that oscillates in proportion to engine vibration. (The term piezoelectric refers to the property of certain crystals that produce a voltage when subjected to a mechanical stress.) The oscillation of the piezoelectric crystal produces a voltage output that is monitored by the PCM, which retards the ignition timing when the oscillation exceeds a certain threshold. When the engine is operating normally, the Knock Sensor (KS) oscillates consistently and its voltage signal is steady. When detonation occurs, engine vibration increases, and the oscillation of the Knock Sensor (KS) exceeds a design threshold. (Detonation is an uncontrolled explosion, after the spark occurs at the spark plug, which spontaneously combusts the remaining air/fuel mixture, resulting in a "pinging" or "slapping" sound.) If allowed to continue, the engine could be damaged.

On 2.7L V6 and 3.5L V6 engines, the knock sensor is located on top of the block, in the valley between the cylinder heads, under the intake manifold. On V8 engines the knock sensors are located on each side of the block, below the exhaust manifolds.

13 **Manifold Absolute Pressure (MAP) sensor** - As the altitude increases, the air becomes thinner. Because the air density changes with altitude, the PCM needs to know whether the vehicle is at sea level or at some higher elevation. Altitude and barometric pressure are inversely proportional: as the altitude increases, the barometric pressure decreases. The MAP sensor monitors the pressure or vacuum downstream from the throttle plate, inside the intake manifold. The MAP sensor measures intake manifold pressure and vacuum on the absolute scale, i.e. from zero psi, not from sea-level atmospheric pressure (14.7 psi). The MAP sensor converts the absolute pressure into a variable voltage signal that changes with the pressure or vacuum. The PCM uses this signal to calculate intake manifold pressure or vacuum, barometric pressure, engine load, injector pulse-width, spark advance, shift points, idle speed and deceleration fuel shut-off.

On 2.7L V6 engines the MAP sensor is located on the intake manifold, near the throttle body. On 3.5L V6 engines the MAP sensor is located on the left side of the intake manifold. On V8 engines, the MAP sensor is located at the rear of the intake manifold, near the cowl/hood seal.

14 **Oxygen sensors** - An oxygen sensor is a galvanic battery that generates a small variable voltage signal in proportion to the difference between the oxygen content in the exhaust stream and the oxygen content in the ambient air. The PCM uses the voltage signal from the upstream oxygen sensor to maintain a "stoichiometric" air/fuel ratio of 14.7:1 by constantly adjusting the "on-time" of the fuel injectors. On vehicles with the Federal Emission Package, there are two oxygen sensors: the upstream (1/1) sensor is located just ahead of the catalytic converter, at the junction of the two exhaust downpipes from the exhaust manifolds. The downstream (1/2) oxygen sensor is located right behind the catalytic converter. On vehicles with the California Emission Package, there are four oxygen sensors: two upstream (1/1 and 2/1) and two downstream (1/2 and 2/2). The left upstream (1/1) sensor is located in the left exhaust downpipe, just ahead of the mini-converter; the left downstream (1/2) sensor is located right behind the mini-converter. The right upstream (2/1) sensor is located in the right exhaust downpipe, just ahead of the mini-converter; the right downstream (2/2) sensor is located right behind the mini-converter.

15 **Throttle Position (TP) sensor** - The TP sensor is a potentiometer that receives constant voltage input from the PCM and sends back a voltage signal that varies in relation to the opening angle of the throttle plate inside the throttle body. This voltage signal tells the PCM when the throttle is closed, half-open, wide open or anywhere in between. The PCM uses this data, along with information from other sensors, to calculate injector "pulse width" (the interval of time during which an injector solenoid is energized by the PCM). All models use an Electronic Throttle Control (ETC) system. The throttle body used in the ETC system has two TP sensors, but they're an integral part of the throttle body's ETC motor assembly and cannot be serviced separately.

16 **Transmission speed sensors** - There are two transmission speeds sensors on 45RFE and 545RFE automatic transmissions, the Input Shaft Speed (ISS) sensor and the Output Shaft Speed (OSS) sensor. Both sensors are located on the left side of the transmission housing. The ISS sensor is the unit closer to the front of the gear case. The OSS is the rear sensor. The ISS is a magnetic pick-up coil that generates an alternating current (AC) signal output to the Transmission Control Module (TCM) that's proportional to the speed of rotation of the input shaft. The OSS is also a magnetic pick-up coil that generates an AC signal output to the TCM that's proportional to the speed of rotation of the rear planetary carrier lugs (the TCM interprets this data as output shaft rpm). The TCM compares the ISS and OSS signals to determine the correct transmission gear ratio, to detect a speed ratio error, Torque Converter Clutch (TCC) slippage and to calculate parameters such as the torque converter element speed ratio. The ISS sensor is located on the left side of the overdrive gear case. There are two speed sensors

on the left side of the transmission; the other one is the Output Shaft Speed (OSS) sensor (see Step 16).

17 **Oxygen sensors** - An oxygen sensor is a galvanic battery that generates a small variable voltage signal in proportion to the difference between the oxygen content in the exhaust stream and the oxygen content in the ambient air. The PCM uses the voltage signal from the upstream oxygen sensor to maintain a "stoichiometric" air/fuel ratio of 14.7:1 by constantly adjusting the "on-time" of the fuel injectors. On four-cylinder models, there are two oxygen sensors: the upstream sensor is located on the exhaust manifold, right above the flange, and the downstream sensor is located behind the catalyst.

There are four oxygen sensors on all engines. The upstream (1/1 and 2/1) oxygen sensors are located on the exhaust manifolds. The downstream (1/2 and 2/2) oxygen sensors are located right behind the outlet ends of the catalytic converters.

18 **Transmission Range (TR) sensor** - The TR sensor (or TR switch) performs the same functions as a Park/Neutral Position (PNP) switch: it prevents the engine from starting in any gear other than Park or Neutral, and it closes the circuit for the back-up lights when the shift lever is moved to Reverse. But the TR switch is also connected to the PCM, which sends a voltage signal to the TR switch, which uses a series of step-down resistors that act as a voltage divider. The PCM monitors the voltage output signal from the switch, which corresponds to the position of the manual lever. Thus the PCM is able to determine the gear selected and is able to determine the correct pressure for the electronic pressure control system of the transaxle.

On the 42RLE (hydraulic, with adaptive electronics) transmission, the TR sensor is located on top of the valve body. On the NAG1 (all-electronic) transmission, there is no "TR sensor." It's been replaced by a "Park/Neutral Contact," which is hard-wired into the electronic control unit, which is an integral part of the electro-hydraulic control unit, which is located on top of the valve body. We don't recommend trying to replace either the TR sensor or the Park/Neutral Contact. Have the work performed by a dealer service department or a qualified automatic transmission shop.

19 **Transmission speed sensors** - The input speed sensor provides the PCM with an output signal that's proportional to the rotational speed of the input shaft. The output speed sensor provides the PCM with an output signal that's proportional to the rotational speed of the output shaft. The PCM uses this information to control the torque converter, to calculate speed scheduling and to determine the correct operating pressure for the transaxle. It also uses the signals from the two sensors to determine the condition of the transmission and to predict its probable failure.

On the 42RLE (hydraulic, with adaptive electronics) transmission, the input speed and output speed sensors are located on the left side of the transmission housing. The input speed sensor is the forward unit. The output speed sensor is the rear unit. You have to raise the vehicle to replace either sensor. On the NAG1 (all-electronic) transmission, there are two input speed sensors (no output speed sensor), but they're located inside the electronic control unit, which is an integral part of the electro-hydraulic control unit, which is located on top of the valve body. We don't recommend trying to replace either speed sensor on an NAG1 transmission. Have the work performed by a dealer service department or a qualified automatic transmission shop.

POWERTRAIN CONTROL MODULE (PCM)

20 The PCM is a computer. Think of it as the "brain" of the engine management system. Like all computers, the PCM receives data inputs, processes the data and outputs commands. The PCM receives data from all of the information sensors described above (input), compares the data to its program and calculates the appropriate responses (processing), then turns the output actuators on or off, or changes their pulse width or duty cycle (output) to keep everything running smoothly, cleanly and efficiently. The PCM is located in the right rear corner of the engine compartment, inside the right end of the cowl area.

OUTPUT ACTUATORS

21 **EVAP canister purge solenoid** - The EVAP canister purge solenoid is a PCM-controlled solenoid that controls the purging of evaporative emissions from the EVAP canister to the intake manifold. The EVAP purge solenoid is never turned on during cold start warm-ups or during hot start time delays. But once the engine reaches a specified temperature and enters closed-loop operation the PCM will energize the canister purge solenoid between 5 and 10 times a second. When the solenoid is energized by the PCM, it allows the fuel vapors that are stored in the EVAP canister to be drawn into the intake manifold, where they're mixed with intake air, then burned along with the normal air/fuel mixture, under certain operating conditions. The PCM regulates the flow rate of the vapors by controlling the pulse-width of the solenoid (the length of time during which the solenoid is turned on) in accordance with operating conditions. The EVAP canister purge solenoid is located in the right rear corner of the engine compartment, where it's bolted to the right strut tower.

22 **EVAP Natural Vacuum Leak Detection (NVLD) system** - Vehicles with a current-generation PCM, referred to by Dodge as a "New Generation Controller" (NGC), use a Natural Vacuum Leak Detection (NVLD) system instead of a Leak Detection Pump (LDP). The NVLD system is based on the principle that the pressure inside a sealed system (such as the EVAP system) will change if the temperature changes, i.e. if the temperature goes up, so does the pressure, and vice versa. So if during a leak test the PCM notes that the pressure inside the EVAP system isn't proportional to the temperature, it sets a Diagnostic Trouble Code (DTC) for a leak. The NVLD unit is located at the EVAP canister, which is located under the right rear corner of the vehicle, behind the splash shield for the right rear wheel. You must raise the vehicle, remove the right rear wheel and remove the splash shield to access the NVLD assembly or the EVAP canister.

23 **Exhaust Gas Recirculation (EGR) valve** - When the engine is put under a load (hard acceleration, passing, going up a steep hill, pulling a trailer, etc.), combustion chamber temperature increases. When combustion chamber temperature exceeds 2500-degrees F (1380-degrees C), excessive amounts of oxides of nitrogen (NOx) are produced. NOx is a precursor of photochemical smog. When combined with hydrocarbons (HC), other "reactive organic compounds" (ROCs) and sunlight, it forms ozone, nitrogen dioxide and nitrogen nitrate and other nasty stuff. The PCM-controlled EGR valve allows exhaust gases to be recirculated back to the intake manifold where they dilute the incoming air/fuel mixture, which lowers the combustion chamber temperature and decreases the amount of NOx produced during high-load conditions.

On 2.7L and 3.5L V6 engines, the EGR valve is located at the rear of the engine and is bolted to the rear end of the right cylinder head. (But the two V6 engines do not use the same EGR valve.) On V8 engines, the electronic EGR valve and solenoid assembly is located on the front of the right cylinder head.

24 **Fuel injectors** - The fuel injectors, which spray a fine mist of fuel into the intake ports, where it is mixed with incoming air, are inductive coils under PCM control. The injectors are installed between the fuel rail and the intake ports that connect the intake manifold run-

ners to the combustion chambers. For more information about the injectors, see Chapter 4.

25 **Ignition coils** - The ignition coils are controlled by the Powertrain Control Module (PCM). There is no separate ignition control module. This function is handled inside the PCM, which controls the ground path for the primary side of each coil. For more information about the ignition coils refer to Chapter 5.

26 **Intake manifold tuning valve actuator and short runner valve actuator** - The manifold tuning valve actuator and short runner valve actuator are components of the Intake Manifold Tuning (IMT) valve system used on 2.7L and 3.5L V6 engines (the 3.5L system uses both components; the 2.7L system just uses the manifold tuning valve actuator).

The manifold tuning valve actuator controls a small flap inside the intake manifold plenum. A partition divides the intake manifold plenum into upper and lower plenums. Intake air in the upper plenum enters three intake runners and air entering the lower plenum enters the other three runners. The two plenums are connected at one end by a small hole. The manifold tuning valve actuator controls the flap that opens and closes this hole, which alters the acoustical tuning properties of the manifold.

When commanded by the PCM, the short runner valve actuator alters the effective length of the intake manifold runners. Below 5000 rpm incoming air travels the full length of the intake runners, which improves the engine's torque. Above 5000 rpm the intake manifold tuning valve actuator and/or short runner solenoid close off part of the intake manifold, routing the incoming air through shorter, more direct intake runners, which improves power.

27 **Multi-Displacement System (MDS) control valve/solenoids** - V8 engines are equipped with MDS, which deactivates cylinders 1, 4, 6 and 7 under light-load cruising conditions, effectively turning the V8 into a four-cylinder engine. There are four control valve/solenoids. Each PCM-controlled solenoid can activate and deactivate the cylinder that it controls by closing the intake and exhaust valves, deactivating the lifters and turning the piston into a big air spring. They're located in the valley of the V8 engine, under the intake manifold and between the cylinder heads. When the engine is subjected to heavy load conditions such as acceleration, the PCM commands the four solenoids to activate the cylinders in firing order.

OBTAINING AND CLEARING DIAGNOSTIC TROUBLE CODES (DTCS)

28 All models covered by this manual are equipped with on-board diagnostics. When the PCM recognizes a malfunction in a monitored emission control system, component or circuit, it turns on the Malfunction Indicator Light (MIL) on the dash. The PCM will continue to display the MIL until the problem is fixed and the Diagnostic Trouble Code (DTC) is cleared from the PCM's memory. You'll need a scan tool to access any DTCs stored in the PCM. Before outputting any DTCs stored in the PCM, thoroughly inspect ALL electrical connectors and hoses. Make sure that all electrical connections are tight, clean and free of corrosion. And make sure that all hoses are correctly connected, fit tightly and are in good condition (no cracks or tears). Also, make sure

2.29 The Data Link Connector (DLC), or diagnostic connector, is located under the left end of the instrument panel

that the engine is tuned up. A poorly running engine is probably one of the biggest causes of emission-related malfunctions. Often, simply giving the engine a good tune-up will correct the problem.

Accessing the DTCs

▶ **Refer to illustration 2.29**

29 On the vehicles covered in this manual, all of which are equipped with On-Board Diagnostic II (OBD-II) systems, the Diagnostic Trouble Codes (DTCs) can only be accessed with a scan tool. Simply plug the connector of the scan tool into the Data Link Connector (DLC) or diagnostic connector, which is located under the lower edge of the dash, near the hood release handle (see illustration). Then follow the instructions included with the scan tool to extract the DTCs.

30 Once you have outputted all of the stored DTCs look them up on the accompanying DTC chart.

31 After troubleshooting the source of each DTC make any necessary repairs or replace the defective component(s).

Clearing the DTCs

32 Clear the DTCs with the scan tool in accordance with the instructions provided by the scan tool's manufacturer.

DIAGNOSTIC TROUBLE CODES

33 The accompanying tables are a list of the Diagnostic Trouble Codes (DTCs) that can be accessed by a do-it-yourselfer working at home (there are many more DTCs available to professional service technicians with proprietary scan tools and software, but those codes cannot be accessed by a generic scan tool). If, after you have checked and repaired the connectors, wire harness and vacuum hoses (if applicable) for an emission-related system, component or circuit, the problem persists, have the vehicle checked by a dealer service department.

OBD-II DIAGNOSTIC TROUBLE CODES (DTCS)

➡**Note: Not all trouble codes apply to all models.**

Code	Possible cause
P000B	Bank 1, camshaft 2 position, slow response
P0013	Bank 1, camshaft 2 position, actuator circuit open
P0016	Crankshaft/camshaft timing misalignment
P0031	Oxygen sensor (1/1)* heater circuit, low voltage
P0032	Oxygen sensor (1/1)* heater circuit, high voltage
P0037	Oxygen sensor (1/2)* heater circuit, low voltage
P0038	Oxygen sensor (1/2)* heater circuit, high voltage
P0051	Oxygen sensor (2/1)* heater circuit, low voltage
P0052	Oxygen sensor (2/1)* heater circuit, high voltage
P0057	Oxygen sensor (2/2)* heater circuit, low voltage
P0058	Oxygen sensor (2/2)* heater circuit, high voltage
P0071	Ambient air temperature sensor performance
P0072	Ambient air temperature sensor circuit, low voltage
P0073	Ambient air temperature sensor circuit, high voltage
P0107	Manifold Absolute Pressure (MAP) sensor circuit, low voltage
P0108	Manifold Absolute Pressure (MAP) sensor circuit, high voltage
P0111	Intake Air Temperature (IAT) sensor rationality
P0112	Intake Air Temperature (IAT) sensor circuit, low voltage
P0113	Intake Air Temperature (IAT) sensor circuit, high voltage
P0116	Engine Coolant Temperature (ECT) sensor circuit performance problem
P0117	Engine Coolant Temperature (ECT) sensor circuit, low voltage
P0118	Engine Coolant Temperature (ECT) sensor circuit, high voltage
P0121	Throttle Position (TP) sensor 1 performance
P0122	Throttle Position (TP) sensor 1 circuit, low voltage
P0123	Throttle Position (TP) sensor 1 circuit, high voltage
P0125	Insufficient coolant temperature for closed-loop fuel control
P0128	Thermostat rationality
P0129	Barometric pressure out-of-range (too low)
P0131	Oxygen sensor (1/1)* circuit, low voltage
P0132	Oxygen sensor (1/1)* circuit, high voltage
P0133	Oxygen sensor (1/1)* circuit, slow response

OBD-II DIAGNOSTIC TROUBLE CODES (DTCS) (CONTINUED)

➡**Note: Not all trouble codes apply to all models.**

Code	Possible cause
P0135	Oxygen sensor (1/1)* circuit, heater performance problem
P0137	Oxygen sensor (1/2)* circuit, low voltage
P0138	Oxygen sensor (1/2)* circuit, high voltage
P0139	Oxygen sensor (1/2)* circuit, slow response
P013A	Oxygen sensor (1/2)* circuit, slow rich-to-lean response
P013C	Oxygen sensor (2/2)* circuit, slow rich-to-lean response
P0141	Oxygen sensor (1/2)* circuit, heater performance problem
P0151	Oxygen sensor (2/1)* circuit, low voltage
P0152	Oxygen sensor (2/1)* circuit, high voltage
P0153	Oxygen sensor (2/1)* circuit, slow response
P0155	Oxygen sensor (2/1)*, heater performance problem
P0157	Oxygen sensor (2/2)* circuit, low voltage
P0158	Oxygen sensor (2/2)* circuit, high voltage
P0159	Oxygen sensor (2/2)* circuit, slow response
P0161	Oxygen sensor (2/2)* circuit, heater performance problem
P0171	Fuel system too lean (cylinder bank no. 1)
P0172	Fuel system too rich (cylinder bank no. 1)
P0174	Fuel system too lean (cylinder bank no. 2)
P0175	Fuel system too rich (cylinder bank no. 2)
P0196	Engine oil temperature sensor, circuit performance
P0197	Engine oil temperature sensor circuit, low voltage
P0198	Engine oil temperature sensor circuit, high voltage
P0201	Fuel injector circuit malfunction - cylinder no. 1
P0202	Fuel injector circuit malfunction - cylinder no. 2
P0203	Fuel injector circuit malfunction - cylinder no. 3
P0204	Fuel injector circuit malfunction - cylinder no. 4
P0205	Fuel injector circuit malfunction - cylinder no. 5
P0206	Fuel injector circuit malfunction - cylinder no. 6
P0207	Fuel injector circuit malfunction - cylinder no. 7
P0208	Fuel injector circuit malfunction - cylinder no. 8
P0221	Throttle Position (TP) sensor 2 performance

Code	Possible cause
P0222	Throttle Position (TP) sensor 2 circuit, low voltage
P0223	Throttle Position (TP) sensor 2 circuit, high voltage
P0298	Engine oil temperature too high
P0300	Multiple cylinder misfire detected
P0301	Cylinder no. 1 misfire detected
P0302	Cylinder no. 2 misfire detected
P0303	Cylinder no. 3 misfire detected
P0304	Cylinder no. 4 misfire detected
P0305	Cylinder no. 5 misfire detected
P0306	Cylinder no. 6 misfire detected
P0307	Cylinder no. 7 misfire detected
P0308	Cylinder no. 8 misfire detected
P0315	No Crankshaft Position (CKP) sensor learned
P0325	Knock sensor 1 circuit malfunction
P0330	Knock sensor 2 circuit malfunction
P0335	Crankshaft Position (CKP) sensor, circuit malfunction
P0339	Crankshaft Position (CKP) sensor, circuit intermittent
P0340	Camshaft Position (CMP) sensor circuit malfunction
P0344	Camshaft Position (CMP) sensor, circuit intermittent
P0401	Exhaust Gas Recirculation (EGR) system, performance problem
P0403	Exhaust Gas Recirculation (EGR) solenoid circuit malfunction
P0404	Exhaust Gas Recirculation (EGR) position sensor performance
P0405	Exhaust Gas Recirculation (EGR) sensor circuit, low voltage
P0406	Exhaust Gas Recirculation (EGR) sensor circuit, high voltage
P0420	Catalyst system efficiency below threshold (cylinder bank no. 1)
P0430	Catalyst system efficiency below threshold (cylinder bank no. 2)
P0440	General Evaporative Emission Control (EVAP) system failure
P0441	Evaporative Emission Control (EVAP) purge system performance problem
P0442	Evaporative Emission Control (EVAP) purge system, medium leak detected
P0443	Evaporative Emission Control (EVAP) purge solenoid circuit malfunction
P0452	Natural Vacuum Leak Detection (NVLD) system, pressure switch stuck closed
P0453	Natural Vacuum Leak Detection (NVLD) system, pressure switch stuck open
P0455	Evaporative Emission Control (EVAP) system, large leak

OBD-II DIAGNOSTIC TROUBLE CODES (DTCS) (CONTINUED)

➡ Note: Not all trouble codes apply to all models.

Code	Possible cause
P0456	Evaporative Emission Control (EVAP) system, small leak
P0457	Loose fuel cap
P0461	Fuel level sensor 1, performance problem
P0462	Fuel level sensor 1, low voltage
P0463	Fuel level sensor 1, high voltage
P0480	Cooling fan 1, control circuit malfunction
P0481	Cooling fan 2, control circuit malfunction
P0498	Natural Vacuum Leak Detection (NVLD) canister vent valve solenoid, low voltage
P0499	Natural Vacuum Leak Detection (NVLD) canister vent valve solenoid, high voltage
P050B	Cold start ignition timing performance
P050D	Cold start rough idle
P0501	Vehicle Speed Sensor (VSS) 1, performance problem
P0503	Vehicle Speed Sensor (VSS) 1 erratic
P0506	Idle speed performance lower than expected
P0507	Idle speed performance higher than expected
P0513	Invalid Sentry Key Immobilizer System (SKIM) key
P0520	Engine oil pressure sensor circuit
P0521	Engine oil pressure sensor performance problem
P0522	Engine oil pressure sensor circuit, low voltage
P0523	Engine oil pressure sensor circuit, high voltage
P0524	Engine oil pressure too low
P0532	Air conditioning refrigerant pressure sensor circuit, low voltage
P0533	Air conditioning refrigerant pressure sensor circuit, high voltage
P0551	Power Steering Pressure (PSP) switch, performance problem
P0562	Battery voltage low
P0563	Battery voltage high
P0571	Brake switch 1 performance problem
P0572	Brake switch 1 stuck on
P0573	Brake switch no. 1 stuck off
P0579	Speed control switch 1 performance
P0580	Speed control switch 1 circuit, low voltage

Code	Possible cause
P0581	Speed control switch 1 circuit, high voltage
P0585	Speed control switch 1/2 correlation
P0591	Speed control switch performance
P0592	Speed control switch 2 circuit, low voltage
P0593	Speed control switch 2 circuit, high voltage
P0600	Serial communication link
P0601	Powertrain Control Module (PCM) internal memory checksum invalid
P0606	Internal Powertrain Control Module (PCM) processor
P060B	Electronic Throttle Control (ETC) analog-to-digital (A/D) ground performance problem
P060D	Electronic Throttle Control (ETC) level 2 Accelerator Pedal Position (APP) sensor performance problem
P060E	Electronic Throttle Control (ETC) level 2 Throttle Position (TP) sensor performance problem
P060F	Electronic Throttle Control (ETC) level 2 Engine Coolant Temperature (ECT) sensor performance problem
P061A	Electronic Throttle Control (ETC) level 2 torque performance problem
P061C	Electronic Throttle Control (ETC) level 2 rpm performance problem
P0622	Generator field control circuit
P0627	Fuel pump relay circuit
P062C	Electronic Throttle Control (ETC) level 2 mph performance problem
P0630	Vehicle Identification Number (VIN) not programmed in Powertrain Control Module (PCM)
P0632	Odometer not programmed in Powertrain Control Module (PCM)
P0633	Sentry Key Immobilizer System (SKIM) secret key not stored in Powertrain Control Module (PCM)
P0642	Sensor reference voltage no. 1 circuit low
P0643	Primary 5-volt supply circuit, high voltage
P0645	Air conditioning clutch relay circuit
P0652	Sensor reference voltage 2 circuit low
P0653	Sensor reference voltage 2 circuit high
P0660	Manifold Tune Valve solenoid circuit
P0685	Auto Shutdown (ASD) relay control circuit
P0688	Auto Shutdown (ASD) relay sense circuit low
P0700	Transmission control system (Malfunction Indicator Light request)
P0703	Brake switch no. 2 performance problem
P0850	Park/Neutral switch performance

* (1/1) = Bank 1, upstream oxygen sensor; (1/2) = Bank 1, downstream oxygen sensor; (2/1) = Bank 2, upstream oxygen sensor; (2/2) Bank 2, downstream oxygen sensor.

➥**Note: Bank 1 is the bank, or row of cylinders, containing cylinder no. 1. Bank 2 is the other bank of cylinders.**

3 Accelerator Pedal Position Sensor (APPS) - replacement

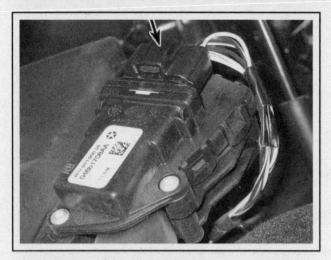

3.1 To disconnect the electrical connector from the APPS assembly, depress this release tab and pull the connector straight up

3.2 On vehicles with adjustable pedals, disconnect the electrical connector (A) and the adjuster motor drive cable (B). To disconnect the cable, simply pull it straight up

▶ Refer to illustrations 3.1, 3.2 and 3.3

➡ **Note:** The Accelerator Pedal Position Sensor (APPS) is an integral component of the accelerator pedal assembly - to replace the APPS, you must replace the pedal assembly.

1   If the vehicle is not equipped with adjustable pedals, disconnect the electrical connector from the APPS (see illustration).

2   If the vehicle is equipped with adjustable pedals, disconnect the electrical connector and the adjuster cable from the APPS assembly (see illustration).

3   Remove the three APPS assembly mounting nuts (see illustration).

4   Remove the APPS assembly.

5   Installation is the reverse of removal. If the vehicle is equipped with adjustable pedals, synchronize the pedals (see Chapter 9).

3.3 To detach the APPS assembly, remove these three mounting nuts

4 Ambient air temperature sensor - replacement

▶ Refer to illustration 4.3

➡ **Note:** The ambient air temperature sensor is located on the trailing edge of the front bumper, below the right horn.

1   Raise the vehicle and place it securely on jackstands.

2   Remove the front splash shield that protects the area under the front part of the engine compartment, right behind the trailing edge of the front bumper cover (see Chapter 2).

3   Disconnect the electrical connector from the ambient air temperature sensor (see illustration).

4   Detach the sensor mounting bracket pushpin from the bumper and remove the sensor.

5   Installation is the reverse of removal.

4.3 To remove the ambient air temperature sensor, depress the tab (A) and pull off the connector, then pull out the pushpin (B) and detach the sensor from the bumper

5   Camshaft Position (CMP) sensor - replacement

V6 ENGINES

2.7L engine

▶ **Refer to illustrations 5.2 and 5.4**

➡**Note: The CMP sensor is located at the front end of the left cylinder head.**

1   Raise the front end of the vehicle and support it securely on jackstands.

2   Disconnect the electrical connector from the CMP sensor (see illustration).

3   Detach the wiring harness clip, if applicable, from the CMP sensor mounting stud.

4   Remove the sensor mounting bolt (see illustration) and remove the CMP sensor.

5   Installation is the reverse of removal.

3.5L engine

▶ **Refer to illustrations 5.6 and 5.7**

➡**Note: The CMP sensor is located ahead of the left cylinder head, on top of the timing belt cover.**

6   Unlock and disconnect the electrical connector from the CMP sensor (see illustration).

7   Remove the CMP sensor mounting bolt (see illustration) and remove the CMP sensor.

8   If you're installing the old CMP sensor, scrape off the old spacer and install a new paper spacer.

9   If you're installing a new CMP sensor, it will be equipped with a new paper spacer.

10 Installation is the reverse of removal.

5.2 To disconnect the electrical connector from the CMP sensor on a 2.7L V6, depress the release tab and pull off the connector. Before removing the sensor, disengage the harness clip (A), if applicable, from the sensor mounting stud by carefully prying it off

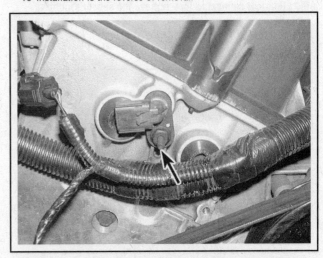

5.4 To detach the CMP sensor from the cylinder head on a 2.7L V6, remove this nut, then pull the sensor straight out

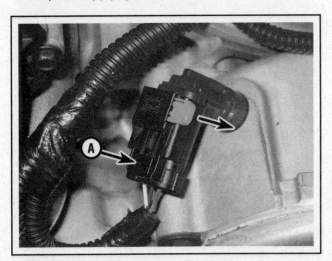

5.6 To remove the CMP sensor from the timing belt cover on a 3.5L V6, push the lock in the direction of the arrow, then depress the release tab (A) and pull off the connector

5.7 To detach the CMP sensor from the timing belt cover on a 3.5L V6, remove the sensor mounting bolt

5.11 To detach the CMP sensor from the timing chain cover on a V8 engine, depress the release tab (A) and disconnect the electrical connector, then remove the sensor mounting bolt (B)

5.13 Remove the old CMP sensor O-ring and inspect it for cracks, tears and deterioration. If it's damaged, replace it (V8 engine)

V8 ENGINE

▶ **Refer to illustrations 5.11 and 5.13**

➡**Note: The CMP sensor is located on the upper right side of the timing chain cover.**

11 Disconnect the electrical connector from the CMP sensor (see illustration).

12 Remove the CMP sensor mounting bolt and remove the CMP sensor from the timing chain cover.

13 Remove the old CMP sensor O-ring (see illustration) and inspect it for cracks, tears and deterioration. If the old O-ring is damaged, replace it.

14 When installing the CMP sensor, apply a small dab of clean engine oil to the sensor O-ring, then use a slight rocking motion to work the O-ring into the sensor mounting bore. Do NOT use a twisting motion or you will damage the O-ring.

15 Make sure that the CMP sensor mounting flange is fully seated flat against the mounting surface around the sensor mounting hole.

❈❈❈ **CAUTION:**

If the CMP sensor is not fully seated against its mounting surface, the sensor mounting tang will be damaged when the sensor mounting bolt is tightened.

16 Installation is otherwise the reverse of removal.

6   Crankshaft Position (CKP) sensor - replacement

V6 ENGINES

▶ **Refer to illustration 6.2**

➡**Note: The CKP sensor is located on the upper right side of the transmission bellhousing.**

1 Raise the front end of the vehicle and place it securely on jackstands.

2 Unlock and disconnect the electrical connector from the CKP sensor (see illustration).

3 Remove the CKP sensor mounting bolt and remove the sensor from the transmission bellhousing.

4 Installation is the reverse of removal.

6.2 To detach the CKP sensor from the transmission bellhousing on a V6 engine, push the lock in the direction of the arrow, depress the release tab (A), disconnect the electrical connector and remove the sensor mounting bolt (B)

V8 ENGINE

▶ **Refer to illustration 6.8**

➡**Note: The CKP sensor is located on the right rear side of the block.**

5   Disconnect the cable from the negative terminal of the battery (see Chapter 5).

6   Raise the front end of the vehicle and place it securely on jackstands.

7   Remove the starter motor (see Chapter 5).

8   Disconnect the electrical connector from the CKP sensor (see illustration).

9   Remove the CKP sensor mounting bolt and remove the sensor from the engine.

10 Remove the CKP sensor O-ring and inspect it for cracks, tears and deterioration. If it's damaged, replace it.

11 Apply a small amount of engine oil on the O-ring and, using a slight rocking motion, push the sensor into its mounting hole in the engine block until the sensor is fully seated.

12 Installation is otherwise the reverse of removal.

6.8 To detach the CKP sensor (A) from the (right-rear side of the) block on a V8 engine, disconnect the electrical connector (B) and remove the sensor mounting bolt (C)

7   Engine Coolant Temperature (ECT) sensor - replacement

✳✳ WARNING:

Wait until the engine is completely cool before beginning this procedure.

1   Partially drain the cooling system, to a level that's slightly below the cylinder heads (see Chapter 1).

V6 ENGINES

▶ **Refer to illustrations 7.2a, 7.2b and 7.4**

➡**Note: The ECT sensor is located at the front of the lower intake manifold.**

2   Disconnect the electrical connector from the ECT sensor

(see illustrations).

3   Using a deep socket, unscrew the ECT sensor from the lower intake manifold.

4   To prevent leakage and thread corrosion, wrap the threads of the ECT sensor with Teflon sealing tape (see illustration) before installing the sensor. (Seal the sensor threads whether you're installing the old sensor or a new unit.)

5   Installation is otherwise the reverse of removal. Be sure to tighten the ECT sensor to the torque listed in this Chapter's Specifications.

6   Refill the cooling system (see Chapter 1).

V8 ENGINE

▶ **Refer to illustration 7.8**

➡**Note: The ECT sensor is located on the front end of the engine block, below the air conditioning compressor.**

7   Remove the accessory drivebelt (see Chapter 1), unbolt the air conditioning compressor (see Chapter 3) and set it aside. Do NOT disconnect any of the air conditioning pressure or return line fittings.

7.2a To remove the ECT sensor from a 2.7L V6, depress the release tab (1) and disconnect the electrical connector, then unscrew the ECT sensor (2) from the lower intake manifold

7.2b To remove the ECT sensor from a 3.5L V6, push the lock toward the harness, depress the release tab (A) and disconnect the electrical connector, then unscrew the ECT sensor (B) from the lower intake manifold

7.4 Before installing the ECT sensor, be sure to wrap the threads of the sensor with Teflon tape to prevent leaks

8   Disconnect the electrical connector from the ECT sensor (see illustration).

9   Using a deep socket, unscrew the ECT sensor from the intake manifold.

10   To prevent leakage and thread corrosion, wrap the threads of the ECT sensor with Teflon sealing tape (see illustration 7.4) before installing the sensor. (Seal the sensor threads whether you're installing the old sensor or a new unit.)

7.8 To remove the ECT sensor from the intake manifold on a V8 engine, disconnect the electrical connector (A) and unscrew the sensor (B) from the manifold

11   Installation is otherwise the reverse of removal. Be sure to tighten the ECT sensor to the torque listed in this Chapter's Specifications.

12   Refill the cooling system (see Chapter 1).

8   Intake Air Temperature (IAT) sensor - replacement

▶ Refer to illustrations 8.1a, 8.1b and 8.3

➡Note: The IAT sensor is located on the air intake duct on all engines. Though the exact location on the duct varies with the engine, the same IAT sensor is used on all engines.

1   Unlock and disconnect the electrical connector from the IAT sensor (see illustrations).

2   Note the orientation of the IAT sensor. When you install a new (or the old) sensor, it MUST be correctly oriented in order to function correctly.

3   To remove the IAT sensor from the air intake duct, grasp it firmly and pull it out (see illustration).

4   Installation is the reverse of removal.

8.1a A typical IAT sensor on a 3.5L V6. To disconnect the electrical connector, push the lock toward the harness, then depress the release tab (A) and pull off the connector

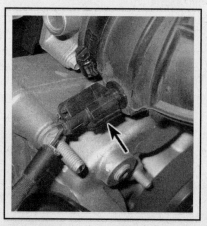

8.1b A typical IAT sensor on a V8 engine. Remove it the same way you would remove the IAT sensor from a V6

8.3 To remove the IAT sensor, note the orientation of the sensor (it must be installed in the exact same orientation), then grasp the sensor firmly and pull it straight out of the air intake duct (3.5L V6 shown, other engines similar)

9   Knock sensor - replacement

V6 ENGINES

➡Note: The knock sensor is located on top of the block, in the valley between the cylinder heads, underneath the lower intake manifold.

1   Remove the upper and lower intake manifolds (2.7L engine, see Chapter 2A; 3.5L engine, see Chapter 2B).

2   On 2.7L V6 engines, remove the right (passenger side) cylinder head (see Chapter 2A).

3   Disconnect the electrical connector from the knock sensor.

4   Remove the knock sensor mounting bolt and remove the knock sensor.

5   Installation is the reverse of removal. Be sure to tighten the knock sensor mounting bolt to the torque listed in this Chapter's Specifications.

✳✳ CAUTION:

Over- or under-tightening the knock sensor mounting bolts will affect knock sensor performance, which might affect the PCM's spark control ability.

9.7 The left knock sensor on a V8 engine is protected by this heat shield. To remove it, grasp it firmly with a pair of pliers and pull it off

V8 ENGINE

▶ Refer to illustrations 9.7 and 9.8

➡Note: There are two knock sensors. One is located on the left side of the block, below the exhaust manifold, and the other is located in the same place on the right side of the block.

6   Raise the front of the vehicle and place it securely on jackstands.

7   If you're removing the left knock sensor, pull off the galvanized heat shield (see illustration).

8   Disconnect the electrical connector from the knock sensor (see illustration).

9   Remove the knock sensor mounting bolt and remove the knock sensor from the engine.

➡Note: The foam strips on the knock sensor mounting bolt threads are used to retain the bolts during vehicle assembly at the manufacturing plant. They have no other purpose. They are not some form of adhesive, thread sealant or locking compound. Do NOT use any type of adhesive, thread sealant or locking compound when installing these bolts again.

10 Installation is the reverse of removal. Be sure to tighten the knock sensor mounting bolts to the torque listed in this Chapter's Specifications.

9.8 To detach a knock sensor from the block on a V8 engine, disconnect the electrical connector (A) and remove the knock sensor mounting bolt (B) (left knock sensor shown, right sensor identical)

✳✳ CAUTION:

Over- or under-tightening the knock sensor mounting bolts will affect knock sensor performance, which might affect the PCM's spark control ability.

10 Manifold Absolute Pressure (MAP) sensor - replacement

V6 ENGINES

▶ Refer to illustrations 10.1, 10.2 and 10.3

➡Note: The MAP sensor is located on top of the intake manifold. The photos accompanying this section depict the MAP sensor on a 3.5L V6 engine. The MAP sensor on a 2.7L V6 is a little closer to the throttle body, but it's the same unit, and is removed the same way.

1   Unlock and disconnect the electrical connector from the MAP sensor (see illustration).

2   Rotate the MAP counterclockwise 1/4-turn (see illustration) and pull it straight up and out of the intake manifold.

3   Remove the MAP sensor O-ring (see illustration) and inspect it for cracks, tears and deterioration. If the O-ring is damaged, replace it.

4   Installation is the reverse of removal.

V8 ENGINE

▶ Refer to illustration 10.6

➡Note: The MAP sensor is located on the rear part of the intake manifold, near the firewall.

5   Disconnect the electrical connector from the MAP sensor (see illustration 10.1).

6   Rotate the MAP sensor 1/4-turn counterclockwise and remove it from the intake manifold (see illustration).

7   Remove the old MAP sensor O-ring (see illustration 10.3) and inspect it for cracks, tears and deterioration. If it's damaged, replace it.

8   To install the MAP sensor, place it in position, insert it into the mounting hole in the intake manifold and turn it 1/4-turn clockwise.

9   Installation is otherwise the reverse of removal.

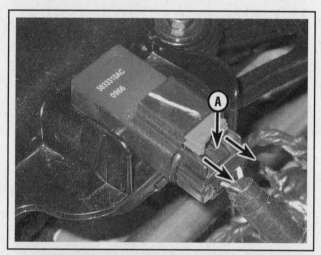

10.1 To disconnect the electrical connector from the MAP sensor on a V6 engine, pull out the lock, then depress the release tab (A) and detach the connector (3.5L V6 shown, 2.7L V6 similar)

10.2 To remove the MAP sensor from the intake manifold, rotate it counterclockwise 1/4-turn and pull it straight up and out of the manifold (3.5L V6 shown, 2.7L V6 similar)

10.3 Remove the MAP sensor O-ring and inspect it for cracks, tears and deterioration; if it's damaged, replace it

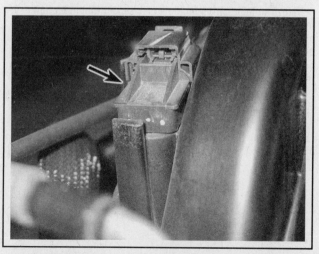

10.6 To remove the sensor from the intake manifold on a V8 engine, rotate it 1/4-turn counterclockwise and pull it out of its mounting hole

11 Oxygen sensors - general description and replacement

DESCRIPTION

1 The oxygen in the exhaust reacts with the elements inside the oxygen sensor to produce a voltage output that varies from 0.1 volt (high oxygen, lean mixture) to 0.9 volt (low oxygen, rich mixture). The pre-converter oxygen sensor (mounted in the exhaust system before the catalytic converter) provides a feedback signal to the PCM that indicates the amount of leftover oxygen in the exhaust. The PCM monitors this variable voltage continuously to determine the required fuel injector pulse width and to control the engine air/fuel ratio. A mixture ratio of 14.7 parts air to 1 part fuel is the ideal ratio for minimum exhaust emissions, as well as the best combination for fuel economy and engine performance. Based on oxygen sensor signals, the PCM tries to maintain this air/fuel ratio of 14.7:1 at all times.

2 The post-converter oxygen sensor (mounted in the exhaust system after the catalytic converter) has no effect on PCM control of the air/fuel ratio. However, the post-converter sensor is identical to the pre-converter sensor and operates in the same way. The PCM uses the post-converter signal to monitor the efficiency of the catalytic converter. A post-converter oxygen sensor will produce a slower fluctuating voltage signal that reflects the lower oxygen content in the post-catalyst exhaust.

3 There are four oxygen sensors on all vehicles. The two upstream sensors (1/1 and 2/1) are located in the exhaust manifolds and the downstream sensors (1/2 and 2/2) are located downstream from and right behind the catalytic converters.

4 An oxygen sensor produces no voltage when it is below its normal operating temperature of about 600-degrees F. During this warm-up period, the PCM operates in an open-loop fuel control mode. It does not use the oxygen sensor signal as a feedback indication of residual oxygen in the exhaust. Instead, the PCM controls fuel metering based on the inputs of other sensors and its own programs.

5 An oxygen sensor depends on four conditions in order to operate correctly:

   a) *Electrical - The low voltage generated by the sensor requires good, clean connections. Always check the connectors whenever an oxygen sensor problem is suspected or indicated.*
   b) *Outside air supply - The sensor needs air circulation to*

the internal portion of the sensor. Whenever the sensor is installed, make sure that the air passages are not restricted.
   c) *Correct operating temperature - The PCM will not react to the sensor signal until the sensor reaches approximately 600-degrees F. This factor must be considered when evaluating the performance of the sensor.*
   d) *Unleaded fuel - Unleaded fuel is essential for correct sensor operation.*

6 The PCM can detect several different oxygen sensor problems and set Diagnostic Trouble Codes (DTCs) to indicate the specific fault (see Section 2). When an oxygen sensor DTC occurs, the PCM disregards the oxygen sensor signal voltage and reverts to open-loop fuel control as described previously.

REPLACEMENT

> ✳✳ **WARNING:**
>
> **Be careful not to burn yourself during the following procedure.**

➡**Note: Since the exhaust pipe contracts when cool, the oxygen sensor may be hard to loosen. To make sensor removal easier, start the engine and let it run for a minute or two, then turn it off.**

Upstream oxygen sensors

◆ **Refer to illustrations 11.8a, 11.8b, 11.8c and 11.9**

➡**Note: The upstream oxygen sensors are located in the exhaust manifolds, right above the flanges. Both of the connectors for the upstream sensors, and the sensors themselves, are more easily accessed from below.**

7 Raise the vehicle and place it securely on jackstands.

8 Locate the upstream sensor that you want to replace, then trace the sensor's lead to the electrical connector (see illustrations) and disconnect it.

9 There isn't enough room to remove an upstream oxygen sensor with a wrench; use an oxygen sensor socket (see illustration). Oxygen

11.8a The left upstream oxygen sensor is screwed into the left exhaust manifold

11.8b Trace the electrical lead up the connector, then depress the release tab (A) and disconnect the two halves of the connector

11.8c The right upstream oxygen sensor (A) and electrical connector (B) (3.5L V6 shown, other engines similar)

11.9 If there isn't enough room to put a wrench on an upstream oxygen sensor, use an oxygen sensor socket (this photo depicts an oxygen sensor socket on a downstream sensor to show you how it fits onto the sensor) (3.5L V6 shown, other engines similar)

sensor sockets are available at most auto parts stores.

10 Clean the threads inside the sensor mounting hole in the exhaust manifold with an 18 mm X 1.5 + 6E tap.

11 If you're installing the old sensor, clean off the threads, then apply a coat of anti-seize compound (such as Loctite® 771-64 or a suitable equivalent) to the threads before installing the sensor. If you're installing a new sensor, do NOT apply anti-seize compound; new sensors are already coated with anti-seize.

12 Installation is otherwise the reverse of removal. Be sure to tighten the oxygen sensor to the torque listed in this Chapter's Specifications.

11.14b Right downstream oxygen sensor (A) and electrical connector (B) (3.5L V6 shown, other engines similar)

11.14a Left downstream oxygen sensor (A) and electrical connector (B) (3.5L V6 shown, other engines similar)

Downstream oxygen sensors

▶ Refer to illustrations 11.14a and 11.14b

➡ **Note: The downstream oxygen sensors are located right behind the catalytic converters.**

13 Raise the vehicle and place it securely on jackstands.

14 Locate the downstream sensor that you want to replace, then trace the sensor's electrical lead to the sensor electrical connector (see illustrations) and disconnect it.

15 All you need to remove one of the downstream sensors is a combination wrench. An oxygen sensor socket isn't really necessary.

16 Clean the threads inside the sensor mounting hole in the exhaust pipe with an 18 mm X 1.5 + 6E tap.

17 If you're installing the old sensor, clean off the threads, then apply a coat of anti-seize compound (such as Loctite® 771-64 or a suitable equivalent) to the threads before installing the sensor. If you're installing a new sensor, do NOT apply anti-seize compound; new sensors are already coated with anti-seize.

18 Installation is otherwise the reverse of removal. Be sure to tighten the oxygen sensor to the torque listed in this Chapter's Specifications.

All sensors

19 Disconnect the cable from the negative terminal of the battery and leave it disconnected for a couple of minutes (see Chapter 5, Section 1). This will erase the old operating values that the Powertrain Control Module (PCM) has learned, allowing it to learn the characteristics of the new sensor. (If this isn't done, the vehicle may exhibit driveability problems.)

➡ **Note: Whenever the battery is disconnected, stored operating parameters may be lost from the PCM, which may cause the engine to run rough for a period of time while the PCM relearns the information.**

12 Transmission speed sensors - replacement

▶ Refer to illustrations 12.2 and 12.3

➡Note: This procedure applies only to the 42RLE (hydraulic, with adaptive electronics) automatic transmission. The input speed and output speed sensors are located on the left side of the transmission housing. The input speed sensor is the forward unit. The output speed sensor is the rear one. On the NAG1 (all-electronic) transmission, there are also two speed sensors, but they're located inside the control unit, which is located inside the transmission, on top of the valve body. Replacing either of these sensors is a job for a professional automatic transmission specialist.

1   Raise the vehicle and place it securely on jackstands.
2   Locate the transmission speed sensor that you're going to replace (see illustration). Place a drip pan underneath it. Some ATF will leak out when you remove the sensor.
3   Disconnect the electrical connector from the speed sensor that you want to replace (see illustration).
4   Remove the mounting bolt from the speed sensor that you want to replace (see illustration 12.3).
5   Installation is the reverse of removal. If you're installing the old sensor, make sure the O-ring is in good condition. Also, apply a non-hardening thread locking compound to the threads of the mounting bolt.

12.2 On 42RLE automatic transmissions, the transmission speed sensors are located on the left side of the transmission

A   *Input speed sensor*   B   *Output speed sensor*

12.3 To remove an input or output speed sensor from the transmission, disconnect the electrical connector (1), then remove the sensor mounting bolt (2)

13 Powertrain Control Module (PCM) - removal and installation

▶ Refer to illustrations 13.2, 13.3 and 13.4

❊❊ CAUTION:

Avoid static electricity damage to the Powertrain Control Module (PCM) by grounding yourself to the body of the vehicle before touching the PCM and using a special anti-static pad on which to store the PCM once it's removed.

➡Note 1: The PCM is located in the right rear corner of the engine compartment, inside the cowl area.

➡Note 2: Whenever the PCM is replaced with a new unit, it must be reprogrammed with a scan tool by a dealership service department or other qualified repair shop.

➡Note 3: Whenever the battery is disconnected, stored operating parameters may be lost from the PCM, causing the engine to run rough for a period of time while the PCM relearns the information.

1   Disconnect the cable from the negative terminal of the battery (see Chapter 5, Section 1).

13.2 To detach the PCM mounting bracket from the cowl, remove this bolt

2   Remove the bolt that secures the PCM mounting bracket to the cowl (see illustration).

13.3 Lift the PCM out of the cowl area, then unlock and disconnect the electrical connectors. To do so, push each sliding lock toward the harness, then depress the release tab (A) and pull off the connector

13.4 To detach the mounting bracket from the PCM, remove these two bolts. Then bolt the mounting bracket onto the new PCM unit

3   Carefully lift the PCM out of the cowl area and disconnect the electrical connectors from the PCM (see illustration).

4   If you're replacing the PCM, remove the two bolts that secure the

mounting bracket to the PCM and attach the bracket to the new PCM (see illustration).

5   Installation is the reverse of removal.

14 Catalytic converter - description, check and replacement

➡**Note: Because of a Federally-mandated extended warranty which covers emission-related components such as the catalytic converter, check with a dealer service department before replacing the converter at your own expense.**

GENERAL DESCRIPTION

1   A catalytic converter (or catalyst) is an emission control device in the exhaust system that reduces certain pollutants in the exhaust gas stream. There are two types of converters. An oxidation catalyst reduces hydrocarbons (HC) and carbon monoxide (CO). A reduction catalyst reduces oxides of nitrogen (NOx). A catalyst that can reduce all three pollutants is known as a "Three-Way Catalyst" (TWC).

2   All models covered by this manual are equipped with two TWCs, one below each exhaust manifold flange. The upper end of each catalyst has a short inlet pipe with a mounting flange that bolts to the exhaust manifold flange. The lower end of each catalyst is welded to a longer outlet pipe. The left and right catalyst outlet pipes are secured to the rest of the exhaust system by large screw-type clamps.

CHECK

3   The test equipment for a catalytic converter (a "loaded-mode" dynamometer and a 5-gas analyzer) is expensive. If you suspect that the converter on your vehicle is malfunctioning, take it to a dealer or

authorized emission inspection facility for diagnosis and repair.

4   Whenever you raise the vehicle to service underbody components, inspect the converter for leaks, corrosion, dents and other damage. Carefully inspect the welds and/or flange bolts and nuts that attach the front and rear ends of the converter to the exhaust system. If you note any damage, replace the converter.

5   Although catalytic converters don't break too often, they can become clogged or even plugged up. The easiest way to check for a restricted converter is to use a vacuum gauge to diagnose the effect of a blocked exhaust on intake vacuum.

   a) *Connect a vacuum gauge to an intake manifold vacuum source (see Chapter 2D).*

   b) *Warm the engine to operating temperature, place the transaxle in Park (automatic models) or Neutral (manual models) and apply the parking brake.*

   c) *Note the vacuum reading at idle and write it down.*

   d) *Quickly open the throttle to near its wide-open position and then quickly get off the throttle and allow it to close. Note the vacuum reading and write it down.*

   e) *Do this test three more times, recording your measurement after each test.*

   f) *If your fourth reading is more than one in-Hg lower than the reading that you noted at idle, the exhaust system might be restricted (the catalytic converter could be plugged, OR an exhaust pipe or muffler could be restricted).*

14.7a To disconnect the inlet pipe flange of either catalytic converter from the exhaust manifold flange, spray the threads of the bolts and nuts with penetrant, then remove these nuts. Replace the nut(s) and bolt(s) when installing the catalyst(s)

14.7b To disconnect either catalyst outlet pipe from the support bracket, remove the bolt from above (not the nut). To disconnect the outlet pipe of either catalytic converter, remove the nut from the clamp bolt (B)

REPLACEMENT

▶ **Refer to illustrations 14.7a and 14.7b**

✳✳ WARNING:

Make sure that the exhaust system is completely cooled down before proceeding. If the vehicle has just been driven, the catalytic converter can be hot enough to cause serious burns.

➡**Note: The photos accompanying this section depict the catalytic converters used on a 3.5L V6 model, but all models use essentially the same setup. Also, this procedure applies to both catalytic converters.**

6   Raise the vehicle and place it securely on jackstands.

7   Spray a liberal amount of penetrating oil onto the threads of the exhaust pipe-to-exhaust manifold bolts and the clamp bolt nut that connects the catalyst outlet pipe to the rest of the exhaust system. Also spray some penetrant on the two bolts and nuts that secure the small bracket between the two catalyst outlet pipes (see illustrations). Wait awhile for the penetrant to loosen things up.

8   While you're waiting for the penetrant to do its work, disconnect the electrical connector for the downstream oxygen sensor and remove the downstream oxygen sensor (see Section 11).

9   Unscrew the upper exhaust pipe-to-exhaust manifold flange bolt nuts (see illustration 14.7a). If they're still difficult to loosen, spray the threads with some more penetrant, wait awhile and try again.

10   Remove the bolt that secures the catalyst outlet pipe to the small support bracket between the catalyst outlet pipes (see illustration 14.7b). If you're removing both catalytic converters, remove the both bolts and remove the support bracket.

➡**Note: The nuts are tack-welded to the bracket, so don't try to unscrew them. Instead, unscrew the bolts from above.**

11   Remove the nut from the clamp bolt that secures the slip joint between the catalyst outlet pipe and the rest of the exhaust system (see illustration 14.7b). If it's still difficult to loosen, spray the threads with some more penetrant, wait awhile and try again. If you're removing both catalytic converters, remove the nuts from both clamps.

12   Remove the catalytic converter. Remove and discard the old flange gasket.

13   Installation is the reverse of removal. Be sure to use a new flange gasket and new bolts and nuts at the exhaust manifold mounting flange. The manufacturer also recommends using a new clamp at the slip joint between the catalyst outlet pipe and the exhaust pipe. Coat the threads of the clamp bolt and the exhaust manifold bolts with anti-seize compound to facilitate future removal. Tighten the fasteners securely.

14   Once the catalytic converter is reattached to the exhaust manifold and to the rest of the exhaust system, install the small support bracket. Again, it's a good idea to use new nuts and bolts and to coat the threads of the bolts with anti-seize compound. Tighten the nuts and bolts securely.

15 Evaporative Emissions Control (EVAP) system - description and component replacement

GENERAL DESCRIPTION

1   The Evaporative Emissions Control (EVAP) system prevents fuel system vapors (which contain unburned hydrocarbons) from escaping into the atmosphere. On warm days, vapors trapped inside the fuel tank expand. When the pressure reaches a certain threshold, these vapors are routed from the fuel tank through the fuel vapor vent valve and the fuel vapor control valve to the EVAP canister, where they're stored temporarily, until they can be consumed by the engine during normal operation. Under certain conditions (engine warmed up, vehicle up to speed, moderate or heavy loads, etc.) the Powertrain Control Module (PCM) opens the canister purge solenoid, which allows intake vacuum to pull fuel vapors from the EVAP canister into the intake manifold, where they mix with the air/fuel mixture before being consumed in the combustion chambers. This system is complex and virtually impossible to troubleshoot without the right tools and training. However, the

15.8 To disconnect the electrical connector from the EVAP canister purge solenoid, push the lock sideways, then depress the release tab (A) and pull off the connector (3.5L V6 model shown, other models similar)

15.9 To remove the EVAP canister purge solenoid, disconnect the EVAP inlet hose (A) and the outlet hose (B), then disengage the solenoid from its mounting bracket by pulling it straight up and off the bracket (3.5L V6 model shown, other models similar)

following description should give you a good idea of how the system works and where the components are located:

2 The EVAP canister, which contains activated charcoal, is the repository for storing fuel vapors produced by gasoline as it heats up inside the fuel tank. You'll have to raise the vehicle to inspect or replace the canister, but the canister is designed to be maintenance-free and should last the life of the vehicle. The EVAP canister is located in the right rear corner of the vehicle, above the right rear wheel. You'll have to raise the vehicle, remove the right rear wheel and remove the wheel well splash shield to access the EVAP canister.

3 The Natural Vacuum Leak Detection (NVLD) assembly is also located in the same spot as the EVAP canister. The NVLD unit monitors the temperature of the unburned hydrocarbon vapors inside the EVAP system. As the temperature increases, so does the pressure; as the temperature decreases, so does the pressure. But this effect can occur only if the system is fully sealed. If there's a leak, the relationship between pressure and temperature will diverge from the pressure-temperature relationship that the Powertrain Control Module (PCM) is programmed to expect. When this divergence between the pressure and the temperature of the fuel vapors inside the fuel tank and the EVAP system occurs, the PCM concludes that the system is leaking and it sets a Diagnostic Trouble Code (DTC) indicating either a small, medium or large leak in the EVAP system. Diagnosis of the NVLD assembly and detection system is beyond the scope of the home mechanic. If a DTC indicates a problem with the NVLD system, have a dealer service department or other qualified repair shop fix the vehicle. But a defective NVLD assembly is easy to replace, and you'll find the instructions to do so later in this section.

4 The EVAP canister purge solenoid (the manufacturer calls it a proportional purge solenoid) regulates the flow of vapors being purged from the EVAP canister into the intake manifold. The canister purge solenoid is controlled by the Powertrain Control Module (PCM). The canister purge solenoid is normally closed. It opens only when directed to do so by the PCM, which uses the availability of intake manifold vacuum and data from various information sensor inputs to determine when and how long to open the valve. The interval of time during which the purge valve is opened by the PCM is known as its "duty cycle." The canister purge solenoid is located at the right rear corner of the engine compartment on all models.

GENERAL SYSTEM CHECKS

5 The most common symptom of a faulty EVAP system is a strong fuel odor (particularly during hot weather). If you smell fuel while driving or (more likely) right after you park the vehicle and turn off the engine, check the fuel filler cap first. Make sure that it's screwed onto the fuel filler neck all the way.

6 If the odor persists, inspect all EVAP hose connections, both in the engine compartment and under the vehicle. You'll have to raise the vehicle and place it securely on jackstands to inspect most of the EVAP system, since it's located under the vehicle. Be sure to inspect each hose attached to the canister for damage and leakage along its entire length. Repair or replace as necessary. Inspect the canister for damage and look for fuel leaking from the bottom. If fuel is leaking or the canister is otherwise damaged, replace it.

7 Poor idle, stalling, and poor driveability can be caused by a defective fuel vapor vent valve or canister purge solenoid, a damaged canister, cracked hoses, or hoses connected to the wrong tubes. Fuel loss or fuel odor can be caused by fuel leaking from fuel lines or hoses, a cracked or damaged canister, or a defective vapor valve.

COMPONENT REPLACEMENT

EVAP canister purge solenoid

▶ Refer to illustrations 15.8 and 15.9

➡Note: The EVAP canister purge solenoid is located in the right rear corner of the engine compartment, on a small bracket attached to the right strut tower.

8 Disconnect the electrical connector from the EVAP canister purge solenoid (see illustration).

9 Clearly label the EVAP hoses (see illustration), then disconnect them from the EVAP canister purge solenoid.

10 To disengage the EVAP canister purge solenoid from its mounting bracket, pull it straight up.

11 Installation is the reverse of removal.

15.14a Typical EVAP canister and NVLD assembly (Chrysler 300 shown, other models similar):

A   NVLD air filter
B   Natural Vacuum Leak
    Detection (NVLD) pump
C   Electrical connector for
    NVLD pump
D   EVAP canister
E   EVAP line
F   EVAP line quick-connect
    fitting

NVLD filter, NVLD pump and EVAP canister

♦ Refer to illustrations 15.14a, 15.14b, 15.15, 15.16a and 15.16b

➡Note: The NVLD filter, NVLD pump and EVAP canister are located in the upper part of the right rear wheel well, above the wheel well splash shield. The easiest way to replace any of these three components is to simply remove the entire assembly, then to remove the component that you want to replace.

12 Loosen the right rear wheel lug nuts, raise the vehicle and place it securely on jackstands.

13 Remove the splash shield from the right rear wheel well (see Chapter 11).

14 Disconnect the NVLD electrical connector (see illustrations).

15 Disconnect the EVAP line from the EVAP canister (see illustration).

16 Remove the EVAP canister/NVLD assembly mounting nut (see

15.14b To disconnect the electrical connector from the NVLD pump, push the lock to the side, then depress the release tab (A) and pull off the connector

15.15 To disconnect the EVAP line quick-connect fitting from the EVAP canister, squeeze these two tabs and pull off the fitting

illustration), then slide the slots in the two mounting bosses on the lower end of the canister off their corresponding mounting brackets (see illustration). Place the assembly on a clean workbench for further disassembly.

15.16a To detach the EVAP canister/NVLD assembly from the vehicle, remove this nut . . .

15.16b . . . then disengage the two slots in the lower end of the canister from their corresponding mounting brackets

15.18 Natural Vacuum Leak Detection (NVLD) assembly:

A   NVLD air filter
B   Air filter-to-NVLD pump hose
C   NVLD pump
D   NVLD pump-to-EVAP canister hose

15.23 To detach the NVLD pump from its mounting bracket, push the mounting tab toward the pump housing to disengage the retainer tooth (A) from the bracket

15.27 To detach the NVLD filter/NVLD pump mounting bracket from the EVAP canister, remove these two nuts

15.19 To detach the NVLD air filter from its mounting bracket, disengage the mounting tab (A) from its slot in the mounting bracket, then swing the filter out from the bracket and unsnap the hinge (B) from its hinge pin

NVLD filter

▶ **Refer to illustrations 15.18 and 15.19**

17 Remove the EVAP canister/NVLD assembly (see Steps 12 through 15).

18 Disconnect the hose from the air filter (see illustration).

19 Disengage the filter mounting tab from the mounting bracket (see illustration), disengage the hinge from its hinge pin and remove the filter.

20 Installation is the reverse of removal.

NVLD pump

▶ **Refer to illustration 15.23**

21 Remove the EVAP canister/NVLD assembly (see Steps 12 through 15).

22 Disconnect the air filter-to-NVLD pump hose and the NVLD pump-to-EVAP canister hose (see illustration 15.18).

23 Unsnap the NVLD pump from its mounting bracket (see illustration).

24 Installation is the reverse of removal.

EVAP canister

▶ **Refer to illustrations 15.27 and 15.28**

25 Remove the EVAP canister/NVLD assembly (see Steps 12 through 15).

26 Remove the NVLD filter (see Steps 18 and 19) and the NVLD pump (see Steps 22 and 23).

27 Remove the NVLD filter/NVLD pump mounting bracket nuts (see illustration) and remove the bracket from the EVAP canister.

28 Inspect the condition of the rubber insulators inside the two canister mounting bosses (see illustration).

29 Installation is the reverse of removal.

EVAP line

▶ **Refer to illustration 15.31**

30 Disconnect the EVAP line from the EVAP canister (see illustration 15.15).

31 Disconnect the EVAP line quick-connect fitting at the lower end of the EVAP line (see illustration).

15.28 Inspect the condition of the rubber insulators inside the two EVAP canister mounting bosses

15.31 To disconnect the quick-connect fitting at the lower end of the EVAP line, squeeze the two sides together and pull it off

16 Exhaust Gas Recirculation (EGR) system - description and component replacement

DESCRIPTION

1   Oxides of nitrogen, nitrogen oxide, or simply NOx, is a compound that is formed in the combustion chambers when the oxygen and nitrogen in the incoming air mix together. NOx is a natural byproduct of high combustion chamber temperatures (2500 degrees F and higher). When NOx is emitted from the tailpipe, it mixes with reactive organic compounds (ROCs), hydrocarbons (HC) and sunlight to form ozone and photochemical smog. The EGR system reduces NOx by recirculating exhaust gases from the exhaust manifold, through the EGR valve and intake manifold, then back to the combustion chambers, where it mixes with the incoming air/fuel mixture before being consumed. These recirculated exhaust gases dilute the incoming air/fuel mixture, which cools the combustion chambers, thereby reducing NOx emissions.

2   All engines covered by this manual use an EGR system.

16.7 To disconnect the electrical connector from the EGR valve, slide the lock sideways, then depress the release tab (A) and pull off the connector

3   The EGR system consists of the Powertrain Control Module (PCM), the EGR valve and various information sensors (ECT, TP, MAP, IAT, RPM and VSS sensors) that the PCM uses to determine when to open the EGR valve. When the PCM closes the power/control circuit for the EGR valve, a solenoid inside the EGR valve is energized. This creates an electromagnetic field, which causes an armature to pull up, lifting the pintle off its seat. The exhaust gas then flows from the exhaust manifold port to the intake manifold.

4   Once activated by the PCM, the EGR valve uses a position feedback circuit to control the position of the pintle valve. The feedback circuit, which functions like a potentiometer, puts out a variable output voltage signal with an operating range between 0.5 and 5.4 volts. This variable output enables the PCM to control the position of the pintle with a high degree of precision. A pintle position sensor monitors the position of the pintle, and the PCM adjusts the current to match the actual pintle position to the optimal pintle position.

5   If there is too much EGR flow at idle, cruise or during cold running conditions, the engine will stop after a cold start, stop at idle after deceleration, surge during cruising speeds or idle roughly. If there is too little EGR flow, combustion chamber temperature can become too high during acceleration or under a heavy load, which can cause spark knock (detonation) and/or engine overheating.

COMPONENT REPLACEMENT

V6 engines

▶ **Refer to illustration 16.7**

➡**Note: The EGR valve is bolted to the rear end of the right cylinder head. The lower EGR pipe connects the right exhaust manifold to the EGR valve. The upper EGR pipe connects the EGR valve to the intake manifold. You must perform the first two steps below before you can remove any of the three components.**

6   Remove the EVAP purge solenoid valve (see Section 15).

7   Disconnect the electrical connector from the EGR valve (see illustration) and set it aside.

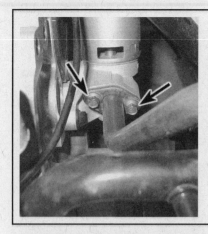

16.12 To disconnect the lower end of the upper EGR pipe from the EGR valve, remove these two bolts (3.5L V6 shown, 2.7L V6 similar)

16.13 To disconnect the upper end of the upper EGR pipe from the intake manifold, grasp it firmly and pull it out

Lower EGR pipe (2.7L engine only)

8   Remove the two bolts that secure the lower EGR pipe to the exhaust manifold.

9   Remove the two bolts that secure the lower EGR pipe to the EGR valve and remove the lower EGR pipe.

10 Remove the old gasket from the EGR pipe mounting flange and discard it.

11 Installation is the reverse of removal. Be sure to use a new gasket and tighten the EGR pipe mounting bolts to the torque listed in this Chapter's Specifications.

Upper EGR pipe

▶ **Refer to illustrations 16.12, 16.13, 16.14 and 16.15**

➡**Note: The photos accompanying this Section depict the EGR system on a 3.5L V6 model. Except for the lower EGR pipe (see above), the rest of the two systems are virtually identical.**

12 Remove the two bolts that secure the lower end of the upper EGR pipe to the EGR valve (see illustration).

13 Disconnect the upper end of the upper EGR pipe from the intake manifold (see illustration) and remove the upper EGR pipe.

14 Remove the old gasket from the EGR pipe flange (see illustration).

15 Remove the old rubber silicone seals from the EGR pipe (see illustration). The smaller black seal is the actual O-ring; the larger

blue seal is a dust seal. To ensure a positive seal, you should always replace both of these seals whenever you disconnect the EGR pipe.

16 Installation is the reverse of removal. Be sure to use a new gasket and new rubber silicone seals and tighten the EGR pipe mounting flange bolts to the torque listed in this Chapter's Specifications.

EGR valve

▶ **Refer to illustration 16.18**

17 Disconnect the upper EGR pipe and, on 2.7L engines, the lower EGR pipe, from the EGR valve.

18 Remove the EGR mounting bolts (see illustration) and remove the EGR valve from the right cylinder head.

19 Clean the EGR valve mounting surfaces on the cylinder head and on the valve itself.

20 Installation is the reverse of removal. Be sure to tighten the EGR valve mounting bolts to the torque listed in this Chapter's Specifications.

V8 ENGINE

EGR valve

▶ **Refer to illustration 16.21**

➡**Note: The EGR valve is located on the front of the right cylinder head.**

21 Disconnect the electrical connector from the EGR valve (see illustration).

16.14 Always replace the gasket between the flange at the lower end of the upper EGR pipe and the mounting surface on the EGR valve

16.15 Always replace these two seals on the upper (intake manifold) end of the upper EGR pipe (3.5L V6 shown, 2.7L V6 similar):

A   Dust seal
B   O-ring

16.18 To detach the EGR valve from the cylinder, remove these two bolts (3.5L V6 shown, 2.7L V6 similar)

16.21 To remove the EGR valve from a V8 engine, slide the lock on the connector out, depress the tab (1) and detach the connector, remove the EGR pipe flange bolts (2), then remove the EGR valve bolts (3)

22 Remove the EGR pipe mounting flange bolts (see illustration 16.16).

23 Remove the EGR valve mounting bolts (see illustration 16.21) and remove the EGR valve. Remove and discard the old gasket.

24 Clean the EGR valve mounting surfaces on the cylinder head and on the valve itself.

25 Installation is the reverse of removal. Be sure to use new gaskets between the EGR valve and the cylinder head and between the EGR pipe mounting flange and the EGR valve and tighten the EGR valve and EGR pipe mounting bolts to the torque listed in this Chapter's Specifications.

EGR pipe

▶ Refer to illustration 16.28

➡Note: The EGR pipe connects the EGR valve to the intake manifold.

26 Remove the engine cover.

27 Remove the EGR pipe mounting flange bolts (see illustration 16.21). Remove and discard the old EGR pipe mounting flange gasket.

28 Disconnect the EGR pipe from the intake manifold (see illustration).

29 Remove the old gasket from the EGR pipe flange (see illustration 16.14) and replace it with a new one. Remove the old rubber silicone seals from the EGR pipe (see illustration 16.21). The smaller black seal is the actual O-ring; the larger blue seal is a dust seal. To ensure a

16.28 To disconnect the upper end of the EGR pipe from the intake manifold, grasp it firmly and pull it straight out of the manifold

positive seal, you should always replace both of these seals whenever you disconnect the EGR pipe.

30 Clean the EGR pipe mounting surfaces on the EGR valve and on the EGR pipe mounting flange.

31 Installation is the reverse of removal. Be sure to tighten the EGR pipe mounting flange bolts to the torque listed in this Chapter's Specifications.

17 Positive Crankcase Ventilation (PCV) system - description and check

DESCRIPTION

▶ Refer to illustration 17.2a, 17.2b, 17.2c, 17.3a, 17.3b and 17.3c

1   The Positive Crankcase Ventilation (PCV) system reduces hydrocarbon emissions by scavenging crankcase vapors, which are rich in unburned hydrocarbons. A PCV valve regulates the flow of gases into the intake manifold in proportion to the amount of intake vacuum available. At idle, when intake vacuum is very high, the PCV valve restricts the flow of vapors so that the engine doesn't run poorly. As the throttle plate opens and intake vacuum begins to diminish, the PCV valve opens more to allow vapors to flow more freely.

2   On V6 engines, the PCV system consists of the fresh air inlet hose, the PCV valve and the crankcase ventilation hose (or PCV hose). The fresh air inlet hose (see illustration) connects the air filter housing to a pipe on top and at the front of the left valve cover. The crankcase ventilation hose (or PCV hose) connects the PCV valve on the rear end of the right valve cover to the intake manifold (see illustration). The PCV valve is screwed into the rear end of the right valve cover (see illustration). To remove it, simply unscrew it.

3   On V8 engines, the PCV system consists of the fresh air inlet

17.2a On V6 engines, the PCV fresh air inlet hose connects the air filter housing to a pipe on the left valve cover (3.5L V6 shown, 2.7L V6 similar)

17.2b On V6 engines, the crankcase ventilation hose (or PCV hose) connects the PCV valve to the intake manifold (3.5L V6 shown, 2.7L V6 similar)

17.2c On V6 engines, the PCV valve is screwed into the rear end of the right valve cover (3.5L V6 shown, 2.7L V6 similar)

hose, the PCV valve and the crankcase ventilation hose (or PCV hose). The fresh air inlet hose (see illustration) connects the air filter housing to the oil filler neck on top of the left valve cover, which is on the right side of the intake manifold. The crankcase ventilation hose, or PCV hose (see illustration), connects the PCV valve to the intake manifold. The PCV valve (see illustration) is located in the right side of the intake manifold. To remove it, turn it 90-degrees and pull it out.

INSPECTION

4   An engine that is operated without a properly functioning crankcase ventilation system can be damaged. So anytime you're servicing the engine, be sure to inspect the PCV system hose(s) for cracks, tears, deterioration and other damage. Disconnect the hose(s) and inspect it/them for damage and obstructions. If a hose is clogged, clean it out. If you're unable to clean it satisfactorily, replace it.

5   A plugged PCV hose might cause any or all of the following conditions: A rough idle, stalling or a slow idle speed, oil leaks or sludge in the engine. So if the engine is running roughly, stalling and idling at a lower than normal speed, or is losing oil, or has oil in the throttle

17.3a On V8 engines, the fresh air inlet hose connects the air filter housing (A) to the oil filler neck pipe (B) on top of the left valve cover

17.3b On V8 engines, the crankcase ventilation hose (A), or PCV hose, connects the PCV valve (B) to the intake manifold

17.3c On V8 engines, the PCV valve is located in the right side of the intake manifold. To remove it, disconnect the PCV hose (A), then turn it counterclockwise 90-degrees

body or air intake manifold plenum, or has a build-up of sludge, a PCV system hose might be clogged. Repair or replace the hose(s) as necessary.

6   A leaking PCV hose might cause any or all of the following conditions: a rough idle, stalling or a high idle speed. So if the engine is running roughly, stalling and idling at a higher than normal speed, a PCV system hose might be leaking. Repair or replace the hose(s) as necessary.

7   Here's an easy functional check of the PCV system on a vehicle with a fresh air inlet hose and a crankcase ventilation hose with a PCV valve in it:

a) *Disconnect the crankcase ventilation hose (the crankcase ventilation hose, or simply "the PCV hose," is the hose that connects the PCV valve to the intake manifold).*

b) *Start the engine and let it warm up to its normal idle.*

c) *Verify that there is vacuum at the PCV hose. If there is no vacuum, look for a plugged hose or a clogged port or pipe on the intake manifold. Also look for a hose that collapses when it's blocked (i.e. when vacuum is applied). Replace clogged or deteriorated hoses.*

d) *Remove the engine oil dipstick and install a vacuum gauge on the upper end of the dipstick tube.*

e) *Pinch off or plug the PCV system's fresh air inlet hose.*

f) *Run the engine at 1500 rpm for 30 seconds, then read the vacuum gauge while the engine is running at 1500 rpm.*

g) *If there's vacuum present, the crankcase ventilation system is operating correctly.*

h) *If there's NO vacuum present, the engine might be drawing in outside air. The PCV system won't function correctly unless the engine is a sealed system. Inspect the valve cover(s), oil pan gasket or other sealing areas for leaks.*

i) *If the vacuum gauge indicates positive pressure, look for a plugged hose or engine blow-by.*

8   If the PCV system is functioning correctly, but there's evidence of engine oil in the throttle body or air filter housing, it could be caused by excessive crankcase pressure. Have the crankcase pressure tested by a dealer service department.

9   In the PCV system, excessive blow-by (caused by worn rings, pistons and/or cylinders, or by constant heavy loads) is discharged into the intake manifold and consumed. If you discover heavy sludge deposits or a dilution of the engine oil, even though the PCV system is functioning correctly, look for other causes (see Troubleshooting and Chapter 2D) and correct them as soon as possible.

18 Intake Manifold Tuning (IMT) Valve System - description and component replacement

DESCRIPTION

▶ **Refer to illustration 18.1**

1   The Intake Manifold Tuning (IMT) Valve System, which is used on V6 engines, improves the acoustical tuning qualities of the intake manifold, which increases torque at engine speeds below 5000 rpm and horsepower at speeds above 5000 rpm. 2.7L engines are equipped with an intake manifold tuning valve actuator, which is located at the front of the intake manifold. 3.5L engines are equipped with a manifold tuning valve actuator and a short runner valve actuator. On 3.5L engines (see illustration), the manifold tuning valve actuator is located on the right front end of the intake manifold and the short runner valve actuator is located on the left front end of the manifold. Both actuators are solenoids that open or close flaps inside the manifold in response to commands from the Powertrain Control Module (PCM).

2   The intake manifold plenum on V6 engines is divided into two equal-volume upper and lower plenums by a horizontal partition running the length of the plenum. Air entering the upper half of the plenum is directed through three of the intake runners; air entering the lower half of the plenum enters the other three intake runners. The manifold tuning valve actuator controls a small valve that opens or closes a hole in the partition at the opposite end of the plenum from the throttle body. When the valve is open, the upper and lower partitions are closed off from one another, preventing the incoming air inside these two smaller plenums from mixing. When the valve is closed, the upper and lower partitions are connected through this hole, allowing incoming air inside the two plenums to mix.

3   The short runner valve solenoid, which is used only on 3.5L engines, directs airflow through the longer route - the air intake plenum and six longer intake runners - or through six shorter intake runners that bypass the plenum and the long runners. Below 5000 rpm, a but-

18.1 Typical Intake Manifold Tuning (IMT) system (3.5L V6 engine shown, 2.7L engine similar):

A *Manifold tuning valve actuator (used on 2.7L and 3.5L V6 engines)*
B *Short runner valve actuator (used only on the 3.5L engine)*

terfly valve inside each runner prevents intake air from entering the short intake runners, forcing it to travel the long way around, through the intake manifold plenum, then through six longer intake runners, before it enters the combustion chambers. This gives the slow-moving mass of air time to build inertia so that it fills the combustion chambers more effectively, improving torque. Above 5000 rpm, the PCM commands the short runner valve solenoid to open the butterfly valves inside the six shorter intake runners, which allows incoming air to travel a much shorter path, bypassing the longer route through the plenum and long runners, increasing horsepower.

18.4 To remove the intake manifold tuning valve actuator from a V6 engine, depress the release tab (1), disconnect the electrical connector and remove the two mounting bolts (2) (3.5L engine shown, 2.7L engine similar)

COMPONENT REPLACEMENT

Intake manifold tuning valve actuator

◗ Refer to illustration 18.4 and 18.6

➡Note: On 2.7L engines, the intake manifold tuning valve actuator is located on the front end of the intake manifold. On 3.5L engines, the manifold tuning valve actuator is located on the right front end of the intake manifold.

4   Disconnect the electrical connector from the manifold tuning valve actuator (see illustration).

5   Remove the manifold tuning valve actuator mounting bolts (see illustration 18.4) and remove the manifold tuning valve actuator.

6   Remove the old manifold tuning valve actuator O-ring (see illustration) and discard it.

7   Installation is the reverse of removal. Be sure to use a NEW O-ring whether you're installing the old actuator or a new unit. Tighten the manifold tuning valve actuator mounting bolts to the torque listed in this Chapter's Specifications.

Short runner valve actuator

◗ Refer to illustration 18.8

➡Note: The short runner valve actuator, which is used only on 3.5L engines, is located on the left front end of the intake manifold.

8   Disconnect the electrical connector from the short runner valve actuator (see illustration).

18.6 Be sure to remove and discard the old actuator O-ring from the intake manifold tuning valve actuator (shown) or short runner valve actuator. Use a new O-ring whether you're installing the old actuator or a new unit

18.8 To remove the short runner valve actuator from a 3.5L engine, depress the release tab (1), disconnect the electrical connector and remove the two mounting bolts (2)

9   Remove the short runner valve actuator mounting bolts (see illustration 18.8) and remove the short runner valve actuator.

10 Remove the old short runner valve actuator O-ring (see illustration 18.6) and discard it.

11 Installation is the reverse of removal. Be sure to use a NEW O-ring whether you're installing the old actuator or a new unit. Tighten the short runner valve actuator mounting bolts to the torque listed in this Chapter's Specifications.

19 Multi-Displacement System (MDS) - description and component replacement

DESCRIPTION

1   The Multi Displacement System (MDS) improves the fuel economy of the V8 engine by deactivating four of the cylinders when certain conditions are met. Under acceleration or heavy loads, the engine runs on all eight cylinders, allowing full power. But when the conditions are right - cruising at light loads or driving in city traffic, for example - the Powertrain Control Module (PCM) deactivates cylinders 1, 4, 6 and 7 (cylinders 2, 3, 5 and 8 run all the time).

2   The MDS components include an oil temperature sensor, four control valve/solenoids, special roller lifters that can be deactivated, the wiring harness that connects these components and a specially-designed camshaft.

COMPONENT REPLACEMENT

Control valve/solenoid

➡**Note: The four solenoids are located in the valley between the cylinder heads. This procedure applies to any of the four units.**

3   Remove the intake manifold (see Chapter 2C).
4   Disconnect the electrical connector from the solenoid.
5   Remove the solenoid hold-down bolt and remove the solenoid.
6   Installation is the reverse of removal.

Lifters and camshaft

7   Refer to Chapter 2C.

Specifications

Torque specifications
Ft-lbs (unless otherwise indicated)

EGR valve (all engines)	
Lower EGR pipe mounting flange bolts	
(2.7L V6 only)	
At exhaust manifold	23
At EGR valve	95 in-lbs
Upper EGR pipe mounting flange bolts	
(at EGR valve)	95 in-lbs
EGR valve mounting bolts	23
Engine coolant temperature sensor	
V6 engines	20
V8 engine	97 in-lbs
Knock sensor mounting bolt	
V6 engine	88 in-lbs
V8 engine	176 in-lbs
Oxygen sensors	22

Notes

Section

Reference to other Chapters

7

AUTOMATIC TRANSMISSION

1 General information

The vehicles covered in this manual are equipped with a four-speed (42RLE) or five-speed (NAG1) automatic transmission. All transmissions are equipped with a Torque Converter Clutch (TCC) system that increases fuel economy. The TCC engages in Drive and Overdrive modes. The TCC system consists of a solenoid, controlled by the Powertrain Control Module (PCM), that locks the torque converter when the vehicle is cruising on level ground and the engine is fully warmed up.

All automatic transmissions covered in this Chapter are equipped with transmission oil coolers which are mounted in front of the air conditioning condenser and serviced as a single unit with the condenser.

All vehicles with an automatic transmission are equipped with a Brake Transmission Shift Interlock (BTSI) system that locks the shift lever in the PARK position and prevents the driver from shifting out of PARK unless the brake pedal is depressed. The BTSI system also pre-vents the ignition key from being turned to the LOCK or ACCESSORY position unless the shift lever is in the PARK position.

Due to the complexity of the automatic transmissions covered in this manual and the need for specialized equipment to perform most service operations, this Chapter is limited to general diagnosis, routine maintenance, adjustments and removal and installation procedures.

If the transmission requires major repair work, leave it to a dealer service department or a transmission repair shop. However, even if a transmission shop does the repairs, you can save some money by removing and installing the transmission yourself. Keep in mind that a faulty transmission should not be removed before the vehicle has been diagnosed by a knowledgeable technician equipped with the proper tools, as troubleshooting must be performed with the transmission installed in the vehicle.

2 Diagnosis - general

➡**Note: Automatic transmission malfunctions may be caused by five general conditions: poor engine performance, incorrect adjustments, hydraulic malfunctions, mechanical malfunctions or malfunctions in the computer or its signal network. Diagnosis of these problems should always begin with a check of the easily repaired items: fluid level and condition (see Chapter 1) and shift cable adjustment. Next, perform a road test to determine if the problem has been corrected or if more diagnosis is necessary. If the problem persists after the preliminary tests and corrections are completed, additional diagnosis should be done by a dealer service department or transmission repair shop. Refer to the Troubleshooting section at the front of this manual for information on symptoms of transmission problems.**

PRELIMINARY CHECKS

1   Drive the vehicle to warm up the transmission to its normal operating temperature.

2   Check the fluid level as described in Chapter 1:

   a) *If the fluid level is unusually low, add enough fluid to bring the level to the correct mark (see Section 26 in Chapter 1), then check for external leaks (see below). The manufacturer states that routine checks of the automatic transmission fluid are not necessary; the procedure in Chapter 1 should only be used when refilling the transmission after the fluid has been drained, unless an obvious leak has been detected. Low fluid level can lead to slipping or loss of drive, while overfilling can cause foaming and loss of fluid.*

➡**Note: To check the fluid level you'll have to obtain a dipstick (part number 9336), which you'll have to obtain through a dealer parts department (unlike most vehicles, a dipstick is not present in the transmission filler tube). A scan tool capable of reading the temperature of the automatic transmission fluid will also be required.**

   b) *If the fluid level is abnormally high, it might have been overfilled. Drain off the excess.*

   c) *If the fluid is foaming, drain it and refill the transmission, then check for coolant in the fluid that was drained. If fluid is present, the transmission fluid cooler in the radiator is faulty.*

3   Check the engine idle speed.

➡**Note: If the engine is malfunctioning, do not proceed with the preliminary checks until it has been repaired and runs normally.**

4   Inspect the shift cable (see Section 3). Make sure it's properly adjusted and that it operates smoothly.

FLUID LEAK DIAGNOSIS

5   Most fluid leaks are usually easy to locate because they leave a visible stain and/or wet spot. Most repairs are simply a matter of replacing a seal or gasket. If a leak is more difficult to find, the following procedure will help.

6   Identify the fluid. Make sure that it's transmission fluid, not engine oil or brake fluid. One way to positively identify Automatic Transmission Fluid (ATF) is by its red color.

7   Try to pinpoint the source of the leak. Drive the vehicle several miles, then park it over a large sheet of cardboard. After a minute or two, you should be able to locate the leak by determining the source of the fluid dripping onto the cardboard.

8   Make a careful visual inspection of the suspected component and the area immediately around it. Pay particular attention to gasket mating surfaces. A flashlight and mirror are often helpful for finding leaks in areas that are hard to see.

9   If you still can't find the leak, thoroughly clean the suspected area with a degreaser or solvent, then dry it off.

10 Drive the vehicle for several miles at normal operating temperature and varying speeds. After driving the vehicle, visually inspect the suspected component again.

11 Once you have located the leak, you must determine the source before you can repair it properly. For example, if you replace a pan gasket but the sealing flange is warped or bent, the new gasket won't stop the leak. The flange must first be straightened.

12 Before attempting to repair a leak, verify that the following conditions are corrected or they might cause another leak.

➡**Note: Some of the following conditions cannot be fixed without highly specialized tools and expertise. Such problems must be referred to a transmission repair shop or a dealer service department.**

Gasket leaks

13 Inspect the pan periodically. Make sure that the bolts are tight, that no bolts are missing, that the gasket is in good condition and that the pan is flat (dents in the pan might indicate damage to the valve body inside).

14 If the pan gasket is leaking, the fluid level or the fluid pressure might be too high, the vent might be plugged, the pan bolts might be too tight, the pan sealing flange might be warped, the sealing surface of the transmission housing might be damaged, the gasket might be damaged or the transmission casting might be cracked or porous. If sealant instead of gasket material has been used to form a seal between the pan and the transmission housing, it may be the wrong type sealant.

Seal leaks

15 If a transmission seal is leaking, the fluid level or pressure might be too high, the vent might be plugged, the seal bore might be dam-

aged, the seal itself might be damaged or incorrectly installed, the surface of the shaft protruding through the seal might be damaged or a loose bearing might be causing excessive shaft movement.

16 Make sure that the dipstick tube seal is in good condition and that the tube is correctly seated.

Case leaks

17 If the case itself appears to be leaking, the casting is porous. A porous casting must be repaired or replaced.

18 Make sure that the oil cooler hose fittings are tight and in good condition.

Fluid comes out vent pipe or fill tube

19 If this condition occurs, the transmission is overfilled, there is coolant in the fluid, the case is porous, the dipstick is incorrect, the vent is plugged or the drain-back holes are plugged.

---

3   Shift cable - check, adjustment and replacement

✳✳ WARNING:

The models covered by this manual are equipped with a Supplemental Restraint System (SRS), more commonly known as airbags. Always disable the airbag system before working in the vicinity of any airbag system component to avoid the possibility of accidental deployment of the airbag(s), which could cause personal injury (see Chapter 12). Do not use a memory saving device to preserve the PCM or radio memory when working on or near airbag system components.

CHECK

1   Firmly apply the parking brake and try to momentarily operate the starter in each shift lever position. The starter should only operate when the shift lever is in the PARK or NEUTRAL positions. If the starter operates in any position other than PARK or NEUTRAL, adjust the shift cable (see below). If, after adjustment, the starter still operates in positions

other than PARK or NEUTRAL, the Transmission Range (TR) sensor may be defective (see Chapter 6, Section 2).

ADJUSTMENT

▶ Refer to illustrations 3.4 and 3.6

2   Place the shift lever in the PARK position.
3   Remove the center console (see Chapter 11).
4   If equipped, remove the shield that covers the shift cable and the BTSI cable. Loosen the shift cable adjustment bolt (see illustration).
5   Raise the vehicle and support it securely on jackstands.

➡ Note: The rear of the vehicle must also be raised, so the driveshaft can be turned in Step 8 (to verify that the transmission is completely engaged in PARK).

6   Working at the transmission, pry the shift cable end from the transmission shift lever (see illustration).
7   Verify that the manual shift lever on the transmission is all the

3.4 Location of the shift cable adjustment bolt on the shift lever assembly

3.6 Use a screwdriver or trim panel tool to pry the shift cable off the shift lever at the transmission

3.16a To remove the shift cable from the transmission, detach the shift cable end from the shift lever (A) and remove the two mounting bolts (B) from the cable bracket

3.16b Press the two lock tabs and slide the shift cable through the bracket

way to the rear, in the last detent. (This is the PARK position.)

8   Verify that the park lock pawl inside the transmission is engaged by trying to rotate the driveshaft. The driveshaft will not rotate if the transmission is correctly engaged in PARK.

9   Reconnect the shift cable to the manual shift lever on the transmission.

10 Lower the vehicle.

11 With the parking brake firmly applied, make sure the engine starts (don't move the shift lever from PARK yet).

12 Tighten the adjuster screw to the torque listed in this Chapter's Specifications.

13 If the linkage appears to be adjusted correctly, but the starter still operates in any other position(s) besides PARK and NEUTRAL, the Transmission Range (TR) sensor might be faulty (see Chapter 6, Section 2).

REPLACEMENT

▶ **Refer to illustrations 3.16a, 3.16b, 3.19 and 3.20**

14 Place the shift lever in the PARK position.

15 Raise the vehicle and support it securely on jackstands.

16 Working at the transmission, pry the shift cable end from the transmission shift lever, remove the bolts from the shift cable bracket (see illustrations) and remove the shift cable from the transmission.

17 Lower the vehicle and remove the center console (see Chapter 11).

18 Remove the shield that covers the shift cable and the BTSI cable, if equipped.

19 Working at the shift lever assembly, lift the shift cable from the slots in the mounting bracket, then remove the shift cable from the shift lever stud (see illustration).

20 Working in the engine compartment, disengage the rubber grommet from the firewall and pull the shift cable through the firewall (see illustration).

21 Installation is the reverse of removal. When you're done, adjust the cable (see Steps 2 through 12).

3.19 To remove the shift cable, disengage it from the slots (A) in the bracket, then separate the cable end from the stud (B). To adjust the shift cable, loosen the adjustment bolt (C) and allow the cable tension to release

3.20 The shift cable passes through the firewall between the heater hoses and the power brake booster

4 Brake Transmission Shift Interlock (BTSI) system

> ### ✳✳ WARNING:
>
> **The models covered by this manual are equipped with a Supplemental Restraint System (SRS), more commonly known as airbags. Always disable the airbag system before working in the vicinity of any airbag system component to avoid the possibility of accidental deployment of the airbag(s), which could cause personal injury (see Chapter 12). Do not use a memory saving device to preserve the PCM or radio memory when working on or near airbag system components.**

➡Note: The shift lever and BTSI solenoid is one complete assembly. In the event of failure, replace the shift lever assembly as a complete unit. Check with a dealer parts department or other qualified automotive parts distributor.

DESCRIPTION

1   The Brake Transmission Shift Interlock (BTSI) system is a solenoid-operated device, located on the shift cable, that locks the shift lever into the PARK position when the ignition key is in the LOCK or ACCESSORY position. When the ignition key is in the RUN position, a magnetic holding device, inline with the park lock cable, is energized. When the system is functioning correctly, the only way to unlock the shift lever and move it out of PARK is to depress the brake pedal. The BTSI system also prevents the ignition key from being turned to the LOCK or ACCESSORY position unless the shift lever is fully locked into the PARK position.

CHECK

2   Verify that the ignition key can be removed only in the PARK position.

3   When the shift lever is in the PARK position, you should be able to rotate the ignition key from OFF to LOCK. But when the shift lever is in any gear position other than PARK (including NEUTRAL), you should not be able to rotate the ignition key to the LOCK position.

4   You should not be able to move the shift lever out of the PARK position when the ignition key is turned to the OFF position.

5   You should not be able to move the shift lever out of the PARK position when the ignition key is turned to the RUN or START position until you depress the brake pedal.

6   You should not be able to move the shift lever out of the PARK position when the ignition key is turned to the ACC or LOCK position (brake pedal NOT depressed).

7   Once in gear, with the ignition key in the RUN position, you

4.13a Push the BTSI cable back slightly and lift the cable through the notch in the BTSI solenoid

4.11 To release the Brake Transmission Shift Interlock (BTSI) cable from the key lock cylinder, place the ignition key in the ON position, press the tab on the BTSI cable and pull the cable from the key lock cylinder housing (housing removed for clarity)

should be able to move the shift lever between gears, or put it into NEUTRAL or PARK, without depressing the brake pedal.

8   If the BTSI system doesn't operate as described, try adjusting it (see Steps 16 through 20).

BTSI CABLE REPLACEMENT

▶ **Refer to illustrations 4.11, 4.13a and 4.13b**

9   Remove the center console and the driver's knee bolster and reinforcement (see Chapter 11).

10 Put the shift lever in the PARK position. Switch the ignition key to the ON position.

11 Working under the steering column, remove the key lock cylinder (see Chapter 12). Disconnect the shift lock cable from the key lock cylinder (see illustration).

12 Working at the center console, remove the shift cable and the BTSI cable shield, if equipped.

13 Disconnect the BTSI cable end from the solenoid (see illustration) and lift the BTSI cable adjuster from the bracket (see illustration).

14 Remove the BTSI cable.

15 Installation is the reverse of removal.

4.13b Lift the BTSI cable adjuster assembly from the slot in the bracket (A); (B) is the BTSI lock button

4.23a Lift the bin from the center console to expose the override button . . .

4.23b . . . and, while pressing the override button, move the console shifter out of the Park position

BTSI CABLE ADJUSTMENT

16 Remove the center console (see Chapter 11).

17 Put the shift lever in the PARK position. Switch the ignition key to the LOCK position.

18 Pull UP on the BTSI lock button (see illustration 4.13b).

➡**Note: If a new BTSI cable is being installed, remove the cable adjuster lock pin.**

19 Check that the BTSI cable is ready for adjustment by pushing the cable to the rear and releasing.

20 Push the lock button down until it snaps into position. At this point, the lock button should be recessed approximately 1 to 2 mm into the cable adjustment housing.

21 Install the center console (see Chapter 11).

SHIFT LOCK OVERRIDE FEATURE

▶ **Refer to illustrations 4.23a and 4.23b**

22 In the event the Brake Transmission Shift Interlock (BTSI) system fails and the shift lever cannot be moved out of gear, the system is equipped with an override feature.

23 Remove the bin to the right of the shift lever (see illustration). Depress the brake pedal (and keep it depressed) and start the engine (or, if you just want to shift out of PARK without starting the engine, turn the ignition key to the ACC position). Locate the button alongside the right side of the shift gate (see illustration), press the button and move the shifter out of the PARK position.

24 Repair the BTSI system (or have it repaired) as soon as possible.

---

5 Extension housing oil seal - replacement

▶ **Refer to illustration 5.8**

1 Oil leaks frequently occur due to wear of the extension housing oil seal. Replacement of this seal is relatively easy, since the repair can be performed without removing the transmission from the vehicle.

2 If you suspect a leak at the extension housing seal, raise the vehicle and support it securely on jackstands. The extension housing seal is located at the rear end of the transmission, where the driveshaft is attached. If the extension housing seal is leaking, transmission lubricant will be evident on the front of the driveshaft and may be dripping from the rear of the transmission.

3 Remove the driveshaft (see Chapter 8).

4 Position the shift lever into PARK, if not already done. Remove the output shaft flange nut. Slide the output shaft flange off the extension housing.

5 Using a screwdriver, prybar or seal removal tool, carefully pry out the extension housing seal. Do not damage the splines on the transmission output shaft.

6 Using a seal driver or a large deep socket with an outside diameter the same as that of the seal, install the new extension housing seal. Drive it into the bore squarely and make sure it's completely seated.

7 Install the output shaft flange and nut and tighten it to the torque listed in this Chapter's Specifications.

5.8 Use a punch or a chisel to stake the flange nut to the output shaft and be sure to repeat the procedure on the opposite side of the flange nut

8 Use a punch to stake the flange nut to the output shaft to prevent rotation (see illustration).

9 Install the driveshaft (see Chapter 8).

6   Transmission mount - check and replacement

CHECK

▶ **Refer to illustration 6.2**

1   Raise the vehicle and support it securely on jackstands.

2   Insert a large screwdriver or prybar into the space between the transmission extension housing and the crossmember and try to pry the transmission up slightly (see illustration).

3   The transmission should not move much at all and the rubber in the center of the mount should fully insulate the center of the mount from the mount bracket around it.

REPLACEMENT

▶ **Refer to illustrations 6.4a and 6.4b**

4   Support the transmission with a jack, remove the bolts attaching the crossmember to the chassis and mount and the bolts attaching the mount to the transmission (see illustrations).

5   Raise the transmission slightly with the jack and remove the mount.

6   Installation is the reverse of the removal procedure. Be sure to tighten all fasteners to the Specifications listed in this Chapter.

6.2 To check the transmission mount, insert a large screwdriver between the extension housing and the crossmember and try to lever the transmission up

6.4a Location of the crossmember-to-frame mounting bolts (A) and the crossmember-to-mount bolts (B)

6.4b Transmission mount-to-transmission bolts (two of four shown)

7   Transmission Control Module (TCM) - replacement

❋❋ WARNING:

The models covered by this manual are equipped with a Supplemental Restraint System (SRS), more commonly known as airbags. Always disable the airbag system before working in the vicinity of any airbag system component to avoid the possibility of accidental deployment of the airbag(s), which could cause personal injury (see Chapter 12). Do not use a memory saving device to preserve the PCM or radio memory when working on or near airbag system components.

❋❋ CAUTION:

The TCM is an Electro-Static Discharge (ESD) sensitive electronic device, meaning a static electricity discharge from your body could possibly damage electrical components. Be sure to properly ground yourself and the TCM before handling it. Avoid touching the electrical terminals of the TCM.

➡Note: Do not interchange TCMs from different year vehicles. Whenever the TCM is replaced with a new unit, it must be programmed with a scan tool by a dealership service department or other qualified repair shop. This may require having the vehicle towed to the facility that will perform this procedure.

NAG1 TRANSMISSION

♦ **Refer to illustration 7.5**

1   Disconnect the cable from the negative terminal of the battery (see Chapter 5, Section 1).
2   Remove the knee bolster (see Chapter 11).
3   Remove the knee bolster reinforcement panel (see Chapter 11).
4   Disconnect the TCM electrical connectors.
5   Remove the TCM screws (see illustration) and detach the TCM from the instrument panel frame.
6   Installation is the reverse of removal.

42RLE TRANSMISSION

7   On models equipped with the 42RLE transmission, the TCM is an integral part of the Powertrain Control Module (PCM). Refer to Chapter 6 for the PCM removal and installation procedure.

7.5 On models with the NAG1 transmission, the TCM is located under the left side of the instrument panel; it's secured by four screws

8   Automatic transmission - removal and installation

♦ **Refer to illustrations 8.3, 8.8, 8.13, 8.19, 8.24, 8.26 and 8.27**

✳✳ CAUTION:

The transmission and torque converter must be removed as a single assembly. If you try to leave the torque converter attached to the driveplate, the converter driveplate, pump bushing and oil seal will be damaged. The driveplate is not designed to support the load, so none of the weight of the transmission should be allowed to rest on the driveplate during removal.

1   Disconnect the cable from the negative terminal of the battery (see Chapter 5, Section 1).
2   Raise the vehicle and support it securely on jackstands.
3   Remove the middle engine splash shield (see illustration).
4   Remove the driveshaft (see Chapter 8).

5   Remove the starter (see Chapter 5).
6   Disconnect the oxygen sensor connectors, separate the harness connectors from the transmission brace and position the wiring harness off to the side.
7   Drain the transmission fluid, then reinstall the fluid pan (see Chapter 1).
8   Remove the torque converter access cover, if equipped (see illustration).
9   On 42RLE transmissions, disconnect the output speed sensor and input speed sensor connectors (see Chapter 6).
10   On 2.7L V6 engines, remove the transmission-to-oil pan support brace (see Chapter 2A).
11   Remove the transmission heat shield, if equipped.
12   Mark the relationship of the torque converter to the driveplate to ensure that their dynamic balance is maintained when the converter is reattached to the driveplate.

8.3 Front engine splash shield (1) and middle engine splash shield (2) fasteners

8.8 Remove this bolt and separate the torque converter cover from the transmission

8.13 Remove the driveplate-to-torque converter bolts (3.5L V6 engine with NAG1 transmission shown)

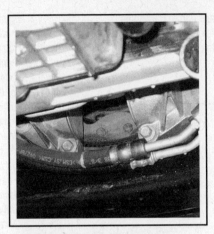

8.19 Use a flare-nut wrench to remove the transmission fluid cooler lines from the transmission

8.24 Remove the nut and detach the ground strap at the upper right transmission-to-engine bolt

13 Remove the driveplate-to-torque converter bolts (see illustration). Turn the crankshaft clockwise for access to each bolt, using a socket and breaker bar placed on the crankshaft pulley bolt.

14 Disconnect all electrical connectors from the transmission. Generally speaking, the connectors to various electrical and/or electronic devices on the transmission are different in shape, color and the number of terminals, so there's little danger of accidentally reconnecting a connector to the wrong device. The wiring harness is also designed so that each connector will only reach the device to which it's supposed to be connected. However, if any of the connectors look identical or look like they could be accidentally reconnected to the wrong device, be sure to mark them to prevent mix-ups.

15 Disconnect the shift cable from the transmission (see Section 3).

16 Rotate the harness connector bayonet lock counterclockwise and disconnect the large wiring harness from the terminal connector at the transmission.

17 Support the transmission with a transmission jack (available at most equipment rental facilities) and secure the transmission to the jack with safety chains.

18 Unbolt and remove the transmission crossmember (see illustration 6.4a).

19 Disconnect the transmission cooler lines from the transmission (see illustration). Plug the ends of the lines to prevent fluid from leaking out after you disconnect them.

20 Disconnect the range sensor (see Chapter 6), the crankshaft position sensor (see Chapter 6) and all other harness connectors.

21 Remove the transmission dipstick tube. Don't lose the tube seal (unless it's damaged, in which case you should replace it).

22 Detach the transmission fluid cooler lines from the frame (see Chapter 3).

23 Lower the jack supporting the transmission and allow it and the engine to angle down as far as possible (if you're using a transmission jack, you'll have to readjust the angle of the jack head).

24 On 3.5L V6 engines, remove the ground strap mounting nut and strap at the upper right transmission mounting bolt (see illustration).

25 On 3.5L V6 engines, remove the nuts and detach the harness bracket from the upper transmission stud bolts (see illustration).

26 Support the engine with a jack. Use a block of wood under the oil pan to spread the load.

27 Remove the bolts securing the transmission to the engine (see illustration). A long extension and a U-joint socket will greatly simplify this step.

8.25 Remove the two nuts and separate the wiring harness bracket from the studs

8.27 The oil pan on the 3.5L V6 engine is equipped with bolts that mount to the transmission

28 Move the transmission to the rear to disengage it from the engine block dowel pins. Make sure the torque converter is detached from the driveplate and stays with the transmission. Lower the transmission with the jack.

INSTALLATION

29 Installation is the reverse of the removal procedure, noting the following points:

a) *Prior to installation, make sure the torque converter is securely engaged in the pump. If you've removed the converter, spread transmission fluid on the torque converter rear hub, where the transmission front seal rides. With the front of the transmission facing up, rotate the converter back and forth. It should drop down into the transmission front pump in stages. To make sure the converter is fully engaged, lay a straightedge across the transmission-to-engine mating surface and make sure the converter lugs are at least 3/4-inch below the straightedge.*

b) *When mating the transmission to the engine, turn the torque converter to line up the marks on the torque converter and driveplate made during removal.*

c) *Move the transmission forward carefully until the dowel pins and the transmission are engaged. Make sure the transmission mates with the engine with no gap. If there's a gap, make sure there are no wires or other objects pinched between the engine and transmission and also make sure the torque converter is completely engaged in the transmission front pump. Try to rotate the converter - if it doesn't rotate easily, it's probably not fully engaged in the pump. If necessary, lower the transmission and install the converter fully.*

d) *Install the transmission-to-engine bolts and tighten them to the torque listed in this Chapter's Specifications. As you're tightening the bolts, make sure that the engine and transmission mate completely at all points. If not, find out why. Never try to force the engine and transmission together with the bolts or you'll break the transmission case!*

e) *Install the driveplate-to-torque converter bolts. Tighten them to the torque listed in this Chapter's Specifications.*

➡**Note: Install all of the bolts before tightening any of them.**

f) *If you're working on a 2.7L V6 engine, install the transmission-to-oil pan support brace and tighten the bolts to the torque listed in the Chapter 2A Specifications, in the sequence indicated in Oil pan - removal and installation.*

g) *The remainder of installation is the reverse of removal.*

h) *When you're done, refill the transmission with the specified fluid (see Chapter 1), run the engine and check for fluid leaks.*

9 Automatic transmission overhaul - general information

In the event of a fault occurring, it will be necessary to establish whether the fault is electrical, mechanical or hydraulic in nature, before repair work can be contemplated. Diagnosis requires detailed knowledge of the transmission's operation and construction, as well as access to specialized test equipment, and so is deemed to be beyond the scope of this manual. It is therefore essential that problems with the automatic transmission are referred to a dealer service department or other qualified repair facility for assessment.

Note that a faulty transmission should not be removed before the vehicle has been assessed by a knowledgeable technician equipped with the proper tools, as troubleshooting must be performed with the transmission installed in the vehicle.

Specifications

General

Transmission fluid type	See Chapter 1

Torque specifications	Ft-lbs
Output shaft flange nut	148
Driveplate-to-torque converter bolts	
2005 and 2006	31
2007 and later	
42RLE	65
NAG1	31
Transmission mount-to-transmission bolts	35
Transmission crossmember-to-mount bolts	39
Transmission crossmember-to-frame bolts	50
Transmission-to-engine bolts	
NAG1 models	29
42RLE	
2005 and 2006	29
2007 and later	
Transmission-to-engine bolts	50
Oil pan-to-transmission bolts	29

Notes

Section

8

DRIVEAXLES

1 Driveshaft - removal and installation

♦ **Refer to illustrations 1.2, 1.4, 1.5 and 1.6**

➡**Note: Driveshaft center bearing replacement requires the use of a hydraulic press. Remove the driveshaft and have a repair shop or automotive machine shop remove the bearing.**

1 Raise the vehicle and support it securely on jackstands and place the selector lever in Neutral.

2 Remove the crossmember brace (see illustration).

3 Remove the rear portion of the exhaust pipe(s) (see Chapter 4). Also remove the heat shield above the exhaust system.

4 Use chalk or a scribe to mark the relationship of the driveshaft to the transmission flange. This ensures correct alignment when the driveshaft is reinstalled (see illustration).

5 Remove the fasteners securing the driveshaft to the transmission flange (see illustration).

6 Remove the fasteners securing the center support bearing (see illustration).

7 Use chalk or a scribe to mark the relationship of the driveshaft to the differential pinion flange (see illustration 1.4).

8 Remove the fasteners securing the driveshaft flange to the differential pinion flange.

9 Carefully remove the driveshaft from the vehicle.

10 Installation is the reverse of removal. Be sure to align the marks made in Steps 4 and 7, and tighten the fasteners to the torque listed in this Chapter's Specifications.

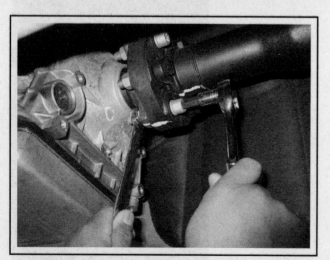

1.2 Remove the fasteners securing the crossmember brace

1.4 Mark the relationship of the driveshaft to the transmission flange

1.5 Remove the fasteners securing the driveshaft to the transmission flange

1.6 Remove the two fasteners securing the center support bearing

2 Driveshaft coupler/damper - removal and installation

▶ **Refer to illustration 2.3**

1   Raise the vehicle and support it securely on jackstands and place the selector lever in Neutral.

2   Depending on which end of the driveshaft you're working on, disconnect the driveshaft from the differential pinion flange or the transmission flange as outlined in Section 1.

➡ **Note: Support the driveshaft - do not let it hang from the center bearing.**

3   Remove the fasteners securing the coupler/damper to the driveshaft, then remove it from the driveshaft (see illustration).

. 4   Installation is the reverse of removal. Tighten the fasteners to the torque listed in this Chapter's Specifications.

2.3 While supporting the driveshaft, remove the fasteners securing the coupler/damper to the driveshaft

3 Driveaxles - removal and installation

➡ **Note: If a driveaxle boot has failed, the entire shaft assembly must be replaced. Boots are not serviceable separately.**

REMOVAL

▶ **Refer to illustration 3.6**

1   Remove the wheel cover or hub cap. Break the driveaxle/hub nut loose with a socket and large breaker bar.

2   Block the front wheels to prevent the vehicle from rolling. Loosen the wheel lug nuts, raise the rear of the vehicle and support it securely on jackstands. Remove the wheel.

3   Remove the driveaxle/hub nut and discard it.

3.6 Carefully pry the inner CV joint out of the differential just far enough to release the snap-ring

4   Drain the gear lubricant from the differential (see Chapter 1).

5   Disconnect the driveshaft from the differential (see Section 1). Remove the rear exhaust pipe and muffler (see Chapter 4).

6   Pry the inner CV joint out of the differential just far enough to release the snap-ring (see illustration).

➡ **Note: The driveaxles can't be removed from the differential until the differential has been lowered.**

7   Support the differential with a floor jack.

8   Remove the mounting fasteners securing the differential to the crossmember and differential mount (see Section 5).

9   Carefully lower the differential enough to separate the driveaxle(s) from the differential.

10 Pull the driveaxle out of the hub flange. If it sticks, tap it out with a soft-faced hammer.

INSTALLATION

11 Installation is the reverse of removal, noting the following points:

a) *Remove the rubber isolation washer from the outer CV joint stub shaft and inspect it. Replace it if necessary.*

b) *Tighten the differential mounting bolts to the torque listed in this Chapter's Specifications.*

c) *Install a new driveaxle/hub nut. Tighten the hub nut securely, but don't try to tighten it to the actual torque specification until you've lowered the vehicle to the ground.*

d) *Fill the differential with the type and amount of lubricant specified in Chapter 1.*

e) *Install the wheels and lower the vehicle to the ground. Tighten the wheel lug nuts to the torque listed in the Chapter 1 Specifications.*

f) *Tighten the driveaxle/hub nut to the torque listed in this Chapter's Specifications. Install the wheel cover or hub cap.*

4 Differential oil seals - replacement

1 Oil leaks frequently occur due to wear of the differential oil seals. Replacement of these seals is relatively easy, since the repair can usually be performed without removing the transmission from the vehicle.

2 Driveaxle oil seals are located at the sides of the differential, where the driveaxles are attached. The driveshaft seal is located behind the differential flange. If leakage at the seal is suspected, raise the vehicle and support it securely on jackstands. If the seal is leaking, lubricant will be found below the seals.

DRIVEAXLE SEALS

3 Refer to Section 3 and remove the driveaxle(s).

4 Use a screwdriver or prybar to carefully pry the oil seal out of the differential bore.

5 If the oil seal cannot be removed with a screwdriver or prybar, a special oil seal removal tool (available at auto parts stores) will be required.

6 Using a seal installation tool or a large deep socket (slightly smaller than the outside diameter of the seal) as a drift, install the new oil seal. Drive it into the bore squarely and make sure it's completely seated. Coat the seal lip with transmission lubricant.

7 Install the driveaxle(s). Be careful not to damage the lip of the new seal.

PINION SEAL

♦ **Refer to illustrations 4.10 and 4.12**

8 Loosen the rear wheel lug nuts, raise the rear of the vehicle and support it securely on jackstands. Refer to Section 1 and remove the driveshaft.

✳ CAUTION:

This procedure disturbs the pinion bearing preload adjustment. Follow the procedure very carefully to reset the pinion bearing preload during reassembly.

9 Remove the rear wheels and brake calipers (see Chapter 9).

➡**Note: It is recommended that you remove the wheels and brake calipers to eliminate the added pinion shaft rotation resistance that otherwise might contribute to a false pinion shaft rotation preload torque value.**

10 Using an inch-pound torque wrench (scale from approximately 0 to 40 inch-pounds) on the drive pinion nut, measure and record the torque necessary to rotate the drive pinion in a load-free state (see illustration).

11 Mark the drive pinion-to-companion flange orientation for proper reassembly.

12 Using a chain wrench or a flange holding tool (available at most auto parts stores), unscrew the pinion flange locknut. Discard the nut - a new one must be used upon reassembly (see illustration).

13 Using a two-jaw puller, remove the companion flange from the drive pinion shaft.

➡**Note: Some fluid loss may occur.**

14 Remove the seal by tapping on the metal flange with a hammer and chisel.

15 Prior to installing the new seal, clean the seal mating surfaces.

16 Lubricate the lips of the new seal with high-temperature grease and tap it evenly into position with a seal installation tool or a large socket. Make sure it enters the housing squarely and is tapped in to its full depth.

17 Align the mating marks made before disassembly and install the companion flange and a new nut. If necessary, tighten the pinion nut to draw the flange into place. Do not try to hammer the flange into position.

18 Using a suitable holding tool, secure the companion flange while tightening the nut to the torque listed in this Chapter's Specifications.

✳ CAUTION:

Don't overtighten the nut.

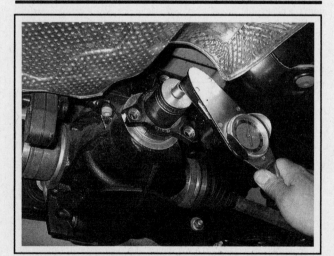

4.10 Use an inch-pound torque wrench to check the torque necessary to rotate the pinion shaft

4.12 A chain wrench can be used to hold the pinion flange while the nut is loosened

19 Measure the torque required to rotate the pinion; it should be equal to the torque recorded in Step 10. If too little torque is required to turn it, tighten the nut in small increments until it matches the figure recorded in Step 10. To compensate for the drag of the new oil seal, the nut should be tightened more until the rotational torque of the pinion exceeds the earlier recording by no more than 5 in-lbs.

✳ CAUTION:

If the nut is tightened too much, resulting in a rotational torque beyond the specified range listed in this Chapter's Specifications, the differential will have to be removed and disassembled, and a new collapsible spacer installed on the pinion shaft.

20 Using a hammer and punch, stake the pinion flange locknut.

21 The remainder of installation is the reverse of removal. Be sure to check the differential lubricant level and add if required (see Chapter 1).

5   Rear differential - removal and installation

REMOVAL

▶ **Refer to illustrations 5.6a and 5.6b**

1   Raise the rear of the vehicle and support it securely on jackstands.

2   Drain the lubricant from the differential (see Chapter 1).

3   Disconnect the driveshaft from the rear differential (see Section 1). Remove the rear exhaust pipe and muffler (see Chapter 4).

4   Pry the inner CV joint out of the differential just far enough to release the snap-ring (see illustration 3.6).

➡**Note: The driveaxles can't be removed from the differential until the differential has been lowered from the vehicle.**

5   Support the differential with a floor jack.

6   Remove the mounting fasteners that attach the differential to the rear crossmember (see illustrations).

7   Lower the differential enough to separate the driveaxles from the differential.

8   Carefully lower the differential and remove it from under the vehicle.

9   With the differential removed from the vehicle, now would be a good time to check or replace the rubber mounts for the differential mounting brackets and/or the rear crossmember.

INSTALLATION

10 Place the differential on the jack head and position it directly underneath the mounting bracket and crossmember.

11 Raise the differential enough to install the driveaxles into the differential.

12 Raise the differential into position and install the rear mounting fasteners loosely. Then install the front mounting fastener. Tighten the mounting fasteners to the torque listed in this Chapter's Specifications.

13 Install the driveshaft (see Section 1).

14 Fill the differential with the type and amount of lubricant specified in Chapter 1.

15 Install the wheels, remove the jack and lower the vehicle to the ground. Tighten the wheel lug nuts to the torque listed in the Chapter 1 Specifications.

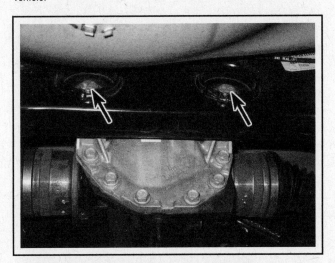

5.6a Remove the differential mounting fasteners at the rear . . .

5.6b . . . and at the front of the differential

Specifications

General

Differential pinion shaft preload (amount of torque required to turn the pinion shaft under no load)	19 to 22 inch-pounds

Torque specifications	Ft-lbs
Differential-to-rear crossmember bolts	162
Differential front mount insulator bolt/nut	48
Driveaxle/hub nut	157
Driveshaft center support bearing	20
Driveshaft-to-differential companion flange	43
Driveshaft-to-transmission flange	43
Pinion flange nut	100
Wheel lug nuts	See Chapter 1

Section

Reference to other Chapters

9

BRAKES

1 General information

The vehicles covered by this manual are equipped with hydraulically operated front and rear disc brake systems. These disc type brakes are self-adjusting and automatically compensate for pad wear.

HYDRAULIC SYSTEM

The hydraulic system consists of two separate circuits. In the event of a leak or failure in one hydraulic circuit, the other circuit will remain operative.

POWER BRAKE BOOSTER

The power brake booster is mounted on the firewall in the engine compartment. It uses engine manifold vacuum and atmospheric pressure to provide assistance to the hydraulically operated brakes.

PARKING BRAKE

The parking brake actuates a pair of parking brake shoes mounted inside the drum (hub) portion of each rear brake disc. The parking brake cable tension is adjusted automatically and requires no service.

SERVICE

After completing any operation involving disassembly of any part of the brake system, always test-drive the vehicle to check for proper braking performance before resuming normal driving. When testing the brakes, perform the tests on a clean, dry, flat surface. Conditions other than these can lead to inaccurate test results.

Test the brakes at various speeds with both light and heavy pedal pressure. The vehicle should stop evenly without pulling to one side or the other. Avoid locking the brakes, because this slides the tires and diminishes braking efficiency and control of the vehicle.

Tires, vehicle load and wheel alignment are other factors that affect braking performance as well.

PRECAUTIONS

There are some general cautions and warnings involving the brake system on this vehicle:

a) *Use only brake fluid conforming to DOT 3 specifications.*

b) *The brake pads and linings contain fibers which are hazardous to your health if inhaled. Whenever you work on brake system components, clean all parts with brake system cleaner. Do not allow the fine dust to become airborne. Also, wear an approved filtering mask.*

c) *Safety should be paramount whenever any servicing of the brake components is performed. Do not use parts or fasteners which are not in perfect condition, and be sure that all clearances and torque specifications are adhered to. If you are at all unsure about a certain procedure, seek professional advice. Upon completion of any brake system work, test the brakes carefully in a controlled area before putting the vehicle into normal service. If a problem is suspected in the brake system, don't drive the vehicle until it's fixed.*

d) *Clean up any spilled brake fluid immediately and then wash the area with large amounts of water. This is especially true for any finished or painted surfaces.*

2 Anti-lock Brake System (ABS) - general information

➡**Note: Models equipped with an Anti-lock Brake System (ABS) will have one of two different systems installed: one is MK25 (the earlier ABS system) and can be identified by a pressure sensor mounted to the bottom of the master cylinder. The other is MK25E (the later ABS system) and the master cylinder appears typical and is not equipped with a pressure sensor on the bottom. Use this information to determine which system is on your vehicle. Knowing which system you have is important regarding part identification and torque specifications.**

1 The Anti-lock Brake System (ABS) is designed to help maintain vehicle steerability, directional stability and optimum deceleration under severe braking conditions and on most road surfaces. The ABS system is primarily designed to prevent wheel lockup during heavy or panic braking situations. It works by monitoring the rotational speed of each wheel and controlling the brake line pressure to each wheel when engaged. The data provided by the ABS wheel speed sensors is shared with another optional system called the Electronic Stability Program (ESP) which aids in vehicle control and handling. This system helps with traction control, over/under-steering and acceleration control when the base brakes are engaged or under acceleration when the system

is turned on manually by the switch on the instrument panel. Another system added to vehicles with ESP is the Brake Assist System (BAS). This system works with the ABS system to maximize brake system performance in panic braking situations.

COMPONENTS

Actuator assembly

▶ **Refer to illustration 2.2**

2 The actuator assembly is mounted in the engine compartment and consists of an electric hydraulic pump and solenoid valves (see illustration).

a) *The electric pump provides hydraulic pressure to charge the reservoirs in the actuator, which supplies pressure to the braking system. The pump and reservoirs are housed in the actuator assembly.*

b) *The solenoid valves modulate brake line pressure during ABS operation.*

2.2 The ABS actuator assembly is mounted in the right front corner of the engine compartment

Wheel speed sensors

3   These sensors are located at each wheel and generate small electrical pulsations when the hubs are turning, sending a signal to the electronic controller indicating wheel rotational speed.

4   The front speed sensors are mounted to the front steering knuckle in close relationship to the magnetic encoders, which are pressed into the back of the hub and bearing assemblies.

5   The rear wheel sensors are bolted to the rear suspension knuckles. The sensor rings are integrated with the rear hub assemblies.

ABS computer

6   The ABS computer is mounted with the actuator and is the brain for the ABS system. The function of the computer is to accept and process information received from the wheel speed sensors to control the hydraulic line pressure, avoiding wheel lock up. The computer also constantly monitors the system, even under normal driving conditions, to find faults within the system.

DIAGNOSIS AND REPAIR

7   If a dashboard warning light comes on and stays on while the vehicle is in operation, the ABS system requires attention. Although special electronic ABS diagnostic testing tools are necessary to properly diagnose the system, you can perform a few preliminary checks before taking the vehicle to a dealer service department.

2.11b Press the spring down to release the ABS harness connector

2.11a A wheel speed sensor wire harness and connector (front shown, rear similar)

a) Check the brake fluid level in the reservoir.
b) Verify that the computer electrical connectors are securely connected.
c) Check the electrical connectors at the hydraulic control unit.
d) Check the fuses.
e) Follow the wiring harness to each wheel and verify that all connections are secure and that the wiring is undamaged.

8   If the above preliminary checks do not rectify the problem, the vehicle should be diagnosed by a dealer service department or other qualified repair shop. Due to the complexity of this system, all actual repair work must be done by a qualified automotive technician.

✳✳ WARNING:

Do NOT try to repair an ABS wiring harness. The ABS system is sensitive to even the smallest changes in resistance. Repairing the harness could alter resistance values and cause the system to malfunction. If the ABS wiring harness is damaged in any way, it must be replaced.

✳✳ CAUTION:

Make sure the ignition is turned off before unplugging or reattaching any electrical connections.

WHEEL SPEED SENSOR - REMOVAL AND INSTALLATION

▶ Refer to illustrations 2.11a, 2.11b, 2.12a and 2.12b

9   Loosen the wheel lug nuts, raise the vehicle and support it securely on jackstands. Remove the wheel.

10   Make sure the ignition key is turned to the Off position.

11   Trace the wiring back from the sensor, detaching all brackets and clips while noting its correct routing, then disconnect the electrical connector (see illustrations).

2.12a Front wheel speed sensor

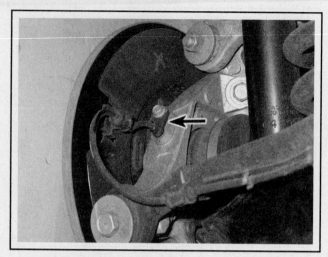

2.12b The rear wheel speed sensor

12 Remove the mounting bolt and carefully pull the sensor out from the knuckle (see illustrations).

13 Installation is the reverse of the removal procedure. Tighten the mounting fastener securely.

14 Install the wheel and lug nuts, tightening them securely. Lower the vehicle and tighten the lug nuts to the torque listed in the Chapter 1 Specifications.

3 Disc brake pads - replacement

▶ Refer to illustrations 3.5 and 3.6a through 3.6m

✳✳ WARNING:

Disc brake pads must be replaced on both front or on both rear wheels at the same time - never replace the pads for only one wheel. Also, the dust created by the brake system is harmful to your health. Never blow it out with compressed air and don't inhale any of it. An approved filtering mask should be worn when working on the brakes. Do not, under any circumstances, use petroleum-based solvents to clean brake parts. Use brake system cleaner only!

➡Note: This procedure applies to both the front and rear disc brakes.

1 Remove the cap from the brake fluid reservoir.

2 Loosen the wheel lug nuts, raise the front or rear of the vehicle and support it securely on jackstands. Block the wheels at the opposite end.

3 Remove the wheels. Work on one brake assembly at a time, using the assembled brake for reference if necessary.

4 Inspect the brake disc carefully as outlined in Section 5. If machining is necessary, follow the information in that Section to remove the disc, at which time the pads can be removed as well.

3.5 Before removing the caliper, slowly depress the piston into the caliper bore by using a large C-clamp between the outer brake pad and the back of the caliper

3.6a Always wash the brakes with brake cleaner before disassembling anything

3.6c If you're replacing the front pads, pivot the caliper up and secure it with a piece of wire in this position; do not allow the caliper to hang by the flexible brake hose. Be careful not to damage the guide pin boots while rotating the caliper

3.6b If you're replacing the front pads, remove the lower caliper bolt while holding the caliper guide pin. On rear calipers, remove the upper caliper bolt

5   Push the piston back into its bore to provide room for the new brake pads. A C-clamp can be used to accomplish this (see illustration). As the piston is depressed to the bottom of the caliper bore, the fluid in the master cylinder will rise. Make sure that it doesn't overflow. If necessary, siphon off some of the fluid.

6   Follow the accompanying photos (illustrations 3.6a through

3.6m) for the actual pad replacement procedure. Be sure to stay in order and read the caption under each illustration.

7   When reinstalling the caliper, be sure to tighten the mounting bolts to the torque listed in this Chapter's Specifications. After the job has been completed, firmly depress the brake pedal a few times to bring the pads into contact with the disc. Check the level of the brake fluid, adding some if necessary. Check the operation of the brakes carefully before placing the vehicle into normal service.

3.6d On rear calipers, pivot the caliper down

3.6e Remove inner pad . . .

3.6f . . . and the outer pad

3.6g Remove the upper and lower anti-rattle clips; make sure they fit tightly and aren't worn. Replace them if necessary

3.6h Install the clean or new anti-rattle clips

3.6i Pull out the upper and lower guide pins and clean them. Then apply a coat of high-temperature grease to the pins and reinstall them. Be careful not to damage the guide pin boots and replace any boots that are worn or damaged

3.6j Install the outer pad, making sure that the ends are seated correctly into the anti-rattle clips . . .

3.6k . . . then install the inner pad in the same way

3.6l Place the caliper back into position over the brake pads and onto the caliper mounting bracket

3.6m Install the caliper bolt and tighten it to the torque listed in this Chapter's Specifications

4   Disc brake caliper - removal and installation

✳✳ WARNING:

Dust created by the brake system is harmful to your health. Never blow it out with compressed air and don't inhale any of it. An approved filtering mask should be worn when working on the brakes. Do not, under any circumstances, use petroleum-based solvents to clean brake parts. Use brake system cleaner only!

➡Note: Always replace the calipers in pairs - never replace just one of them.

REMOVAL

◆ **Refer to illustrations 4.2a and 4.2b**

1   Loosen the wheel lug nuts, raise the vehicle and support it securely on jackstands. Remove the wheels.
2   Remove the brake hose banjo bolt and disconnect the hose from

the caliper. Plug the hose to keep contaminants out of the brake system and to prevent losing any more brake fluid than is necessary (see illustrations).

➡**Note:** If you're just removing the caliper for access to other components, don't detach the hose.

3   Remove the caliper mounting bolts, lift the caliper from the bracket and, if the hose is still attached, support it with a length of wire.

INSTALLATION

4   Install the caliper by reversing the removal procedure. Tighten the caliper mounting bolts to the torque listed in this Chapter's Specifications. Install new sealing washers, one on each side of the brake hose fitting, then tighten the banjo bolt to the torque listed in this Chapter's Specifications.
5   Bleed the brake system (see Section 8).
6   Install the wheels and lug nuts. Lower the vehicle and tighten the lug nuts to the torque listed in the Chapter 1 Specifications.

4.2a Brake caliper mounting details (front caliper shown - rear caliper similar)

1   Caliper mounting bolts
2   Brake hose and banjo fitting bolt

4.2b Using a piece of rubber hose of the appropriate size, plug the brake line banjo fitting to prevent brake fluid from leaking out and to prevent dirt and moisture from contaminating the fluid in the hose

5   Brake disc - inspection, removal and installation

INSPECTION

◆ **Refer to illustrations 5.4, 5.5a, 5.5b, 5.6a and 5.6b**

➡**Note: The manufacturer suggests using a specialized (on-vehicle) brake lathe that can cut the disc while it is still installed on the vehicle for disc refinishing (machining); although, it is not essential. Moreover, this service requires a repair facility to have the specialized tool and to have the vehicle as opposed to your taking the brake discs to a machine shop for refinishing.**

1   Loosen the wheel lug nuts, raise the vehicle and support it securely on jackstands. Remove the wheel.

2   Remove the brake caliper as outlined in Section 4. It's not necessary to disconnect the brake hose for this procedure. After removing the caliper bolts, suspend the caliper out of the way with a piece of wire. Don't let the caliper hang by the hose and don't stretch or twist the hose.

3   Reinstall the lug nuts (inverted) to hold the disc against the hub. It may be necessary to install washers between the disc and the lug nuts to take up space.

4   Visually check the disc surface for score marks, cracks and other damage. Light scratches and shallow grooves are normal after use and may not always be detrimental to brake operation. Deep score marks or cracks may require disc refinishing by an automotive machine shop or disc replacement (see illustration). Be sure to check both sides of the

5.4 The brake pads on this vehicle were obviously neglected, as they wore down completely and cut deep grooves into the disc - wear this severe means the disc must be replaced

5.5a Use a dial indicator to check disc runout; if the reading exceeds the maximum allowable runout limit, the disc will have to be machined or replaced

disc. If the brake pedal pulsates during brake application, suspect disc runout.

➡Note: The most common symptoms of damaged or worn brake discs are pulsation in the brake pedal when the brakes are applied or loud grinding noises caused from severely worn brake pads. If these symptoms are extreme, it is very likely that the disc(s) will need to be replaced.

5   To check disc runout, place a dial indicator at a point about 1/2-inch from the outer edge of the disc (see illustration). Set the indicator to zero and turn the disc. An indicator reading that exceeds .003 of an inch could cause pulsation upon brake application and will require disc refinishing by an automotive machine shop or disc replacement.

➡Note: If disc refinishing or replacement is not necessary, you can deglaze the brake pad surface on the disc with emery cloth or sandpaper (use a swirling motion to ensure a non-directional finish) (see illustration).

6   The disc must not be machined to a thickness less than the specified minimum refinish thickness. The minimum wear (or discard) thickness is cast into either the front or backside of the disc (see illustration). The disc thickness can be checked with a micrometer (see illustration).

REMOVAL AND INSTALLATION

▶ **Refer to illustrations 5.7 and 5.8**

7   Remove the caliper mounting bracket (see illustration).

8   Mark the disc in relation to the hub so that it can be installed in it's original position on the hub and then remove the disc. If it's stuck, make sure you have removed any lug nuts installed during inspection. If the disc has never been removed, there may be wave washers on the wheel studs securing it to the hub flange. Simply cut them off and discard them (see illustration).

➡Note: On rear discs, make sure the parking brake is released.

9   Clean the hub flange and the inside of the brake disc thoroughly, removing any rust or corrosion, then install the disc onto the hub assembly.

10   Install the caliper mounting bracket and tighten the bolts to the torque listed in this Chapter's Specifications.

11   Install the brake pads and caliper, tightening the bolts to the torque listed in this Chapter's Specifications.

12   Install the wheel, then lower the vehicle to the ground. Tighten the wheel lug nuts to the torque listed in the Chapter 1 Specifications.

5.5b Using a swirling motion, remove the glaze from the disc surface with sandpaper or emery cloth

5.6a The minimum wear dimension is usually cast into the back side of the disc (typical shown)

5.6b Use a micrometer to measure disc thickness

5.7 The caliper mounting bracket is retained by these two bolts (rear shown - front similar)

Depress the brake pedal a few times to bring the brake pads into contact with the disc. Bleeding of the system will not be necessary unless

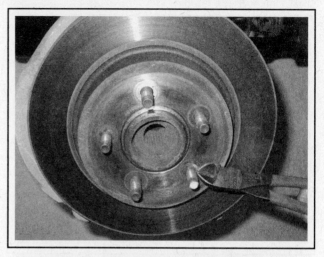

5.8 Cut off any retainers that may be holding the disc onto the hub and discard them (there is no need to replace them)

the brake hose was disconnected from the caliper. Check the operation of the brakes carefully before placing the vehicle into normal service.

6 Master cylinder - removal and installation

REMOVAL

▶ **Refer to illustrations 6.3 and 6.6**

❊❊ **CAUTION:**

Brake fluid will damage paint or finished surfaces. Cover all body parts and be careful not to spill fluid during this procedure. Clean up any spilled brake fluid immediately and then wash the area with large amounts of water.

➡Note: Vehicle models equipped with an Anti-lock brake system (ABS) will have one of two different factory systems installed: one is MK25 (the earlier ABS system) and can be identified by a pressure sensor mounted to the bottom of the

master cylinder. The other is MK25E (the later ABS system) and the master cylinder appears typical and is not equipped with a pressure sensor on the bottom. Use this information to determine which system is on your vehicle. Knowing which system you have is important regarding part identification and torque specifications.

1   Disconnect the cable(s) from the negative battery terminal(s) (see Chapter 5, Section 1).

2   Firmly depress the brake pedal several times to remove all vacuum from the power brake booster.

3   Remove the master cylinder access cover in the cowl (see illustration).

4   Clean the master cylinder and reservoir thoroughly with brake cleaner.

5   Remove as much fluid as possible from the reservoir with a syringe.

6   Unplug the electrical connector for the brake fluid level warning switch (see illustration).

6.3 Lift up the access cover on the cowl

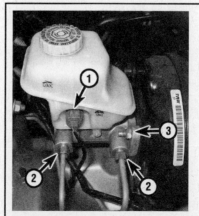

6.6 Master cylinder details

1   *Electrical connector*
2   *Brake line fittings*
3   *Mounting nut (one hidden - located on other side of mounting flange)*

6.12 Place the master cylinder in a vise by its mounting flange, attach the bleed tubes as shown and push the piston with a blunt tool several times to bench bleed the master cylinder

➡Note: Some models have additional electrical connectors on the master cylinder and the power brake booster for the ESP system. Simply disconnect these connectors when necessary to remove the master cylinder.

7　Place rags under the fittings and prepare caps or plastic bags to cover the ends of the lines once they're disconnected.

8　Loosen the fittings at the ends of the brake lines where they enter the master cylinder. To prevent rounding off the corners on the fittings, use a flare-nut wrench.

9　Carefully move the brake lines away from the master cylinder and plug the ends to prevent contamination.

10　Remove the master cylinder mounting nuts. Pull the master cylinder off the studs to remove it. Again, be careful not to spill fluid or bend the brake lines as this is done.

INSTALLATION

◆ **Refer to illustrations 6.12, 6.17 and 6.21**

11　Bench bleed the new master cylinder before installing it. Because it will be necessary to depress the master cylinder piston and, at the same time, control flow from the brake line outlets, it is recommended that the master cylinder be mounted in a vise.

➡Note: If the replacement master cylinder is not equipped with a reservoir, remove the reservoir from the old master cylinder and place it on the new one using new seals.

12　Attach a pair of master cylinder bleeder tubes to the outlet ports of the master cylinder (see illustration).

13　Fill the reservoir with brake fluid of the recommended type (see Chapter 1).

14　Slowly push the pistons into the master cylinder (a large Phillips screwdriver can be used for this) - air will be expelled from the pressure chambers and into the reservoir. Because the tubes are submerged in fluid, air can't be drawn back into the master cylinder when you release the pistons.

15　Repeat the procedure until no more air bubbles are present.

16　Remove the bleed tubes, one at a time, and install plugs in the open ports to prevent fluid leakage and air from entering.

17　Install a new vacuum seal on the master cylinder (see illustration).

6.17 Replace the vacuum seal on the master cylinder every time the cylinder is removed (typical shown)

6.21 Loosen the fittings on the master cylinder to bleed it when it is installed on the vehicle (typical shown)

❋❋ WARNING:

This must be done every time the master cylinder is removed.

18　Install the reservoir cover, then install the master cylinder over the studs on the power brake booster and tighten the attaching nuts only finger tight at this time.

19　Thread the brake line fittings into the master cylinder. Since the master cylinder is still a bit loose, it can be moved slightly in order for the fittings to thread in easily. Do not strip the threads as the fittings are tightened.

20　Tighten the mounting nuts to the torque listed in this Chapter's Specifications and tighten the brake line fittings securely.

21　Fill the master cylinder reservoir with the correct fluid (see Chapter 1), then bleed the brake system as described in Section 8. To bleed the master cylinder on the vehicle, have an assistant pump the brake pedal several times slowly and then hold the pedal to the floor. Loosen the line fittings one at a time to allow air and fluid to escape. Repeat this procedure on both fittings until the fluid is clear of air bubbles (see illustration).

Have plenty of rags on hand to catch the fluid - brake fluid will ruin painted surfaces.

22 The remainder of installation is the reverse of removal. Test the operation of the brake system carefully before placing the vehicle into normal service.

Do not operate the vehicle if you are in doubt about the effectiveness of the brake system. On models equipped with ABS, it is possible for air to become trapped in the anti-lock brake system hydraulic control unit, so, if the pedal continues to feel spongy after repeated bleedings or the BRAKE or ANTI-LOCK light stays on, have the vehicle towed to a dealer service department or other qualified shop to be bled with the aid of a scan tool.

7 Brake hoses and lines - inspection and replacement

INSPECTION

1 About every six months, with the vehicle raised and supported securely on jackstands, the rubber hoses which connect the steel brake lines with the front and rear brake assemblies should be inspected for cracks, chafing of the outer cover, leaks, blisters and other damage. These are important and vulnerable parts of the brake system and inspection should be complete. A light and mirror will be helpful for a thorough check. If a hose exhibits any of the above conditions, replace it with a new one.

REPLACEMENT

Front brake hose

▶ **Refer to illustrations 7.3a and 7.3b**

2 Loosen the wheel lug nuts, raise the vehicle and support it securely on jackstands. Remove the wheel.

3 At the frame bracket, unscrew the brake line fitting from the hose (see illustrations). Use a flare-nut wrench to prevent rounding off the corners.

4 Remove the U-clip from the female fitting at the frame bracket with a pair of pliers (see illustration 7.3b), then pass the hose through the bracket.

5 At the caliper end of the hose, remove the banjo fitting bolt, then separate the hose from the caliper. Note that there are two copper sealing washers, one on each side of the fitting - they should be replaced with new ones during installation.

6 Remove the fastener from the hose bracket at the steering knuckle and then detach it.

➡**Note: The replacement hose should come equipped with a steering knuckle bracket like the original one.**

7 To install the hose, attach the hose bracket to the steering knuckle, then connect the fitting to the caliper with the banjo bolt and new sealing washers. Tighten the bolt to the torque listed in this Chapter's Specifications.

8 Push the metal support into the frame bracket and install the U-clip. Make sure the hose isn't twisted between the caliper and the steering knuckle bracket.

9 Connect the brake line fitting, starting the threads by hand, then tighten the fitting securely.

10 Bleed the caliper (see Section 8).

11 Install the wheel and lug nuts, lower the vehicle and tighten the lug nuts to the torque listed in the Chapter 1 Specifications.

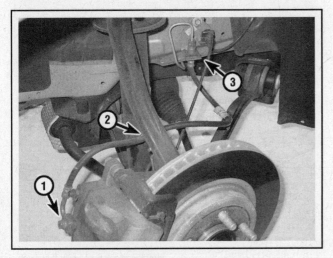

7.3a Front brake hose details:

1   Hose fitting at brake caliper
2   Location of steering knuckle bracket (actual bracket hidden behind knuckle)
3   Brake hose and line fitting secured to frame bracket

7.3b Front brake hose/line fitting details:

1   Line fitting (loosen with flare-nut wrench
2   U-clip (remove with pliers)
3   Female hose fitting (remove from frame bracket)

Rear brake hose

▶ **Refer to illustration 7.12**

12 The rear brake hose has a fitting and a bracket that is fastened to the rear frame. Otherwise, refer to the previous steps for rear brake hose replacement (see illustration).

Metal brake lines

13 When replacing brake lines, be sure to use the correct parts. Don't use copper tubing for any brake system components. Purchase genuine steel brake lines from a dealer or auto parts store.

14 Prefabricated brake line, with the tube ends already flared and fittings installed, is available at auto parts stores and dealer parts departments.

15 When installing the new line, make sure it's securely supported in the brackets and has plenty of clearance between moving or hot components.

16 After installation, check the master cylinder fluid level and add fluid as necessary. Bleed the brake system (see Section 8) and test the brakes carefully before driving the vehicle in traffic.

7.12 The rear brake hose/line fitting bracket

---

8 Brake hydraulic system - bleeding

▶ **Refer to illustration 8.8**

✳✳ WARNING:

Wear eye protection when bleeding the brake system. If the fluid comes in contact with your eyes, immediately rinse them with water and seek medical attention.

➡ **Note: Bleeding the hydraulic system is necessary to remove any air that manages to find its way into the system when it's been opened during removal and installation of a hose, line, caliper or master cylinder.**

1 You'll probably have to bleed the system at all four brakes if air has entered it due to low fluid level, or if the brake lines have been disconnected at the master cylinder.

2 If a brake line was disconnected only at a wheel, then only that caliper must be bled. If a brake line is disconnected at a fitting located between the master cylinder and any of the brakes, that part of the system served by the disconnected line must be bled.

3 Raise the rear of the vehicle about one foot and secure it on jackstands.

➡ **Note: This step is recommended by the manufacturer to ensure that all the air is bled from the ABS hydraulic actuator assembly or the junction block for non-ABS equipped vehicles efficiently.**

4 Remove any residual vacuum from the brake power booster by applying the brake several times with the engine off.

5 Remove the master cylinder reservoir cover and fill the reservoir with brake fluid. Reinstall the cover.

➡ **Note: Check the fluid level often during the bleeding operation and add fluid as necessary to prevent the fluid level from falling low enough to allow air bubbles into the master cylinder.**

6 Have an assistant on hand, as well as a supply of new brake fluid, a clear container partially filled with clean brake fluid, a length of tubing to fit over the bleeder valve and a wrench to open and close the

8.8 When bleeding the brakes, a hose is connected to the bleeder valve at the caliper and the other end is submerged in brake fluid. Air will be seen as bubbles in the tube and container. All air must be expelled before moving to the next wheel (typical shown)

bleeder valve.

7 Beginning at the right rear wheel, loosen the bleeder valve slightly, then tighten it to a point where it's snug but can still be loosened quickly and easily.

8 Place one end of the tubing over the bleeder valve and submerge the other end in brake fluid in the container (see illustration).

9 Have the assistant depress the brake pedal slowly, then hold the pedal down firmly.

10 While the pedal is held down, open the bleeder valve just enough to allow a flow of fluid to leave the valve. Watch for air bubbles to exit the submerged end of the tube. When the fluid flow slows after a couple of seconds, close the valve and have your assistant release the pedal.

11 Repeat Steps 9 and 10 until no more air is seen leaving the tube,

then tighten the bleeder valve and proceed to the left rear wheel, the right front wheel and the left front wheel, in that order, and perform the same procedure. Be sure to check the fluid in the master cylinder reservoir frequently.

12 Never use old brake fluid. It contains moisture that can boil, rendering the brake system inoperative.

13 Refill the master cylinder with fluid at the end of the operation.

14 Check the operation of the brakes. The pedal should feel solid when depressed, with no sponginess. If necessary, repeat the entire process.

✳✳ WARNING:

Do not operate the vehicle if you are in doubt about the effectiveness of the brake system. It's possible for air to become trapped in the ABS hydraulic control unit, so, if the pedal continues to feel spongy after repeated bleedings or the BRAKE or ANTI-LOCK (ABS) light stays on, have the vehicle towed to a dealer service department or other qualified shop to be bled with the aid of a scan tool.

---

9   Power brake booster - check, removal and installation

➡Note: Vehicle models equipped with an Anti-lock brake system (ABS) will have one of two different factory systems installed: one is MK25 (the earlier ABS system) and can be identified by a pressure sensor mounted to the bottom of the master cylinder. The other is MK25E (the later ABS system) and the master cylinder appears typical and is not equipped with a pressure sensor on the bottom. Use this information to determine which system is on your vehicle. Knowing which system you have is important regarding part identification and torque specifications.

OPERATING CHECK

1 Depress the brake pedal several times with the engine off and make sure there's no change in the pedal reserve distance.

2 Depress the pedal and start the engine. If the pedal goes down slightly, operation is normal.

AIRTIGHTNESS CHECK

3 Start the engine and turn it off after one or two minutes. Depress the brake pedal slowly several times. If the pedal depresses less each time, the booster is airtight.

4 Depress the brake pedal while the engine is running, then stop the engine with the pedal depressed. If there's no change in the pedal reserve travel after holding the pedal for 30 seconds, the booster is airtight.

REMOVAL

▶ Refer to illustrations 9.10 and 9.12

➡Note 1: The power brake booster is not serviceable and is replaced with a new or rebuilt unit.

➡Note 2: Models that are equipped with ESP may have additional components integrated with power brake booster resulting in electrical connectors attached to it. The new or rebuilt unit must also have all of the original components.

5 With the engine off, press the brake pedal several times to remove any stored vacuum in the power brake booster.

6 Move the driver's seat to the rearmost position, then disconnect the cable(s) from the negative battery terminal(s) (see Chapter 5, Section 1).

7 Remove the windshield wiper motor (see Chapter 12).

8 Remove the brake master cylinder (see Section 6).

9 Remove any electrical connectors attached to the power brake booster, if applicable.

10 Carefully disconnect the vacuum hose from the brake booster check valve (see illustration).

✳✳ WARNING:

Do not remove the check valve from the brake booster.

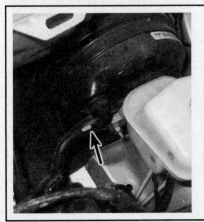

9.10 Remove the vacuum hose from the power booster by carefully pulling it off the check valve. Do not remove the check valve to remove the vacuum hose

9.12 Power brake booster mounting details:

1   Retaining clip
2   Mounting fasteners

11 Inside the vehicle, remove the brake light switch (see Section 12).

12 Pry the retaining clip off of the brake pedal pin, then disconnect the booster push rod (see illustration).

13 Remove the booster mounting fasteners. Slide the booster straight out from the firewall until the studs clear the holes and remove it from the engine compartment (see illustration 9.12).

INSTALLATION

14 Installation procedures are basically the reverse of removal while noting the following points:

a) Replace the seal that goes between the power booster and the firewall (over the booster's mounting studs).

b) Tighten the booster mounting nuts to the torque listed in this Chapter's Specifications.

c) Install a new retaining clip securing the booster pushrod to the brake pedal pin.

d) Bleed the brake system (see Section 8) and test the operation of the brakes before putting the vehicle into normal service.

---

10 Parking brake shoes - replacement

◆ **Refer to illustrations 10.4a through 10.4r and 10.6**

❋❋ WARNING 1:

Dust created by the brake system is hazardous to your health. Never blow it out with compressed air and don't inhale any of it. An approved filtering mask should be worn when working on the brakes. Do not, under any circumstances, use petroleum-based solvents to clean brake parts. Use brake system cleaner only!

❋❋ WARNING 2:

Parking brake shoes must be replaced on both wheels at the same time - never replace the shoes on only one wheel.

1 Remove the brake disc (see Section 5).

2 Remove the hub and bearing assembly if necessary (see Chapter 10).

10.4a Turn the adjuster until it's at its shortest setting (the threads disappear into the adjuster)

10.4b Remove the adjuster spring

10.4c Remove the return spring

10.4d Remove the adjuster

10.4e Remove the lower shoe hold-down clip, pin and shoe

10.4f Remove the upper shoe hold-down clip, pin and shoe

10.4g Parking brake shoes and component details:

1	Brake shoes	4	Adjuster assembly
2	Return spring	5	Hold-down pins
3	Adjuster spring	6	Hold-down clips

10.4h Clean the backing plate thoroughly, then lubricate the brake shoe contact areas on the plate with high-temperature grease

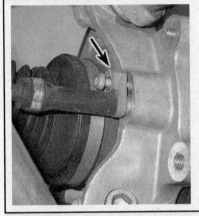

10.4i Loosen the fastener that anchors the parking brake cable to the knuckle and withdraw it enough to disengage the actuator from the end of the parking brake cable

10.4j Remove the actuator from the end of the parking brake cable and inspect it for wear. Place it back into position and then secure the parking brake cable to the knuckle

➡Note: It is possible to perform the shoe replacement procedure without removing the hub and bearing assembly, although working room is limited.

   3   Wash off the brake parts with brake system cleaner.

   4   Follow the accompanying illustrations for the brake shoe replacement procedure (see illustrations 10.4a through 10.4r). Be sure to stay

in order and read the caption under each illustration.

   5   Install the brake disc and caliper (see Sections 4 and 5) and then install the wheel. Proceed to the shoe replacement on the opposite rear wheel.

10.4k Place the upper shoe and hold-down pin in position while engaging the brake actuator

10.4l Install the upper shoe hold-down clip

10.4m Place the lower shoe and hold-down pin in position while engaging the brake actuator

10.4n Install the lower shoe hold-down clip

10.4o Lubricate the adjuster threads

10.4p Install the adjuster

10.4q Install the return spring

10.4r Install the adjuster spring

6   With both sides complete and wheels installed, remove the rubber plug from the brake backing plate to access the parking brake adjuster (see illustration).

7   Turn the adjuster star wheel with a brake adjusting tool or screwdriver until the shoes contact the drum the vehicle's wheel can't be turned. Back off the adjuster six notches to achieve the appropriate shoe-to-drum clearance, then replace the rubber plug.

8   Perform the brake shoe adjustment for both wheels.

9   Set the parking brake and confirm proper operation. Re-adjust the shoe clearance if necessary.

10   Lower the vehicle and tighten the wheel lug nuts to the torque specified in Chapter 1.

10.6 Remove the rubber plug to access the adjuster for the parking brake shoes through the backing plate

11 Proportioning valve - removal and installation

➡Note 1: Vehicle models equipped with an Anti-lock brake system (ABS) are not equipped with a proportioning valve or junction block.

➡Note 2: The proportioning valve is integrated with a junction block and they are replaced as an assembly.

1   Disconnect the cable(s) from the negative battery terminal(s) (see Chapter 5, Section 1).

2   Use a suitable tool to depress and hold the brake pedal down by 1 inch.

➡Note: Holding the pedal down by an inch will minimize fluid loss in the hydraulic circuits while the brake lines are open.

3   Locate the junction block in the right front portion of the engine compartment. It can be recognized as a solid looking aluminum part with several hydraulic brake lines attached to it. It is mounted to the chassis with three rubber grommets.

4   Using a flare-nut wrench, disconnect all line fittings to the junction block.

5   Pull the junction block up to remove it from the mounting grommets.

6   Installation is the reverse of removal. Tighten all line fittings securely and bleed the brake system (see Section 8). Test the operation of the brakes before putting the vehicle into normal service.

12 Brake light switch - removal and installation

▸ Refer to illustration 12.2

1   Remove the lower instrument panel insulator below the driver's side knee bolster for access (see Chapter 11).

2   The brake light switch is mounted to a bracket attached to the brake pedal assembly (see illustration).

3   Depress and hold the brake pedal.

4   Rotate the switch about 30 degrees counterclockwise and remove it from its bracket.

5   Disconnect the electrical connector for the brake light switch.

6   To install the switch, pull the plunger on the switch out fully.

7   Depress the brake pedal as far as it will go and then install the switch in its bracket in the opposite manner it was removed.

8   Release the brake pedal and gently pull up on it to make sure it's fully released. The switch is now fully adjusted and installed.

12.2 Location of the brake light switch

13 Adjustable brake pedal - removal and installation

▸ Refer to illustrations 13.4 and 13.8

➡Note 1: Not all models are equipped with adjustable brake and accelerator pedals.

➡Note 2: The adjustable brake pedal mechanism is driven by a cable from a motor in the accelerator pedal assembly. The motor moves the accelerator pedal up and down directly. Although the brake and accelerator pedal mechanisms are two separate assemblies, their movement is synchronized by a drive cable between them; the result is equal upward and downward motion of both pedals simultaneously.

1   Using the pedal adjusting switch, move the pedals to the lowest position, if possible.

2   Move the drivers seat to the rearmost position, then disconnect the cable(s) from the negative battery terminal(s) (see Chapter 5, Section 1).

3   Remove the lower instrument panel insulator below the driver's side knee bolster for access (see Chapter 11).

4   Disconnect the drive cable from the motor on the accelerator pedal assembly by gently prying up on the cable mounting flange (see illustration).

13.4 The drive cable attaches to the motor on the accelerator pedal assembly

13.8 The brake pedal assembly mounting nuts (two hidden)

5 Remove the brake light switch (see Section 12).

6 Disconnect the booster pushrod from the brake pedal (see Section 9).

7 Disconnect any electrical connectors attached to the brake pedal assembly.

8 Remove the brake pedal assembly mounting fasteners (see illustration).

9 Gently move the power brake booster forward towards the engine compartment. Be careful not to cause any damage.

10 Remove the brake pedal assembly.

11 Installation is the same as removal noting the following points:

 a) *It may be necessary to remove the drive cable and gear from the brake pedal assembly to install on a replacement assembly.*

 b) *Tighten the brake pedal assembly mounting fasteners to the torque listed in this Chapter's Specifications.*

 c) *A drill or equivalent tool attached to the end of the drive cable can be used to adjust the brake pedal mechanism to its down-most position. This is necessary to synchronize the brake pedal assembly with the accelerator assembly.*

❋❋ WARNING:

If the two mechanisms are not synchronized properly they can become damaged. Make certain that both mechanisms are in the same position (either in their most upward or downward position) before installing the drive cable to the accelerator pedal assembly motor.

 d) *Test the operation of the adjustable brake and accelerator pedals before driving the vehicle.*

Specifications

General

Brake fluid type	See Chapter 1

Disc brakes

Minimum brake pad thickness	See Chapter 1
Disc minimum thickness	Cast into disc
Disc runout limit	0.0014 inch
Parking brake shoe minimum thickness	1/32-inch

Torque specifications   Ft-lbs (unless otherwise indicated)

➡ Note: One foot-pound (ft-lb) of torque is equivalent to 12 inch-pounds (in-lbs) of torque. Torque values below approximately 15 ft-lbs are expressed in inch-pounds, since most foot-pound torque wrenches are not accurate at these smaller values.

Adjustable brake pedal assembly nuts	18
Caliper mounting bolts	
Front	44
Rear	23
Caliper bracket mounting bolts	
Front	70
Rear	85
Brake hose-to-caliper banjo bolt	37
Master cylinder-to-brake booster nuts	
MK25	18
MK25E	133 in-lbs
Power brake booster mounting nuts	18
Wheel lug nuts	See Chapter 1

Notes

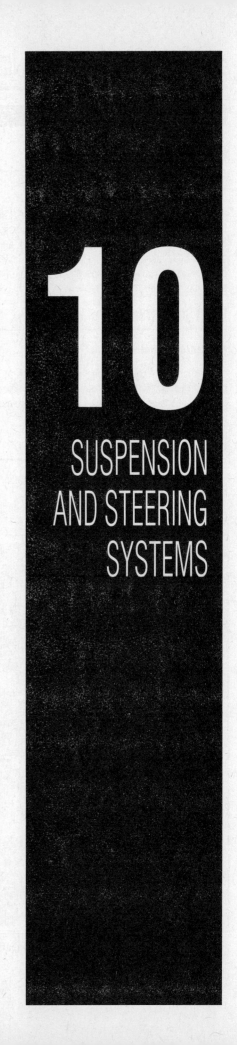

10

SUSPENSION
AND STEERING
SYSTEMS

Section

1 General information

FRONT SUSPENSION

▶ **Refer to illustration 1.1**

All models are equipped with an independent, long-arm/short-arm, front suspension system with upper and lower control arms, tension links and shock absorber/coil spring assemblies. A stabilizer bar controls body roll. Each steering knuckle is positioned by a series of balljoints at the ends of the upper and lower control arms and the tension links (see illustration).

REAR SUSPENSION

▶ **Refer to illustration 1.2**

All models are equipped with an independent multi-link suspension consisting of shock absorbers, coil springs and several specialized links. Some models incorporate a stabilizer bar to control body roll (see illustration).

STEERING

The steering system consists of a rack-and-pinion steering gear and two adjustable tie-rods. Power assist is standard.

Frequently, when working on the suspension or steering system components, you may come across fasteners which seem impossible to loosen. These fasteners on the underside of the vehicle are continually subjected to water, road grime, mud, etc., and can become rusted or "frozen," making them extremely difficult to remove. In order to unscrew these stubborn fasteners without damaging them (or other components), be sure to use lots of penetrating oil and allow it to soak in for a while. Using a wire brush to clean exposed threads will also ease removal of the nut or bolt and prevent damage to the threads. Sometimes a sharp blow with a hammer and punch is effective in breaking the bond between a nut and bolt threads, but care must be taken to prevent the punch from slipping off the fastener and ruining the threads. Heating the stuck fastener and surrounding area with a torch sometimes helps too, but isn't recommended because of the obvious dangers associated with fire. Long breaker bars and extension, or "cheater," pipes will increase leverage, but never use an extension pipe on a ratchet - the ratcheting mechanism could be damaged. Sometimes, turning the nut or bolt in the tightening (clockwise) direction first will help to break it loose. Fasteners that require drastic measures to unscrew should always be replaced with new ones.

Since most of the procedures that are dealt with in this Chapter involve jacking up the vehicle and working underneath it, a good pair of jackstands will be needed. A hydraulic floor jack is the preferred type of jack to lift the vehicle, and it can also be used to support certain components during various operations.

1.1 Front suspension and steering components

1	Stabilizer bar	4	Lower balljoint ballstud (tension strut)	7	Steering gear
2	Lower control arm	5	Tie-rod end	8	Shock absorber/coil spring assembly
3	Lower balljoint (control arm)	6	Tension strut	9	Upper control arm

1.2 Rear suspension components

1	*Subframe*	*3*	*Shock absorber*	*5*	*Compression link*
2	*Coil spring*	*4*	*Toe link*	*6*	*Spring link*

✳✳ WARNING:

Never, under any circumstances, rely on a jack to support the vehicle while working on it. Also, whenever any of the suspension or steering fasteners are loosened or removed they must be inspected and, if necessary, be replaced with new ones of the same part number or of original equipment quality and design. Torque specifications must be followed for proper reassembly and component retention. Never attempt to heat or straighten any suspension or steering components. Instead, replace any bent or damaged part with a new one.

2 Shock absorber/coil spring assembly (front) - removal and installation

✳✳ WARNING:

Always replace shock absorbers or shock absorber/coil spring assemblies in pairs - never replace just one of them.

➡Note: These vehicle models are equipped with shock absorber/coil spring assemblies. It is possible to replace the shocks or springs individually but the unit will have to be disassembled by a qualified repair shop with the proper equipment. This will add considerable cost to the project. You can compare the cost of replacing the complete assemblies yourself to the cost of replacing individual components (with the help of a shop).

REMOVAL

♦ **Refer to illustrations 2.1 and 2.4**

1   Remove the cap on the shock tower (if equipped) and remove the fasteners that attach the upper end of the shock to the frame (see illustration).

2   Loosen the front wheel lug nuts. Raise the front of the vehicle and support it securely on jackstands. Remove the front wheels.

3   Disconnect the stabilizer bar link from the shock assembly (see Section 3).

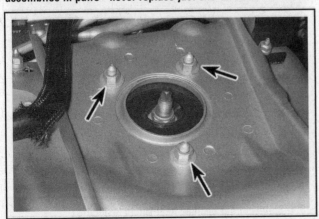

2.1 Upper shock absorber mounting fasteners

4   Remove the fasteners attaching the lower end of the shock absorber to the lower control arm (see illustration).

5   Pull down on the lower control arm and remove the shock absorber towards the rear of the vehicle.

6   Inspect the shock absorber for leaking fluid, dents, cracks and other damage. Inspect the coil spring for chips and cracks which could cause premature failure. Inspect the spring seats for hardness and general deterioration. If any of the components of the assembly are worn or damaged, have the unit serviced by a qualified repair shop or replace it.

INSTALLATION

7   Installation is the reverse of removal. Tighten the mounting fasteners to the torque listed in the Chapter's Specifications.

➡Note: Raise the lower control arm with a floor jack to simulate normal ride height before tightening lower shock absorber mounting fasteners.

8   Tighten the wheel lug nuts to the torque listed in the Chapter 1 Specifications.

2.4 Lower shock absorber mounting fastener

3   Stabilizer bar, bushings and links (front) - removal and installation

▶ **Refer to illustrations 3.3 and 3.4**

1   Raise the front of the vehicle and support it securely on jackstands. Remove the front wheels.

2   Remove the engine splash shield from under the vehicle (see Chapter 2).

3   Remove the lower nut from the stabilizer bar link and separate it from the bar (see illustration).

➡Note: The stabilizer bar link can be separated from the shock absorber assembly by removing the upper nut on the link.

4   Remove the heat shields covering the stabilizer bar brackets (see illustration).

5   Remove the stabilizer bar bracket fasteners and remove the brackets.

6   Remove the stabilizer bar. Remove the rubber bushings from the stabilizer bar. Note that the slit in the bushing is facing towards the rear of the vehicle and must be installed in the same direction.

7   Clean the stabilizer bar where the bushings contact it. Inspect all rubber bushings for wear and damage. If any of the rubber parts are cracked, torn or generally deteriorated, replace them.

8   Check each stabilizer link for signs of excessive wear and replace them as necessary.

9   Installation is the reverse of removal. Be sure to tighten all the fasteners to the torque listed in this Chapter's Specifications.

3.4 Stabilizer bar bushing heat shield fasteners

3.3 Stabilizer bar mounting details:

1   *Link nuts*
2   *Link ballstud (hold with wrench while loosening or tightening link nuts)*
3   *Stabilizer bar bracket fasteners*
4   *Stabilizer bar bushing*

4   Tension strut - removal and installation

▶ **Refer to illustrations 4.3a, 4.3b, 4.4, and 4.6**

➡**Note: A special tool, available at most auto parts stores, is necessary to separate the balljoint from the steering knuckle.**

1   Loosen the front wheel lug nuts. Raise the front of the vehicle and support it securely on jackstands. Remove the front wheel.

2   Remove the engine splash shield from under the vehicle (see Chapter 2).

3   Separate the balljoint on the tension strut from the steering knuckle (see illustrations).

➡**Note: Be careful not to damage the balljoint seal during this step.**

4   Inspect the tension strut-to-subframe mounting bolt for grooves by looking at the end where the threads can be seen (see illustration).

➡**Note: Grooved mounting bolts may or may not be installed on the vehicle you're working on. They are installed for wheel alignment adjustment when necessary (see Section 24).**

5   Hold the tension strut-to-subframe mounting bolt while loosening the nut (see illustration 4.3a).

✳✳ CAUTION:

DO NOT turn the tension strut mounting bolt if there are grooves in it or considerable damage will occur.

4.3a   Tension strut mounting details:

1   *Balljoint stud nut*
2   *Tension strut-to-subframe mounting bolt (hold the bolt with wrench and remove the nut - do not turn the bolt)*
3   *Mounting nut*

4.4   The tension strut may have a grooved mounting bolt like the one illustrated

6   Remove the nut and slowly withdraw the bolt while noting its placement in the notched portion of the bushing (see illustration).

➡**Note: If the bolt has no grooves in it, then it is installed in between the notches in the center of the bushing.**

7   Remove the tension strut.

8   Installation is the reverse of removal. Use a new balljoint stud nut. Tighten all fasteners to the torque listed in this Chapter's Specifications.

➡**Note: Before tightening the tension strut-to-subframe nut, raise the outer end of the lower control arm with a floor jack to simulate normal ride height.**

9   Install the wheel, remove the jackstands and lower the vehicle.

10 Tighten the wheel lug nuts to the torque listed in the Chapter 1 Specifications.

11 Have the front end alignment checked, and if necessary, adjusted.

4.3b   To separate the strut mounted balljoint from the steering knuckle, loosen the balljoint stud nut and then install the tool as shown

4.6   The tension strut bushing's center area has notches to engage grooved mounting bolts. Regular (non-grooved) mounting bolts are placed in between the notches - directly in the center

5 Upper control arm - removal and installation

REMOVAL

▶ **Refer to illustrations 5.1, 5.3, 5.6 and 5.8**

➡**Note: A special tool, available at most auto parts stores, is necessary to separate the balljoint from the steering knuckle.**

1   For right upper control arm removal, move the engine compartment fuse and relay box aside for access (see illustration). For left upper control arm removal, move the coolant expansion tank aside (see Chapter 3).

2   Remove the upper fasteners for the shock absorber so that it can be moved outward in order to remove the control arm fasteners (see Section 2).

3   Remove the upper control arm mounting nuts from within the engine compartment (see illustration).

4   Loosen the wheel lug nuts, raise the front of the vehicle and support it securely on jackstands placed under the frame rails. Remove the wheel.

5   Remove the ABS wheel speed sensor harness from the frame bracket where the brake hose and brake line fitting are (see Chapter 9).

6   Loosen (but don't remove) the nut on the upper balljoint stud, then disconnect the balljoint from the steering knuckle with a balljoint removal tool (see illustration).

7   Carefully secure the steering knuckle aside, then move the shock absorber outward.

8   Remove the control arm mounting flag bolts and pull the upper arm from its frame brackets (see illustration).

INSTALLATION

9   Installation is the reverse of removal. Use a new balljoint stud nut. Tighten all fasteners to the torque values listed in this Chapter's Specifications.

➡**Note: Raise the lower control arm with a floor jack to simulate normal ride height before tightening upper control arm mounting nuts at the shock tower.**

10 Install the wheel and lug nuts. Lower the vehicle and tighten the lug nuts to the torque listed in the Chapter 1 Specifications.

11 Have the front end alignment checked and, if necessary, adjusted.

5.1 Release the tabs on the fuse and relay box to lift it off its mounting brackets and move it aside

5.3 The mounting nuts for the upper control arm are on each side of the shock tower

5.6 Back off the nut a few turns, then separate the balljoint from the steering knuckle (leaving the nut on the ballstud will prevent the balljoint from separating violently)

5.8 Upper control arm flag bolt fasteners

6 Lower control arm - removal and installation

REMOVAL

▶ **Refer to illustrations 6.3, 6.5, 6.6 and 6.9**

➡**Note: A special tool, available at most auto parts stores, is necessary to separate the balljoint from the lower control arm.**

1   Loosen the wheel lug nuts, raise the front of the vehicle and support it securely on jackstands placed under the frame rails. Remove the wheel.

2   Remove the engine splash shield from under the vehicle (see Chapter 2).

3   Remove the stabilizer bar brackets to gain access to the lower control arm-to-subframe mounting bolt (see Section 3) (see illustration).

4   Inspect the lower control arm-to-subframe mounting bolt for grooves by looking at the end where the threads can be seen (see illustration 4.4).

➡**Note: Grooved mounting bolts may or may not be installed on the vehicle you're working on. They are installed for wheel alignment adjustment when necessary (see Section 24).**

6.3 Lower control arm mounting details:

1   Balljoint stud nut
2   Shock absorber mounting fastener
3   Lower control arm-to-subframe mounting bolt (hold the bolt with wrench and remove the nut - do not turn the bolt)

6.6 The lower control arm bushing's center area has notches to engage grooved mounting bolts. Regular (non-grooved) mounting bolts are placed in between the notches - directly in the center

5   Hold the lower control arm-to-subframe mounting bolt while loosening the nut (see illustration).

✳✳ CAUTION:

DO NOT turn the lower control arm mounting bolt if there are grooves in it or considerable damage will occur.

6   Remove the nut and slowly withdraw the bolt while noting its placement in the notched portion of the bushing (see illustration).

➡**Note: If the bolt has no grooves in it, then it is installed in between the notches in the center of the bushing.**

7   Remove the shock absorber lower mounting fasteners (see illustration 6.3).

8   Remove the ABS wheel speed sensor harness from the frame bracket where the brake hose and brake line fitting are (see Chapter 9).

9   Loosen (but don't remove) the nut on the balljoint stud, then disconnect the balljoint from the lower control arm with a balljoint removal tool (see illustration).

6.5 Hold the mounting bolt while loosening the nut

6.9 To separate the balljoint from the lower control arm, loosen the balljoint stud nut and install the tool as shown (leaving the nut on the ballstud will prevent the balljoint from separating violently)

10 Remove the balljoint stud nut and pry the knuckle down to remove the balljoint stud from the lower control arm. Move the steering knuckle away from the control arm until they are separated.

11 Remove the lower control arm by sliding it out of the subframe bracket.

INSTALLATION

12 Installation is the reverse of removal. Use a new balljoint stud nut. Be sure to tighten all fasteners to the torque values listed in this Chapter's Specifications.

➡**Note: Raise the lower control arm with a floor jack to simulate normal ride height before tightening the lower control arm mounting nut at the subframe and the lower shock absorber mounting fasteners.**

13 Install the wheel and lug nuts. Lower the vehicle and tighten the lug nuts to the torque listed in the Chapter 1 Specifications.

14 Have the front end alignment checked and, if necessary, adjusted.

7 Balljoints - check and replacement

1 Inspect the control arm balljoints for looseness anytime either of them is separated from the steering knuckle. See if you can turn the ballstud in its socket with your fingers. If the balljoint is loose, or if the ballstud can be turned, replace the balljoint. You can also check the balljoints with the suspension assembled as follows.

UPPER BALLJOINT

2 Loosen the front wheel lug nuts, raise the front of the vehicle and support it securely on jackstands, then remove the wheel. Raise the lower control arm with a floor jack to simulate normal ride height.

3 Using a large prybar inserted between the upper control arm and the steering knuckle, pry upwards on the upper control arm. The manufacturer specifies up to 0.059-inch movement is allowed; a dial indicator can be used to check for play. If you are unable to accurately measure balljoint play, have the balljoint checked at an automotive repair shop.

4 If replacement is indicated, replace the upper control arm (see Section 5); the balljoint cannot be replaced separately.

LOWER BALLJOINT

▶ **Refer to illustration 7.7**

5 Raise the vehicle and support it securely on jackstands.

6 Place a floor jack under the lower control arm, near the outer end, and raise it until it is supporting the vehicle's weight.

7 Now, insert the prybar against the lower control arm or tension strut and pry the steering knuckle up (see illustration). The manufacturer specifies up to 0.059-inch movement is allowed; a dial indicator

7.7 Pry up on the steering knuckle to check for wear

can be used to check for play. If you are unable to accurately measure balljoint play, have the balljoint checked at an automotive repair shop.

8 If replacement is indicated, remove the steering knuckle or tension strut (see Sections 4 or 9); the balljoint is press fit in the steering knuckle and tension strut, which necessitates the use of a special press tool and receiver cup to remove and install the balljoint. Equipment rental yards and some auto parts stores have these tools available for rent. If you don't have access to this tool, take the vehicle (or the steering knuckle) to an automotive machine shop or other qualified repair facility to have the balljoint replaced.

8 Hub and bearing assembly (front) - removal and installation

✳✳ WARNING:

The dust created by the brake system is harmful to your health. Never blow it out with compressed air and don't inhale any of it. Do not, under any circumstances, use petroleum-based solvents to clean brake parts. Use brake system cleaner only.

➡**Note: The hub and bearing assembly is sealed-for-life. If any part is worn or damaged, it must be replaced as a unit.**

REMOVAL

▶ **Refer to illustrations 8.3 and 8.4**

1 Loosen the wheel lug nuts, raise the front of the vehicle and support it securely on jackstands placed under the frame rails. Remove the wheel.

2 Remove the brake disc (see Chapter 9).

3 Remove the dust cap (see illustration).

4 Remove the hub nut (see illustration).

5 Remove the hub from the steering knuckle spindle.

8.3 Carefully remove the dust cover using a sharp chisel or suitable tool

8.4 Remove the hub nut and slide the hub off the steering knuckle spindle

INSTALLATION

6   Installation is the reverse of removal, noting the following points:

  a) *Tighten the hub nut to the torque listed in this Chapter's Specifications.*

  b) *Tighten the brake caliper mounting bracket and brake caliper mounting bolts to the torque listed in the Chapter 9 Specifications.*

  c) *Install the wheel, lower the vehicle and tighten the lug nuts to the torque listed in the Chapter 1 Specifications.*

9   Steering knuckle - removal and installation

✳✳ WARNING:

The dust created by the brake system is harmful to your health. Never blow it out with compressed air and don't inhale any of it. Do not, under any circumstances, use petroleum-based solvents to clean brake parts. Use brake system cleaner only.

1   Loosen the wheel lug nuts, raise the front of the vehicle and support it securely on jackstands. Remove the wheel.

2   Remove the brake disc, the wheel speed sensor and the small bracket that holds the brake hose and ABS wheel speed sensor harness to the knuckle (see Chapter 9).

3   Disconnect the tie-rod end from the steering knuckle (see Section 18).

4   Separate the upper control arm from the steering knuckle (see Section 5).

5   Separate the tension strut from the steering knuckle (see Section 4).

6   Separate the lower control arm from the steering knuckle (see Section 6).

7   Carefully inspect the steering knuckle for cracks, especially around the steering arm and spindle mounting area. Also inspect the balljoint stud holes. If they're elongated, or if you find any cracks in the knuckle, replace the steering knuckle.

8   Remove the hub, brake dust shield or lower balljoint as necessary for replacement.

➡**Note: Balljoint removal will require special tools. The knuckle can be taken to a dealership service department or qualified repair facility for removal.**

9   Installation is the reverse of removal. Be sure to tighten all suspension fasteners to the torque listed in this Chapter's Specifications. Refer to the torque values listed in the Chapter 9 Specifications for brake related fasteners.

10 Tighten the wheel lug nuts to the torque listed in the Chapter 1 Specifications.

10 Shock absorber (rear) - removal and installation

➡ **Note: Some models may have optional automatic load-leveling shock absorbers. They can be identified by their considerably larger diameters. Removal and installation of these shocks requires lowering the rear subframe one side at a time. The job is a lot more difficult than changing typical shock absorbers.**

1 Loosen the wheel lug nuts, raise the rear of the vehicle and support it securely on jackstands placed under the frame rails. Remove the wheel.

REGULAR SHOCK ABSORBERS

▸ **Refer to illustrations 10.2, 10.3 and 10.4**

2 Support the spring link with a floor jack to keep the suspension in place when the shock is removed (see illustration).

3 Remove the fasteners that attach the upper end of the shock absorber to the frame (see illustration). If the bolts won't loosen because of rust, apply some penetrating oil and allow it to soak in for awhile.

4 Remove the fasteners that attach the lower end of the shock to the spring link (see illustration). Again, if the nut is frozen, apply some

penetrating oil, wait awhile and try again.

5 Installation is the reverse of removal. Tighten the mounting fasteners to the torque listed in the Chapter's Specifications.

➡ **Note: Raise the spring link with a floor jack to simulate normal ride height before tightening the lower shock absorber mounting fasteners (see illustration 10.2).**

LOAD-LEVELING SHOCK ABSORBERS

▸ **Refer to illustrations 10.8, 10.11a and 10.11b**

6 When servicing the left shock absorber, remove the rubber hose between the fuel filler neck and the gas tank, and then move the filler neck aside (see Chapter 4).

7 On vehicles with dual exhaust, or when servicing the right shock absorber, lower the exhaust by removing it from its hangers and support it with jackstand or another jack (see Chapter 4).

➡ **Note: There is no need to disconnect the exhaust pipes from the resonator(s) or muffler(s), simply lower and support them.**

8 Place a floor jack under the rear differential and use it to support the suspension and subframe (see illustration).

10.2 Use a wood block and a floor jack to support or raise the spring link

10.3 Rear shock absorber upper mounting fasteners

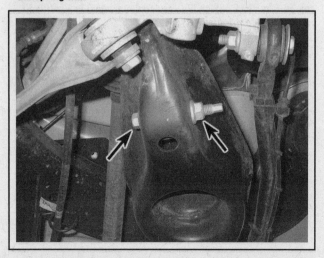

10.4 Rear shock absorber lower mounting fasteners

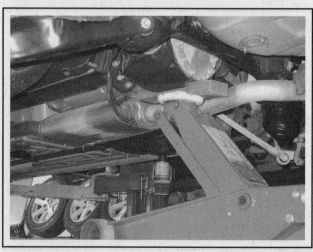

10.8 Use a wood block and a floor jack to support, lower and raise the rear subframe and differential

10.11a The location of the subframe mounting bolts on the right side

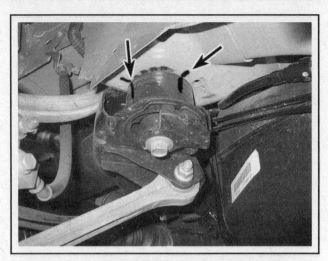

10.11b Place reference marks on the subframe and the vehicle chassis so that the subframe can be placed back into the same position when reinstalled

9 Support the spring link with a floor jack and wood block (see illustration 10.2). Remove the fasteners that attach the upper end of the shock absorber to the frame (see illustration 10.3). If the bolt won't loosen because of rust, apply some penetrating oil and allow it to soak in for awhile. Slowly lower the floor jack supporting the spring link.

10 Remove the fasteners that attach the lower end of the shock to the spring link (see illustration 10.4). Again, if the nut is frozen, apply some penetrating oil, wait awhile and try again.

11 Mark the subframe in relation to the chassis, then remove the front and rear subframe fasteners on the side you're working on (see illustrations).

➡**Note: Only service one side at a time to avoid changing the rear wheel alignment.**

12 SLOWLY lower the differential with the floor jack just enough to remove the shock absorber.

❋❋ **CAUTION:**

The other side of the subframe and suspension will flex to accommodate lowering the side of the suspension you're working on. Do not lower the subframe any more than necessary to remove the shock or damage to other suspension components will occur.

13 Installation is the reverse of removal noting the following points:
  a) *Install the lower shock absorber fasteners before raising the subframe into position, but do not tighten them yet.*
  b) *When raising the subframe into position, be sure that the coil spring and insulators are seated into their original positions and that the subframe is matched to the reference marks made previously.*
  c) *The subframe mounting bolts have two different lengths; the longer bolts are installed to the rear of the subframe while the shorter bolts are installed to the front.*
  d) *Make sure to reinstall the brake, fuel tank, driveline and exhaust system components.*
  e) *Raise the spring link with a floor jack to simulate normal ride height, then tighten the lower shock absorber mounting fasteners to the torque listed in this Chapter's Specifications (see illustration 10.2).*
  f) *Be sure to tighten all suspension fasteners to the torque listed in this Chapter's Specifications.*
  g) *Have the wheel alignment checked and, if necessary, adjusted.*

11 Stabilizer bar, bushings and links (rear) - removal and installation

▶ **Refer to illustrations 11.5, 11.7 and 11.19**

❋❋ **WARNING:**

The removal of the rear stabilizer bar involves lowering the subframe and drivetrain components. This job is very involved and can be considered hazardous even with the proper equipment. Use extreme caution throughout the following procedures to avoid injury.

➡**Note 1: A transmission jack or equivalent is necessary for the following procedure.**

➡**Note 2: It is recommended that additional help from an assistant be used during this procedure.**

1 Disconnect the cable from the negative battery terminal (see Chapter 5, Section 1).

2 Loosen the wheel lug nuts, raise the rear of the vehicle and support it securely on jackstands placed under the frame rails. Remove the wheel.

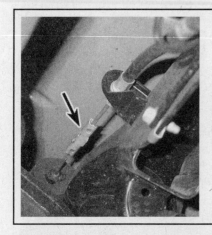

11.5 The brake equalizer is just above the rear differential

11.7 Location of the rear subframe mounting fasteners (one hidden)

3 Remove the rear exhaust system (see Chapter 4).

4 Disconnect the driveshaft from the rear differential (see Chapter 8).

5 Separate and detach the parking brake equalizer from the front parking brake cable (see illustration).

6 Remove the bracket that holds the parking brake cable to the subframe.

7 Mark the subframe in relation to the chassis at all four mounting locations (see illustration 10.11b and the accompanying illustration).

❋❋ CAUTION:

If the subframe is not returned to its original position, the rear wheel alignment will be adversely affected.

8 Support the spring link with a floor jack and wood block (see illustration 10.2), then remove the shock absorber lower mounting fasteners (see Section 10). Slowly lower the floor jack supporting the spring link.

9 Remove the brake calipers and secure them so that the brake hoses will not be affected when the subframe is lowered (see Chapter 9).

10 Disconnect and remove the ABS wheel speed harnesses from the chassis (see Chapter 9).

11 Place a transmission jack (or equivalent) under the differential and attach it securely.

➡**Note: Do not secure the rear stabilizer bar along with the differential when securing it to the transmission jack.**

12 Remove the fuel filler neck (see Chapter 4).

13 With the transmission jack in place and securing the differential and subframe, remove all four subframe bolts.

14 SLOWLY lower the subframe enough to separate the driveshaft from the differential.

15 Continue lowering the subframe until there is adequate access to the stabilizer bar retainers.

➡**Note: Do not lower the subframe any more than necessary to remove the stabilizer bar.**

16 Stabilize the subframe and suspension assembly with additional jackstands or equivalent.

17 Remove the stabilizer bar bracket fasteners and remove the brackets. Remove the bushings from the bar while noting the direction of the slits.

18 Clean the stabilizer bar where the bushings contact it. Inspect the bushings for wear and damage. If they are cracked, torn or generally deteriorated, replace them.

11.19 Rear stabilizer bar link mounting fasteners - right side shown

19 Remove the stabilizer bar links and inspect them for wear or damage; replace them if necessary (see illustration).

20 Installation is the reverse of removal noting the following points:

a) *Install the lower shock absorber fasteners before raising the subframe into position, but do not tighten them yet.*

b) *When raising the subframe into position, be sure that the coil spring and insulators are seated into their original positions and that the subframe is matched to the reference marks made previously. Install the driveshaft to the rear differential as the subframe is being raised. Guide the top of the shock absorbers to the chassis as the subframe nears its installed position.*

c) *The subframe mounting bolts are two different lengths; the longer bolts are installed to the rear of the subframe while the shorter bolts are installed to the front.*

d) *Make sure to reinstall the brake, fuel tank, driveline and exhaust system components.*

e) *Raise the spring link with a floor jack to simulate normal ride height, then tighten the lower shock absorber and stabilizer bar link mounting fasteners (see illustration 10.2).*

f) *Be sure to tighten all suspension fasteners to the torque listed in this Chapter's Specifications.*

g) *Have the wheel alignment checked and, if necessary, adjusted.*

12 Suspension links (rear) - removal and installation

➡**Note: The subframe must be lowered one side at a time to remove the camber and tension links or the left toe link; a good floor jack, jackstands and wood blocks will be necessary.**

COMPRESSION LINK

▸ **Refer to illustration 12.2**

1 Raise the rear of the vehicle and support it securely on jackstands.

2 Remove the compression link mounting fasteners from the rear knuckle (see illustration).

3 Remove the compression link mounting fasteners from the rear subframe and remove the link.

4 Inspect all rubber bushings for wear and damage. If any of the rubber parts are cracked, torn or generally deteriorated, replace them.

5 Installation is the reverse of removal. Tighten the mounting fasteners to the torque listed in this Chapter's Specifications.

➡**Note: Raise the spring link with a floor jack to simulate normal ride height before tightening the compression link mounting fasteners (see illustration 10.2).**

CAMBER LINK

▸ **Refer to illustration 12.7**

6 Follow the procedures in Section 10 for the removal of the load-leveling type shock absorbers for the side of the vehicle you're working on. Remove the shock absorber in this manner regardless if it is the regular or load leveling type.

7 Remove the camber link mounting fasteners at the knuckle (see illustration).

8 Remove the camber link mounting fasteners at the subframe, note the position of the link and then remove it.

➡**Note: The thicker end of the link is attached to the subframe with the bend giving space for the coil spring.**

9 Inspect all rubber bushings for wear and damage. If any of the rubber parts are cracked, torn or generally deteriorated, replace them.

10 For installation, refer to the same procedure in Section 10 for load-leveling shock absorbers.

12.2 Compression link mounting fasteners

➡**Note: Raise the spring link with a floor jack to simulate normal ride height before tightening the camber link mounting fasteners (see illustration 10.2).**

TENSION LINK

▸ **Refer to illustration 12.12**

11 Follow the procedures in Section 10 for the removal of the load-leveling type shock absorbers for the side of the vehicle you're working on. Remove the shock absorber in this manner regardless if it is the regular or load leveling type.

12 Remove the tension link mounting fasteners at the knuckle (see illustration).

13 Remove the tension link mounting fasteners at the subframe, note the position of the link and then remove it.

14 Inspect all rubber bushings for wear and damage. If any of the rubber parts are cracked, torn or generally deteriorated, replace them.

15 For installation, refer to the same procedure in Section 10 for load-leveling shock absorbers.

12.7 Camber link mounting fasteners

12.12 Tension link mounting fasteners - one hidden

12.18 Mark the relationship of the toe adjusting cam bolt to the subframe to preserve the rear wheel alignment when the fasteners are reinstalled

➡Note: Raise the spring link with a floor jack to simulate normal ride height before tightening the tension link mounting fasteners (see illustration 10.2).

TOE LINK

Right toe link

▶ Refer to illustrations 12.18 and 12.19

16 Loosen the wheel lug nuts, raise the rear of the vehicle and support it securely on jackstands placed under the frame rails. Remove the wheel.

17 Remove the ABS harness from the toe link, if equipped.

18 Mark the relationship of the toe adjusting cam bolt to the subframe (see illustration).

19 Remove the toe link mounting fasteners from the rear knuckle (see illustration).

➡Note: Lower the exhaust if you need more room for access. There is no need to detach the pipes from the muffler or resonator - simply lower it and rest it on jackstands.

20 Hold the cam bolt while loosening the toe link mounting nut from the rear subframe. Note the position of the link and then remove it.

21 Inspect all rubber bushings for wear and damage. If any of the rubber parts are cracked, torn or generally deteriorated, replace them.

22 Installation is the reverse of removal. Tighten the mounting fasteners to the torque listed in this Chapter's Specifications.

➡Note: Raise the spring link with a floor jack to simulate normal ride height before tightening the toe link mounting fasteners (see illustration 10.2).

12.19 Toe link mounting fasteners

Left toe link

23 Follow the procedures in Section 10 for the removal of the load-leveling type shock absorbers for the side of the vehicle you're working on. Remove the shock absorber in this manner regardless if it is the regular or load leveling type.

24 Remove the ABS harness from the toe link, if equipped.

25 Mark the relationship of the toe adjusting cam bolt to the subframe (see illustration 12.18).

26 Remove the toe link mounting fasteners at the knuckle (see illustration 12.19).

27 Hold the cam bolt while loosening the toe link mounting nut from the rear subframe. Note the position of the link and then remove it.

28 Inspect all rubber bushings for wear and damage. If any of the rubber parts are cracked, torn or generally deteriorated, replace them.

29 For installation, refer to the same procedure in Section 10 for load-leveling shock absorbers.

➡Note: Raise the spring link with a floor jack to simulate normal ride height before tightening the toe link mounting fasteners (see illustration 10.2).

SPRING LINK

30 The bushing in the spring link, where it connects to the rear knuckle, has a metal sleeve installed in it. The metal sleeve must be withdrawn from the link before it can be separated from the knuckle. Special tools are required to remove the sleeve from the link's bushing. However, the spring link and knuckle can be removed together and taken to a dealer service department or qualified repair shop for separation. Special tools are also necessary for the link and knuckle to be rejoined with a new metal sleeve installed. Refer to Section 14 for removal of the spring link with the rear knuckle.

13 Coil spring (rear) - removal and installation

▶ **Refer to illustration 13.2**

➡**Note: The subframe must be lowered one side at a time to remove the coil spring; a good floor jack, jackstands and wood blocks will be necessary.**

1   Follow the procedures in Section 10 for the removal of the load-leveling type shock absorbers for the side of the vehicle you're working on. Remove the shock absorber in this manner regardless if it is the regular or load leveling type. Continue to lower the subframe until the coil spring is extended.

2   Remove the coil spring and the upper and lower insulators (see illustration).

3   Inspect insulators for wear and damage. If the rubber is cracked, torn or generally deteriorated, replace them.

4   For installation, refer to the same procedure in Section 10 for load-leveling shock absorbers.

➡**Note: Be sure to follow the instructions in Section 10 regarding the tightening of the suspension fasteners.**

13.2 The coil spring (A) and the insulators (B)

14 Knuckle (rear) - removal and installation

▶ **Refer to illustration 14.6**

➡**Note 1: The bushing in the spring link, where it connects to the rear knuckle, has a metal sleeve installed in it. The metal sleeve must be withdrawn from the link before it can be separated from the knuckle. Special tools are required to remove the sleeve from the link's bushing. However, the spring link and knuckle can be removed together and taken to a dealer service department or qualified repair shop for separation. Special tools are also necessary for the link and knuckle to be rejoined with a new metal sleeve installed.**

➡**Note 2: The subframe must be lowered one side at a time to remove the spring link and knuckle; a good floor jack, jackstands and wood blocks will be necessary.**

1   Loosen the wheel lug nuts, raise the rear of the vehicle and support it securely on jackstands placed under the frame rails. Remove the wheel.

2   Remove the ABS wheel speed sensor and unclip the harness from the brake backing plate (see Chapter 9).

3   Remove the hub and bearing assembly (see Section 15).

4   Remove the rear parking brake shoes and disconnect the parking brake cable from the knuckle (see Chapter 9).

5   Follow the procedures in Section 13 for the removal of the coil spring.

6   Detach the spring link-to-subframe mounting fasteners (see illustration).

14.6 Spring link-to-subframe pivot bolt

7   Remove all links connected to the knuckle except the spring link and carefully remove the knuckle (see Section 12).

8   Installation is the reverse of removal.

➡**Note: Raise the spring link with a floor jack to simulate normal ride height, then tighten the suspension component mounting fasteners to the torque listed in this Chapter's Specifications (see illustration 10.2).**

15 Hub and bearing assembly (rear) - removal and installation

▶ **Refer to illustrations 15.4 and 15.5**

1   Loosen the driveaxle/hub nut (see Chapter 8).

2   Loosen the wheel lug nuts, raise the rear of the vehicle and support it securely on jackstands placed under the frame rails. Remove the wheel.

3   Remove the brake caliper and disc. Also remove the wheel speed sensor from the steering knuckle (see Chapter 9).

4   Remove the hub mounting bolts from the back of the steering knuckle enough to release the hub assembly (see illustration).

➡**Note: The hub bolts can stay in the knuckle to support the brake backing plate.**

5   Remove the driveaxle/hub nut and push the driveaxle through the hub splines as the hub and bearing assembly is removed. If the driveaxle sticks in the hub, it's best to push it out with a puller (see illustration).

✳✳ CAUTION:

Be careful not to overextend the inner CV joint. Once the hub has been removed, support the outer end of the driveaxle with a length of wire or rope.

6   Installation is the reverse of removal, noting the following points:

a) Tighten the hub mounting bolts to the torque listed in this Chapter's Specifications.

b) Tighten the brake caliper mounting bracket bolts, caliper mounting bolts and the wheel speed sensor bolt to the torque listed in the Chapter 9 Specifications.

c) Tighten the driveaxle/hub nut to the torque listed in the Chapter 8 Specifications.

d) Tighten the wheel lug nuts to the torque listed in the Chapter 1 Specifications.

15.4 Hub and bearing assembly mounting bolts - one hidden

15.5 If the driveaxle is stuck tightly to the hub, install a puller to remove it

16 Steering wheel - removal and installation

✳✳ WARNING:

These models are equipped with airbags. Always disable the airbag system whenever working in the vicinity of any airbag system component to avoid the possibility of accidental airbag deployment, which could cause personal injury (see Chapter 12).

REMOVAL

▶ **Refer to illustrations 16.3, 16.4, 16.5a, 16.5b and 16.6**

➡**Note: A new steering wheel mounting bolt is necessary for installation.**

1   Park the vehicle with the front wheels in the straight-ahead position.

✳✳ WARNING:

Do NOT turn the steering shaft during or after steering wheel removal. If the shaft is turned while the steering wheel is removed, a mechanism known as the clockspring can be damaged. The clockspring, which maintains a continuous electrical circuit between the wiring harness and the airbag module, consists of a flat, ribbon-like electrically conductive tape which winds and unwinds as the steering wheel is turned.

2   Disconnect the cable from the negative battery terminal, (see Chapter 5, Section 1).

3   Remove the two airbag module retaining screws (see illustration) and lift off the airbag module.

16.3 Remove the airbag module retaining screws

16.4 Lift the airbag off the steering wheel and unplug the electrical connectors for the airbag, horn, etc.

⁑ WARNING:

Carry the airbag module with the trim cover (upholstered side) facing away from you, and set the airbag module in a safe location with the trim cover facing up.

---

4   Unplug the electrical connectors for the airbag, horn and other components (if equipped) (see illustration).

5   Remove the steering wheel bolt and note the relationship of the steering wheel hub to the steering shaft before removing the steering wheel (see illustration).

➡Note: **The steering wheel hub is 'keyed' with one larger spline to fit the steering shaft in one position (see illustration). Slide the steering wheel off the shaft.**

6   If it is necessary to remove the clockspring, remove the mounting screws and lift the clockspring from the steering column (see illustration).

➡Note: **Use tape to keep the clockspring in the centered position.**

16.5a Remove the mounting bolt and discard it

16.5b After removing the bolt, note the keyed area of the steering wheel hub and its relationship of the wheel to the shaft

16.6 Clockspring mounting details:

1 Mounting screws	3 Tab that engages with
2 Alignment arrows	steering wheel
(pointing up)	

INSTALLATION

7   When installing the clockspring, make absolutely sure that the airbag clockspring is centered with the arrows on the clockspring rotor and case lined up (see illustration 16.6). This shouldn't be a problem as long as you have not turned the steering shaft while the wheel was removed. If for some reason the shaft was turned, center the clockspring as follows:

   a) *Rotate the clockspring clockwise until it stops (don't apply too much force, though).*
   b) *Rotate the clockspring counterclockwise about 2-1/2 turns until the arrows on the clockspring rotor and case line up.*

8   Installation is the reverse of removal, noting the following points:

   a) *Make sure the airbag clockspring is centered before installing the steering wheel (see Step 7).*
   b) *When installing the steering wheel, align the tab on the clockspring with the steering wheel hub.*
   c) *Install a NEW steering wheel bolt and tighten it to the torque listed in this Chapter's Specifications.*
   d) *Install the airbag module on the steering wheel and tighten the mounting screws to the torque listed in this Chapter's Specifications.*
   e) *Enable the airbag system (see Chapter 12).*

17 Steering column - removal and installation

※※ WARNING:

These models are equipped with airbags. Always disable the airbag system whenever working in the vicinity of any airbag system component to avoid the possibility of accidental airbag deployment, which could cause personal injury (see Chapter 12).

➡**Note: The manufacturer recommends using new mounting fasteners for installation.**

REMOVAL

◆ **Refer to illustrations 17.6, 17.7, 17.9, 17.11, 17.13 and 17.14**

1   Park the vehicle with the wheels pointing straight ahead. Extend the column all the way out. Disconnect the cable(s) from the negative battery terminal(s) (see Chapter 5, Section 1). Wait at least two minutes before proceeding (to allow the backup power supply for the airbag system to become depleted).

➡**Note: On models equipped with electric telescoping columns, place the column in the mid-tilt position.**

2   Remove the steering wheel (see Section 16), then turn the ignition key to the LOCK position to prevent the steering shaft from turning.

※※ CAUTION:

If this is not done, the airbag clockspring could be damaged.

3   Loosen (but don't remove) one of the clockspring mounting fasteners to keep the clockspring centered (see illustration 16.6).

4   Remove the knee bolster and reinforcement panel underneath it (see Chapter 11).

5   Remove the Steering Column Control Module (SCCM) (see Chapter 12).

6   Remove the mounting screws for the plastic shroud at the end of the column and detach the tilt adjuster handle, if equipped (see illustration).

7   Remove the lower steering column mounting fasteners at the firewall (see illustration).

8   Remove the instrument cluster (see Chapter 12).

9   Detach the electrical wiring harness for the column (see illustration).

10 Raise the front of the vehicle and support it securely on jackstands.

11 From under the vehicle, mark the steering shaft to the lower coupling shaft and remove the pinch bolt (see illustration). Separate the shafts.

12 On vehicles equipped with electric telescoping columns, remove

17.6 The steering column shroud mounting fasteners

17.7 Lower steering column mounting fasteners

17.9 Remove the wiring harness by releasing the tabs that hold the connector to the column

17.11 Mark the relationship of the steering shaft to the lower coupling shaft (A) and remove the coupler pinch bolt (B)

17.13 Column pivot bolt

the brace attached to dash support and the column (inside the vehicle and under the dash on the left side of the column).

13 Remove the pivot bolt on the column (see illustration).

14 Remove the upper steering column mounting bolts and remove the column (see illustration).

✳✳ CAUTION:

Handle the steering column with care to avoid damaging it.

INSTALLATION

15 Guide the steering column into position and install the top and pivot mounting fasteners, but don't tighten them yet.

➡**Note: Make sure the lower boot is properly seated on the column before placing it into position through the firewall.**

16 Install the brace removed in Step 12 if equipped.

17 The remainder of installation is the reverse of removal.

17.14 Steering column upper mounting bolts

18 Tighten the mounting fasteners to the torque listed in this Chapter's Specifications.

18 Tie-rod ends - removal and installation

REMOVAL

▶ **Refer to illustrations 18.2, 18.3, and 18.4**

1 Loosen the wheel lug nuts, raise the front of the vehicle and support it securely on jackstands. Apply the parking brake. Remove the wheel.

2 Loosen the tie-rod end jam nut (see illustration).

3 Mark the relationship of the tie-rod end to the threaded portion of the tie-rod. This will ensure the toe-in setting is restored when reassembled (see illustration).

4 Loosen (but don't remove) the nut on the tie-rod end ballstud and disconnect the tie-rod end from the steering knuckle arm with a puller (see illustration).

➡**Note: If the ballstud turns while loosening the nut, hold the ballstud with a wrench while removing the nut.**

18.2 Hold the tie-rod with a wrench while loosening the jam nut

18.3 Mark the position of the tie-rod end in relation to the threads

5   If you're replacing the tie-rod end, unscrew the tie-rod end from the tie-rod, then thread the new tie-rod end onto the tie-rod to the marked position.

INSTALLATION

6   Connect the tie-rod end to the steering knuckle arm. Install the

18.4 Back-off the ballstud nut a few turns, then separate the tie-rod end from the steering knuckle with a puller (leaving the nut on the ballstud will prevent the tie-rod end from separating violently)

nut on the ballstud and tighten it to the torque listed in this Chapter's Specifications. Install the wheel. Lower the vehicle and tighten the lug nuts to the torque listed in the Chapter 1 Specifications.

7   Have the front end alignment checked and, if necessary, adjusted.

19 Steering gear boots - replacement

▶ **Refer to illustration 19.3**

1   Loosen the wheel lug nuts, raise the front of the vehicle and support it securely on jackstands. Remove the wheel.

2   Remove the tie-rod end and jam nut (see Section 18).

3   Remove the steering gear boot clamps and slide the boot off (see illustration).

➡**Note: Check for the presence of power steering fluid in the boot. If there is a substantial amount, it means the steering gear seals are leaking and the power steering gear should be replaced with a new or rebuilt unit.**

4   Before installing the new boot, wrap the threads and serrations on the end of the steering rod with a layer of tape so the small end of the new boot isn't damaged.

5   Slide the new boot into position on the steering gear until it seats in the grooves, then install new clamps.

6   Remove the tape and install the tie-rod end (see Section 18).

7   Install the wheel and lug nuts. Lower the vehicle and tighten the lug nuts to the torque listed in the Chapter 1 Specifications.

8   Have the front end alignment checked and, if necessary, adjusted.

19.3 Remove both clamps to remove the steering gear boot

20 Steering gear - removal and installation

▶ Refer to illustrations 20.3, 20.4 and 20.5

❊❊ WARNING:

Make sure the steering column shaft is not turned while the steering gear is removed or you could damage the airbag system clockspring. To prevent the shaft from turning, turn the ignition key to the lock position before beginning work, and run the seat belt through the steering wheel and clip it into its latch.

1   Park the vehicle with the wheels pointing straight ahead. Loosen the front wheel lug nuts, raise the front of the vehicle and support it securely on jackstands. Apply the parking brake. Remove the wheels.

2   Detach the tie-rod ends from the steering knuckles (see Section 18).

3   Mark the relationship of the intermediate shaft coupler to the steering gear input shaft, remove the pinch bolt and separate the coupler from the input shaft (see illustration).

4   Position a drain pan under the steering gear. Using a flare-nut wrench, disconnect the power steering pressure and return lines from the steering gear (see illustration). Cap the lines to prevent leakage.

5   Remove the mounting fasteners and then remove the steering gear (see illustration).

6   Inspect all rubber bushings for wear and damage. If any of the rubber parts are cracked, torn or generally deteriorated, replace them.

7   Installation is the reverse of removal, noting the following points:

a) Tighten the steering gear mounting bolts and the lower coupler pinch bolt to the torque values listed in this Chapter's Specifications.

20.3 Mark the relationship of the steering shaft coupler to the steering input shaft (A) and then remove the lower coupler pinch bolt

b) Tighten the wheel lug nuts to the torque listed in the Chapter 1 Specifications.

c) Check the power steering fluid level and add some, if necessary (see Chapter 1) and then bleed the system as described in Section 22.

d) Re-check the power steering fluid level.

20.4 Use a flare-nut wrench to remove the line fittings from the steering gear

20.5 Steering gear mounting fasteners

21 Power steering pump - removal and installation

▶ Refer to illustrations 21.5 and 21.6

1   Disconnect the cable from the negative battery terminal, (see Chapter 5, Section 1).

2   Using a large syringe or suction gun, suck as much fluid out of the power steering fluid reservoir as possible.

3   Remove the air filter housing (see Chapter 4).

4   Remove the drivebelt (see Chapter 1).

5   Position a drain pan under the power steering pump, then disconnect the pressure line and the supply hose (see illustration). Plug the openings to prevent excessive fluid loss and the entry of contaminants.

21.5 Detach the supply hose (A) and the pressure line fitting (B)

21.6 Use a socket through the pulley to remove the power steering pump mounting bolts

6   Remove the pump mounting bolts. The bolts can be accessed through the holes in the power steering pump pulley (see illustration).

7   Lift the pump from the engine compartment, being careful not to let any power steering fluid drip on the vehicle's paint.

➡**Note: The pulley can be removed from the pump if necessary.**

Special tools for this are available at most auto parts stores.

8   Installation is the reverse of removal. Be sure to tighten all fasteners securely. Fill the power steering reservoir with the recommended fluid (see Chapter 1) and bleed the system following the procedure described in Section 22. Re-check the power steering fluid level.

22 Power steering system - bleeding

1   The power steering system must be bled whenever a line is disconnected. Bubbles can be seen in power steering fluid that has air in it and the fluid will often have a milky appearance. Low fluid level can cause air to mix with the fluid, resulting in a noisy pump as well as foaming of the fluid.

2   Open the hood and check the fluid level in the reservoir, add-ing the specified fluid necessary to bring it up to the proper level (see Chapter 1).

3   Start the engine and slowly turn the steering wheel several times from left-to-right and back again. Do not turn the wheel completely from lock-to-lock. Check the fluid level, topping it up as necessary until it remains steady and no more bubbles are visible.

23 Wheels and tires - general information

▶ **Refer to illustration 23.1**

All models covered by this manual are equipped with radial tires (see illustration). Use of other size or type of tires may affect the ride and handling of the vehicle. Don't mix different types of tires, such as radials and bias belted tires, on the same vehicle - handling may be seriously affected. It's recommended that tires be replaced in pairs on the same axle, but if only one tire is being replaced, be sure it's the same size, structure and tread design as the other tire on the same axle.

Because tire pressure has a substantial effect on handling and wear, the pressure of all tires should be checked at least once a month or before any extended trips are taken (see Chapter 1).

Wheels must be replaced if they are bent, dented, leak air, have elongated bolt holes, are heavily rusted, out of vertical symmetry or if the lug nuts won't stay tight. Wheel repairs that use welding or peening are not recommended.

Tire and wheel balance are important to the overall handling, braking and performance of the vehicle. Unbalanced wheels can adversely affect handling and ride characteristics as well as tire life. Whenever a tire is installed on a wheel, the tire and wheel should be balanced by a shop with the proper equipment and expertise.

23.1 Metric tire size code

24 Wheel alignment - general information

▶ **Refer to illustration 24.1**

➡**Note: Since wheel alignment requires special equipment and techniques, it is beyond the scope of this manual. This Section is intended only to familiarize the reader with the basic terms used and procedures followed during a typical wheel alignment.**

The three basic checks made when aligning a vehicle's front wheels are camber, caster and toe-in (see illustration).

Camber and caster are the angles at which the wheels and suspension are inclined in relation to a vertical centerline. Camber is the angle of the wheel in the lateral, or side-to-side plane, while caster is the tilt between the steering axis and the vertical plane, as viewed from the side. Camber angle affects the amount of tire tread which contacts the road and compensates for changes in suspension geometry as the vehicle travels around curves and over bumps. Caster angle affects the self-centering action of the steering, which governs straight-line stability.

Toe-in is the amount the front wheels are angled in relationship to the center line of the vehicle. For example, in a vehicle with zero toe-in, the distance measured between the front edges of the wheels and the distance measured between the rear edges of the wheels are the same. In other words, the wheels are running parallel with the centerline of the vehicle. Toe-in is adjusted by lengthening or shortening the tie-rods. Incorrect toe-in will cause the tires to wear improperly by allowing them to "scrub" against the road surface.

Proper wheel alignment is essential for safe steering and even tire wear. Symptoms of alignment problems are pulling of the steering to one side or the other and uneven tire wear. If these symptoms are present, check for the following before having the alignment adjusted:

a) *Loose steering gear mounting bolts*
b) *Damaged or worn steering gear mounts*
c) *Worn or damaged wheel bearings*
d) *Bent tie-rods*
e) *Worn balljoints*
f) *Improper tire pressures*
g) *Mixing tires of different construction*

Front wheel alignment should be left to an alignment shop with the proper equipment and experienced personnel.

CAMBER ANGLE (FRONT VIEW)

CASTER ANGLE (SIDE VIEW)

TOE-IN (TOP VIEW)

24.1 Wheel alignment details

A minus B = C (degrees camber)
D = degrees caster
E minus F = toe-in (measured in inches)
G = toe-in (expressed in degrees)

Torque specifications   Ft-lbs (unless otherwise indicated)

➤Note: One foot-pound (ft-lb) of torque is equivalent to 12 inch-pounds (in-lbs) of torque. Torque values below approximately 15 ft-lbs are expressed in inch-pounds, since most foot-pound torque wrenches are not accurate at these smaller values.

Front suspension

Hub nut	184
Shock absorber	
Upper mounting nuts	20
Lower mounting nut/bolt	128
Stabilizer bar	
Link nuts	95
Bracket bolts	44
Tension strut	
Strut-to-subframe nut	130
Balljoint-to-steering knuckle nut	
Step 1	50
Step 2	Tighten an additional 90 degrees
Upper control arm	
Arm-to-shock tower nuts	55
Balljoint-to-steering knuckle nut	
Step 1	35
Step 2	Tighten an additional 90 degrees
Lower control arm	
Arm-to-subframe nut	130
Balljoint-to-steering knuckle nut	
Step 1	50
Step 2	Tighten an additional 90 degrees

Rear suspension

Camber link	
Link-to-subframe nut/bolt	63
Link-to-knuckle nut/bolt	72
Compression link	
Link-to-subframe nut/bolt	63
Link-to-knuckle nut/bolt	60
Hub/bearing assembly mounting bolts	50
Shock absorber	
Upper mounting bolts	38
Lower mounting nut/bolt	53
Spring link	
Link-to-subframe nut/bolt	80
Stabilizer bar	
Link nuts/bolts	45
Bracket bolts	45
Tension link	
Link-to-subframe nut/bolt	63
Link-to-knuckle nut/bolt	72
Toe link	
Link-to-subframe nut/bolt	80
Link-to-knuckle nut/bolt	60

Torque specifications   Ft-lbs (unless otherwise indicated)

➡Note: One foot-pound (ft-lb) of torque is equivalent to 12 inch-pounds (in-lbs) of torque. Torque values below approximately 15 ft-lbs are expressed in inch-pounds, since most foot-pound torque wrenches are not accurate at these smaller values.

Steering

Airbag module-to-steering wheel screws	89 in-lbs
Steering wheel bolt	52
Steering column mounting fasteners	
Upper bolts	22
Pivot bolt	22
Lower nuts	62 in-lbs
Steering shaft pinch bolts	
Steering shaft-to-lower coupling shaft	62 in-lbs
Lower coupler-to-steering gear input shaft	36
Steering gear mounting bolts	70
Tie-rod-to-steering knuckle (ballstud) nut	63
Wheel lug nuts	See Chapter 1

Notes

Section

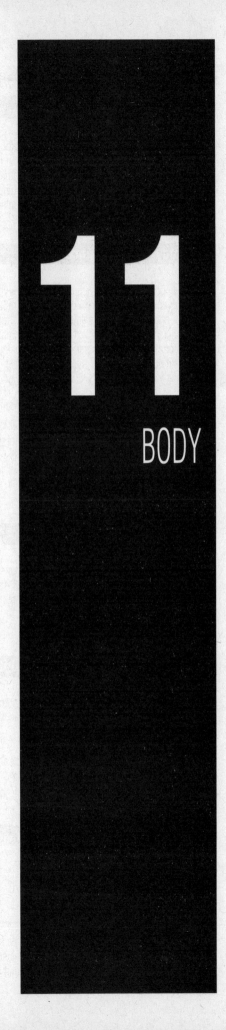

11

BODY

1 General information

These models feature a "unibody" construction, using a floor pan with front and rear frame side rails which support the body components, front and rear suspension systems and other mechanical components. Certain components are particularly vulnerable to accident damage and can be unbolted and repaired or replaced. Among these parts are the body moldings, front fenders, bumpers, hood, doors, trunk lid and all glass.

Only general body maintenance practices and body panel repair procedures within the scope of the do-it-yourselfer are included in this Chapter.

2 Body - maintenance

1   The condition of your vehicle's body is very important, because the resale value depends a great deal on it. It's much more difficult to repair a neglected or damaged body than it is to repair mechanical components. The hidden areas of the body, such as the wheel wells, the frame and the engine compartment, are equally important, although they don't require as frequent attention as the rest of the body.

2   Once a year, or every 12,000 miles, it's a good idea to have the underside of the body steam cleaned. All traces of dirt and oil will be removed and the area can then be inspected carefully for rust, damaged brake lines, frayed electrical wires, damaged cables and other problems. The front suspension components should be greased after completion of this job.

3   At the same time, clean the engine and the engine compartment with a steam cleaner or water soluble degreaser.

4   The wheel wells should be given close attention, since undercoating can peel away and stones and dirt thrown up by the tires can cause the paint to chip and flake, allowing rust to set in. If rust is found, clean down to the bare metal and apply an anti-rust paint.

5   The body should be washed about once a week. Wet the vehicle thoroughly to soften the dirt, then wash it down with a soft sponge and plenty of clean soapy water. If the surplus dirt is not washed off very carefully, it can wear down the paint.

6   Spots of tar or asphalt thrown up from the road should be removed with a cloth soaked in solvent.

7   Once every six months, wax the body and chrome trim. If a chrome cleaner is used to remove rust from any of the vehicle's plated parts, remember that the cleaner also removes part of the chrome, so use it sparingly.

3 Vinyl trim - maintenance

Don't clean vinyl trim with detergents, caustic soap or petroleum-based cleaners. Plain soap and water works just fine, with a soft brush to clean dirt that may be ingrained. Wash the vinyl as frequently as the rest of the vehicle.

After cleaning, application of a high quality rubber and vinyl protectant will help prevent oxidation and cracks. The protectant can also be applied to weatherstripping, vacuum lines and rubber hoses (which often fail as a result of chemical degradation) and to the tires.

4 Upholstery and carpets - maintenance

1   Every three months remove the floor mats and clean the interior of the vehicle (more frequently if necessary). Vacuum the upholstery and carpets to remove loose dirt and dust.

2   Leather upholstery requires special care. Stains should be removed with warm water and a very mild soap solution. Use a clean, damp cloth to remove the soap, then wipe again with a dry cloth. Never use alcohol, gasoline, nail polish remover or thinner to clean leather upholstery.

3   After cleaning, regularly treat leather upholstery with a leather wax. Never use car wax on leather upholstery.

4   In areas where the interior of the vehicle is subject to bright sunlight, cover leather seats with a sheet if the vehicle is to be left out for any length of time.

5 Body repair - minor damage

♦ See photo sequence

REPAIR OF MINOR SCRATCHES

1   If the scratch is superficial and does not penetrate to the metal of the body, repair is very simple. Lightly rub the scratched area with a fine rubbing compound to remove loose paint and built-up wax. Rinse the area with clean water.

2   Apply touch-up paint to the scratch, using a small brush. Continue to apply thin layers of paint until the surface of the paint in the scratch is level with the surrounding paint. Allow the new paint at least two weeks to harden, then blend it into the surrounding paint by rubbing with a very fine rubbing compound. Finally, apply a coat of wax to the scratch area.

3   If the scratch has penetrated the paint and exposed the metal of the body, causing the metal to rust, a different repair technique is required. Remove all loose rust from the bottom of the scratch with a

pocket knife, then apply rust inhibiting paint to prevent the formation of rust in the future. Using a rubber or nylon applicator, coat the scratched area with glaze-type filler. If required, the filler can be mixed with thinner to provide a very thin paste, which is ideal for filling narrow scratches. Before the glaze filler in the scratch hardens, wrap a piece of smooth cotton cloth around the tip of a finger. Dip the cloth in thinner and then quickly wipe it along the surface of the scratch. This will ensure that the surface of the filler is slightly hollow. The scratch can now be painted over as described earlier in this Section.

REPAIR OF DENTS

4   When repairing dents, the first job is to pull the dent out until the affected area is as close as possible to its original shape. There is no point in trying to restore the original shape completely as the metal in the damaged area will have stretched on impact and cannot be restored to its original contours. It is better to bring the level of the dent up to a point which is about 1/8-inch below the level of the surrounding metal. In cases where the dent is very shallow, it is not worth trying to pull it out at all.

5   If the back side of the dent is accessible, it can be hammered out gently from behind using a soft-face hammer. While doing this, hold a block of wood firmly against the opposite side of the metal to absorb the hammer blows and prevent the metal from being stretched.

6   If the dent is in a section of the body which has double layers, or some other factor makes it inaccessible from behind, a different technique is required. Drill several small holes through the metal inside the damaged area, particularly in the deeper sections. Screw long, self-tapping screws into the holes just enough for them to get a good grip in the metal. Now the dent can be pulled out by pulling on the protruding heads of the screws with locking pliers.

7   The next stage of repair is the removal of paint from the damaged area and from an inch or so of the surrounding metal. This is done with a wire brush or sanding disk in a drill motor, although it can be done just as effectively by hand with sandpaper. To complete the preparation for filling, score the surface of the bare metal with a screwdriver or the tang of a file, or drill small holes in the affected area. This will provide a good grip for the filler material. To complete the repair, see the subsection on filling and painting later in this Section.

REPAIR OF RUST HOLES OR GASHES

8   Remove all paint from the affected area and from an inch or so of the surrounding metal using a sanding disk or wire brush mounted in a drill motor. If these are not available, a few sheets of sandpaper will do the job just as effectively.

9   With the paint removed, you will be able to determine the severity of the corrosion and decide whether to replace the whole panel, if possible, or repair the affected area. New body panels are not as expensive as most people think and it is often quicker to install a new panel than to repair large areas of rust.

10   Remove all trim pieces from the affected area except those which will act as a guide to the original shape of the damaged body, such as headlight shells, etc. Using metal snips or a hacksaw blade, remove all loose metal and any other metal that is badly affected by rust. Hammer the edges of the hole in to create a slight depression for the filler material.

11   Wire brush the affected area to remove the powdery rust from the surface of the metal. If the back of the rusted area is accessible, treat it with rust inhibiting paint.

12   Before filling is done, block the hole in some way. This can be

done with sheet metal riveted or screwed into place, or by stuffing the hole with wire mesh.

13   Once the hole is blocked off, the affected area can be filled and painted. See the following subsection on filling and painting.

FILLING AND PAINTING

14   Many types of body fillers are available, but generally speaking, body repair kits which contain filler paste and a tube of resin hardener are best for this type of repair work. A wide, flexible plastic or nylon applicator will be necessary for imparting a smooth and contoured finish to the surface of the filler material. Mix up a small amount of filler on a clean piece of wood or cardboard (use the hardener sparingly). Follow the manufacturer's instructions on the package, otherwise the filler will set incorrectly.

15   Using the applicator, apply the filler paste to the prepared area. Draw the applicator across the surface of the filler to achieve the desired contour and to level the filler surface. As soon as a contour that approximates the original one is achieved, stop working the paste. If you continue, the paste will begin to stick to the applicator. Continue to add thin layers of paste at 20-minute intervals until the level of the filler is just above the surrounding metal.

16   Once the filler has hardened, the excess can be removed with a body file. From then on, progressively finer grades of sandpaper should be used, starting with a 180-grit paper and finishing with 600-grit wet-or-dry paper. Always wrap the sandpaper around a flat rubber or wooden block, otherwise the surface of the filler will not be completely flat. During the sanding of the filler surface, the wet-or-dry paper should be periodically rinsed in water. This will ensure that a very smooth finish is produced in the final stage.

17   At this point, the repair area should be surrounded by a ring of bare metal, which in turn should be encircled by the finely feathered edge of good paint. Rinse the repair area with clean water until all of the dust produced by the sanding operation is gone.

18   Spray the entire area with a light coat of primer. This will reveal any imperfections in the surface of the filler. Repair the imperfections with fresh filler paste or glaze filler and once more smooth the surface with sandpaper. Repeat this spray-and-repair procedure until you are satisfied that the surface of the filler and the feathered edge of the paint are perfect. Rinse the area with clean water and allow it to dry completely.

19   The repair area is now ready for painting. Spray painting must be carried out in a warm, dry, windless and dust free atmosphere. These conditions can be created if you have access to a large indoor work area, but if you are forced to work in the open, you will have to pick the day very carefully. If you are working indoors, dousing the floor in the work area with water will help settle the dust which would otherwise be in the air. If the repair area is confined to one body panel, mask off the surrounding panels. This will help minimize the effects of a slight mismatch in paint color. Trim pieces such as chrome strips, door handles, etc., will also need to be masked off or removed. Use masking tape and several thickness of newspaper for the masking operations.

20   Before spraying, shake the paint can thoroughly, then spray a test area until the spray painting technique is mastered. Cover the repair area with a thick coat of primer. The thickness should be built up using several thin layers of primer rather than one thick one. Using 600-grit wet-or-dry sandpaper, rub down the surface of the primer until it is very smooth. While doing this, the work area should be thoroughly rinsed with water and the wet-or-dry sandpaper periodically rinsed as well. Allow the primer to dry before spraying additional coats.

21   Spray on the top coat, again building up the thickness by using

These photos illustrate a method of repairing simple dents. They are intended to supplement Body repair - minor damage in this Chapter and should not be used as the sole instructions for body repair on these vehicles.

1   If you can't access the backside of the body panel to hammer out the dent, pull it out with a slide-hammer-type dent puller. In the deepest portion of the dent or along the crease line, drill or punch hole(s) at least one inch apart . . .

2   . . . then screw the slide-hammer into the hole and operate it. Tap with a hammer near the edge of the dent to help 'pop' the metal back to its original shape. When you're finished, the dent area should be close to its original contour and about 1/8-inch below the surface of the surrounding metal

3   Using coarse-grit sandpaper, remove the paint down to the bare metal. Hand sanding works fine, but the disc sander shown here makes the job faster. Use finer (about 320-grit) sandpaper to feather-edge the paint at least one inch around the dent area

4   When the paint is removed, touch will probably be more helpful than sight for telling if the metal is straight. Hammer down the high spots or raise the low spots as necessary. Clean the repair area with wax/silicone remover

5   Following label instructions, mix up a batch of plastic filler and hardener. The ratio of filler to hardener is critical, and, if you mix it incorrectly, it will either not cure properly or cure too quickly (you won't have time to file and sand it into shape)

6   Working quickly so the filler doesn't harden, use a plastic applicator to press the body filler firmly into the metal, assuring it bonds completely. Work the filler until it matches the original contour and is slightly above the surrounding metal

7 Let the filler harden until you can just dent it with your fingernail. Use a body file or Surform tool (shown here) to rough-shape the filler

8 Use coarse-grit sandpaper and a sanding board or block to work the filler down until it's smooth and even. Work down to finer grits of sandpaper - always using a board or block - ending up with 360 or 400 grit

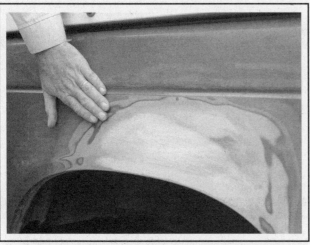

9 You shouldn't be able to feel any ridge at the transition from the filler to the bare metal or from the bare metal to the old paint. As soon as the repair is flat and uniform, remove the dust and mask off the adjacent panels or trim pieces

10 Apply several layers of primer to the area. Don't spray the primer on too heavy, so it sags or runs, and make sure each coat is dry before you spray on the next one. A professional-type spray gun is being used here, but aerosol spray primer is available inexpensively from auto parts stores

11 The primer will help reveal imperfections or scratches. Fill these with glazing compound. Follow the label instructions and sand it with 360 or 400-grit sandpaper until it's smooth. Repeat the glazing, sanding and respraying until the primer reveals a perfectly smooth surface

12 Finish sand the primer with very fine sandpaper (400 or 600-grit) to remove the primer overspray. Clean the area with water and allow it to dry. Use a tack rag to remove any dust, then apply the finish coat. Don't attempt to rub out or wax the repair area until the paint has dried completely (at least two weeks)

several thin layers of paint. Begin spraying in the center of the repair area and then, using a circular motion, work out until the whole repair area and about two inches of the surrounding original paint is covered. Remove all masking material 10 to 15 minutes after spraying on the final coat of paint. Allow the new paint at least two weeks to harden, then use a very fine rubbing compound to blend the edges of the new paint into the existing paint. Finally, apply a coat of wax.

6 Body repair - major damage

1   Major damage must be repaired by an auto body shop specifically equipped to perform these repairs. Most shops have the specialized equipment required to do the job properly.

2   If the damage is extensive, the body must be checked for proper alignment or the vehicle's handling characteristics may be adversely affected and other components may wear at an accelerated rate.

3   Due to the fact that all of the major body components (hood, fenders, etc.) are separate and replaceable units, any seriously damaged components should be replaced rather than repaired. Sometimes the components can be found in a wrecking yard that specializes in used vehicle components, often at considerable savings over the cost of new parts.

7 Hinges and locks - maintenance

Once every 3000 miles, or every three months, the hinges and latch assemblies on the doors, hood and trunk should be given a few drops of light oil or lock lubricant. The door latch strikers should also be lubricated with a thin coat of grease to reduce wear and ensure free movement. Lubricate the door and trunk locks with spray-on graphite lubricant.

8 Windshield and fixed glass - replacement

Replacement of the windshield and fixed glass requires the use of special fast-setting adhesive/caulk materials and some specialized tools. It is recommended that these operations be left to a dealer or a shop specializing in glass work.

9 Hood - removal, installation and adjustment

➡Note: The hood is heavy and somewhat awkward to remove and install - at least two people should perform this procedure.

REMOVAL AND INSTALLATION

▶ Refer to illustrations 9.2 and 9.4

1   Use blankets or pads to cover the cowl area of the body and fenders. This will protect the body and paint as the hood is lifted off.

2   Make marks or scribe a line around the hood hinge to ensure proper alignment during installation (see illustration).

3   Disconnect any cables or wires that will interfere with removal.

4   Have an assistant support one side of the hood while you support the other. Simultaneously remove the hinge-to-hood nuts (see illustration).

5   Lift off the hood.

6   Installation is the reverse of removal.

9.2 Before removing the hood, draw a mark around the hinge plate

9.4 Support the hood with your shoulder while removing the hood bolts

ADJUSTMENT

▶ **Refer to illustrations 9.10 and 9.11**

7   Fore-and-aft and side-to-side adjustment of the hood is done by moving the hinge plate slot after loosening the bolts or nuts.

8   Mark around the each hinge plate so you can determine the amount of movement (see illustration 9.2).

9   Loosen the bolts or nuts and move the hood into correct alignment. Move it only a little at a time. Tighten the hinge bolts and carefully lower the hood to check the position.

10 If necessary after installation, the hood latch can be adjusted up-and-down as well as from side-to-side on the radiator support so the hood closes securely and flush with the fenders. To make the adjustment, scribe a line or mark around the hood latch mounting bolts to provide a reference point, then loosen them and reposition the latch, as necessary (see illustration). Following adjustment, retighten the mounting bolts.

11 Finally, adjust the hood bumpers on the radiator support so the hood, when closed, is flush with the fenders (see illustration).

12 The hood latch assembly, as well as the hinges, should be periodically lubricated with white, lithium-base grease to prevent binding and wear.

9.10 Make a mark around the latch to use as a reference point. To adjust the hood latch, loosen the retaining bolts, move the latch and retighten bolts, then close the hood to check the fit

9.11 Adjust the hood closing height by turning the hood bumpers in or out

10 Hood latch and release cable - removal and installation

LATCH

1   Scribe a line around the latch to aid alignment when reinstalling the latch assembly.

2   Remove the latch retaining bolts securing the latch to the radiator support (see illustration 9.10) and remove the latch.

3   Disconnect the hood release cable by disengaging the cable from the back of the latch assembly.

4   Installation is the reverse of the removal procedure.

➡**Note: Adjust the latch so the hood engages securely when closed and the hood bumpers are slightly compressed.**

CABLE

5   Remove the hood latch as described earlier in this Section, then detach the cable from the latch.

6   Remove the left-side headlight housing (see Chapter 12).

7   Attach a length of wire to the end of the cable (in the engine compartment). This will be used to pull the new cable back into the engine compartment.

8   Working in the engine compartment, detach the cable from all of its retaining clips. It may be necessary to cut some of the clips to free the cable.

9   Working under the instrument panel, remove the screws and detach the hood release handle. Dislodge the grommet and pull the cable through the firewall and into the cab.

10   Detach the wire from the old cable, then attach it to the end of the new cable.

➡**Note: Make sure the new cable is equipped with a grommet.**

11   Pull the new cable through the firewall and into the engine compartment. Seat the grommet in the firewall.

12   The remainder of installation is the reverse of removal.

11   Radiator grille - removal and installation

▶ **Refer to illustration 11.2**

1   Remove the bumper cover (see Section 12).

2   Remove the fasteners securing the grille to the bumper cover (see illustration).

3   Installation is the reverse of removal.

11.2   Radiator grille mounting fasteners

12   Bumper covers - removal and installation

1   Bumpers on all models are composed of a plastic fascia, or bumper cover, fascia support and a structural beam.

FRONT BUMPER COVER

▶ **Refer to illustrations 12.3, 12.4, 12.5 and 12.6**

2   Raise the vehicle and support it securely on jackstands.

3   Working in the front wheelwell, remove the fasteners securing the ends of the bumper to the inner fender splash shield (see illustration).

4   Remove the engine splash shield (see illustration).

5   Working in the front wheelwell, remove the fasteners securing the bumper cover to the fender (see illustration).

6   Remove the bumper cover upper mounting fasteners and remove the bumper cover (see illustration).

7   Disconnect the fog lamps, if equipped, then carefully remove the bumper cover from the vehicle.

8   Installation is the reverse of removal.

12.3   Remove the fasteners securing the ends of the bumper to the inner fender splash shield

12.4   Remove the fasteners securing the engine splash shield

12.5 Remove the fasteners securing the bumper cover to the fender

12.6 Bumper cover upper mounting fasteners

REAR BUMPER COVER

▶ **Refer to illustrations 12.10, 12.11a and 12.11b**

9   Raise the vehicle and support it securely on jackstands,

10 Working in the rear wheelwell, remove the fasteners securing the bumper cover to the rear quarter panel (see illustration).

11 Remove the remaining bumper cover mounting fasteners and remove the bumper cover (see illustrations).

12 Installation is the reverse of removal.

12.10 Remove the fasteners securing the bumper cover to the rear quarter panel

12.11a Bumper cover lower mounting fasteners

12.11b Bumper cover upper mounting fasteners

13 Front fender - removal and installation

▶ **Refer to illustrations 13.2, 13.5a, 13.5b and 13.5c**

1   Loosen the wheel lug nuts, then raise the vehicle and support it securely on jackstands and. Remove the front wheel.

2   Remove the fasteners retaining the fender inner splash shield (see illustration).

3   Remove the front bumper cover (see Section 12).

4   Remove the headlight housings (see Chapter 12).

5   Remove the fender mounting bolts (see illustrations).

6   Detach the fender. It's a good idea to have an assistant support the fender while it's being moved away from the vehicle to prevent damage to the surrounding body panels.

7   Installation is the reverse of removal.

13.2 Remove the fender inner splash shield mounting fasteners

13.5a Fender-to-door pillar fasteners

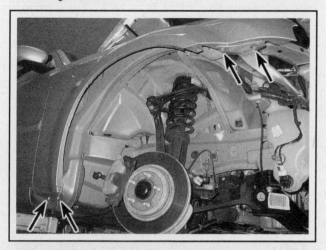

13.5b Fender lower mounting bolts

13.5c Fender upper mounting bolts

14 Door trim panels - removal and installation

REMOVAL

▶ **Refer to illustrations 14.1a, 14.1b, 14.2 and 14.3**

1 Remove all door trim panel retaining fasteners (see illustrations).
2 Disconnect the handle link rod (see illustration), disconnect any wiring harness connectors then remove the trim panel from the vehicle.
3 For access to the inner door, carefully peel back the plastic watershield (see illustration).

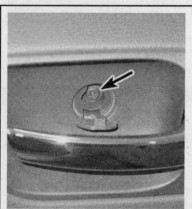

14.1a Remove the handle retaining screw

14.1b Door panel retaining fasteners

14.2 Rotate the plastic retaining clip off the handle link rod and detach the rod from the handle

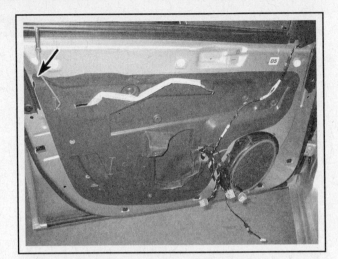

14.3 From the corner, carefully peel back the plastic watershield

INSTALLATION

4   Connect the wiring harness connectors and place the panel in position on the door. Connect the handle link rod.

5   The remainder of installation is the reverse of removal.

15 Door - removal, installation and adjustment

▶ **Refer to illustrations 15.1 and 15.5**

1   Open the door and disconnect the door wire harness electrical connector at the A-pillar (see illustration).

2   Place a jack under the door or have an assistant on hand to support it when the hinge fasteners are removed.

➡**Note: If a jack is used, place a few rags between it and the door to protect the door's painted surfaces.**

3   Scribe around the hinges with a marking pen, remove the fasteners and carefully lift off the door.

4   Installation is the reverse of removal, making sure to align the hinge with the marks made during removal before tightening the fasteners.

5   Following installation of the door, check the alignment and adjust the hinges, if necessary. Adjust the door lock striker, centering it in the door latch (see illustration).

6   Rear doors are removed and installed as described above for front doors, except that the door is attached to the body "B" pillar.

15.1 Pull out the boot and disconnect the door wire harness electrical connector at the A-pillar

15.5 The latch striker on the door jamb can be adjusted slightly up/down or in/out

16 Door latch, lock cylinder and handle - removal and installation

LATCH

▶ **Refer to illustrations 16.3 and 16.5**

1 Raise the window completely and remove the door trim panel and watershield (see Section 14).

2 Remove the door speaker (see Chapter 12).

3 Remove the fasteners at the rear glass run channel and move the channel away from the latch (see illustration). This provides a little extra working room in the latch area inside the door.

4 Rotate the plastic retaining clips off the rods, then detach the latch links. Disconnect the electrical connector.

5 Remove the three mounting screws (it may be necessary to use an impact-type screwdriver to loosen them), then remove the latch from the door (see illustration).

6 Place the latch in position and install the screws. Tighten the screws securely.

7 Connect the link rods and electrical connector to the latch.

8 The remainder of installation is the reverse of removal.

LOCK CYLINDER

9 Remove the outside door handle (see Step 12).

10 Withdraw the lock cylinder from the door handle.

11 Installation is the reverse of removal.

OUTSIDE HANDLE

▶ **Refer to illustration 16.15**

12 Remove the door trim panel (see Section 14).

13 Remove the door speaker (see Chapter 12).

14 Remove the fasteners at the rear glass run channel and move the channel away from the latch (see illustration 16.3). This provides a little extra working room in the latch area inside the door.

15 Disconnect the link rods from the outside handle, remove the mounting fasteners and carefully detach the handle from the door (see illustration).

16 Place the handle in position, attach the link and install the nuts. Tighten the fasteners securely.

17 The remainder of installation is the reverse of removal.

16.3 Remove the fasteners securing the pull cup bracket

16.5 Remove the latch mounting screws

16.15 Door handle mounting fasteners

17 Door window glass - removal and installation

FRONT

▶ **Refer to illustration 17.4**

1   Remove the door trim panel and watershield (see Section 14).
2   Remove the door speaker (see Chapter 12).
3   Pry the inner weather seal out of the door glass opening.
4   Lower the window to access the glass retaining fasteners, then remove the fasteners (see illustration).
5   Remove the window by tilting it forward, then lifting it out of the door.
6   To install, lower the glass into the door, slide it into position and install the nuts.
7   The remainder of installation is the reverse of removal.

REAR

8   The rear doors are serviced similarly to the front doors.

17.4 Align the window so that the fasteners can be removed from the glass track

18 Door window glass regulator - removal and installation

▶ **Refer to illustration 18.3**

1   Remove the door trim panel and watershield (see Section 14).
2   Unbolt the window glass from the regulator (see Section 17). Push the glass all the way up and tape it to the door frame.
3   Remove the window regulator-to-door and track mounting fasteners (see illustration).
4   Unplug the electrical connector.
5   Remove the regulator from the door.
6   Installation is the reverse of removal.

18.3 Door window regulator mounting bolt locations

19 Mirrors - removal and installation

OUTSIDE MIRRORS

▶ **Refer to illustration 19.2**

1   Remove the door trim panel (see Section 14).
2   Pull back the window trim molding, on power mirrors, unplug the electrical connector, then remove the fasteners and detach the mirror from the door (see illustration).
3   Installation is the reverse of removal.

INSIDE MIRROR

4   Remove the setscrew, then slide the mirror up off the support base on the windshield. On models with optional automatic day/night mirror, disconnect the electrical connector.

19.2 Disconnect the electrical connector (A), then remove the mirror mounting fasteners (B)

5   Installation is the reverse of removal.
6   If the support base for the mirror has come off the windshield, it can be reattached with a special mirror adhesive kit available at auto parts stores. Clean the glass and support base thoroughly and follow the directions on the adhesive package.

---

20 Liftgate (Magnum models) - removal and installation

1   Open the liftgate and cover the upper body area around the opening with pads or cloths to protect the painted surfaces when the liftgate is removed.
2   Using a trim stick, remove the upper headliner trim panel, then disconnect the body-to-liftgate electrical connectors.
3   Make alignment marks around the liftgate hinge flanges.
4   While an assistant supports the liftgate, detach the support struts (see Section 21).

5   Remove the hinge bolts and detach the liftgate from the vehicle.
6   Installation is the reverse of removal.
7   After installation, close the liftgate and make sure it's in proper alignment with the surrounding body panels.
8   If the liftgate needs to be adjusted, loosen the hinge bolts slightly, gently close the liftgate and verify that it's centered (the striker should center it). Then carefully open the liftgate and retighten the hinge bolts.

---

21 Liftgate panels, outside handle, latch and support struts (Magnum models) - removal and installation

INTERIOR TRIM PANELS

1   Remove the fasteners securing the lower trim panel inside the pull handle.
2   Using a trim stick, carefully pry around the lower trim panel to release the clips securing the trim panel.
3   With the lower panel pulled away from the liftgate, disconnect the electrical connectors at the courtesy lights.
4   Remove the two fasteners securing the upper trim panel.
5   Using a trim stick, carefully pry around the upper trim panel to release the clips securing the trim panel.
6   Remove the upper trim panel by pulling it outward carefully to free it from the spring clips.
7   Installation is the reverse of the removal procedure.

OUTSIDE HANDLE

8   Remove the interior lower liftgate panel.

9   Working through the liftgate access hole, disconnect the handle electrical connector, then remove the handle mounting fasteners.
10 Installation is the reverse of the removal procedure.

LATCH

11 Remove the interior lower liftgate panel.
12 Working through the liftgate access hole, disconnect the latch electrical connector, then remove the latch mounting fasteners.
13 Installation is the reverse of the removal procedure.

SUPPORT STRUTS

14 Open the liftgate and prop it securely in the full open position.
15 Using a small screwdriver, detach the retaining clip at the ends of the support strut. Then pry or pull sharply to detach it from the vehicle.
16 Installation is the reverse of the removal procedure.

---

22 Trunk lid - removal, installation and adjustment

➡**Note: The trunk lid is heavy and somewhat awkward to remove and install - at least two people should perform this procedure.**

REMOVAL AND INSTALLATION

◆ **Refer to illustrations 22.2 and 22.3**

1   Open the trunk lid and cover the edges of the trunk compartment with pads or cloths to protect the painted surfaces when the lid is removed.
2   Disconnect any cables or wire harness connectors attached to the trunk lid that would interfere with removal. Remove the trunk lid support struts (see illustration).

3   Make alignment marks around the hinge mounting bolts with a marking pen, then while an assistant supports the trunk lid, remove the lid-to-hinge bolts (see illustration) on both sides of the trunk and lift it off.
4   Installation is the reverse of removal.
➡**Note: When reinstalling the trunk lid, align the lid-to-hinge bolts with the marks made during removal.**

ADJUSTMENT

5   Fore-and-aft and side-to-side adjustment of the trunk lid is accomplished by moving the lid in relation to the hinge after loosening the bolts or nuts.

22.2 Use a small screwdriver to detach the retaining clip at the top end of the support strut

22.3 Before removing the trunk lid, draw a mark around the hinge plate

6   Scribe a line around the entire hinge plate as described earlier in this Section so you can determine the amount of movement.

7   Loosen the bolts or nuts and move the trunk lid into correct alignment. Move it only a little at a time. Tighten the hinge bolts or nuts and carefully lower the trunk lid to check the alignment.

8   If necessary after installation, the entire trunk lid striker assembly can be adjusted up and down as well as from side to side on the trunk

lid so the lid closes securely and is flush with the rear quarter panels. To do this, scribe a line around the trunk lid striker assembly to provide a reference point. Then loosen the bolts and reposition the striker as necessary. Following adjustment, retighten the mounting bolts.

9   The trunk lid latch assembly, as well as the hinges, should be periodically lubricated with white lithium-base grease to prevent sticking and wear.

23 Trunk lid latch - removal and installation

TRUNK LID LATCH

▶ **Refer to illustrations 23.1 and 23.3**

1   Open the trunk and remove the latch trim cover (see illustration).

2   Scribe a line around the trunk lid latch assembly for a reference point to aid the installation procedure.

3   Disconnect the electrical connector (see illustration).

4   Detach the mounting fasteners and remove the latch.

5   Installation is the reverse of removal.

23.1 Remove the latch trim cover fasteners

23.3 Remove the latch electrical connector

24 Cowl cover - removal and installation

▶ Refer to illustrations 24.2 and 24.3

1 Remove the windshield wiper arms (see Chapter 12).
2 Remove the fasteners securing the right side of the cowl cover, then remove the right side cover (see illustration).

3 Remove the fasteners securing the left side of the cowl cover, then remove the cover (see illustration).
4 Disconnect the windshield washer hose.
5 Installation is the reverse of removal.

24.2 Remove the fasteners securing the right side of the cowl cover

24.3 Remove the fasteners from the left side of the cowl cover

25 Center console - removal and installation

▶ Refer to illustrations 25.2, 25.3, 25.4a and 25.4b

❉❉ WARNING:

The models covered by this manual are equipped with Supplemental Restraint Systems (SRS), more commonly known as airbags. Always disable the airbag system before working in the vicinity of any airbag system components to avoid the possibility of accidental deployment of the airbags, which could cause personal injury (see Chapter 12).

1 Place the shift lever in the Neutral position.
2 Remove the mat at the front of the console, then remove the fasteners securing the shifter trim bezel (see illustration). Remove the shifter trim bezel.
3 Open the lid to the console bin and remove the mat, then remove the bolts securing the console to the floorpan (see illustration).
4 Remove the fasteners at the front of the console (see illustrations).
5 Unplug any electrical connectors and remove the console from the vehicle.
6 Installation is the reverse of removal.

25.2 After removing the mat at the front of the console, remove the two console fasteners

25.3 Remove the bolts securing the console to the floorpan

25.4a Using a trim removal tool, carefully pry off the ashtray trim panel

25.4b Remove the two fasteners at the front of the center console

26 Dashboard trim panels - removal and installation

INSTRUMENT CLUSTER BEZEL

▶ **Refer to illustrations 26.1 and 26.2**

1   Using a trim removal tool or a flat-blade screwdriver with the tip taped, carefully remove the ignition switch bezel (see illustration).

2   Use a trim removal tool or a flat-blade screwdriver with the tip taped to pry around the complete edge of the instrument cluster bezel (see illustration).

3   Pull the panel out far enough to disconnect any electrical connectors.

4   Installation is the reverse of removal.

26.1 Carefully remove the ignition switch bezel

LOWER INSTRUMENT PANEL INSULATOR

▶ **Refer to illustration 26.5**

5   Remove the fasteners securing the panel insulator (see illustration).

26.2 Pry around the complete edge of the instrument cluster bezel to release the clips

26.5 Remove the fasteners securing the panel insulator

26.8 Remove the fasteners securing the driver's knee bolster

26.11 Pry around the edges of the panel to release it from the clips

6   Remove the lower instrument panel insulator.
7   Installation is the reverse of removal.

KNEE BOLSTER

♦ Refer to illustration 26.8

8   Remove the fasteners securing the driver's knee bolster, then grasp the bolster securely and pull out sharply to detach the retaining clips (see illustration).
9   Detach the parking brake release cable and disconnect any electrical connectors, then remove the bolster from the vehicle.
10 Installation is the reverse of removal.

INSTRUMENT PANEL CENTER BEZEL

♦ Refer to illustration 26.11

11 Use a dull, flat-bladed tool to pry around the edges of the panel to release it from the clips (see illustration).
12 Disconnect any electrical connectors, then remove the bezel from the vehicle.
13 Installation is the reverse of removal.

GLOVE BOX

♦ Refer to illustrations 26.15 and 26.16

14 Open the glove box door.
15 Squeeze the two sides of the glove compartment bin together and pull the door down until the bumpers on the bin have cleared the stops (see illustration).
16 Detach the glove box support strap (see illustration).
17 Pull the glove box door away from the instrument panel.
18 Installation is the reverse of removal.

26.15 Push on the sides of the glove box until the stops clear the instrument panel

26.16 Detach the glove box support strap

27 Seats - removal and installation

✱✱ WARNING:

These models are equipped with seat belt pre-tensioners, which are pyrotechnic (explosive) devices that tighten the seat belts during an impact of sufficient force to deploy the airbags. Always disable the airbag system before working in the vicinity of any restraint system component to avoid the possibility of accidental deployment of the airbag(s) and seat belt pre-tensioners, which could cause personal injury (see Chapter 12).

FRONT SEAT

▸ **Refer to illustrations 27.3a and 27.3b**

1   Disconnect the cable from the negative battery terminal (see Chapter 5, Section 1).
2   Remove the plastic cover, then remove the seat belt anchor bolt.

3   Remove the seat track-to-floor bolts and remove the front seat assembly (see illustrations).

➡**Note: This is a job for two people.**

Disconnect any electrical connectors.
4   Installation is the reverse of removal.

REAR SEAT

▸ **Refer to illustrations 27.5 and 27.6**

5   Pull up on the front of the seat cushion, to release the retainer loops (see illustration). Remove the cushion.
6   Fold the left and right seat backs forward, then remove the fasteners securing each unit (see illustration).
7   Remove the seat assembly.
8   Installation is the reverse of removal.

27.3a Remove the rear bolts from the front seat . . .

27.3b . . . then remove the front bolts

27.5 Pull up on the front of the seat cushion, to release the retainer loops

27.6 Remove the fasteners securing the seat backs

28 Rear package tray - removal and installation

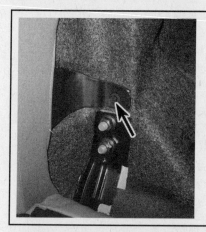

28.3a Remove the fastener securing the sides of the seat back

▶ **Refer to illustrations 28.3a, 28.3b, 28.3c, 28.4a and 28.4b**

1 Remove the rear seat cushion (see Section 27).
2 Unlock and flip forward the seat backs.
3 Remove the C-pillar trim panels (see illustrations).
4 Remove the fastener securing the package tray, then remove the tray from the vehicle (see illustration).
5 Installation is the reverse of removal.

28.3c Remove the fasteners securing the lower portion of the C-pillar trim

28.3b Remove the upper trim panel by pulling it outward carefully to free it from the spring clips

28.4a Remove the fastener at the center portion of the package tray . . .

28.4b . . . then remove the package tray

29 Rear spoiler - removal and installation

1 Remove the liftgate upper trim panel (see Section 21).
2 Disconnect the rear washer fluid hose.
3 Disconnect any electrical connectors, then remove the spoiler

mounting fasteners.
4 Remove the spoiler from the liftgate.
5 Installation is the reverse of removal.

Section

12

CHASSIS
ELECTRICAL
SYSTEM

1 General information

The electrical system is a 12-volt, negative ground type. A lead/acid-type battery that is charged by the alternator supplies power for the lights and all electrical accessories.

This Chapter covers repair and service procedures for the various electrical components not associated with the engine. Information on the battery, alternator, distributor and starter motor can be found in Chapter 5.

❈❈ WARNING:

When working on the electrical system, disconnect the cable from the negative battery terminal to prevent electrical shorts and/or fires (see Chapter 5, Section 1).

2 Electrical troubleshooting - general information

◆ **Refer to illustrations 2.5a, 2.5b, 2.6, 2.9 and 2.15**

A typical electrical circuit consists of an electrical component, any switches, relays, motors, fuses, fusible links or circuit breakers related to that component and the wiring and connectors that link the component to both the battery and the chassis. To help you pinpoint an electrical circuit problem, wiring diagrams are included at the end of this Chapter.

Before tackling any troublesome electrical circuit, first study the appropriate wiring diagrams to get a complete understanding of what makes up that individual circuit. You can often narrow down trouble spots, for instance, by noting whether other components related to the circuit are operating correctly. If several components or circuits fail at one time, chances are that the problem is in a fuse or ground connection, because several circuits are often routed through the same fuse and ground connections.

Electrical problems usually stem from simple causes, such as loose or corroded connections, a blown fuse, a melted fusible link or a failed relay. Visually inspect the condition of all fuses, wires and connections in a problem circuit before troubleshooting the circuit.

If test equipment and instruments are going to be utilized, use the diagrams to plan ahead of time where you will make the necessary connections in order to accurately pinpoint the trouble spot.

For electrical troubleshooting you'll need a circuit tester or voltmeter, a continuity tester, which includes a bulb, battery and set of test

2.5a The most useful tool for electrical troubleshooting is a digital multimeter that can check volts, amps, and test continuity

leads, and a jumper wire, preferably with a circuit breaker incorporated, which can be used to bypass electrical components (see illustrations). Before attempting to locate a problem with test instruments, use the wiring diagram(s) to decide where to make the connections.

2.5b A simple test light is a very handy tool for testing voltage

2.6 In use, a basic test light's lead is clipped to a known good ground, then the pointed probe can test connectors, wires or electrical sockets - if the bulb lights, battery voltage is present at the test point

2.9 With a multimeter set to the ohm scale, resistance can be checked across two terminals - when checking for continuity, a low reading indicates continuity, a very high or infinite reading indicates lack of continuity

2.15 To backprobe a connector, insert a small, sharp probe (such as a straight-pin) into the back of the connector alongside the desired wire until it contacts the metal terminal inside; connect your meter leads to the probes - this allows you to test a functioning circuit

VOLTAGE CHECKS

Voltage checks should be performed if a circuit is not functioning properly. Connect one lead of a circuit tester to either the negative battery terminal or a known good ground. Connect the other lead to a connector in the circuit being tested, preferably nearest to the battery or fuse (see illustration). If the bulb of the tester lights, voltage is present, which means that the part of the circuit between the connector and the battery is problem free. Continue checking the rest of the circuit in the same fashion. When you reach a point at which no voltage is present, the problem lies between that point and the last test point with voltage. Most of the time the problem can be traced to a loose connection.

➡Note: Keep in mind that some circuits receive voltage only when the ignition key is in the ACC or RUN position.

FINDING A SHORT

One method of finding shorts in a circuit is to remove the fuse and connect a test light or voltmeter to the fuse terminals. There should be no voltage present in the circuit when it is turned off. Move the wiring harness from side-to-side while watching the test light. If the bulb goes on, there is a short to ground somewhere in that area, probably where the insulation has rubbed through. The same test can be performed on each component in the circuit, even a switch.

GROUND CHECK

Perform a ground test to check whether a component is properly grounded. Disconnect the battery and connect one lead of a continuity tester or multimeter (set to the ohm scale), to a known good ground. Connect the other lead to the wire or ground connection being tested. If the resistance is low (less than 5 ohms), the ground is good. If the bulb on a self-powered test light does not go on, the ground is not good.

CONTINUITY CHECK

A continuity check determines whether there are any breaks in a circuit, i.e. whether it's conducting electricity correctly. With the circuit off (no power in the circuit), use a self-powered continuity tester or multimeter to check the circuit. Connect the test leads to both ends of the circuit (or to the "power" end and a good ground). If the test light comes on, the circuit is conducting current correctly (see illustration). If the resistance is low (less than 5 ohms), there is continuity; if the reading is 10,000 ohms or higher, there is a break somewhere in the circuit. The same procedure can be used to test a switch, by connecting the continuity tester to the switch terminals. With the switch turned on, the test light should come on (or low resistance should be indicated on a meter).

FINDING AN OPEN CIRCUIT

When diagnosing for possible open circuits, it is often difficult to locate them by sight because the connectors hide oxidation or terminal misalignment. Merely wiggling a connector on a sensor or in the wiring harness may correct the open circuit condition. Remember this when an open circuit is indicated when troubleshooting a circuit. Intermittent problems may also be caused by oxidized or loose connections.

Electrical troubleshooting is simple if you keep in mind that all electrical circuits are basically electricity running from the battery, through the wires, switches, relays, fuses and fusible links to each electrical component (light bulb, motor, etc.) and to ground, from which it is passed back to the battery. Any electrical problem is an interruption in the flow of electricity to and from the battery.

CONNECTORS

Most electrical connections on these vehicles are made with multi-wire plastic connectors. The mating halves of many connectors are secured with locking clips molded into the plastic connector shells. The mating halves of large connectors, such as some of those under the instrument panel, are held together by a bolt through the center of the connector.

To separate a connector with locking clips, use a small screwdriver to pry the clips apart carefully, then separate the connector halves. Pull only on the shell, never pull on the wiring harness as you may damage the individual wires and terminals inside the connectors. Look at the connector closely before trying to separate the halves. Often the locking clips are engaged in a way that is not immediately clear. Additionally, many connectors have more than one set of clips.

Each pair of connector terminals has a male half and a female half. When you look at the end view of a connector in a diagram, be sure to understand whether the view shows the harness side or the component side of the connector. Connector halves are mirror images of each other, and a terminal shown on the right side end-view of one half will be on the left side end view of the other half.

It is often necessary to take circuit voltage measurements with a connector connected. Whenever possible, carefully insert a small straight pin (not your meter probe) into the rear of the connector shell to contact the terminal inside, then clip your meter lead to the pin. This kind of connection is called "backprobing" (see illustration). When inserting a test probe into a male terminal, be careful not to distort the terminal opening. Doing so can lead to a poor connection and corrosion at that terminal later. Using the small straight pin instead of a meter probe results in less chance of deforming the terminal connector.

3 Fuses and fusible links - general information

FUSES

♦ **Refer to illustrations 3.1a, 3.1b and 3.3**

The electrical circuits of the vehicle are protected by a combination of fuses and relays. The engine compartment fuse and relay box is located at the right front corner of the engine compartment (see illustrations). You can access either fuse and relay box by simply opening the cover.

At a dealer parts department you might hear the phrase "Integrated Power Module" or "Power Distribution Center." These are the Chrysler/Dodge terms for the fuse and relay boxes. In this manual, we use the simpler term "fuse and relay box." However, you should know the location of each specific fuse and relay box by its factory name so that you can communicate with a Chrysler or Dodge parts department if you have to buy fuses or relays. The Integrated Power Module is located at the right front corner of the engine compartment; it's also referred to as the "Front Power Distribution Center." The Rear Power Distribution Center is located in the trunk, under the spare tire access panel.

Each fuse is designed to protect a specific circuit, and the various circuits are identified (in a highly abbreviated way) on the fuse panel itself. Different sizes of fuses are employed. There are "mini" and "maxi" sizes, with the larger located in the fuse and relay box. You'll need to use electronics needle-noise pliers or a small plastic fuse-puller tool to remove most fuses. There should be one of these

3.1a The engine compartment fuse and relay box is located at the right front corner of the engine compartment. To open the lid, pull out the latch and swing up the lid

fuse-puller tools in the fuse and relay box. If an electrical component fails, always check the fuse first. The best way to check the fuses is with a test light. Check for power at the exposed terminal tips of each fuse. If power is present at one side of the fuse but not the other, the fuse is

3.1b The rear fuse and relay box is located in the trunk, beneath the spare tire access panel. To open the lid, pull back the latch on the left end of the lid and swing the lid up. Arrows indicate circuit breaker locations

Bad   **Good**

3.3 When a fuse blows, the element between the terminals melts

blown. A blown fuse can also be identified by visually inspecting it (see illustration).

Be sure to replace blown fuses with the correct type. Fuses of different ratings are physically interchangeable, but only fuses of the proper rating should be used. Replacing a fuse with one of a higher or lower value than specified is not recommended. Each electrical circuit needs a specific amount of protection. The amperage rating of each fuse is molded into the fuse body.

If the replacement fuse immediately fails, don't replace it again until the cause of the problem is isolated and corrected. In most cases, the cause will be a short circuit in the wiring caused by a broken or deteriorated wire.

FUSIBLE LINKS

The wiring between the alternator and the starter is protected by two fusible links. These links functions like a fuse, in that they melt when the circuit is overloaded, but they resemble a large-gauge wire. To replace a fusible link, first disconnect the negative cable from the battery. Disconnect the burned-out link and replace it with a new one (available from your dealer or auto parts store). Always determine the cause for the overload that melted the fusible link before installing a new one.

4   Circuit breakers - general information

Circuit breakers protect certain heavy-load circuits. Depending on the vehicle's accessories, there will be one to three circuit breakers located in the rear fuse and relay box (see illustration 3.1b).

Because the circuit breakers reset automatically, an electrical overload in a circuit-breaker-protected system will cause the circuit to fail momentarily, then come back on. If the circuit does not come back on, check it immediately.

For a basic check, pull the circuit breaker up out of its socket on the fuse panel, but just far enough to probe with a voltmeter. The breaker should still contact the sockets.

With the voltmeter negative lead on a good chassis ground, touch each end prong of the circuit breaker with the positive meter probe. There should be battery voltage at each end. If there is battery voltage only at one end, the circuit breaker must be replaced.

5   Relays - general information and testing

1   Many electrical accessories in the vehicle utilize relays to transmit current to the component. If the relay is defective, the component won't operate properly.

2   Most relays are located in the engine compartment fuse and relay box (see illustration 3.1a or 3.1b).

3   Some relays are located in other parts of the vehicle or in various wiring harnesses underneath the instrument panel.

4   If a faulty relay is suspected, it can be removed and tested using the procedure below or by a dealer service department or a repair shop. Defective relays must be replaced as a unit.

TESTING

▸ **Refer to illustrations 5.5a and 5.5b**

5   Most of the relays used in these vehicles are of a type often called "ISO" relays, which refers to the International Standards Organization. The terminals of ISO relays are numbered to indicate their usual circuit connections and functions. There are two basic layouts of terminals on the relays used in the vehicles covered by this manual (see illustrations).

6   Refer to the wiring diagram for the circuit to determine the proper connections for the relay you're testing. If you can't determine the correct connection from the wiring diagrams, however, you may be able to

5.5a Typical ISO relay designs, terminal numbering and circuit connections

5.5b Most relays are marked on the outside to easily identify the control circuit and power circuits - this one is of the four-terminal type

determine the test connections from the information that follows.

7 Two of the terminals are the relay control circuit and connect to the relay coil. The other relay terminals are the power circuit. When the relay is energized, the coil creates a magnetic field that closes the larger contacts of the power circuit to provide power to the circuit loads.

8 Terminals 85 and 86 are normally the control circuit. If the relay contains a diode, terminal 86 must be connected to battery positive (B+) voltage and terminal 85 to ground. If the relay contains a resistor, terminals 85 and 86 can be connected in either direction with respect to B+ and ground.

9 Terminal 30 is normally connected to the battery voltage (B+) source for the circuit loads. Terminal 87 is connected to the ground side of the circuit, either directly or through a load. If the relay has several alternate terminals for load or ground connections, they usually are numbered 87A, 87B, 87C, and so on.

10 Use an ohmmeter to check continuity through the relay control coil.

   a) Connect the meter according to the polarity shown in illustration 5.5a for one check; then reverse the ohmmeter leads and check continuity in the other direction.

   b) If the relay contains a resistor, resistance will be indicated on the meter, and should be the same value with the ohmmeter in either direction.

   c) If the relay contains a diode, resistance should be higher with the ohmmeter in the forward polarity direction than with the meter leads reversed.

   d) If the ohmmeter shows infinite resistance in both directions, replace the relay.

11 Remove the relay from the vehicle and use the ohmmeter to check for continuity between the relay power circuit terminals. There should be no continuity between terminal 30 and 87 with the relay de-energized.

12 Connect a fused jumper wire to terminal 86 and the positive battery terminal. Connect another jumper wire between terminal 85 and ground. When the connections are made, the relay should click.

13 With the jumper wires connected, check for continuity between the power circuit terminals. Now there should be continuity between terminals 30 and 87.

14 If the relay fails any of the above tests, replace it.

6 Front Control Module (FCM) - replacement

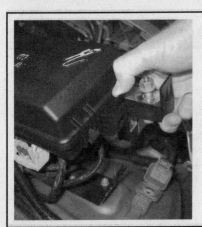

6.2 Pull back the tang and swing the Power Distribution Center up . . .

♦ Refer to illustrations 6.2, 6.3 and 6.4

➡ Note: The Front Control Module (FCM) is located on the front of the front Power Distribution Center (the engine compartment fuse and relay box). Chrysler/Dodge refers to the FCM/Power Distribution Center assembly as the Integrated Power Module (IPM). The IPM is connected directly to the battery and provides the primary means of circuit protection and power distribution for all vehicle electrical systems, including:

   Air conditioning condenser cooling fan
   Daytime Running Lights (DRL) system
   Front and rear hazard warning light system (there is no conventional hazard flasher relay)
   Front turn signal lights
   Horns
   Radiator fans
   Rear window defroster power and timing
   Brake lights, turn signal lights and taillights
   Windshield and, on Magnums, liftgate wiper/washer systems

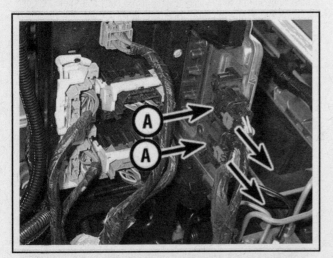

6.3 . . . then, to disconnect each electrical connector from the Front Control Module (FCM), slide the red locks toward the wiring harness, then depress the release tabs (A) and pull off the connectors

6.4 To detach the FCM from the engine compartment fuse and relay box, remove these four screws

1   Disconnect the cable from the negative battery terminal (see Chapter 5, Section 1).

2   Disconnect the positive battery cable from the front Power Distribution Center, then pull back the tang and lift the Power Distribution Center up (see illustration).

3   Disconnect the electrical connectors from the FCM (see illustration).

4   Remove the FCM mounting screws (see illustration) and remove the FCM.

5   Installation is the reverse of removal.

7   Steering Column Control Module (SCCM) - component replacement

▶ **Refer to illustrations 7.3, 7.4, 7.5, 7.6, 7.7, 7.8a, 7.8b, 7.9, 7.10, 7.11 and 7.12**

✳✳ WARNING:

The models covered by this manual are equipped with a Supplemental Restraint System (SRS), more commonly known as airbags. Always disarm the airbag system before working in the vicinity of any airbag system component to avoid the possibility of accidental deployment of the airbag, which could cause personal injury (see Section 26). Do not use a memory-saving device to preserve the PCM's memory when working on or near airbag system components.

➡ **Note: The Steering Column Control Module (SCCM) includes the clockspring for the steering wheel airbag, the multi-function switch, the speed control switch, the Steering Angle Sensor (SAS), if equipped with Electronic Stability Program, and the Steering Column Module (SCM).**

1   Disconnect the cable from the negative battery terminal (see Chapter 5, Section 1).

2   Remove the steering wheel airbag and the steering wheel (see Chapter 10).

3   To prevent the clockspring from uncentering itself, loosen - BUT DON'T REMOVE - at least one clockspring screw (see illustration).

4   Back out the setscrew through the access hole in the bottom of the SCCM (see illustration).

5   Remove the SCCM from the steering column (see illustration) and place the SCCM on a clean workbench.

6   Loosen all three clockspring screws (see illustration) just enough to detach the clockspring from the SCCM.

7.3 To keep the clockspring from uncentering itself, loosen - BUT DON'T REMOVE - at least one of the three clockspring screws

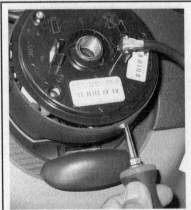

7.4 To release the SCCM from the steering column, insert a screwdriver through the access hole in the bottom of the SCCM and back out the setscrew

7.5 To remove the SCCM from the steering column, pull it to the rear

7.6 To detach the clockspring from the SCCM, loosen these three screws just enough to pull off the clockspring, but not so much that the clockspring unwinds

7.7 Separate the clockspring from the SCCM

7.8a To detach the Steering Angle Sensor (SAS) from the SCCM, remove this retaining screw . . .

7.8b . . . then lift the SAS out of the SCCM

7.9 On vehicles with a manual telescoping steering column, remove these two Phillips screws (A) and remove the strut (B). On all vehicles, remove these two speed control switch screws (C) . . .

7.10 . . . and remove the speed control switch

7.11 To detach the multi-function switch and Steering Control Switch (SCM) from the SCCM shroud, remove these three screws, then pull the SCM and multi-function switch out of the shroud

7.12 Separate the SCM (A) from the multi-function switch (B)

✻✻ CAUTION:

Do NOT completely unscrew the clockspring screws or the clockspring will unwind.

7 Remove the clockspring from the SCCM (see illustration).
8 Remove the Steering Angle Sensor (SAS) retaining screw and remove the SAS (see illustrations).
9 If the vehicle is equipped with a manual telescoping steering column, remove the strut screws (see illustration) and remove the strut. If the vehicle is equipped with an electronic telescoping steering column, remove the switch mounting screws and remove the switch and stalk.
10 Remove the speed control switch retaining screws (see illustra-

tion 7.9) and remove the speed control switch (see illustration).
11 On vehicles with an SCCM assembly on which the steering column tilt/telescoping lever is an integral part of the SCCM assembly, remove the two-lever assembly retaining screws and remove the lever assembly. (On some models, the tilt lever is located underneath the steering column and its removal is not necessary for this procedure.)
12 Remove the three screws at the bottom of the SCCM shroud (see illustration) for the multi-function switch and the Steering Control Module (SCM), then remove the switch and SCM as a single assembly.
13 Separate the multi-function switch from the SCM.
14 No further disassembly is possible.
15 Installation is the reverse of removal.

8 Key lock cylinder and ignition switch - replacement

✻✻ WARNING:

The models covered by this manual are equipped with a Supplemental Restraint System (SRS), more commonly known as airbags. Always disarm the airbag system before working in the vicinity of any airbag system component to avoid the possibility of accidental deployment of the airbag, which could cause personal injury (see Section 26). Do not use a memory-saving device to preserve the PCM's memory when working on or near airbag system components.

➡Note: If the key is difficult to turn, the problem might not be in the ignition switch or the key lock cylinder. The transmission shift cable or the Brake Transmission Shift Interlock (BTSI) cable might be out of adjustment (see Chapter 7).

KEY LOCK CYLINDER

▸ **Refer to illustrations 8.4 and 8.5**

✻✻ CAUTION:

Make sure that you obtain the correct key lock cylinder for your ignition key BEFORE you install the lock cylinder. Otherwise, you will find that once you have installed a new key lock cylinder the key won't fit! Take your ignition key and your vehicle's Vehicle Identification Number (VIN) with you when you purchase a new key lock cylinder. If you lose an ignition key and have to replace it, you might be in trouble. The ignition key contains a transponder with its own unique encrypted Radio Frequency (RF) signal, and a new key will have to be programmed to work with the Sentry Key Remote Entry Module (SKREEM) (see below).

1 Disconnect the cable from the negative battery terminal (see Chapter 5, Section 1).
2 Using a trim stick, carefully pry off the ignition switch bezel (the small circular trim piece around the key lock cylinder) and remove the instrument cluster bezel (see Chapter 11).
3 Insert the ignition key into the key lock cylinder and turn it to the ON position.
4 Insert a small awl, punch or scribe into the hole for the key lock cylinder retaining pin, depress the retaining pin and pull the key lock cylinder out of the steering column (see illustration).
5 Before installing the key lock cylinder, make sure that the ignition key is still in the ON position. Align the D-shaped lug on the end of the

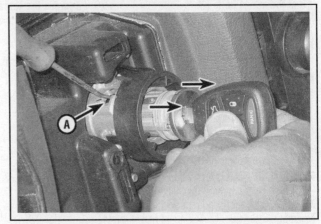

8.4 To remove the key lock cylinder, turn the ignition key to the ON position, depress the spring-loaded retaining lug with a small screwdriver, or with an awl, punch or scribe, and pull out the key lock cylinder

8.5 Lock cylinder installation details

A must align with B   *E must align with F*
C must align with D

key lock cylinder with the D-shaped socket in the bottom of the lock cylinder housing (see illustration) and push the lock cylinder into the ignition switch until it clicks into place.
6 Installation is otherwise the reverse of removal.

8.10 To detach the key lock cylinder/ ignition switch housing from the instrument panel, remove this nut (1) and these two bolts (2)

8.11a To disconnect the electrical connector from the ignition switch, slide the red lock sideways, then depress the release tab (A) and pull off the connector

8.11b To disconnect the electrical connector from the Sentry Key Remote Entry Module (SKREEM), depress this release tab and pull off the connector

IGNITION SWITCH

▶ **Refer to illustrations 8.10, 8.11a, 8.11b, 8.12, 8.13, 8.14a and 8.14b**

7 Disconnect the cable from the negative battery terminal (see Chapter 5, Section 1).

8 Disable the airbag system (see Section 26).

9 Remove the knee bolster and the knee bolster reinforcement panel (see Chapter 11).

10 Remove the lower mounting nut and the two front mounting bolts (see illustration) and remove the key lock cylinder/ignition switch assembly.

11 Disconnect the electrical connectors from the ignition switch and from the Sentry Key Remote Entry Module (see illustrations).

12 Disconnect the Brake Transmission Shift Interlock (BTSI) cable (see illustration).

13 Remove the ignition switch mounting screw (see illustration).

14 Depress the release tabs (see illustrations) and remove the ignition switch

15 Installation is the reverse of removal.

8.12 To disconnect the Brake Transmission Shift Interlock (BTSI) cable from the ignition switch/key lock cylinder assembly, depress this release tab and pull off the cable

8.13 To detach the ignition switch from the key lock cylinder housing, remove this Torx screw

8.14a To remove the ignition switch from the key lock cylinder housing, depress these two release tabs . . .

8.14b . . . with a pair of needle-nose pliers

SENTRY KEY REMOTE ENTRY MODULE (SKREEM)/ WIRELESS CONTROL MODULE (WCM)

The SKREEM, also sometimes referred to as the Wireless Control Module (WCM), is the small black plastic module mounted on the left side of the ignition switch/key lock cylinder housing. The SKREEM/ WCM is part of the Sentry Key Remote Entry System (SKREES). When you press the UNLOCK button on the ignition key, a transponder inside the key produces its own unique encrypted Radio Frequency (RF) signal, which the SKREEM/WCM recognizes as a valid signal. The SKREEM/WCM unlocks the door locks (one push to unlock the driver door, two pushes to unlock the other doors), activates the vehicle's electronic modules via the Controller Area Network (CAN) and allows you to start the engine. When you press the LOCK button, the transponder's RF signal tells the SKREEM to lock the doors, activate the security system and disable all electronic modules. The SKREEM/WCM and the ignition key are programmed to work together. If you replace the key or the SKREEM/WCM, you must have them reprogrammed at a dealership, so we don't recommend trying to replace the SKREEM at home.

9   Instrument panel switches and clock- replacement

✳✳ WARNING:

The models covered by this manual are equipped with a Supplemental Restraint System (SRS), more commonly known as airbags. Always disarm the airbag system before working in the vicinity of any airbag system component to avoid the possibility of accidental deployment of the airbag, which could cause personal injury (see Section 26). Do not use a memory-saving device to preserve the PCM's memory when working on or near airbag system components.

HEADLIGHT SWITCH

▶ **Refer to illustrations 9.3 and 9.4**

1   Disconnect the cable from the negative battery terminal (see Chapter 5, Section 1).
2   Remove the knee bolster (see Chapter 11).
3   Push the headlight switch out of the instrument panel from

behind (see illustration).
4   Disconnect the electrical connector from the headlight switch (see illustration).
5   Installation is the reverse of removal.

INSTRUMENT PANEL SWITCH POD

▶ **Refer to illustration 9.7**

6   Remove the instrument panel center bezel (see Chapter 11).
7   Disconnect the electrical connector from the instrument panel switch pod (see illustration).
8   Remove the instrument panel switch pod mounting screws.
9   Remove the instrument panel switch pod from the instrument panel center bezel.
10   Installation is the reverse of removal.

9.3 To remove the headlight switch from the instrument panel, push it out from behind

9.4 To disconnect the electrical connector from the headlight switch, slide the red lock (1) toward the wiring harness until it snaps out and overlaps the release tab (2), then depress the red lock and release tab and pull off the connector

9.7 To remove the instrument panel switch pod from the instrument panel center bezel, depress the release tab (1) and disconnect the electrical connector, then remove the two switch pod mounting screws (2) and remove the pod from the center bezel

9.12 To remove the clock from the instrument panel center bezel, depress the release tab (1) and disconnect the electrical connector, then remove the clock mounting screws (2) and remove the clock from the center bezel

CLOCK

▶ **Refer to illustration 9.12**

11 Remove the instrument panel center bezel (see Chapter 11).

12 Disconnect the electrical connector from the clock (see illustration).

13 Remove the clock mounting screws.

14 Remove the clock from the instrument panel center bezel.

15 Installation is the reverse of removal.

10 Instrument cluster - removal and installation

▶ **Refer to illustrations 10.3 and 10.4**

❊❊ WARNING:

The models covered by this manual are equipped with a Supplemental Restraint System (SRS), more commonly known as airbags. Always disarm the airbag system before working in the vicinity of any airbag system component to avoid the possibility of accidental deployment of the airbag, which could cause personal injury (see Section 26). Do not use a memory-saving device to preserve the PCM's memory when working on or near airbag system components.

1 Disconnect the cable from the negative battery terminal (see Chapter 5, Section 1).

2 Remove the instrument cluster bezel (see Chapter 11).

3 Remove the two instrument cluster mounting screws (see illustration).

4 Pull out the cluster and disconnect the electrical connectors from the backside of the cluster (see illustration).

5 Installation is the reverse of removal.

10.3 To detach the instrument cluster from the instrument panel, remove these two screws

10.4 Pull out the instrument cluster, depress the release tabs and disconnect these two electrical connectors (there's another smaller connector, not shown in this photo, at the other end of the cluster)

11 Wiper motors - replacement

11.2 Carefully pry off the protective trim cap from each windshield wiper arm . . .

11.3 . . . then remove the wiper arm retaining nuts and mark the relationship between each wiper arm and its shaft

11.5 To disconnect the electrical connector from the windshield wiper motor, depress the release tab and pull off the connector

WINDSHIELD WIPER MOTOR

▶ **Refer to illustrations 11.2, 11.3, 11.5, 11.6, 11.7, 11.8a, 11.8b and 11.10**

1 Disconnect the cable from the negative battery terminal (see Chapter 5, Section 1).

2 Remove the protective trim cap from each wiper arm, then remove the wiper arm retaining nuts (see illustration).

3 Mark the relationship of the wiper arms to their shafts (see illustration), then remove the wiper arms.

4 Remove the cowl cover (see Chapter 11).

5 Disconnect the electrical connector from the windshield wiper motor (see illustration).

6 Remove the windshield wiper module mounting bolts (see illustration) and remove the module.

7 Disconnect the two link rods from the bellcrank (see illustration).

8 Remove the nut that secures the bellcrank to the motor shaft (see illustration), then use a small puller to remove the bellcrank from the

11.6 To detach the windshield wiper module from the cowl area, remove these two mounting bolts

11.7 To separate the two link rods from the bellcrank pin, pry them off, one at a time, with a trim removal tool or large screwdriver

11.8a To detach the bellcrank from the windshield wiper motor shaft, remove this nut

11.8b Use a small puller to separate the bellcrank from the wiper motor nut. To detach the motor from the wiper module assembly, remove these two Torx screws

11.10 Inspect the condition of the wiper motor's rubber insulator. If it's cracked, torn, deteriorated or otherwise damaged, replace it

11.18 Disconnect the electrical connector (1) from the rear wiper motor, then remove the three wiper motor mounting bolts (2) and remove the wiper motor from the rear liftgate

11.14 Remove the rear wiper arm retaining nut

wiper motor shaft (see illustration).

9   Remove the windshield wiper motor mounting screws and remove the wiper motor from the module.

10 Inspect the condition of the wiper motor's rubber insulator (see illustration)

11 Installation is the reverse of removal.

REAR WIPER MOTOR (MAGNUM MODELS)

▶ Refer to illustrations 11.14 and 11.18

12 Disconnect the cable from the negative battery terminal (see Chapter 5, Section 1).

13 Remove the trim cap from the rear wiper arm.

14 Remove the rear wiper arm retaining nut (see illustration).

15 Mark the relationship of the wiper arm to the wiper motor shaft.

16 Remove the arm from the motor shaft.

17 Remove the rear liftgate trim panel (see Chapter 11).

18 Disconnect the electrical connector from the rear wiper motor (see illustration).

19 Remove the rear wiper motor mounting bolts (see illustration 11.18).

20 Remove the rear wiper motor.

21 Installation is the reverse of removal.

12 Radio and speakers - removal and installation

☀ WARNING:

The models covered by this manual are equipped with a Supplemental Restraint System (SRS), more commonly known as airbags. Always disarm the airbag system before working in the vicinity of any airbag system component to avoid the possibility of accidental deployment of the airbag, which could cause personal injury (see Section 26). Do not use a memory-saving device to preserve the PCM's memory when working on or near airbag system components.

RADIO

▶ Refer to illustrations 12.3 and 12.4

1   Disconnect the cable from the negative battery terminal (see Chapter 5, Section 1).

2   Remove the instrument panel center bezel (see Chapter 11).

3   Remove the radio mounting screws (see illustration) and pull the radio out of the dash.

4   Disconnect the antenna cable and the electrical connectors from the radio (see illustration).

5   Installation is the reverse of removal.

12.3 To detach the radio from the dash, remove these four mounting screws

SPEAKERS

Door speakers

▶ **Refer to illustration 12.8**

6   Disconnect the cable from the negative battery terminal (see Chapter 5, Section 1).

12.8 To detach the speaker from the front door, remove these four mounting screws (rear door speakers similar)

12.12 To remove an instrument panel speaker, carefully pry off the speaker cover with a trim panel removal tool or a trim stick. If you don't have a trim removal tool, use a screwdriver instead, but put a clean shop rag under it to protect the instrument panel

12.4 Pull the radio out of the dash far enough to disconnect the antenna cable (A) and the electrical connectors

7   Remove the door trim panel (see Chapter 11).
8   Remove the four speaker mounting screws (see illustration).
9   Pull out the speaker and disconnect the electrical connector.
10 Installation is the reverse of removal.

Instrument panel speakers

▶ **Refer to illustration 12.12**

11 Disconnect the cable from the negative battery terminal (see Chapter 5, Section 1).
12 Remove the speaker cover (see illustration).
13 Remove the speaker mounting screws.
14 Pull out the speaker and disconnect the electrical connector.
15 Installation is the reverse of removal.

Rear speakers

Sedans

▶ **Refer to illustration 12.18**

16 Disconnect the cable from the negative battery terminal (see Chapter 5, Section 1).
17 Remove the upper C-pillar trim and the lower C-pillar trim from both sides, then remove the rear shelf trim (see Chapter 11).
18 Remove the rear speaker mounting screws (see illustration).
19 Pull out the speaker and disconnect the electrical connector.
20 Installation is the reverse of removal.

12.18 To detach a rear speaker, remove these four screws

Wagons

➡**Note: There are two rear speakers, which are located at the rear corners of the cargo area, on small panels mounted on the rear D-pillars.**

21 Disconnect the cable from the negative battery terminal (see Chapter 5, Section 1).

22 Remove the screw from the speaker bezel, carefully pry the front end of the bezel up, then release the two spring clips holding the bezel to the quarter trim panel.

23 Pass the seat belt trough the slit in the bezel, then move the speaker bezel forward to free it from the trim panel.

24 Remove the rear speaker mounting screws.

25 Pull out the speaker and disconnect the electrical connector.

26 Installation is the reverse of removal.

Subwoofers

➡**Note: The subwoofer, if equipped, is located behind the rear seat, under the rear shelf trim, between the two rear speakers.**

27 Follow the procedure for replacing a rear speaker (see Steps 16 through 20).

---

13 Antenna and antenna module - replacement

ANTENNA

1 The grid-type antenna is bonded to and is an integral component of the rear window glass. If the antenna is faulty the rear glass must be replaced. This is a job best left to a professional.

ANTENNA MODULE

Sedans

▶ **Refer to illustration 13.3**

➡**Note: The antenna module is mounted on the inside of the right C-pillar on sedans.**

2 Remove the right upper C-pillar trim (see Chapter 11).

3 Disconnect the two antenna module electrical connectors from the antenna grid and disconnect the antenna coaxial cable and electrical connector from the module (see illustration).

4 Remove the antenna module mounting bolt (see illustration 13.3) and remove the module.

5 Installation is the reverse of removal.

Wagons

➡**Note: The antenna module is mounted on the inside of the liftgate.**

6 Remove the liftgate trim panel (see Chapter 11).

7 Disconnect the two antenna module electrical connectors from the antenna grid and disconnect the antenna coaxial cable and electrical

13.3 To remove the antenna module:

A   *Disconnect the module electrical connectors from the two antenna grid terminals*

B   *Disconnect the coaxial antenna cable (this cable goes to the radio)*

C   *Disconnect the electrical connector*

D   *Remove the module mounting bolt*

connector from the module (see illustration 13.3).

8 Remove the antenna module mounting bolt and remove the module.

9 Installation is the reverse of removal.

---

14 Rear window defogger - check and repair

1 The rear window defogger consists of a number of horizontal heating elements baked onto the inside surface of the glass. Power is supplied through a relay and fuse from the interior fuse/relay box. A defogger switch on the instrument panel controls the defogger grid.

2 Small breaks in the element can be repaired without removing the rear window.

CHECK

▶ **Refer to illustrations 14.5, 14.6 and 14.8**

3 Turn the ignition and defogger switches to the ON position.

4 Using a voltmeter, place the positive probe against the defogger grid positive side and the negative probe against the ground side. If

14.5 When measuring voltage at the rear window defogger grid, wrap a piece of aluminum foil around the positive probe of the voltmeter and press the foil against the wire with your finger

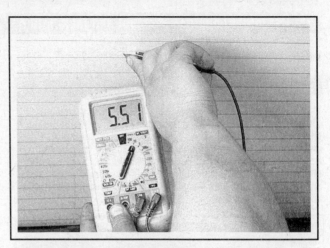

14.6 To determine if a heating element has broken, check the voltage at the center of each element - if the voltage is 6-volts, the element is unbroken

battery voltage is not indicated, check that the ignition switch is On and that the feed and ground wires are properly connected. Check the two fuses, defogger switch, defogger relay and related wiring. The dealer can scan the body control module if necessary. If voltage is indicated, but all or part of the defogger doesn't heat, proceed with the following tests.

5   When measuring voltage during the next two tests, wrap a piece of aluminum foil around the tip of the voltmeter positive probe and press the foil against the heating element with your finger (see illustration). Place the negative probe on the defogger grid ground terminal.

6   Check the voltage at the center of each heating element (see illustration). If the voltage is 5 to 6 volts, the element is okay (there is no break). If the voltage is 0 volts, the element is broken between the center of the element and the positive end. If the voltage is 10 to 12 volts, the element is broken between the center of the element and the ground side. Check each heating element.

7   If none of the elements are broken, connect the negative probe to a good chassis ground. The voltage reading should stay the same, if it doesn't the ground connection is bad.

8   To find the break, place the voltmeter negative probe against the defogger ground terminal. Place the voltmeter positive probe with the foil strip against the heating element at the positive side and slide it

toward the negative side. The point at which the voltmeter deflects from several volts to zero is the point where the heating element is broken (see illustration).

REPAIR

▶ **Refer to illustration 14.14**

9   Repair the break in the element using a repair kit specifically for this purpose, available at most auto parts stores. The kit includes conductive plastic epoxy.

10   Before repairing a break, turn off the system and allow it to cool for a few minutes.

11   Lightly buff the element area with fine steel wool; then clean it thoroughly with rubbing alcohol.

12   Use masking tape to mask off the area being repaired.

13   Thoroughly mix the epoxy, following the kit instructions.

14   Apply the epoxy material to the slit in the masking tape, overlapping the undamaged area about 3/4-inch on either end (see illustration).

15   Allow the repair to cure for 24 hours before removing the tape and using the system.

14.8 To find the break, place the voltmeter negative lead against the defogger ground terminal, place the voltmeter positive lead with the foil strip against the heat wire at the positive terminal end and slide it toward the negative terminal end. The point at which the voltmeter deflects from several volts to zero volts is the point at which the wire is broken

14.14 To use a defogger repair kit, apply masking to the inside of the window at the damaged area, then brush on the special conductive coating

15 Headlight housing - removal and installation

▶ Refer to illustrations 15.2 and 15.3

❄❄ **WARNING:**

This procedure does not apply to the headlight housings on Chrysler 300C (V8) models, which use a High Intensity Discharge (HID) low-beam headlight bulb. If you own one of these models, we don't recommend that you try to remove the headlight housing yourself because you could be accidentally electrocuted when disconnecting the electrical connector from one of these bulbs, which you must do to remove the headlight housing (see the Warning in Section 17).

15.2 To detach the headlight housing, remove these three mounting bolts (lower bolt not visible)

1 On Charger models, remove the bumper cover (see Chapter 11).
2 Remove the two upper and two lower headlight mounting bolts (see illustration).
3 Pull out the headlight housing far enough to disconnect the electrical connectors (see illustration), then remove the headlight housing.
4 Installation is the reverse of removal.

15.3 Pull out the headlight housing and disconnect the electrical connectors for all five headlight housing lights:

A Low-beam headlight   D Inner parking light
B High-beam headlight   E Park/turn signal light
C Outer parking light

16 Headlights - adjustment

HEADLIGHTS

▶ Refer to illustrations 16.1 and 16.2

❄❄ **WARNING:**

The headlights must be aimed correctly. If adjusted incorrectly, they could temporarily blind the driver of an oncoming vehicle and cause an accident or seriously reduce your ability to see the road. The headlights should be checked for proper aim every 12 months and any time a new headlight is installed or front-end bodywork is performed. The following procedure is only intended to provide temporary adjustment until you can have the headlights professionally adjusted by a dealer service department.

1 Open the hood and locate the headlight vertical adjusting screw (see illustration) for each headlight in the upper radiator crossmember. Each headlight has a vertical adjustment screw; there are no horizontal adjustment screws.

16.1 Headlight vertical adjustment screw location

16.2 Headlight adjustment screen details

16.10 Fog light adjustment screw location

5   Adjustment should be made with the vehicle parked 25 feet from the wall, sitting level, the gas tank full and no unusually heavy load in the vehicle.

6   The high intensity zone should be vertically centered with the exact center, about three inches below the horizontal line.

7   Have the headlights adjusted by a qualified technician at the earliest opportunity.

FOG LIGHTS

▶ **Refer to illustration 16.10**

➡**Note: This procedure applies only to vehicles equipped with fog lights.**

8   Park the vehicle 25 feet from the wall.

9   Tape a horizontal line on the wall that represents the height of the fog lights and tape another line four inches below that line.

10   Using the adjusting screw (see illustration) on each fog light, adjust the pattern on the wall so that the top of the fog light beam meets the lower line on the wall. Repeat this procedure for the other fog light.

2   There are several ways to adjust the headlights. The simplest method requires an open area with a blank wall and a level floor (see illustration).

3   Position masking tape vertically on the wall in reference to the vehicle centerline and the centerlines of both headlights.

4   Position a horizontal tape line in reference to the centerline of the headlights.

➡**Note: It might be easier to position the tape on the wall with the vehicle parked only a few inches away.**

17 Headlight bulb - replacement

ALL HEADLIGHT BULBS EXCEPT LOW-BEAM BULBS ON CHRYSLER 300C MODELS

▶ **Refer to illustrations 17.2a, 17.2b and 17.3**

❊❊ **WARNING:**

Halogen bulbs are gas-filled and under pressure and they can shatter if the surface is scratched or the bulb is dropped. Wear eye protection and handle the bulbs carefully, grasping only the base whenever possible. Don't touch the surface of the bulb with your fingers because the oil from your skin could cause it to overheat and fail prematurely. If you do touch the bulb surface, clean it with rubbing alcohol.

➡**Note 1: This procedure applies to both the high- and low-beam headlight bulbs on all models except Chrysler 300C models (300 models with a V8 engine). On these models the low-beam headlight units are High Intensity Discharge (HID) units (see Warning below with "High Intensity Discharge low-beam bulbs on Chrysler 300C models").**

➡**Note 2: This procedure simplifies headlight bulb replacement by showing how to replace a headlight bulb without removing the headlight housing. However, if there's not enough space to work on your vehicle or if your hands are too big, remove the headlight housing first (see Section 15), then replace the bulb.**

1   If you're replacing one of the left headlight bulbs, remove the air filter housing (see Chapter 4).

2   Disconnect the electrical connector from the headlight bulb that you want to replace (see illustrations).

17.2a To replace either headlight bulb, disconnect the electrical connector:

    A *Low-beam headlight connector*
    B *High-beam headlight connector*

3   To remove either headlight bulb from the headlight housing, turn it counterclockwise about 30-degrees (see illustration). The headlight bulb and the bulb socket are a single assembly. No further disassembly is possible. The new bulb will have its own socket.

4   Installation is the reverse of removal.

HIGH INTENSITY DISCHARGE (HID) LOW-BEAM BULBS ON CHRYSLER 300C MODELS

�֍ WARNING:

Chrysler 300C models (300 models with a V8 engine) use a High Intensity Discharge (HID) low-beam bulb instead of a conventional halogen low-beam bulb. According to Daimler/Chrysler, high voltage can remain in the circuit even after the headlight switch has been turned to OFF and the ignition key has been removed. Therefore, for your safety, we don't recommend that you try to replace one of these bulbs yourself. Instead, have this service performed by a dealer service department.

5   300C models use a High Intensity Discharge (HID) low-beam headlight bulb instead of a halogen bulb. According to Daimler/Chrysler, these bulbs put out three times as much light of a standard halogen bulb, use less energy doing so, and last 10 times longer. HID bulbs use an alternating current (AC) electrical charge to ignite xenon gas inside the sealed bulb. They're similar in operation to vapor-filled streetlights. Instead of a filament, the gas inside the bulb is ignited by creating an arc between two electrodes. A ballast module converts battery voltage

17.2b To disconnect either headlight electrical connector, grasp the connector firmly, then pull it out of the bulb socket terminal. You must pull firmly enough to spread the two halves of the split locking tab apart so that they release from the locking lug (A)

17.3 To remove a headlight bulb socket from the headlight housing, rotate it counterclockwise about 30-degrees, then pull it out of the housing

to alternating current, stepping it up from 12 volts DC to 800 volts AC. The HID bulb takes about 10-15 seconds to warm up before it operates normally. The igniter (part of the HID bulb) controls the voltage applied to the electrodes. The igniter steps up the 800 volt AC input to about 25,000 volts to start up the light; once ignited, it reduces voltage to about 85 volts.

18 Bulb replacement

EXTERIOR LIGHTS

Front park/turn signal light bulbs

▶ Refer to illustrations 18.2, 18.3 and 18.4

➡ **Note 1:** The photos accompanying this section depict a typical front park/turn signal unit on a Chrysler 300 model. On these models the front park/turn signal unit is located in the headlight housing, directly below the high-beam headlight bulb. On Magnum models the front park/turn signal unit is also located in the headlight housing, but it's above the low-beam headlight bulb. On Charger models the front park/turn signal unit is located at the lower inner end of the headlight housing. But the park/turn signal unit itself is removed and installed the same way on all models.

➡ **Note 2:** This procedure simplifies front park/turn signal bulb replacement by showing how to replace a park/turn signal bulb without removing the headlight housing. However, if there's not enough space to work on your vehicle or if your hands are too big, remove the headlight housing first (see Section 15), then replace the bulb.

➡ **Note 3:** If you're replacing a front park/turn signal bulb on a Chrysler 300C model, you will have to do it with the headlight housing installed because we don't recommend removing the headlight housing on these models because of the danger of electrocution. Please refer to the Warning in Section 17.

➡ **Note 4:** If you're replacing a front park/turn signal bulb on a Charger model, and decide that you want to remove the headlight housing before doing so, please note that you must first remove the front fascia (front bumper cover) before you can remove either headlight housing.

1　If you're replacing the front park/turn signal bulb in the left headlight housing, remove the air filter housing (see Chapter 4).

2　Disconnect the electrical connector from the holder for the front park/turn signal light bulb (see illustration).

3　Remove the front park/turn signal bulb holder from the headlight housing (see illustration).

4　Remove the front park/turn signal bulb from its holder by sim-

ply pulling it straight out of the socket (see illustration). To install a new bulb into the holder, push it straight into the socket until it's fully seated.

5　Installation is the reverse of removal.

Inner and outer front parking light bulbs (Chrysler 300 models)

▶ Refer to illustration 18.7

➡ **Note 1:** The inner and outer front parking light bulbs are located in the lower part of the headlight housings (see illustration 15.3). These lights are used only on Chrysler 300 models. 300C, Magnum and Charger models are not equipped with these lights.

➡ **Note 2:** This procedure simplifies front parking light bulb replacement by showing how to replace a parking light bulb without removing the headlight housing. However, if there's not enough space to work on your vehicle or if your hands are too big, remove the headlight housing first (see Section 15), then replace the bulb.

➡ **Note 3:** This procedure applies to any of the four parking light bulbs (two in each headlight housing) - they're identical.

6　If you're replacing a front parking light bulb in the left headlight housing, remove the air filter housing (see Chapter 4).

7　Remove the front parking light bulb holder (see illustration).

8　Remove the front parking light bulb from its holder by pulling it straight out. To install a new bulb into the holder, push it straight into the socket until it's fully seated.

9　Installation is the reverse of removal.

Front sidemarker lights

Chrysler 300 models

▶ Refer to illustration 18.12

➡ **Note:** The front sidemarker lights are located in the front bumper cover. They can be accessed from underneath the vehicle or by removing the headlight housing.

10　Remove the headlight housing (see Section 15).

11　OR, raise the vehicle and place it securely on jackstands, then remove the front engine splash shield (see Chapter 2).

18.2 To disconnect the electrical connector from the front park/turn signal bulb holder, slide the red lock toward the harness, then depress the release tab (A) and pull off the connector

18.3 Turn the bulb holder counterclockwise and pull it out

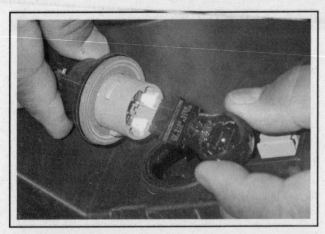

18.4 To remove a front park/turn signal bulb from the holder, simply pull it straight out

12 Disconnect the electrical connector from the sidemarker light bulb holder (see illustration).

13 To remove the front sidemarker light bulb holder, turn it counterclockwise and pull it out.

14 To remove a front sidemarker light bulb from its holder, pull it straight out of the holder. To install a new bulb, push it straight into the socket until it's fully seated.

15 Installation is the reverse of removal.

Dodge models

➡**Note: The front sidemarker light bulbs are located in the headlight housing.**

16 Unbolt and pull out the headlight housing (see Section 15).

17 Disconnect the electrical connector from the sidemarker light bulb holder.

18 To remove the front sidemarker light bulb holder, turn it counterclockwise and pull it out.

19 To remove a front sidemarker light bulb from its holder, pull it straight out of the holder. To install a new bulb, push it straight into the socket until it's fully seated.

20 Installation is the reverse of removal.

18.12 To disconnect the electrical connector from the front sidemarker light bulb holder on a Chrysler 300 model, slide the red lock toward the harness, then depress the release tab (A) and pull off the connector. To remove the holder, turn it counterclockwise and pull it out

18.7 To remove the holder for either front parking light bulb, simply twist it counterclockwise and pull it out of the housing

Fog light bulbs

▶ **Refer to illustrations 18.23 and 18.24**

➡**Note: The fog lights are located in the front bumper cover.**

21 Raise the vehicle and place it securely on jackstands.

22 Remove the front engine splash shield (see Chapter 2).

23 Disconnect the electrical connector from the fog light bulb holder (see illustration).

24 Remove the bulb holder from the fog light housing (see illustration).

25 Installation is the reverse of removal.

Center high-mounted brake lights

➡**Note: The center high-mounted brake light assembly uses LEDs (light emitting diodes). You cannot replace individual bulbs.**

Sedan models

▶ **Refer to illustrations 18.27 and 18.28**

26 Remove the upper and lower C-pillar trim panels and remove the rear shelf trim panel (see Chapter 11).

18.23 To disconnect the electrical connector from the fog light bulb holder, grasp the connector firmly and pull it off. You must pull firmly enough to spread the two halves of the split locking tab apart so that they release from the locking lug

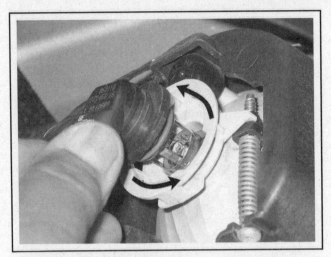

18.24 To remove the fog light bulb holder, turn it counterclockwise and pull it out of the fog light housing

18.28 To detach the center high-mounted brake light housing from the vehicle, remove these two screws

27 Disconnect the electrical connector from the center high-mounted brake light housing (see illustration).

28 Remove the center high-mounted brake light housing mounting screws (see illustration).

18.36 To access the taillight electrical connector and retainers, unscrew this fastener and peel back the carpeting

18.27 To disconnect the electrical connector from the center high-mounted brake light housing, depress the release tab and pull off the connector

29 Remove the center high-mounted brake light housing.
30 Installation is the reverse of removal.

Magnum models

31 Remove the rear spoiler (see Chapter 11).

32 Disconnect the electrical connector from the center high-mounted brake light housing.

33 Remove the fasteners that secure the center high-mounted brake light housing to the rear spoiler.

34 Remove the center high-mounted brake light housing.

35 Installation is the reverse of removal.

Taillight bulbs

Chrysler 300 and Dodge Charger

▶ Refer to illustrations 18.36, 18.37, 18.38 and 18.39

36 Open the trunk, unscrew the fastener that secures the carpeting (see illustration), then pull back the carpeting to expose the taillight electrical connector and retainers.

37 Disconnect the electrical connector from the taillight assembly (see illustration).

18.37 To disconnect the electrical connector from the taillight assembly, slide the red lock sideways, then depress the release tab (A) and pull off the connector

18.38 To detach the taillight assembly from the body, unscrew these two retainers, then pull out the taillight housing to the rear

38 Remove the remaining taillight assembly retainers (see illustration), then pull out the taillight housing to the rear.

39 There are three bulbs in the taillight housing (see illustration).

➡**Note: This illustration depicts the taillight housing on a Chrysler 300 model. If you're replacing a bulb on a Charger model, refer to the bulb replacement section of your owner's manual for the location of each bulb.**

Dodge Magnum

40 Open the liftgate, then pry out the two pushpin fasteners from the taillight housing with a flat-blade screwdriver or some other suitable tool with a flat blade.

41 Pull off the taillight housing to the rear.

All models

▶ **Refer to illustration 18.42**

42 Remove the holder for the bulb that you want to replace (see illustration).

43 Remove the bulb from its holder by pulling it straight out of the holder. To install a new bulb, insert it straight into the socket and push it in until it's fully seated.

44 Installation is the reverse of removal.

License plate light bulb

▶ **Refer to illustrations 18.45 and 18.46**

➡**Note: The license plate light is located in the rear bumper cover on all models.**

45 Remove the license plate light housing retaining screws (see illustration) and pull the housing out of the trunk lid.

18.45 To detach the license plate light assembly from the rear bumper cover, remove these two screws

18.39 There are three bulbs in the taillight housing (Chrysler 300 shown, others slightly different):

A   Brake light/turn signal/taillight bulb
B   Backup light bulb
C   Rear sidemarker light bulb

46 Remove the license plate light bulb socket from the housing (see illustration).

47 Remove the license plate light bulb from its socket, by pulling it straight out.

18.42 To remove a bulb holder from the taillight housing, turn it counterclockwise and pull it out

18.46 To remove the bulb holder from the license plate housing, rotate it counterclockwise 30-degrees and pull it out

18.50 To remove the trunk light lens, push one of the retaining tangs inward

48 To install a new bulb, insert it into the socket and push it in until it's fully seated.

49 Installation is the reverse of removal.

INTERIOR LIGHTS

※※ WARNING:

The models covered by this manual are equipped with a Supplemental Restraint System (SRS), more commonly known as airbags. Always disarm the airbag system before working in the vicinity of any airbag system component to avoid the possibility of accidental deployment of the airbag, which could cause personal injury (see Section 26). Do not use a memory-saving device to preserve the PCM's memory when working on or near airbag system components.

Trunk light

▶ **Refer to illustration 18.50**

➡**Note: This procedure applies to sedan models.**

50 Open the trunk lid and locate the trunk light on the ceiling of the trunk space, ahead of the trunk lid (see illustration).

51 Push one of retaining tangs on the trunk light lens to free it.

52 To remove the trunk light bulb from its socket, pull it straight out. To install a new bulb, push it straight into the socket until it's fully seated.

53 Installation is the reverse of removal.

Reading light bulbs

▶ **Refer to illustrations 18.54, 18.55 and 18.56**

※※ CAUTION:

Removing the lens from one of these reading lights can be tricky. But if you get frustrated and try to force the lens out, you will break it. So proceed carefully.

54 Using a small, thin-blade screwdriver or a trim stick, carefully pry out the front edge (the edge nearest the windshield) of the reading light lens (see illustration), disconnect the switch electrical connectors and remove the switch housing.

18.54 To remove a reading light lens:

1 Carefully pry down the leading edge of the lens with a small screwdriver or a small trim removal stick
2 Push up on the trailing edge of the lens to disengage the rear tab
3 Slide the lens forward until the rear tab clears the light switch

18.55 Before removing the small metal shroud that surrounds the reading light bulb, note its exact location and orientation; it's held in by friction, so you must place it in the exact same spot when installing it (or you won't be able to install the lens)

55 Pull off the small metal housing that surrounds the bulb (see illustration).

56 Remove the reading light bulb from its terminals (see illustration).

18.56 To remove a reading light bulb, pull it straight down out of its terminals (if it's necessary to pry the bulb out, pry only on the metal ends, not the glass)

18.59a To remove a vanity light lens, carefully pry it loose along its lower edge at these three spots only (where there are small recesses to insert a small screwdriver). Pry it off just far enough to disengage the two small retaining tabs at each end . . .

18.59b . . . then flip the visor farther down, carefully insert the screwdriver into these two slots on the upper edge of the lens and pry the lens down until it comes loose

18.60 To remove a vanity light bulb, pull it out of these spring-type conductors (if it's necessary to pry the bulb out, pry only on the metal ends, not the glass)

18.64 Pry the front end of the door courtesy light out of the door panel . . .

18.65 . . . then disengage the wire loops (A) on the bulb from the hooked end of each conductor (B)

18.67 To remove the lens from a rear reading light, insert a small screwdriver into the gap between the forward end of the lens and the light housing, carefully pry the lens down, then move it forward to disengage the tab at the rear

57 To install a reading light bulb, push it up into its terminals until its snaps into place.

58 Installation is the reverse of removal.

Vanity light bulbs

▶ **Refer to illustrations 18.59a, 18.59b and 18.60**

59 Using a small, thin-blade screwdriver, carefully pry off the vanity light lens (see illustrations).

60 Remove the vanity light bulb from its housing by sliding it out to the left with a pair of small needle-nose pliers (see illustration).

61 To install a new vanity light bulb, carefully insert the bulb into the housing, then, using the needle-nose pliers, slide it to the right, back into the housing, until it's fully seated.

62 Installation is the reverse of removal.

Door courtesy lights

▶ **Refer to illustrations 18.64 and 18.65**

➡**Note: The door courtesy lights are located in the bottom of the front door trim panels.**

63 The door courtesy light is located in the bottom of the door trim panel.

64 Pry the forward end of the lens out of the door trim panel and pull the light/lens assembly down (see illustration).

65 Remove the bulb from the door courtesy light (see illustration).

66 Installation is the reverse of removal.

18.68 To remove a bulb from a rear reading light housing, just pull it straight out of the socket

Rear reading lights

▶ **Refer to illustrations 18.67 and 18.68**

67 Insert a small flat-bladed screwdriver into the gap between the forward edge of the lens and the light housing and carefully pry out the lens (see illustration). When the forward end is free, carefully disengage the tab at the rear end of the lens and pull out the lens.

68 Remove the bulb from the rear reading light housing (see illustration). To install a new bulb, insert the bulb straight into its socket until it's fully seated.

69 Installation is otherwise the reverse of removal.

19 Horn - replacement

▶ **Refer to illustrations 19.2a, 19.2b and 19.3**

➡**Note: The horns are located under the plastic covers between the fascia (front bumper cover) and the upper radiator support.**

1 Remove the plastic covers that span the gap between the front

bumper cover and the upper radiator support (see *Radiator - removal and installation* in Chapter 3).

2 Disconnect the electrical connector from the horn that you want to replace (see illustrations).

3 Remove the horn mounting bracket bolt (see illustration).

19.2a The horns are located below two small plastic trim covers that span the gap between the fascia (front bumper cover) and the upper radiator support (trim covers and front bumper cover removed for clarity)

19.2b Disconnect the electrical connector from the horn . . .

4   Remove the horns and mounting bracket as a single assembly, then disconnect the electrical connectors from the horns.

5   To replace either horn, remove the retaining nut for the horn that you want to replace, then remove that horn from the mounting bracket.

6   Installation is the reverse of removal.

19.3 . . . then remove the horn mounting bracket bolt (A), remove the horn and bracket, then remove the nut (B) to separate the horn from the bracket

20 Electric side-view mirrors - general information

1   The electric side-view mirrors can be adjusted up-and-down and left-to-right by a driver's side switch located on the left door trim panel. On models with factory-installed dual power mirrors, each mirror is also equipped with a heater grid behind the mirror glass to clear the mirror surface of fog, ice or snow. On these models, the mirror heater grid is an integral component of each mirror. If a heater grid fails, replace the mirror (see Chapter 11). The heater grid switches and the heated mirror system indicator light are integral components of the heater/air conditioning control panel on the dash. If one of these components fails, replace the heater/air conditioning control assembly (see Chapter 3). The heated mirror relay is located in one of the fuse and relay boxes.

2   The power mirror control switch has a LEFT-RIGHT selector switch that allows you to send voltage to the side-view mirror that you want to adjust. With the ignition switch in the ACC position, roll down the windows and operate the mirror control switch through all functions (left-right and up-down) for both the left and right side-view mirrors.

3   Listen carefully for the sound of the electric motors running in the mirrors.

4   If you can hear the motors but the mirror glass doesn't move, the problem is probably a defective drive mechanism inside the mirror, which will necessitate replacement of the mirror.

5   If the mirrors don't operate and no sound comes from the mirrors, check the fuse in one of the fuse and relay boxes (see Section 3).

6   If the fuse is OK, refer to Chapter 11 and remove the door panel for access to the back of the mirror control switch, without disconnecting the wires attached to it. Turn the ignition ON and check for voltage at the switch. There should be voltage at one terminal. If there's no voltage at the switch, check for an open in the wiring between the fuse panel and the switch.

7   If there's voltage at the switch, disconnect it. Check the switch for continuity in all its operating positions. If the switch does not have continuity, replace it.

8   Reconnect the switch. Locate the wire going from the switch to ground. Leaving the switch connected, connect a jumper wire between this wire and ground. If the mirror works normally with this wire in place, repair the faulty ground connection.

9   If the mirror still doesn't work, remove the mirror and check the wires at the mirror for voltage. Check with the ignition key turned to ON and the mirror selector switch on the appropriate side. Operate the mirror switch in all its positions. There should be voltage at one of the switch-to-mirror wires in each switch position, except the neutral (off) position.

10 If voltage is not present in each switch position, check the wiring between the mirror and control switch for opens and shorts.

11 If there's voltage, remove the mirror and test it off the vehicle with jumper wires. Replace the mirror if it fails this test.

21 Cruise control system - general information

The Powertrain Control Module (PCM) controls the cruise control system electronically via the Electronic Throttle Control (ETC) system. If you have problems with the cruise control system, have it checked by a dealer service department or other qualified repair shop.

22 Power window system - general information

1   The power window system controls the electric motors, mounted inside the doors, that lower and raise the windows. The power window system consists of the control switches, the fuse, the circuit breaker, the motors, the window "regulators" (the scissor-like mechanisms that raise and lower the window glass) and the wiring connecting the switches to the motors. When the ignition switch is turned to ON, current flows through the power window fuse in the engine compartment fuse and relay box to a circuit breaker located in the instrument panel wiring harness (located near the parking brake pedal). From there, current flows to the power window switches.

2   The power windows are wired so that they can be lowered and raised from the master control switch by the driver or by passengers using remote switches located at each passenger window. Each window has a separate motor that is reversible. The position of the control switch determines the polarity and therefore the direction of operation.

3   The power window system will only operate when the ignition switch is turned to ON. In addition, a window lockout switch at the master control switch can, when activated, disable the power window switches on the other doors. Always check these items before troubleshooting a window problem.

4   These procedures are general in nature, so if you can't find the problem using them, take the vehicle to a dealer service department.

5   If the power windows don't work at all, check the fuse or circuit breaker.

6   If only the rear windows are inoperative, or if the windows only operate from the master control switch, check the window lockout switch for continuity in the unlocked position. If it doesn't have continuity, replace it.

7   Check the wiring between the switches and the fuse for continuity. Repair the wiring, if necessary.

8   If only one window is inoperative from the master control switch, try the control switch at the window that doesn't work.

➡**Note: This doesn't apply to the driver's door window.**

9   If the same window works from one switch, but not the other, check the switch for continuity.

10 If the switch tests OK, check for a short or open in the wiring between the affected switch and the window motor.

11 If one window is inoperative from both switches, remove the trim panel from the affected door (see Chapter 11), then check for voltage at the switch and at the motor while operating the switch. First check for voltage at the electrical connectors for the circuit. With the ignition key turned to ON and the connectors all connected, backprobe at the designated wire (see the wiring diagrams at the end of this Chapter) with a grounded test light. Pushing the driver's window switch to the DOWN position, there should be voltage at one terminal. Pushing the same switch to the UP position, there should be voltage at another terminal. If these voltage checks are OK, disconnect the electrical connector at the driver's motor, and check it for voltage when the switch is operated.

12 If voltage is reaching the motor and the switch is OK, disconnect the door glass from its regulator (see Chapter 11). Move the window up and down by hand while checking for binding and damage. Also check for binding and damage to the regulator. If the regulator is not damaged and the window moves up and down smoothly, replace the motor. If there's binding or damage, lubricate, repair or replace parts, as necessary.

13 If voltage isn't reaching the motor, check the wiring in the circuit for continuity between the switches and motors (see the wiring diagram at the end of this Chapter).

14 If you have to replace the main power window switch, pry it out of the door trim panel, then disconnect the electrical connector(s) from the switch.

15 When you're done, test the windows to confirm that the window system is functioning correctly.

23 Power door lock system - general information

1   The power door lock system operates the power door motors, which are integral components of the door latch units in each door. The system consists of a fuse (in the engine compartment fuse and relay box), the instrument cluster, the control switches (in each of the front doors), the power door motors and the electrical wiring harnesses connecting all of these components.

2   The lock mechanisms in the door latch units are actuated by a reversible electric motor in each door. When you push the door lock switch to LOCK, the motor operates one way and locks the latch mechanism. When you push the door lock switch the other way, to the UNLOCK position, the motor operates in the other direction, unlocking the latch mechanism. Because the motors and lock mechanisms are an integral part of the door latch units, they cannot be repaired. If a door lock motor or lock mechanism fails, replace the door latch unit (see Chapter 11).

3   Even if you don't manually lock the doors or press the door lock switch to the LOCK position before driving, the instrument cluster automatically locks the doors when the vehicle speed exceeds 15 mph, as long as all the doors are closed and the accelerator pedal is depressed. (You can turn off this feature if you don't want the doors to lock automatically. Refer to your owner's manual.)

4   Some vehicles have an optional Remote Keyless Entry (RKE) system that allows you to lock and unlock the doors from outside the vehicle. The RKE system consists of the transmitter (the electronic push-button "key") and a receiver located on the instrument cluster. The RKE receiver, which operates all the time, is protected by a fuse in the engine compartment fuse and relay box. Vehicles are shipped from the factory with two RKE transmitters but, if you want to purchase extra units, the RKE receiver can actually handle up to four vehicle access codes.

5   Some features of the door lock system on these vehicles rely on resources that they share with other electronic modules through the Programmable Communications Interface (PCI) data bus network. Professional diagnosis of these modules and the PCI data bus network requires the use of a DRB III, (proprietary factory) scan tool and factory diagnostic information. At-home repairs are therefore limited to inspecting the wiring for bad connections and for minor faults that can be easily repaired. If you are unable to locate the trouble using the following general steps, consult your dealer service department.

6   Always check the circuit fuses (in the engine compartment fuse and relay box) first.

7   When depressed, each power door lock switch locks or unlocks

all of the doors. The easiest way to verify that each door lock switch is operating correctly is to watch the door lock button in each door as you operate the switch. The door lock buttons should all go down when you push the door lock switch to the LOCK position, and go up when you push the door lock switch to the UNLOCK position. Also, with the engine turned off so that you can hear better, operate the door lock switches in both directions and listen for the faint click of the motors locking and unlocking the latch mechanisms.

8 If there's no click, check for voltage at the switches. If no voltage is present, check the wiring between the fuse and the switches for shorts and opens (see the wiring diagrams at the end of this Chapter).

9 If voltage is present, but no clicking sound is apparent, remove the switch from the door trim panel (see Chapter 11) and test it for continuity. If there is no continuity in either direction, replace the switch.

10 If the switch has continuity but the latch mechanism doesn't

click, check the wiring between the switch and the motor in the latch mechanism for continuity. If the circuit is open between the switch and the motor, repair the wiring.

11 If all but one motor is operating, remove the trim panel from the affected door (see Chapter 11) and check for voltage at the motor while operating the lock switch. One of the wires should have voltage in the LOCK position; the other should have voltage in the UNLOCK position.

12 If the inoperative motor is receiving voltage, replace the latch mechanism.

13 If the inoperative motor isn't receiving voltage, check for an open or short in the circuit between the switch and the motor.

➡**Note: It's common for wires to break in the harness between the body and the door because repeatedly opening and closing the door fatigues and eventually breaks the wires.**

24 Power seats - general information

✳✳ WARNING:

The models covered by this manual are equipped with a Supplemental Restraint System (SRS), more commonly known as airbags. Additionally, some models are equipped with seat belt pre-tensioners, which are explosive devices. Always disarm the airbag/restraint system before working in the vicinity of any airbag/restraint system component to avoid the possibility of accidental deployment of the airbag/seat belt pre-tensioners, which could cause personal injury (see Section 26). Do not use a memory-saving device to preserve the PCM's memory when working on or near airbag system components.

1 Some models feature an optional eight-way power seat system that allows the driver and passenger to adjust the front seats up, down, front up, front down, rear up, rear down, forward and rearward. The system consists of the driver's power seat switch, the passenger power seat switch, the driver's power seat track, the passenger power seat track and, on some models, the optional power lumbar adjusters.

2 The power seat switches are located on the outboard side of the seat cushions, on the seat cushion side panels. If the vehicle is equipped with the optional power lumbar adjusters, the lumbar switches are located on the power seat switch assemblies. Each switch assembly is attached to the seat side panel by two Torx screws. Refer to your owner's manual for instructions regarding switch functions. Individual switches in the power seat switch assemblies cannot be repaired or replaced separately. If one of the switches in a power seat switch assembly fails, replace the entire switch assembly.

3 The seats are powered by three reversible motors that are attached to the upper half of the power seat track assembly. These motors are controlled by the power seat switches on the sides of the seats. Each switch changes the direction of seat travel by reversing polarity to the drive motor. The motors are an integral part of the power

seat track assembly and cannot be repaired or replaced separately. If a motor fails, replace the power seat track assembly.

4 The optional power lumbar adjuster and motor are located on the back of the seat, under the seat trim cover and padding, where they're attached to a molded plastic back panel and to the seat back frame. The power lumbar adjuster and motor cannot be repaired or replaced separately from the seat back frame. If either the adjuster or the motor fails, replace the entire seat back frame unit.

5 Diagnosis is usually a simple matter, using the following procedures.

6 Look under the seat for any object which may be preventing the seat from moving.

7 If the seat won't work at all, check the fuse, which is located in the engine compartment fuse and relay box.

8 With the engine off to reduce the noise level, operate the seat controls in all directions and listen for sound coming from the seat motors.

9 If the motor doesn't work or make noise, check for voltage at the motor while an assistant operates the switch.

10 If the motor is getting voltage but doesn't run, test it off the vehicle with jumper wires. If it still doesn't work, replace it. The individual components are not available separately. The whole power-seat track must be purchased as an assembly.

11 If the motor isn't getting voltage, remove the seat side panel to access the switch and check for voltage. If there's no voltage at the switch, check the wiring between the fuse and the switch. If there's voltage at the switch, check for a short or open in the wiring between the switch and the motor. If that circuit is okay, replace the switch. No further testing is recommended. If the power seat system is still malfunctioning at this point, have the system checked out by a dealer service department.

25 Daytime Running Lights (DRL) - general information

Canadian models are equipped with Daytime Running Lights (DRL). The DRL system illuminates the headlights whenever the engine is running and the parking brake is disengaged. The DRL system provides reduced power to the headlights so that they won't be too bright for daytime use and it prolongs the headlight bulbs' service life. It does

this by modulating the pulse-width of the power to the headlights. The duration and interval of these power pulses is programmed into the Front Control Module (FCM), which is located on the instrument cluster. If you want to alter the pulse-width, you must have it done by a dealer service department.

26 Airbag system - general information

These models are equipped with a Supplemental Restraint System (SRS), more commonly called an airbag system. There are at least two airbags, one for the driver and one for the front seat passenger, on all models. The SRS system is designed to protect the driver and passenger from serious injury in the event of a head-on or frontal collision. The airbag control module is located on the transmission tunnel, right below the center of the instrument panel. Some models are also equipped with optional side curtain airbags. Vehicles with this option can be identified by the "SRS - AIRBAG" logo printed on the headliner above the B-pillar.

AIRBAG MODULES

The airbag module houses the airbag and the inflater unit. The inflater unit is mounted on the back of the housing over a hole through which gas is expelled, inflating the bag almost instantaneously when an electrical signal is received from the airbag control module. On the driver's airbag, the specially wound wire that carries this signal to the module is called a "clockspring." The clockspring is a flat, ribbon-like electrically conductive tape that winds and unwinds as the steering wheel is turned so it can transmit an electrical signal regardless of wheel position. The procedure for removing the driver's airbag is part of *Steering wheel - removal and installation* in Chapter 10.

The passenger airbag is located in the top of the dashboard, above the glove box. There's also a passenger airbag ON/OFF switch located at the lower right corner of the center instrument panel bezel. This switch allows you to deactivate the passenger airbag if you're transporting an infant or a young child in a child safety seat. We don't recommend removing the passenger airbag because there is no reason to do so unless it has been activated during an accident and needs to be replaced afterward.

Optional side-curtain airbags, if equipped, are located on each roof side rail, above the headliner, and they extend from the A-pillar to the C-pillar. Again, we don't recommend trying to remove the side-curtain airbags because there is no reason to do so unless they've been deployed in an accident and must be replaced.

AIRBAG CONTROL MODULE (ACM) AND SIDE IMPACT AIRBAG CONTROL MODULES (SIACMS)

The Airbag Control Module (ACM) is the microprocessor that monitors and operates the airbag system. The ACM checks the system every time the vehicle is started. When you start the car, an AIRBAG indicator light comes on for about six seconds, then goes off, if the system is

operating properly. If there is a fault in the system, the ACM stores a Diagnostic Trouble Code (DTC) and illuminates the AIRBAG indicator light, which remains on until the problem is repaired and the ACM memory is cleared of any DTCs. If the AIRBAG indicator light comes on at any time other than the bulb test and remains on, or doesn't come on at all, there's a problem in the system. A DRBIII scan tool is the only means by which the system can be diagnosed. Take the vehicle to your dealer immediately and have the system professionally diagnosed and repaired.

The ACM controls the operation of the standard driver and passenger airbags. Vehicles with optional side-curtain airbags are also equipped with Side Impact Airbag Control Modules (SIACMs). There are two SIACMs, one for each side-curtain airbag. The SIACMs are located behind the B-pillar trim, above the outboard front seat belt retractor inside each B-pillar.

IMPACT SEAT BELT RETRACTORS

All models are equipped with pyrotechnic (explosive) units in the front seat belt retracting mechanisms for both the lap and shoulder belts. During an impact that would trigger the airbag system, the airbag control unit also triggers the seat belt retractors. When the pyrotechnic charges go off, they accelerate the retractors to instantly take up any slack in the seat belt system to more fully prepare the driver and front seat passenger for impact.

The airbag system should be disabled any time work is done to or around the seats.

✳✳ WARNING:

Never strike the pillars or floorpan with a hammer or use an impact-driver tool in these areas unless the system is disabled.

SERVICING COMPONENTS NEAR THE SRS SYSTEM

There are times when you need to remove the steering wheel, the instrument cluster, the radio, the heater/air conditioning control assembly or other components on or near the dashboard. At these times you'll be working around components and wire harnesses for the SRS system. Do not use electrical test equipment on airbag system wires; it could cause the airbag(s) to deploy. ALWAYS DISABLE THE SRS SYSTEM BEFORE WORKING NEAR THE SRS SYSTEM COMPONENTS OR RELATED WIRING.

DISABLING THE SYSTEM

Whenever working in the vicinity of the steering wheel, steering column, floor console or other airbag system components, the system should be disarmed. To do this perform the following steps:

a) *Turn the ignition switch to the OFF position.*

b) *Disconnect the cable from the negative battery terminal (see Chapter 5, Section 1).*

c) *WAIT FOR AT LEAST TWO MINUTES before beginning work (during this two-minute interval the capacitor that provides emergency back-up power to the system loses its charge).*

ENABLING THE SYSTEM

To enable the airbag system, perform the following steps:

a) *Turn the ignition switch to the OFF position.*

b) *Connect the cable to the negative battery terminal.*

c) *Without putting your body in front of either airbag, turn the ignition switch to the ON position. Note whether the airbag indicator light glows for six seconds, then goes out. If it does, this indicates that the system is functioning properly.*

27 Wiring diagrams - general information

Since it isn't possible to include all wiring diagrams for every year covered by this manual, the following diagrams are those that are typical and most commonly needed.

Prior to troubleshooting any circuits, check the fuse and circuit breakers (if equipped) to make sure they are in good condition. Make sure the battery is properly charged and has clean, tight cable connections (see Chapter 1).

When checking the wiring system, make sure that all electrical connectors are clean, with no broken or loose pins. When disconnecting an electrical connector, do not pull on the wires, only on the connector housings.

Starting and Charging Systems

Exterior lighting system (1 of 2)

Exterior Lighting System (2 of 2)

Interior lighting system

Power door locks system (1 of 2)

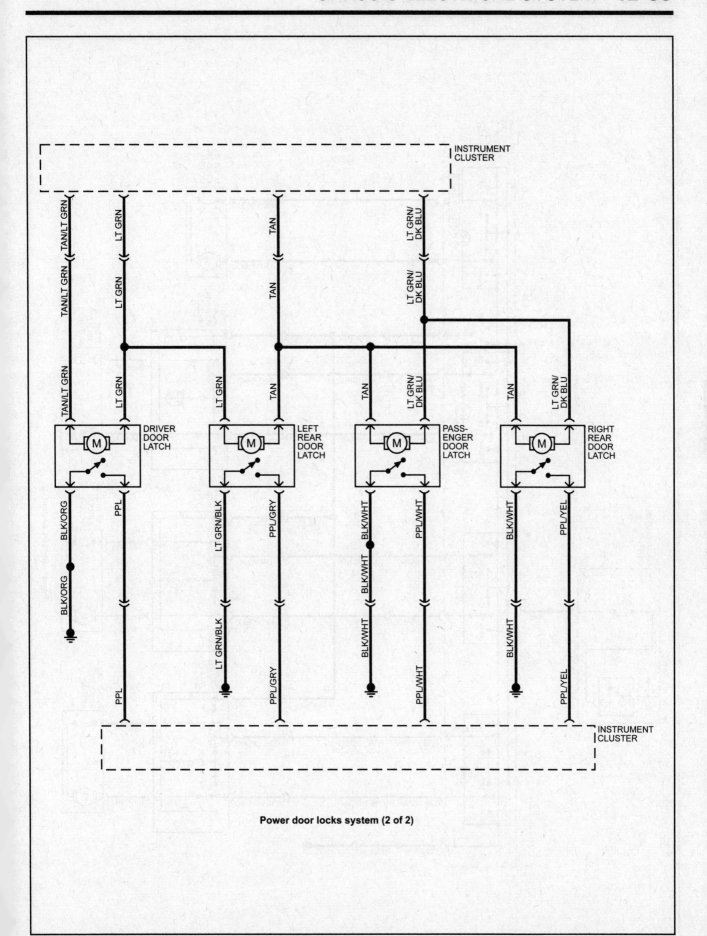

Power door locks system (2 of 2)

Power windows system

Heating and air conditioning system

Base audio system

Cruise control system

Windshield wiper system

Rear wiper system

Note

GLOSSARY

AIR/FUEL RATIO: The ratio of air-to-gasoline by weight in the fuel mixture drawn into the engine.

AIR INJECTION: One method of reducing harmful exhaust emissions by injecting air into each of the exhaust ports of an engine. The fresh air entering the hot exhaust manifold causes any remaining fuel to be burned before it can exit the tailpipe.

ALTERNATOR: A device used for converting mechanical energy into electrical energy.

AMMETER: An instrument, calibrated in amperes, used to measure the flow of an electrical current in a circuit. Ammeters are always connected in series with the circuit being tested.

AMPERE: The rate of flow of electrical current present when one volt of electrical pressure is applied against one ohm of electrical resistance.

ANALOG COMPUTER: Any microprocessor that uses similar (analogous) electrical signals to make its calculations.

ARMATURE: A laminated, soft iron core wrapped by a wire that converts electrical energy to mechanical energy as in a motor or relay. When rotated in a magnetic field, it changes mechanical energy into electrical energy as in a generator.

ATMOSPHERIC PRESSURE: The pressure on the Earth's surface caused by the weight of the air in the atmosphere. At sea level, this pressure is 14.7 psi at 32°F (101 kPa at 0°C).

ATOMIZATION: The breaking down of a liquid into a fine mist that can be suspended in air.

AXIAL PLAY: Movement parallel to a shaft or bearing bore.

BACKFIRE: The sudden combustion of gases in the intake or exhaust system that results in a loud explosion.

BACKLASH: The clearance or play between two parts, such as meshed gears.

BACKPRESSURE: Restrictions in the exhaust system that slow the exit of exhaust gases from the combustion chamber.

BAKELITE: A heat resistant, plastic insulator material commonly used in printed circuit boards and transistorized components.

BALL BEARING: A bearing made up of hardened inner and outer races between which hardened steel balls roll.

BALLAST RESISTOR: A resistor in the primary ignition circuit that lowers voltage after the engine is started to reduce wear on ignition components.

BEARING: A friction reducing, supportive device usually located between a stationary part and a moving part.

BIMETAL TEMPERATURE SENSOR: Any sensor or switch made of two dissimilar types of metal that bend when heated or cooled due to the different expansion rates of the alloys. These types of sensors usually function as an on/off switch.

BLOWBY: Combustion gases, composed of water vapor and unburned fuel, that leak past the piston rings into the crankcase during normal engine operation. These gases are removed by the PCV system to prevent the buildup of harmful acids in the crankcase.

BRAKE PAD: A brake shoe and lining assembly used with disc brakes.

BRAKE SHOE: The backing for the brake lining. The term is, however, usually applied to the assembly of the brake backing and lining.

BUSHING: A liner, usually removable, for a bearing; an anti-friction liner used in place of a bearing.

CALIPER: A hydraulically activated device in a disc brake system, which is mounted straddling the brake rotor (disc). The caliper contains at least one piston and two brake pads. Hydraulic pressure on the piston(s) forces the pads against the rotor.

CAMSHAFT: A shaft in the engine on which are the lobes (cams) which operate the valves. The camshaft is driven by the crankshaft, via a belt, chain or gears, at one half the crankshaft speed.

CAPACITOR: A device which stores an electrical charge.

CARBON MONOXIDE (CO): A colorless, odorless gas given off as a normal byproduct of combustion. It is poisonous and extremely dangerous in confined areas, building up slowly to toxic levels without warning if adequate ventilation is not available.

CARBURETOR: A device, usually mounted on the intake manifold of an engine, which mixes the air and fuel in the proper proportion to allow even combustion.

CATALYTIC CONVERTER: A device installed in the exhaust system, like a muffler, that converts harmful byproducts of combustion into carbon dioxide and water vapor by means of a heat-producing chemical reaction.

CENTRIFUGAL ADVANCE: A mechanical method of advancing the spark timing by using flyweights in the distributor that react to centrifugal force generated by the distributor shaft rotation.

CHECK VALVE: Any one-way valve installed to permit the flow of air, fuel or vacuum in one direction only.

CHOKE: A device, usually a moveable valve, placed in the intake path of a carburetor to restrict the flow of air.

CIRCUIT: Any unbroken path through which an electrical current can flow. Also used to describe fuel flow in some instances.

CIRCUIT BREAKER: A switch which protects an electrical circuit from overload by opening the circuit when the current flow exceeds a predetermined level. Some circuit breakers must be reset manually, while most reset automatically.

COIL (IGNITION): A transformer in the ignition circuit which steps up the voltage provided to the spark plugs.

COMBINATION MANIFOLD: An assembly which includes both the intake and exhaust manifolds in one casting.

COMBINATION VALVE: A device used in some fuel systems that routes fuel vapors to a charcoal storage canister instead of venting them into the atmosphere. The valve relieves fuel tank pressure and allows fresh air into the tank as the fuel level drops to prevent a vapor lock situation.

COMPRESSION RATIO: The comparison of the total volume of the cylinder and combustion chamber with the piston at BDC and the piston at TDC.

CONDENSER: 1. An electrical device which acts to store an electrical charge, preventing voltage surges. 2. A radiator-like device in the air conditioning system in which refrigerant gas condenses into a liquid, giving off heat.

CONDUCTOR: Any material through which an electrical current can be transmitted easily.

CONTINUITY: Continuous or complete circuit. Can be checked with an ohmmeter.

COUNTERSHAFT: An intermediate shaft which is rotated by a mainshaft and transmits, in turn, that rotation to a working part.

CRANKCASE: The lower part of an engine in which the crankshaft and related parts operate.

CRANKSHAFT: The main driving shaft of an engine which receives reciprocating motion from the pistons and converts it to rotary motion.

CYLINDER: In an engine, the round hole in the engine block in which the piston(s) ride.

CYLINDER BLOCK: The main structural member of an engine in which is found the cylinders, crankshaft and other principal parts.

CYLINDER HEAD: The detachable portion of the engine, usually fastened to the top of the cylinder block and containing all or most of the combustion chambers. On overhead valve engines, it contains the valves and their operating parts. On overhead cam engines, it contains the camshaft as well.

DEAD CENTER: The extreme top or bottom of the piston stroke.

DETONATION: An unwanted explosion of the air/fuel mixture in the combustion chamber caused by excess heat and compression, advanced timing, or an overly lean mixture. Also referred to as "ping".

DIAPHRAGM: A thin, flexible wall separating two cavities, such as in a vacuum advance unit.

DIESELING: A condition in which hot spots in the combustion chamber cause the engine to run on after the key is turned off.

DIFFERENTIAL: A geared assembly which allows the transmission of motion between drive axles, giving one axle the ability to turn faster than the other.

DIODE: An electrical device that will allow current to flow in one direction only.

DISC BRAKE: A hydraulic braking assembly consisting of a brake disc, or rotor, mounted on an axle, and a caliper assembly containing, usually two brake pads which are activated by hydraulic pressure. The pads are forced against the sides of the disc, creating friction which slows the vehicle.

DISTRIBUTOR: A mechanically driven device on an engine which is responsible for electrically firing the spark plug at a predetermined point of the piston stroke.

DOWEL PIN: A pin, inserted in mating holes in two different parts allowing those parts to maintain a fixed relationship.

DRUM BRAKE: A braking system which consists of two brake shoes and one or two wheel cylinders, mounted on a fixed backing plate, and a brake drum, mounted on an axle, which revolves around the assembly.

DWELL: The rate, measured in degrees of shaft rotation, at which an electrical circuit cycles on and off.

ELECTRONIC CONTROL UNIT (ECU): Ignition module, module, amplifier or igniter. See Module for definition.

ELECTRONIC IGNITION: A system in which the timing and firing of the spark plugs is controlled by an electronic control unit, usually called a module. These systems have no points or condenser.

END-PLAY: The measured amount of axial movement in a shaft.

ENGINE: A device that converts heat into mechanical energy.

EXHAUST MANIFOLD: A set of cast passages or pipes which conduct exhaust gases from the engine.

FEELER GAUGE: A blade, usually metal, or precisely predetermined thickness, used to measure the clearance between two parts.

FIRING ORDER: The order in which combustion occurs in the cylinders of an engine. Also the order in which spark is distributed to the plugs by the distributor.

FLOODING: The presence of too much fuel in the intake manifold and combustion chamber which prevents the air/fuel mixture from firing, thereby causing a no-start situation.

FLYWHEEL: A disc shaped part bolted to the rear end of the crankshaft. Around the outer perimeter is affixed the ring gear. The starter drive engages the ring gear, turning the flywheel, which rotates the crankshaft, imparting the initial starting motion to the engine.

FOOT POUND (ft. lbs. or sometimes, ft.lb.): The amount of energy or work needed to raise an item weighing one pound, a distance of one foot.

FUSE: A protective device in a circuit which prevents circuit overload by breaking the circuit when a specific amperage is present. The device is constructed around a strip or wire of a lower amperage rating than the circuit it is designed to protect. When an amperage higher than that stamped on the fuse is present in the circuit, the strip or wire melts, opening the circuit.

GEAR RATIO: The ratio between the number of teeth on meshing gears.

GENERATOR: A device which converts mechanical energy into electrical energy.

HEAT RANGE: The measure of a spark plug's ability to dissipate heat from its firing end. The higher the heat range, the hotter the plug fires.

HUB: The center part of a wheel or gear.

HYDROCARBON (HC): Any chemical compound made up of hydrogen and carbon. A major pollutant formed by the engine as a byproduct of combustion.

HYDROMETER: An instrument used to measure the specific gravity of a solution.

INCH POUND (inch lbs.; sometimes in.lb. or in. lbs.): One twelfth of a foot pound.

INDUCTION: A means of transferring electrical energy in the form of a magnetic field. Principle used in the ignition coil to increase voltage.

INJECTOR: A device which receives metered fuel under relatively low pressure and is activated to inject the fuel into the engine under relatively high pressure at a predetermined time.

INPUT SHAFT: The shaft to which torque is applied, usually carrying the driving gear or gears.

INTAKE MANIFOLD: A casting of passages or pipes used to conduct air or a fuel/air mixture to the cylinders.

JOURNAL: The bearing surface within which a shaft operates.

KEY: A small block usually fitted in a notch between a shaft and a hub to prevent slippage of the two parts.

MANIFOLD: A casting of passages or set of pipes which connect the cylinders to an inlet or outlet source.

MANIFOLD VACUUM: Low pressure in an engine intake manifold formed just below the throttle plates. Manifold vacuum is highest at idle and drops under acceleration.

MASTER CYLINDER: The primary fluid pressurizing device in a hydraulic system. In automotive use, it is found in brake and hydraulic clutch systems and is pedal activated, either directly or, in a power brake system, through the power booster.

MODULE: Electronic control unit, amplifier or igniter of solid state or integrated design which controls the current flow in the ignition primary circuit based on input from the pick-up coil. When the module opens the primary circuit, high secondary voltage is induced in the coil.

NEEDLE BEARING: A bearing which consists of a number (usually a large number) of long, thin rollers.

OHM: (Ω) The unit used to measure the resistance of conductor-to-electrical flow. One ohm is the amount of resistance that limits current flow to one ampere in a circuit with one volt of pressure.

OHMMETER: An instrument used for measuring the resistance, in ohms, in an electrical circuit.

OUTPUT SHAFT: The shaft which transmits torque from a device, such as a transmission.

OVERDRIVE: A gear assembly which produces more shaft revolutions than that transmitted to it.

OVERHEAD CAMSHAFT (OHC): An engine configuration in which the camshaft is mounted on top of the cylinder head and operates the valve either directly or by means of rocker arms.

OVERHEAD VALVE (OHV): An engine configuration in which all of the valves are located in the cylinder head and the camshaft is located in the cylinder block. The camshaft operates the valves via lifters and pushrods.

OXIDES OF NITROGEN (NOx): Chemical compounds of nitrogen produced as a byproduct of combustion. They combine with hydrocarbons to produce smog.

OXYGEN SENSOR: Use with the feedback system to sense the presence of oxygen in the exhaust gas and signal the computer which can reference the voltage signal to an air/fuel ratio.

PINION: The smaller of two meshing gears.

PISTON RING: An open-ended ring with fits into a groove on the outer diameter of the piston. Its chief function is to form a seal between the piston and cylinder wall. Most automotive pistons have three rings: two for compression sealing; one for oil sealing.

PRELOAD: A predetermined load placed on a bearing during assembly or by adjustment.

PRIMARY CIRCUIT: the low voltage side of the ignition system which consists of the ignition switch, ballast resistor or resistance wire, bypass, coil, electronic control unit and pick-up coil as well as the connecting wires and harnesses.

PRESS FIT: The mating of two parts under pressure, due to the inner diameter of one being smaller than the outer diameter of the other, or vice versa; an interference fit.

RACE: The surface on the inner or outer ring of a bearing on which the balls, needles or rollers move.

REGULATOR: A device which maintains the amperage and/or voltage levels of a circuit at predetermined values.

RELAY: A switch which automatically opens and/or closes a circuit.

RESISTANCE: The opposition to the flow of current through a circuit or electrical device, and is measured in ohms. Resistance is equal to the voltage divided by the amperage.

RESISTOR: A device, usually made of wire, which offers a preset amount of resistance in an electrical circuit.

RING GEAR: The name given to a ring-shaped gear attached to a differential case, or affixed to a flywheel or as part of a planetary gear set.

ROLLER BEARING: A bearing made up of hardened inner and outer races between which hardened steel rollers move.

ROTOR: 1. The disc-shaped part of a disc brake assembly, upon which the brake pads bear; also called, brake disc. 2. The device mounted atop the distributor shaft, which passes current to the distributor cap tower contacts.

SECONDARY CIRCUIT: The high voltage side of the ignition system, usually above 20,000 volts. The secondary includes the ignition coil, coil wire, distributor cap and rotor, spark plug wires and spark plugs.

SENDING UNIT: A mechanical, electrical, hydraulic or electro-magnetic device which transmits information to a gauge.

SENSOR: Any device designed to measure engine operating conditions or ambient pressures and temperatures. Usually electronic in nature and designed to send a voltage signal to an on-board computer, some sensors may operate as a simple on/off switch or they may provide a variable voltage signal (like a potentiometer) as conditions or measured parameters change.

SHIM: Spacers of precise, predetermined thickness used between parts to establish a proper working relationship.

SLAVE CYLINDER: In automotive use, a device in the hydraulic clutch system which is activated by hydraulic force, disengaging the clutch.

SOLENOID: A coil used to produce a magnetic field, the effect of which is to produce work.

SPARK PLUG: A device screwed into the combustion chamber of a spark ignition engine. The basic construction is a conductive core inside of a ceramic insulator, mounted in an outer conductive base. An electrical charge from the spark plug wire travels along the conductive core and jumps a preset air gap to a grounding point or points at the end of the conductive base. The resultant spark ignites the fuel/air mixture in the combustion chamber.

SPLINES: Ridges machined or cast onto the outer diameter of a shaft or inner diameter of a bore to enable parts to mate without rotation.

TACHOMETER: A device used to measure the rotary speed of an engine, shaft, gear, etc., usually in rotations per minute.

THERMOSTAT: A valve, located in the cooling system of an engine, which is closed when cold and opens gradually in response to engine heating, controlling the temperature of the coolant and rate of coolant flow.

TOP DEAD CENTER (TDC): The point at which the piston reaches the top of its travel on the compression stroke.

TORQUE: The twisting force applied to an object.

TORQUE CONVERTER: A turbine used to transmit power from a driving member to a driven member via hydraulic action, providing changes in drive ratio and torque. In automotive use, it links the driveplate at the rear of the engine to the automatic transmission.

TRANSDUCER: A device used to change a force into an electrical signal.

TRANSISTOR: A semi-conductor component which can be actuated by a small voltage to perform an electrical switching function.

TUNE-UP: A regular maintenance function, usually associated with the replacement and adjustment of parts and components in the electrical and fuel systems of a vehicle for the purpose of attaining optimum performance.

TURBOCHARGER: An exhaust driven pump which compresses intake air and forces it into the combustion chambers at higher than atmospheric pressures. The increased air pressure allows more fuel to be burned and results in increased horsepower being produced.

VACUUM ADVANCE: A device which advances the ignition timing in response to increased engine vacuum.

VACUUM GAUGE: An instrument used to measure the presence of vacuum in a chamber.

VALVE: A device which control the pressure, direction of flow or rate of flow of a liquid or gas.

VALVE CLEARANCE: The measured gap between the end of the valve stem and the rocker arm, cam lobe or follower that activates the valve.

VISCOSITY: The rating of a liquid's internal resistance to flow.

VOLTMETER: An instrument used for measuring electrical force in units called volts. Voltmeters are always connected parallel with the circuit being tested.

WHEEL CYLINDER: Found in the automotive drum brake assembly, it is a device, actuated by hydraulic pressure, which, through internal pistons, pushes the brake shoes outward against the drums.

NOTES

MASTER INDEX

A

Notes